Parks in Hertfordshire since 1500

Parks in Hertfordshire since 1500

Hugh Prince

HERTFORDSHIRE PUBLICATIONS

an imprint of

University of Hertfordshire Press

First published in Great Britain in 2008 by
Hertfordshire Publications
an imprint of the
University of Hertfordshire Press
Learning and Information Services
University of Hertfordshire
College Lane
Hatfield
Hertfordshire AL10 9AB

Hertfordshire Publications, an imprint of the University of Hertfordshire Press, is
published on behalf of the Hertfordshire Association of Local History.

British Library Cataloguing in Publication Data
A catalogue record for this book is available from the British Library

ISBN 978–0–954218–99–7

Design and typesetting by Mathew Lyons
Cover design by John Robertshaw

Printed in Great Britain by Antony Rowe Ltd

Contents

List of Figures

Cover Illustrations

View of Panshanger, 1800. H. Repton, 'Panshanger Red Book', 1800, Plate II. By kind permission of Hertfordshire Archives and Local Studies (HALS), (D/EP/P21A).

Every effort has been made to contact copyright holders in order to seek permission to reproduce images. Where it has been impossible to trace copyright holders, the publishers would be pleased to hear from them.

List of Tables

Preface

THE DATE FOR STARTING THIS NARRATIVE is around 1500. Parks, as distinctive features in the landscape, have a much longer history. Their early development in Hertfordshire is traced in a companion volume by Anne Rowe. She has shared with me her extensive local knowledge and has been unsparingly generous in answering many queries and checking many details as my search proceeded. Anne introduced me to the research group of the Hertfordshire Gardens Trust, whose members have collected much material for the histories of many parks.

My special interest in the economic, social and political history and geography of parks began in the early 1950s when I studied landscape gardens in the Chilterns under the supervision of Henry Clifford Darby. In that project, I received valuable help and advice from Dorothy Stroud, Nikolaus Pevsner and, about landownership, from the economic historian, Michael Thompson. I owe a great deal to John Whitfield, then assistant county archivist, for guiding me through collections of papers from Panshanger, Brocket and Great Gaddesden. Lionel Munby not only provided me with much valuable information on Hertfordshire local history but he also broadened my outlook on the making of the landscape and edited for publication in the Amateur Historian in 1958, lists of parks improved by Charles Bridgeman, William Kent, Lancelot Brown, Richard Woods and Humphry Repton.

Many garden historians and geographers have extended my knowledge of changing tastes and practices of park-making. Among those to whom I am most indebted for new ideas and information are Mavis Batey, David Brown, Ben Cowell, Fiona Cowell, Stephen Daniels, Brent Elliott, Ted Fawcett, Peter Goodchild, Kate Harwood, John Dixon Hunt, David Jacques, John Phibbs, Charles Watkins, Tom Williamson, Peter Willis and Jan Woudstra. I thank them for writing letters and answering verbal enquiries. I have also learned much about the history of county maps from Peter Barber, Catherine Delano-Smith, Roger Kain, Richard Oliver and, in particular, Donald Hodson, the leading authority on maps of Hertfordshire.

Many librarians and archivists have been helpful in finding source material. I am especially grateful to the staff of the British Library, University of London Library, the Institute of Historical Research, the Courtauld Institute of Art, University College London Library, the Architectural Association, Hertfordshire Archives and Local Studies, Hertfordshire Gardens Trust, Watford Central Library, Watford Museum and Bushey Museum. I am especially indebted to Mick Thompson, gardens manager and archivist at Ashridge, John Cox, archivist at Gorhambury, Bryen Wood and Audrey Adams at Bushey Museum, Sarah Priestley at Watford Museum, Victoria Hynes and Katrina Legg at Hertfordshire Archives and Local Studies and Jane Cunningham at the Courtauld Institute of Art for access to important sources.

Colleagues in the Geography Department at University College London, notably John Catt, Richard Dennis, Richard Munton and Peter Wood have been kind enough to offer valuable suggestions about many topics discussed in the book and I thank Hugh Clout for patiently reading and commenting on drafts of all the chapters.

I have been greatly helped by Todd Longstaffe-Gowan in finding sources for illustrations, by Nick Mann who taught me new methods of processing cartographic information on a computer and by Matt Prince who photographed details from early maps and engravings. Miles Irving's graphic skills have transformed rough sketches into accurate, legible maps and diagrams.

At the University of Hertfordshire Press, Jane Housham, Sarah Elvins and their diligent copy editor have taken great pains to improve both text and illustrations.

I wish to thank David Thorpe for his generosity in making a grant towards the collection and preparation of illustrations.

Once again, Sheila has borne the trials and tribulations that attend a long spell of studying and writing. I thank her for her patience.

Chapter I

Parks and Landed Estates in Hertfordshire

HERTFORDSHIRE IS A SMALL COUNTY, but it contains many parks that were represented on printed maps from the late sixteenth century to the present day. Parks here are not typical of those in England as a whole; most are smaller than in other counties and, in addition, they have changed hands and been altered more frequently than those elsewhere. From 1500 to 1880, the creation and expansion of parks was closely related to the increasing size of landed estates, a process which stopped short of forming estates more than 60,000 acres in extent. The Cecils were the only Hertfordshire family to attain a leading position among the nation's great landowners, and the only family to have owned estates in the county for more than four hundred years. Few other families held their estates for more than three generations. Because of its closeness to London and Westminster, Hertfordshire attracted many ambitious and acquisitive newcomers: members of parliament, nabobs, bankers, brewers, churchmen and senior military officers all sought to enter the elite by climbing the property ladder. Most bought and sold estates in rapid succession, but, during their occupation, they left their distinctive marks on the landscape. After 1880, the destruction and adaptation of parks was linked to the reduction in the number and size of landed estates. As the size of estates diminished, the rate at which parks changed hands accelerated.

The central idea behind this book develops an idea put forward by Lawrence and Jeanne Stone for the period from 1540 to 1879. The

Stones related sizes of country houses to the status of landowners and the extent of their estates,[1] estimating the sizes of houses using a variety of sources, including the hearth tax returns of 1662–73 and Jan Drapentier's engravings of twenty-seven houses owned by gentry families, illustrated in Henry Chauncy's *Historical Antiquities of Hertfordshire*, 1700.[2] They also drew upon later county histories by Nathanael Salmon and Robert Clutterbuck which traced descents of manors; John Edwin Cussans and the *Victoria County History*, which in addition followed lineages of mercantile and professional families.[3] The Stones discussed the acquisition of estates by inheritance, marriage and purchase, and explained losses of estates through failures to produce heirs or through debts. Their aim was to elucidate connections between enlarging estates, building houses and joining the ruling elite. In 1992–3, J.T. Smith examined architects' drawings and contemporary illustrations, including over 100 sketches of houses made by H.G. Oldfield in the 1790s and drawings of sixty houses made by John and John Chessell Buckler in the 1830s. These drawings enabled Smith to trace the rebuilding, extending and refacing of country houses to make room for owners to perform new public duties and provide accommodation for household servants.[4]

Instead of relating sizes of houses to sizes of estates, I have examined the relationship between sizes of parks and sizes of estates. Parks were enlarged when their owners had money to spend and their estates expanded. They were altered when heirs succeeded or newcomers bought them. In order to match changes in the number and area of parks with changing fortunes of landowners, it has been necessary to trace the names of owners and occupiers of parks represented on county maps at different dates. John Warburton's map of 1725 and Dury and Andrews' map of 1766 are especially valuable because they inscribed names of owners on the face of their maps. Lists of subscribers, prepared for John Oliver's map in 1695 and A. Bryant's map in 1821 identified many owners of parks. At other dates, it has been difficult to find owners' names. Studies by the Hertfordshire Gardens Trust, directed by Anne Rowe and edited by Tom Williamson and Richard Bisgrove have provided detailed information about individual parks and their owners.[5] Maps present a succession of period pictures of the changing size and character of parks that have been created and altered by a succession of landowners.

The most distinctive feature of sixteenth-century parks was their outer palings, whose primary purpose was to enclose herds of deer. The right of lords to enclose land for private enjoyment conflicted with the rights of commoners to graze sheep and cattle and gather winter fuel on waste lands and commons. The privilege claimed by lords to preserve deer and other game as their exclusive property was widely resented and closures of roads and paths across parks were regarded as infringements of ancient rights of way. When lords rebuilt their seats within park pales, they withdrew from village communities. To administer rural society, Tudor monarchs more than doubled the number of justices of the peace. Magistrates were given wide powers to maintain law and order; they were directed to organise relief for the poor, the old and infirm and were made responsible for repairing roads and bridges. Parks and new country houses thus became seats of local government. Representing two sides of the division between rulers and ruled in the late sixteenth century, John Norden, the map-maker, rejoiced at the presence of thirty-one parks in Hertfordshire, while William Harrison, the topographer, rebuked owners for not converting parks to productive uses, such as growing corn or grazing cattle.[6]

In the early seventeenth century, the number of parks decreased, some being reclaimed for agriculture, others falling into disrepair. At some places, herds of deer were replaced by cattle, sheep and horses. Other parks were transformed into ornamental grounds with large gardens and attractive layouts of trees and lakes. Magnificent renaissance gardens were created at Theobalds, Hatfield, Moor Park and Gorhambury. During the Civil War, many parks were plundered and estates confiscated, and, after the restoration of Charles II, owners struggled to regain their lands and rebuild their houses. A few had enough money to transform old parks into extensive formal gardens but, for most owners, recovery was slow. John Seller's map of 1675 showed only twenty-one parks in Hertfordshire; John Oliver's map of 1695 showed thirty-five and thirty-four appeared on John Warburton's map of 1725.

Landowning families entered into strict settlements in order to secure estates for themselves and future heirs, so that a member of each generation in turn would hold the land as tenant-for-life. Brides brought dowries, while younger children and widows were given portions. The system was widely adopted after 1660. Settlements favoured families that produced a succession of male heirs and settled estates were enlarged by acquiring lands offered for sale on the open market.[7] Throughout the eighteenth century, great estates were able to consolidate their gains and spend fortunes on building and laying out spacious landscape gardens: Dury and Andrews' map of 1766 shows forty-five empaled parks and thirty-four large gardens. While old-established families created large landscapes, many newcomers laid out smaller pleasure grounds, the size and appearance of parks corresponding with the social hierarchy among landowners.

Drawings prepared during the Napoleonic wars by the Ordnance Survey for the first edition one-inch map showed 153 places tinted or stippled as parkland; and in the course of the nineteenth century parks in Hertfordshire reached their maximum extent, covering 7.5 per cent of the surface area on Bryant's map of 1821 and 7.3 per cent on the Ordnance Survey six-inch maps of 1863–81. Some parks shrank a little but many continued to increase in size as planting programmes initiated by earlier generations were extended. A final stage was reached in the enclosure of commons and closure of rights of way to enlarge park boundaries, while conflicts over game preservation remained unresolved at the end of the century. Socially, owners were more isolated from villagers and their own servants than at any time since 1500. The growth of large estates culminated just after the middle of the century. The *Return of Owners of Land* in 1873 recorded that seventy-nine owners of more than 2,000 acres held 48.4 per cent of the surface of the county. Owners of the largest estates possessed all the largest parks and, proportionately, owners of smaller estates owned smaller parks. Victorian parks and small ornamental grounds exhibited a great variety of styles, their chief characteristic being novelty.

The decline of parks began about 1880 with the onset of a deep agricultural depression which led to farm rents in Hertfordshire falling by 40 per cent between 1874 and 1898. As the value of land declined, landowners had to rely on urban property and investments in commerce and industry to pay for the upkeep of parks and country houses; a few decided to cut their losses and sell to developers. During the First World War, some park owners and their heirs were killed and a few houses and parks were badly damaged by wartime occupants. After the war, low rents and high taxes forced many to sell up; some parks were converted into golf courses, a few were taken over as municipal parks and others were built over. In 1932–3 the fifth edition one-inch Ordnance Survey map showed 165 parks in Hertfordshire, eighty-four fewer than in 1863–81. The proportion of the surface area of the county occupied by parkland decreased from 7.3 per cent in 1863–81 to 6 per cent in 1932–3. In the interwar years, the population of Watford and other towns, the volume of road traffic, and the number of people travelling to London by rail all increased. Hertfordshire was thoroughly urbanised. A few concerns were expressed about the spread of suburbia but little was done to prevent unsightly developments and no steps were taken to save parks.

During the Second World War agriculture revived whilst parks and country houses suffered serious damage. Plans to control rural land use were implemented after 1945, creating a green belt around London, protecting sites of outstanding historic or scientific interest in Hertfordshire and neighbouring counties. The preservation of parks was left in the hands of private owners, most of whom could no longer afford to maintain them out of income from greatly reduced estates. Some parks and country houses were acquired by hotels and golf clubs, and some were adapted as colleges, schools and other institutions, but others continued to be demolished.

Notes

1. L. Stone and J.C.F. Stone, 'Country houses and their owners in Hertfordshire, 1540–1879', in W.O. Aydelotte, A.G. Bogue and R.W. Fogel (eds.), *The dimensions of quantitative research in history* (London, 1972) pp.56–123; L. Stone and J.C.F. Stone, *An open elite? England 1540–1880* (Oxford, 1984).

2. H. Chauncy, *The historical antiquities of Hertfordshire* (Bishops Stortford, 1826).

3. N. Salmon, *The history of Hertfordshire* (London, 1728); R. Clutterbuck, *The history and antiquities of the county of Hertford* (London, 1815–27), 3 vols;

J.E. Cussans, *History of Hertfordshire* (Hertford, 1870–81), 3 vols; *Victoria County History, Hertfordshire* (London, 1902–14), 4 vols.

4. J.T. Smith, *English houses: the Hertfordshire evidence* (London, 1992); J.T. Smith, *Hertfordshire houses: selective inventory* (London, 1993); the Oldfield and Buckler drawings are deposited in Hertfordshire Archives and Library Service (HALS D/EOf 1–9).

5. Hertfordshire Gardens Trust and R. Bisgrove, *Hertfordshire gardens on Ermine Street* (Abbots Langley, 1996); Hertfordshire Gardens Trust and T. Williamson, *The parks and gardens of west Hertfordshire* (Letchworth 2000); A. Rowe (ed) *Hertfordshire garden history: a miscellany* (Hatfield 2007).

6. J. Norden, *Speculi Britanniae pars. The description of Hartfordshire* (1598), p.2; G. Edelen (ed.), William Harrison, *the description of England, 1577–1587* (Ithaca NY, 1968), pp.253–63.

7. J. Habakkuk, *Marriage, debt and the estates system: English landownership 1650–1950* (Oxford, 1994), 1–49, 77–239.

Chapter II
Elizabethan Parks

PARKS APPEAR TO BE ANCIENT, almost permanent features in the landscape, but in Hertfordshire during the sixteenth century an exceptional amount of change took place, and Elizabethan maps show many parks that changed hands and changed in character after the Tudors came to power. At the beginning of the century, many old parks were in a poor state of repair: fences were neglected, some had been broken into, deer had been stolen and wood removed. Parks of rebellious lords had been confiscated and those belonging to abbots were seized in the process of dissolving the monasteries. During the second half of the century, loyal servants of the Crown who acquired great estates took over old parks and sought to create new ones. At the same time, population was increasing and food prices were rising, inducing owners to reclaim parkland for agriculture. At the end of the century, the number of old parks that had disappeared exceeded the number of newly created parks.

Most old parks occupied lands that were of little value for cultivation or were situated at the edges of settlements and fields, among woods and heaths along boundaries of parishes and around the county boundary. At the beginning of the sixteenth century, parks were, in the strict legal sense of the term, preserves for beasts of the chase, where privileged persons were licensed to keep and kill deer.[1] Tudor monarchs granted few licences to empark but nobles and gentlemen continued to enclose parks and continued to repair and renew decayed palings,[2] both to prevent deer escaping and causing damage

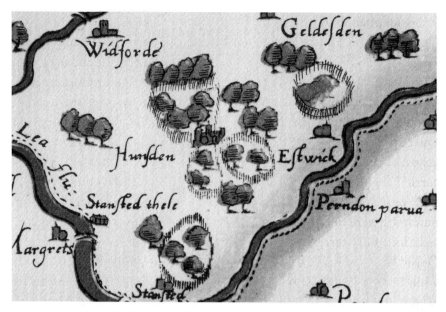

Figure 2.1: Cluster of parks at Hunsdon shown on Saxton's map, 1577. Christopher Saxton depicted three parks enclosed by palings clustered around the village of Hunsdon. These parks, and others at Stanstead and Gilston, had trees growing within and beyond the pales. Photograph by Matt Prince

to neighbours' property, but also to deter trespassers from entering and taking deer and wood. During this period many owners of parks decided to move from old manor houses in villages to new mansions within park pales, where they enjoyed greater privacy and displayed their superiority. These new houses were spacious and comfortable inside and well-proportioned outside; the principal residences faced courts at the back and front and, at the sides, were flanked by walled gardens, orchards, stables and farm buildings. Parks became more ornamental and much effort was spent on forestry and gardening. For Queen Elizabeth and her courtiers, deer hunting remained an important leisure activity, but domestic luxury and magnificent pleasure grounds were marks of greater refinement.

The first comprehensive record of parks in Hertfordshire was made by Christopher Saxton in his map of 1577. Another survey was carried out by John Norden twenty-two years later. These two maps provide the basic information about the number and size of parks and their place in the changing landscape.

Parks mapped by Christopher Saxton and John Norden

Christopher Saxton produced the first atlas of maps of all counties in England and Wales. It was a leading step in the Elizabethan discovery of the kingdom and the mapping of the world[3] and was commissioned by William Cecil, Queen Elizabeth's Secretary, just before he was created Lord Burghley in 1571. Thomas Seckford, Master of the Queen's Requests, financed the project and appointed Saxton, a 30-year-old Yorkshire surveyor, to prepare maps for publication. Saxton carried out the survey by measuring distances between church towers and beacons on hilltops. Courses of rivers and boundaries of hundreds were delineated, sites of settlements were plotted by perambulation, hilly terrain and wooded areas were depicted by symbols. Outlines of twenty-six parks were signified by rings of palings and, while they were not drawn to scale, differences in size were indicated (Figure 2.1). Hatfield, known from other sources to have contained about 1,000 acres, was shown much larger than any other park. A possibility that one or two parks were overlooked cannot be denied — one place not marked on the map is Aspenden Hall, where a park was recorded in an estate survey of 1556[4] — but Saxton would have taken great pains not to cause offence by omitting places belonging to powerful landowners and potential purchasers of his map. When the county surveys were completed, Saxton was granted a licence protecting his copyright for ten years.[5] The map of the county of Hertford, which was published in 1577, was engraved by Nicholas Reynolds at a scale of approximately 1 in 137,740 or about 0.46 inches to a statute mile.[6]

John Norden, the son of a Somerset yeoman farmer, was educated at Oxford University, trained as a lawyer and built up a busy practice as a land surveyor, valuer and estate agent. Among his patrons were the Queen, Lord Burghley and Christopher Hatton. In Hertfordshire, he was employed by Sir John Spencer to survey an estate at Barley in 1593.[7] From his extensive practical knowledge, he wrote an important book on surveying.[8] He was appointed Surveyor of Woods and Forests by Elizabeth I, a position he continued to hold under James I. Norden's map of Hertfordshire was part of a large project to survey the counties of England, sponsored by the Queen and privy council. He spent

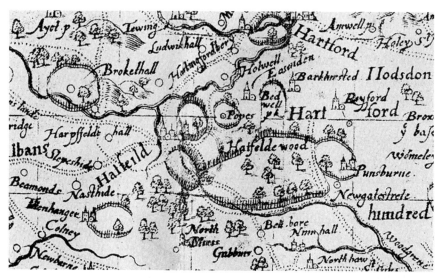

Figure 2.2: Parks around Hatfield shown on Norden's map, 1598. John Norden drew parks of different shapes and sizes, representing them as distinctive features in the landscape. Reproduced by kind permission of Hertfordshire Archives and Library Service

a long time travelling, often begrimed with mud from 'deep and dirty roads,' and complained repeatedly that he had not been paid for his services.[9] The Hertfordshire map was published in 1598 and, although it was engraved at a smaller scale of approximately 1 in 301,720 or about 0.21 inches to one mile, it displayed more information than Saxton's. It showed major roads, market towns, parish churches and other settlements, and, significantly, the delineation of the boundaries of thirty-one parks was more realistic and probably more accurate than Saxton's (Figure 2.2). Norden's description of Hertfordshire, written to accompany the map, commented on the large number of parks in the county: 'This Shire at this day is, and more hath beene heretofore, much repleat with parkes, woodes and rivers.'[10]

Putting information from Saxton's and Norden's maps together, a total of thirty-six parks is shown on Figure 2.3. This Figure and subsequent compilations from county maps have been constructed by plotting the National Grid References of historic parks located on modern maps. The county boundary is that of the historic county before the reorganisation of local government boundaries in 1974. Some Elizabethan parks were situated at a distance from towns:

Table 2.1 Parks in Hertfordshire in 1577 and 1598

Park	Grid reference	Source	Owner in 1598
Ardeley Bury	301269	N	Henry Chauncy
Bedwell Park, Essendon	277076	S N	Sir Edward Denny
Benington Park	310236	S N	Frances, Countess of Clanricarde
Berkhamsted Place	991088	S N	Sir Edward Carey
Brocket Hall, Hatfield	214130	S N	Sir John Brocket
Cassiobury, Watford	081975	N	Sir Charles Morrison
Cheshunt Park	347046	S N	Sir Henry Cock
Digswell House, Welwyn	250151	N	Thomas Perient
Furneux Pelham	427279	S	William Parker, Lord Morley
Gilston Park	441122	S	George Chauncy
Hadham Park, Lt Hadham	452227	S N	Sir Arthur Capel
Hatfield	236084	S N	Queen Elizabeth
Hatfield, Millwards	236065	S N	Queen Elizabeth
Hatfield Wood	247063	S N	Queen Elizabeth
Hatfield Woodhall, Welwyn	235106	S	Robert Cecil, Earl of Salisbury
Hertingfordbury Park	310121	S N	Queen Elizabeth
Hunsdon, Old Park	424143	S N	Henry Carey, Lord Hunsdon
Hunsdon, New Park	414131	S N	Henry Carey, Lord Hunsdon
Hunsdon, Goodmanshyde	419127	S N	Henry Carey, Lord Hunsdon
Kings Langley	063016	S N	Edward Russell, Earl of Bedford
Morehouse, Rickmansworth	075933	N	Edward Russell, Earl of Bedford
Pendley, Tring	943118	S N	Edmund Verney
Ponsbourne Park, Hatfield	304054	S N	Sir John Cocke
Popes, Hatfield	259077	N	Walter Tooke
Rye Park, Stanstead Abbots	387100	N	William Frankland
Salisbury Hall, Shenley	195028	S N	Sir John Cutte
Shingle Hall, Sawbridgeworth	469172	S N	John Leventhorpe
Sopwell, St Albans	155053	N	Humphrey Coningsby
Standon Lordship	392214	S N	Sir Thomas Sadler
Stanstead Bury, Stanstead Abbots	400111	S	Edward Baesh
Stortford Park, Bishops Stortford	470212	N	Sir Edward Denny
Theobalds, Cheshunt	345011	N	Robert Cecil, Earl of Salisbury
Tyttenhanger, Ridge	192047	S N	Sir Thomas Pope
Walkern Park	316247	S N	Henry Capel
Ware Park	333144	S N	Thomas Fanshawe
Woodhall Park, Watton	318189	N	Sir Philip Boteler

Sources: S = Christopher Saxton, map of *Hertfordiae Comitatus* (1577); N = John Norden, map of *Hartford Shire* (1598)

Morehouse, Ardeley Bury, Walkern, Benington Park, Hatfield Wood, Ponsbourne and Cheshunt Park all lay half a mile or more from the nearest town or village and were bordered by woods, commons and heaths. They appear on the map as besieged stockades facing advancing farmland and urban expansion.

Parkland reclaimed for agriculture

During this period, population in Hertfordshire increased rapidly as birth rates rose and peaks of mortality fell; numbers were swollen by net migration into the county and by movement within the county towards London. In the course of the sixteenth century, population in south Hertfordshire doubled.[11] At the same time, transport, commerce and industry prospered. Navigation on the Lea was improved between 1571 and 1581, merchants and innkeepers in St Albans accumulated considerable wealth and paper-making, flour-milling, malting and brewing expanded.[12]

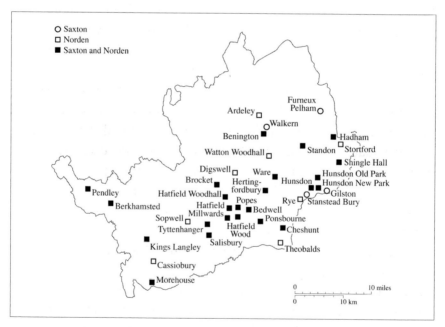

Figure 2.3: Parks in Elizabethan Hertfordshire, 1577 and 1598. Parks have been located within the pre-1974 boundary of Hertfordshire by reference to the National Grid. Full details are listed in Table 2.1. Based on Christopher Saxton, Hertfordiae Comitatus, *1577 and John Norden,* Hartford Shire, *1598. Drawn in the Geography Department Drawing Office at University College, London*

More mouths to feed and more money to spend led to growth in demand for foodstuffs and inflated prices. The fortunes of landlords and yeomen farmers were boosted, while landless labourers were impoverished. From 1500 to 1599, prices of bread and other consumables rose steeply. Figure 2.4 indicates that prices of wheat rose about four and a half times, and those of barley and oats from five to six times, partly impelled by severe scarcities of grain that were experienced from 1549 to 1551, 1554 to 1556, 1585 to 1586 and from 1594 to 1598. During the sixteenth century, prices of live cattle and sheep increased between four- and five-fold, while those of animal produce, including milk, butter, cheese, wool and hides, increased by three or four times.[13] Joan Thirsk describes the 'powerful influence' exerted by the London market on the growth of commercial agriculture: from Rickmansworth in the west to Cheshunt in the east, the breeding of horses, the fattening of cattle, pigs, chickens and geese, and the making of butter were all directed towards consumers in London, while farms in the north-east of the county supplied the metropolis with wheat and malting barley. Boats carrying farm produce down the Lea and Colne returned loaded with town manure.[14] Agriculture and related activities were booming.

Lords responded by engaging in piecemeal clearing of woods, reclaiming heaths, ploughing up pastures and also converting parks into farmland; in 1587, William Harrison lamented that any park should remain occupied by wild and savage beasts, cherished solely for pleasure and delight, rendering no profit.[15] An unrecorded number of parks was lost in the process. The economic incentive to bring new land into cultivation was strongest in southern Hertfordshire, a district which was still thickly wooded in 1500. Extensive stands of tall oaks covered much of Enfield Chase and oakwoods also occupied large tracts in Hatfield, Elstree, Aldenham and Northwood. Dense woodland was interspersed with open glades of birch heath and thickets of gorse and bracken, as at Littleheath, Letchmore Heath, Bushey Heath and Batchworth Heath. Medieval parks at Hoddesdon, Little Berkhamsted and Periers in Cheshunt, on the fringes of densely wooded Enfield Chase, were not marked on Saxton's and Norden's maps. Other medieval parks situated in wooded localities in south

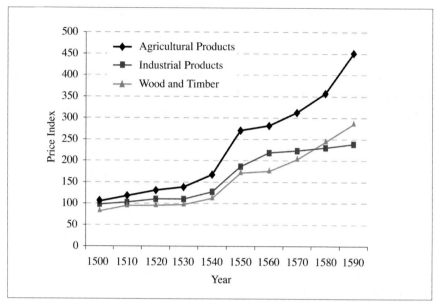

Figure 2.4: Rise in prices 1485–1585, showing that prices of agricultural products rose faster than those of industrial products or wood and timber. Price index 100 = average for 1450–99. Based on P. Bowden in Thirsk, Agrarian history vol. IV, pp. 595, 862. Drawn in the Geography Department, UCL

Hertfordshire, at Boreham Wood and Little Munden adjoining Bricket Wood, were also absent from late sixteenth-century maps. There is no direct evidence that these parks were ploughed up before the Elizabethan maps were surveyed but accounts of sales of timber and decayed trees and leases of coppice from Crown estates in Hertfordshire indicate that extensive areas of woodlands were being cleared in this period.[16] During the sixteenth century prices of wood and timber increased almost three times (Figure 2.4), offering a powerful inducement to landowners to cut down mature trees.[17]

Fears of commoners' hostility at losses of their common grazing rights and fears of an impending timber shortage were frequently expressed. Between 1489 and 1563, a number of ineffective acts of parliament were intended to prevent further enclosure of commons and, in 1543, the first act was passed to protect woodlands. It stipulated that twelve young trees be left standing on each acre cut. Subsequent acts imposed further restrictions on clearance, reserving stands of oak trees for naval shipbuilding and banning clear felling within fourteen miles of navigable water. In districts where scarcity of land was acute, complaints against landowners for clearing woods and enclosing commons were investigated: in 1575, for instance, Queen Elizabeth appointed a commission to inquire into the spoiling of woods belonging to Colney Chapel and, in 1577, another inquiry was set up into the death of deer at Hatfield.[18] Restrictive edicts failed to stop the destruction of timber, and some of the largest clearings were made on royal estates. In Hammersley's opinion, the Crown sold timber 'to the point of national improvidence'.[19] Both Henry VIII and Elizabeth I shamelessly gave away standing timber to their favourite courtiers. Lesser lords sought ways of avoiding legal penalties: in 1598 Francis Heydon of Watford obtained a licence to cut down timber and coppices in his park at Oxhey and convert it into tillage. His plea was accepted that 'the country thereabout was sufficiently replenished with wood'.[20]

Changing ownership of land

The disappearance of medieval parks and the creation of new parks were closely associated with sweeping changes in landownership. Feudal lords who took up arms against the Crown in the Wars of the Roses forfeited their estates by acts of attainder; estates of those who were killed or died without issue reverted to the Crown under common law. Henry VII, Henry VIII and their treasurers were assiduous in resuming possession of lands that had been misappropriated and resolute in raising rents of properties that had been undervalued. Later Tudor administrators were overwhelmed by an increasing workload and corrupt practices were allowed to creep in; under Edward VI and Mary efficiency in collecting rents and receipts from sales of Crown land declined precipitously.[21]

Laxity in the administration of Crown lands was matched by poor estate management among the aristocracy. Few sixteenth-century peers kept accounts that distinguished between capital and income or between recurring and non-recurring payments, and accounts for different estates and households were kept in different places by officers who practised different methods of book-keeping. Many landowners failed to exercise effective control over their finances and failed to increase their incomes.[22] Families of spendthrift and warring lords attempted to avoid financial ruin by selling timber or exploiting minerals, but some were forced to dispose of their lands. The volume of land sales increased relentlessly from the mid-fifteenth century.[23]

After 1500, the market in land expanded at an accelerating rate and a new class of freehold owner emerged. Some new owners held offices of state and were rewarded by gifts of land. John Russell, created earl of Bedford, owed his fortune to the favour of Henry VIII. Descended from Dorset shipowners and wine merchants, he married Anne Sapcote, daughter and heiress of a Huntingdonshire gentleman who owned three manors. In 1538, the king appointed Russell Lord President of the West to settle religious unrest and restrain landlord oppression. In return for his hard work and faithful service he received extensive estates in Devon and Cornwall, and later went on to purchase and exchange many manors in Bedfordshire, Buckinghamshire, Cambridgeshire, Suffolk, London and other parts of England. In Hertfordshire, he was given custody of royal parks at Kings Langley and the Moor at Rickmansworth. He was most active in estate-building during the years 1540 to 1545 and improved the management of his properties, but did not embark on agricultural innovation. His successors, fortunately, could well afford the luxury of keeping parks.[24] John's son, Francis Russell, the second earl, lived at Chenies in Buckinghamshire, marked on Saxton's map. The third earl, Edward Russell, married Lucy Harington and they lived at Moor Park in Hertfordshire.[25] Both Moor Park and Kings Langley Park are marked on Norden's map.

Other newcomers purchased land with money earned in professions, notably in the practice of law, or from the profits of commercial ventures. One of the most successful lawyers to acquire land in Hertfordshire was Sir Nicholas Bacon. Son of the sheep reeve of Bury St Edmunds Abbey, Bacon went to Corpus Christi College, Cambridge, and, after graduating, travelled in France. In 1532, he was admitted to Grays Inn. His practice in the Court of Augmentations, conveying, administering and arranging sales and gifts of monastic lands, brought advancement and wealth; he was appointed attorney in the Court of Wards from 1545 and made Lord

Keeper in 1558. He had opportunities to buy, often at very cheap prices, lands in many parts of eastern England. In Hertfordshire, he acquired Gorhambury and nearby properties at Childwick, Windridge, Burston, Redbourn and Parker's Place, Kings Langley. In 1563, he began building a mansion and enclosed a large park at Gorhambury. At the time of his death, in 1578, income from his Hertfordshire estates alone amounted to £406.[26]

Whilst some of the more established nobility lost their estates or leased parks to farmers, other members of ancient families took advantage of new opportunities to expand their holdings. The turnover of property in the market was remarkably rapid. Lionel Munby has estimated that the 'average Hertfordshire manor changed hands at least two or three times' between 1540 and 1700.[27] These findings are confirmed by Clive Holmes, who concludes that no more than 10 per cent of the leading gentry who took sides in the Civil War were descended from families that had settled in the county before 1485.[28] Similarly, Lawrence and Jeanne Stone have calculated that only two out of sixty-three owners of landed estates in Cashio and Dacorum hundreds in 1663 held those estates before 1500.[29]

Following the dissolution of the monasteries, over a quarter of the surface area of Hertfordshire changed hands. Monastic estates included some of the poorest soils as well as much productive land in the south-west. Out of sixteen parks that passed from monastic to lay owners, only two, Tyttenhanger and Ardeley Bury, were recorded on Saxton's and Norden's maps. The Crown kept the largest share of the confiscated property, while acquisitive large landowners bought former monastic land and other land from the Crown to add to existing holdings; small owners bought and sold land speculatively. Joyce Youings observes that 'very few new or appreciably large estates were built up entirely or even principally out of monastic land'.[30] The Cecil, Russell, Bacon, Fanshawe, Caesar, Baesh, Mildmay and Audley families were simply more active buyers and sellers of land than others: they were the keenest bargain-hunters, enlarging their estates with donations from the Crown and arranging additional purchases and exchanges by private agreements.

New owners, new houses and new parks

Some new owners built fine mansions in brick and stone within the pales of ancient parks. Foremost among the newcomers were high officers appointed by Tudor monarchs. Sir John Cutte, Under-Treasurer to Henry VII and Henry VIII, built a 'very sumptuous house' in Salisbury Park, Shenley, between 1507 and 1519.[31] A much larger mansion was built in a medieval park at Standon Lordship by Sir Ralph Sadler, one of Henry VIII's principal secretaries,[32] and another fine house was erected in 1570–75 in an ancient park at Ware by Thomas Fanshawe, Queen's Remembrancer of the Exchequer.[33] In 1559, Queen Elizabeth gave a palatial estate at Hunsdon to Henry Carey, her first cousin on the Boleyn side. Carey, who was created Lord Hunsdon and appointed Lord Chamberlain of the Household, made three adjoining parks at Hunsdon.[34] Salisbury Park, Standon Lordship, Ware Park and the parks at Hunsdon were created by families advanced and enriched by services to the Crown.

Many other parks marked the rise of landed gentry to positions of eminence in the county. In an old park at Little Hadham, Henry Capel, a new member of the gentry, built Hadham Hall between 1572 and 1578.[35] In the 1570s, another landowner, Sir John Brocket, built a courtyard mansion in a park of just under 100 acres that bears his family's name.[36] A few places were founded by wealthy merchants. Before 1590, Walter Mildmay, a London merchant, built a 'very neat and fair' house within the pales of Pishiobury Park.[37]

Comfortable Tudor houses within parks were secluded from the watchful attention of villagers and their owners were able to withdraw from the daily obligation to play their parts as lords of the manor or ladies bountiful. Many houses were not only set within high park palings but were surrounded by walled gardens and courts, and embellished with trellises, ponds, knotted beds, mounts, sundials and statues. Tudor gardens raised fruit, medicinal herbs and vegetables and some also grew flowers, admired as much for their scent as their colour.[38] Many of the new elite, who were also leading builders, sprang from peasant stock and rose in one or two generations through the ranks of the yeomanry and gentry. Their wealth increased from 'steadily rising selling prices' and fixed expenses.[39] In Hertfordshire, the 'great rebuilding' began much

Figure 2.5: Queen Elizabeth's hunting party. Queen Elizabeth enjoyed hunting at Theobalds Park, surrounded by courtiers and servants. Accompanying 'George Gascoigne, On the commendation of the noble arte of venerie', 1576. Photograph by Anne Rowe

earlier than in other parts of England. Work started in the 1530s and by 1550 foundations for thirty large houses had been laid,[40] many of which were sited in parks shown on late sixteenth-century maps.

Lost parks

Some landowners, particularly absentees, did not follow the fashion. They were more interested in collecting rents and promoting agricultural improvements than spending money on building and keeping parks. Some laid out neat gardens enclosed by high walls or hedges while, at the same time, breaking up old parks. Parks that formerly belonged to monasteries at Boreham Wood, Bramfield Bury, Codicote Bury, Easneye, Little Munden, Oxhey and St Albans, as well as the

Bishop of Ely's old park at Little Berkhamsted and the Bishop of London's former park at Moor Place in Much Hadham, did not appear on Saxton's and Norden's maps. While the representation of park palings on a map is clear evidence for the presence of a park in the landscape, the absence of a park symbol is not conclusive evidence for the disappearance of a park. However, in north-east Hertfordshire, there is a lack of any kind of evidence, whether cartographic or documentary, of medieval parks having survived. It may be inferred that losses there were heavier than elsewhere.

In other parts of the county, several large parks were reduced in size. Most of Ashridge Park was converted to farmland and a survey in 1575 recorded only eighty-three acres of parkland remaining. It was called Bush Park and was represented neither on Saxton's nor on Norden's map.[41] At Knebworth, two parks and a warren together

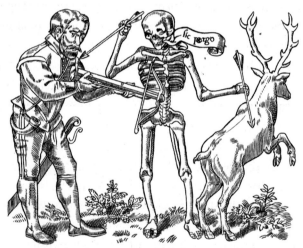

BELOVED OF ALL WHILST HE HAD LYFE
VNMOEND OF NONE WHEN HE DID DIE,
IAMES GRAY, INTERRED OF HIS WIFE
NEER TO THIS DEATHS SIGNE BRASSE DOTH LYE
YEARES THIRTIE FYVE, IN GOOD RENOWNNE
PARKE AND HOVSE KEPER IN THIS TOWNE
OBIIT 12·DIE DECEMBRIS A° DNI 1591
ÆTATIS SVE 69

Figure 2.6: Memorial brass to James Gray, keeper of Hunsdon Park, 1591. Hunsdon Park was owned by Henry Carey, Lord Hunsdon. He was Lord Chamberlain and cousin of Queen Elizabeth. The keeper was a highly respected person. Illustrated in Henry Cokayne Gibbs, The parish registers of Hunsdon, county Hertford (London, 1915), opposite p. 12. Reproduced by kind permission of Hertfordshire Archives and Library Service (HALS)

occupied over 500 acres at the beginning of the sixteenth century, but they were not recorded on Saxton's and Norden's maps.[42] In the 1560s parts of the Great Park were let for pasturing a few cows and horses and at about the same time Rowland Lytton built a new courtyard house to the west of the medieval parks. It is not known whether deer were kept when Queen Elizabeth stayed at Knebworth in 1571 and perhaps again in 1588; it would have been a courtesy to offer the queen the pleasure of a hunt.

By this time Henry VIII and Elizabeth had turned deer hunting into an elaborate ritual in which a deer was driven by hounds along a prepared course towards a 'standing' where bowmen were positioned to shoot the approaching quarry. On these occasions, the royal hunting party would take their refreshments sheltered by trees in the park (Figure 2.5). Park-keepers at places visited by the queen or her courtiers, where formal hunts were arranged, enjoyed respected positions in local communities. Such a person was James Gray, the keeper at Hunsdon Park, whose death in 1591 was commemorated by a brass placed in Hunsdon parish church (Figure 2.6). The brass portrays Gray aiming at a stag while Death aims at him.[43] Ambitious courtiers and status-seeking landowners imitated the monarch by keeping parks but puritan commentators increasingly abhorred their vanity and complained of the waste of land and resources.[44] In the second half of the sixteenth century, opposition to enclosures for deer strengthened and, at the same time, landed gentlemen were inclined to take profits from grazing cattle.[45]

In the sixteenth century, Hertfordshire was seriously troubled by criminal gangs who broke into parks and stole deer. More than any other county, its roads were marauded by highwaymen.[46] In 1533, Sir John Russell, who was entrusted by Henry VIII to keep Moor Park, reported to the king's secretary, Thomas Cromwell, that travellers and wagoners had broken down the hedges and made a highway through the park. Of the 500 deer that had been placed in Russell's care only 100 remained; the rest had escaped from the park or been killed. He ordered 200 oaks to be cut down to make 1,500 stakes for repairing the fence.[47] The depredations of thieves and trespassers further deterred many owners from improving or even maintaining parks.

Parks newly represented on Elizabethan maps

Maps of the late sixteenth century depicted fourteen parks that were not recorded in the medieval period. Some of these were newly imparked. The manor house of Holbeaches in Hatfield was referred to in 1542 as the manor house of Popes Park,[48] and the building of a new house within the park began in 1555. Sopwell had been a small priory of Benedictine nuns and shortly after the dissolution the property was granted to Sir Richard Lee, a military engineer. Lee began building a new house on the site about 1550 and in 1562 he proposed to close the road from St Albans to London via Shenley in order to encircle his new park with palings.[49] Stanstead Bury belonged to the Augustinian abbey of Waltham before the dissolution. In 1559, the decayed manor was granted to Edward Baesh, styled 'General Surveyor of Victuals for the Navy Royal', who, in 1577, obtained a licence to empark 300 acres. When he died in 1587, the estate included the house and grounds, covering fifteen acres, and a park containing 100 deer.[50] Among other places that appeared as new parks on Saxton's and Norden's maps, the park at Brocket was described in 1580 and the building of new houses during the sixteenth century was recorded at Cassiobury, Digswell, Hatfield Woodhall, Tyttenhanger and Woodhall in Watton.[51]

The making of deer parks was dazzlingly outshone by the splendour of the newly built palace at Theobalds and the creation of intricate knot gardens, fragrant herb gardens, luxuriant kitchen gardens, vineyards, orchards, well-stocked fishponds, ingeniously contrived fountains, mounts and gazebos. Theobalds was acquired by Sir William Cecil in 1564 and the building of a palatial mansion began in 1571. The gardens were supervised by John Gerard, the leading English herbalist. In 1585, when the mansion and gardens were almost completed, the park at Theobalds was enclosed by a wall some eight miles in length. James I, who received the property from Robert Cecil in exchange for Hatfield Park, further enlarged the park, and in 1620 the extended park wall was nine and a half miles long.[52] The creation of spacious gardens within the confines of a large park was a precursor to the development of Renaissance gardens in parks in the early seventeenth century.

Decline of parks and change of owners

The dominant motifs in parkland history during the sixteenth century were contraction and replacement. Many old parks were swept away as owners converted land to productive agricultural use. There was a net loss in the number of parks and a reduction in the size of deer herds. Many old estates passed into the hands of up-and-coming families rising from the peasantry, and replacement of owners occurred on a large scale and at a very rapid pace. Among established landowners, the Crown alone increased its holdings.

Possession of a large share of the nation's acres gave Tudor monarchs the strength to overthrow feudal and papal institutions. The monarchy exacted a high price for bringing peace to the country: feudal lords were forced reluctantly to disband private armies; rebels of the highest rank were summarily executed and their estates confiscated; control of the church was wrested from the Pope and the Crown seized vast estates formerly held by monasteries and some bishoprics; feudal retainers and monastic servants were thrown out of work, some joining unemployed apprentices, wounded soldiers, victims of enclosure and strolling players as vagrants and casual labourers. When the church ceased to give alms or help the old and sick, alternative means of caring for the poor and homeless had to be found, and new landowners were left with the formidable tasks of organising poor relief and maintaining law and order in their home localities. Justices of the peace, without retinues of armed men, had to deal with multitudes of poor and dispossessed people. The invasion of Moor Park by travellers and wagoners, an offence against one of Henry VIII's most powerful servants, the Lord Privy Seal, illustrates how precarious was the peace of the realm. By the end of the sixteenth century, the new elite sought wider powers and more resources to protect private property. The outlook for parks was unsettled.

Notes

1. *Oxford English Dictionary* 11 (1989), p.234, defines 'park' as '1. Law. An enclosed tract of land, held by royal grant or prescription for keeping beasts of the chase. Distinguished from a forest or chase by being enclosed and from a forest also by having no special laws or officers.'

2.   As their most distinctive feature, palings were used as symbols for parks on Elizabethan maps.

3.   A.L. Rowse, 'The Elizabethan discovery of England' in A.L. Rowse, *The England of Elizabeth: the structure of society* (London, 1950), pp.31–65.

4.   Smith, *Hertfordshire houses*, p.15.

5.   C. Delano-Smith and R.J.P. Kain, *English maps: a history* (London, 1999), 66–75; J.B. Harley, 'Christopher Saxton and the first atlas of England and Wales 1579–1979', *The Map Collector*, 8 (1979), pp.3–11; I.M. Evans and H. Lawrence, *Christopher Saxton. Elizabethan map-maker* (Wakefield, 1979).

6.   D. Hodson, *Printed maps of Hertfordshire, 1577–1900* (Folkestone, 1974).

7.   F. Kitchen, 'John Norden, c.1547–1625: estate surveyor, topographer, county mapmaker and devotional writer', *Imago Mundi*, 49 (1997), pp.43–61; J. C. Wilkerson (ed.) *John Norden's survey of Barley, Hertfordshire, 1593-1603* (Cambridge, 1974).

8.   J. Norden, *The Surveior's dialogue* (London, 1607).

9.   Kitchen, 'John Norden', p.44.

10. Norden, *Speculi Britanniae pars. The description of Hartfordshire*, p.2.

11. L.M. Munby, *Hertfordshire population statistics, 1563–1801* (Hitchin, 1964), pp.21–3.

12. H.J. Dyos and D.H. Aldcroft, *British transport: an economic survey from the seventeenth century to the twentieth* (Harmondsworth, 1974), pp.24, 40; W. Branch Johnson, *The industrial archaeology of Hertfordshire* (Newton Abbot, 1970), pp.28–61.

13. P. Bowden, 'Agricultural prices, farm profits and rents'; also 'Statistical appendix' Tables I, VIII, IX, XI, XII, XIII, in J. Thirsk (ed.), *The agrarian history of England and Wales*. vol. IV, 1500–1650 (Cambridge, 1967), pp.593–5, 601–9, 817–20, 857–62.

14. J. Thirsk, 'The farming regions of England: four Home Counties', in J. Thirsk (ed.), *The agrarian history of England and Wales*. vol. IV 1500–1650 (Cambridge, 1967), pp.49–52; P. Glennie, 'Continuity and change in Hertfordshire agriculture 1550–1700: I. Patterns of agricultural production', *Agricultural History Review*, 36 (1988), pp.55–76.

15. Edelen, William Harrison, *The description of England*, pp.253–63.

16. G. Hammersley, 'The crown woods and their exploitation in the sixteenth and seventeenth centuries', *Bulletin of the Institute of Historical Research*, 30 (1957), pp.136–61.

17. Bowden, 'Agricultural prices, farm profits and rents', pp.607, 862.

18. J.C. Cox, 'Forestry', in *VCH Hertfordshire*, vol. 4 (London, 1914), p.276.

19. Hammersley, 'Crown woods', p.137; G. Batho, 'Landlords in England: the crown', in J. Thirsk (ed.), *The agrarian history of England and Wales*. vol. IV 1500–1650 (Cambridge, 1967), pp.256–73.

20. Hertfordshire County Record Office (HCRO 10148) cited in G. Longman, *A corner of England's garden: an agrarian history of south-west Hertfordshire 1600–1850* (Bushey, 1977), p.6.

21. J. Youings, *Sixteenth-century England* (Harmondsworth, 1984), pp.52–3, 105–6.

22. Batho, 'Landlords in England', pp.276–85.

23. J.M.W. Bean, 'Landlords: the market for land', in E. Miller (ed.), *The agrarian history of England and Wales*. vol. III 1348–1500 (Cambridge, 1991), pp.562–8.

24. D. Willen, *John Russell, first earl of Bedford: one of the king's men* (London, 1981), pp.23, 31, 56, 62, 74, 115, 126–7.

25. G.E.C., *The complete peerage of England, Scotland and Ireland*, vol. 2 (London, 1912), 77–8.

26. A. Simpson, *The wealth of the gentry 1540–1660: East Anglian studies* (Cambridge, 1961), pp.22–71, 111; J.E.B. Gover, A. Mawer and F.M. Stenton, *The place-names of Hertfordshire*, English Place-Name Society XV (Cambridge, 1938), pp.78, 91, 92, 97.

27. L.M. Munby, *The Hertfordshire landscape* (London, 1977), p.140.

28. C.A. Holmes, *The Eastern Association in the English Civil War* (London, 1974), pp.12–14, Appendix 3, p.231.

29. Stone and Stone, 'Country houses', p.94.

30. J. Youings, *The dissolution of the monasteries* (London, 1971), p.130.

31. *VCH Hertfordshire*, vol. 2 (London, 1908), pp.267–8; Gover, Mawer and Stenton, *Place-Names of Hertfordshire*, pp.68, 274.

32. *VCH Hertfordshire*, vol. 3 (London, 1912), pp.353–4.

33. *VCH Hertfordshire*, vol. 3, pp.385–8; Cussans, *History of Hertfordshire*, vol. 1, p.140.

34. Stone and Stone, *An open elite?*, p.198.

35. *VCH Hertfordshire*, vol. 4 (London, 1914), pp.50–4; W. Minet, *The manor of Hadham Hall* (Little Hadham, 1914).

36. Gover, Mawer and Stenton, *Place-Names of Hertfordshire*, p.127; *VCH Hertfordshire*, vol. 2, pp.101–2.

37. *VCH Hertfordshire*, vol. 3, pp.337–8.

38. M. Hadfield, *A history of British gardening* (London, 1985); T. Hill, *The profitable art of gardening* (1568).

39. W.G. Hoskins, 'The rebuilding of rural England, 1570–1640', *Past and Present*, 4 (1953), pp.44–59, quote from p.50.

40. Stone and Stone, *An open elite?*, pp.429–31.

41. A. Wainwright, *The Ashridge Park survey*, unpublished report for the National Trust (1989), pp.10–12; Hertfordshire Gardens Trust and T. Williamson, *The parks and gardens of west Hertfordshire* (Letchworth, 2000), p.14.

42. A. Rowe, 'The parks of Knebworth', unpublished MS (2004) (HALS Herts Gardens Trust 3898), pp.1–4.

43. N. Pevsner, revised by B. Cherry, *The buildings of England: Hertfordshire* (Harmondsworth, 1992), p.211.

44. Edelen, *William Harrison, Description of England.*

45. J. Thirsk, 'Enclosing and engrossing', in J. Thirsk (ed.), *The agrarian history of England and Wales.* vol. IV 1500–1650 (Cambridge, 1967), p.239.

46. Youings, *Sixteenth century England*, p.222.

47. J. Gairdner, *Letters and Papers of Henry VIII* (London, 1882), vol. 6, nos 347, 426.

48. *VCH Hertfordshire,* vol. 3, p.103.

49. *VCH Hertfordshire,* vol. 2, pp.413, 422–6.

50. *VCH Hertfordshire,* vol. 3, 369; Inquisition Post Mortem, The National Archives: Public Record Office (TNA: C142/ 215/ 269).

51. Smith, *Hertfordshire houses*, pp.202, 206, 208.

52. J. Summerson, 'The building of Theobalds, 1564-1585', *Archaeologia* 97 (1959), pp.107–26; C. Read, *Lord Burghley and Queen Elizabeth* (London, 1960), pp.121–4; C. Read, 'Lord Burghley's household accounts', *Economic History Review*, 2nd ser. 9 (1956), p.344.

Chapter III
Restoration Parks

IN THE SEVENTEENTH CENTURY, parks continued to disappear from the landscape. Protests against enclosures were most vehement where common land was taken into parks, and puritans directed their harshest complaints at lords who exploited the poor in order to indulge in the pleasures of hunting. Some landowners acknowledged that parks were luxuries they could ill afford and many others simply took advantage of whatever opportunities arose to make money. In some places, unsaleable deer were replaced by profit-making cattle or sheep; in others, trees were cut down for sale and to make room for tillage. Throughout the seventeenth century, thrift rather than pride dictated landowners' choices.

Renaissance gardens in parkland settings
King James and a few who shared his tastes ignored the prevailing mercenary attitudes to land use. The king, Robert Cecil, Lucy Harington, William Herbert and Francis Bacon were all enchanted by Renaissance palace gardens in Italy and France and sought to adorn their own parks in a similar manner. At Hatfield, Moor Park and Gorhambury, the beauties of Florentine gardens were transferred to a colder climate and classical terraces were reconstructed on gentle slopes in sylvan settings. They were designed to excite the senses and, above all, to please the eye. Unlike earlier gardens they were not entirely closed in; they were intended to be viewed at a distance, from the windows of the house, and walked through so that visitors might

enjoy at close quarters the colours, textures and scents of plants and hear the sounds of falling water. They also contained wildernesses, composed of selected natural features artistically arranged. The size of these gardens was larger than any previously created.

In Queen Elizabeth's reign, gardens at Theobalds Park were laid out under the direction of William Cecil, first Earl of Salisbury. They were enlarged by James I, who exchanged Theobalds for Hatfield in 1607. William Cecil's son Robert, second Earl of Salisbury, immediately began to plan a splendid new mansion and equally splendid gardens for Hatfield. The gardener from Theobalds, Mountain Jennings, together with Robert Bell, a London merchant and garden expert, drafted the first overall plans. The detailed layout of the east garden was carried out by Thomas Chaundler from 1609 to 1611. After the king came to stay in July 1611, the leading Renaissance gardener, a Huguenot, Salomon de Caus, employed by Queen Anne at Somerset House and Greenwich, took over the supervision of the east garden. De Caus engineered a water garden, constructing a new cistern, fountains and an artificial watercourse, and the garden was laid out as a flight of terraces descending to a new pond. Plots were planted by John Tradescant the elder, who brought 'shiploads of rare trees, fruits, flowers, plants and seeds' from Holland, Flanders and France.[1] Marie de Medici donated 500 exotic fruit trees and 10,000 vines and sent two of her gardeners to attend to their planting. The wife of the French ambassador sent 20,000 vines for the Vineyard, a sunny pleasaunce formed on the banks of the Lea. This was laid out on a rectilinear plan, formally divided into sections by trim yew hedges embellished with topiary work. Fountains were erected at the ends of parallel alleys and water from the basins of these fountains was conducted in narrow channels to the river.[2] The Jacobean gardens at Hatfield were opulent, magnificent and prodigiously spacious, but were not integrated into a unified whole.

Moor Park was inherited by Lucy Harington, Countess of Bedford, whose imagination was fired by Renaissance gardens in Italy. About 1617, she began to build a new house on high ground overlooking the Colne valley. The slope was laid out in three terraces. The house faced a broad, open, gravelled walk flanked on each side by summer houses. A line of clipped standard laurels stood at the edge of this platform and three flights of stone steps descended to the gardens below. The middle terrace was partitioned into quarters by gravel walks. Two quarters were adorned with statues at the four corners; the other two quarters were centred on fountains. The sides of this parterre were ranged with cloisters, sheltered walks open to the gardens. Another two summer houses stood at the ends of the cloisters, overlooking the lowest level. Many steps led down the face of the lower terrace on each side of a grotto decorated with shell rock-work, fountains and waterworks. The lowest garden was a wilderness, planted with fruit trees and crossed by shady walks carpeted with mown grass. It was a balanced and harmonious composition of terrace walk descending to terrace garden, descending again to orchard wilderness. Sir William Temple, who visited Moor Park in 1655, praised the gardens as 'the most beautiful and perfect, at least in Figure and Disposition, that I have ever seen'.[3] Questions about the author-ship of the Italianate gardens remain unanswered. Roy Strong attributes the design to Isaac de Caus, a young relative of Salomon de Caus, who worked at Hatfield. Inigo Jones and Isaac de Caus designed the gardens at Wilton for William Herbert, Earl of Pembroke, and Pembroke took possession of Moor Park after Lucy Harington's death in 1627.[4] The wording of a deed of sale in 1631 implies that there were then two gardens: 'the new garden adjoining the great house to the E lately erected and built by Will. Earl of Pembroke; the other garden with the Bowling Green to the W of the great house', which may refer to the earlier occupation by Edward, late Earl of Bedford, and Lucy, his wife.[5] In the 1670s, the Renaissance gardens were swept away.

At Gorhambury, no more than fragments of a Renaissance garden were completed. When Francis Bacon inherited his father's large estate and Elizabethan house in 1601, he had already thought deeply about gardens. Years passed before he started putting his ideas into practice. He spoke with the Earl of Salisbury about a scheme to con-vert the Pondyards by the river Ver into a place of pleasure and, in July 1608, he drafted a plan to construct islands in a square lake bor-dered by a broad gravel walk, screened by rows of lime and birch trees.[6] In contriving the waterworks, Bacon was assisted by Thomas Bushell, who later created a weird and marvellous hermitage and grotto at Enstone in Oxfordshire.[7] The Pondyards eventually occupied over four acres and, a short distance to the south, Bacon built Verulam House with a balustraded viewing platform on the roof from which to admire the water gardens. At the top of the hill, about a mile from the Pondyards, a grove of oaks and other choice forest trees was described by John Aubrey as 'rarely planted and finely kept in his lordship's time'. To the east of this lay a thicket of plum trees with raspberries, crossed by 'delicate walks' and 'at several good views were erected elegant summer houses, well built of Roman architecture'.[8] After Bacon's death in 1626, much of the park was ploughed up and the garden buildings were left to decay.

The creator's lasting legacy was his essay enunciating new concepts on the relations of art and nature in gardens.[9] Bacon thought that a princely garden 'ought not well to be under thirty acres of ground', larger than Theobalds, Hatfield or any Jacobean garden then existing in Hertfordshire, and he proposed that a green of four acres be laid at the front of the house, 'because nothing is more pleasant to the eye than green grass kept finely shorn.' In the middle, the main garden was to be a square of twelve acres, 'encompassed on all sides with a stately arched hedge'. In the centre of the main garden, there should be a mount about thirty feet high, with a banqueting house on the top. This enclosed space should be flanked on each side by broad alleys four acres in size. Beyond the garden was to be a heath, covering six acres, 'framed, as much as may be, to a natural wilderness', having no trees but thickets made only of sweet briar. The ground was to be set here and there, not in any order, with violets, strawberries, primroses and many other low flowering plants. Bacon wanted plants to appear natural. He disliked topiary work and knot gardens composed of contrasting coloured gravels, and, in choosing plants that blossomed at different seasons, he offered *ver perpetuum*, endless springtime. His vision was spacious and open, looking outward to the landscape beyond the precincts of the house.

None but courtiers or the richest and most powerful lords could afford to emulate the king and queen in creating princely gardens. To commission engineers and gardeners was expensive and the recommendations of professionals who enjoyed royal patronage were proportionately costly in initial outlays and in recurrent labour costs. The glorious blaze of Renaissance gardening was short-lived, being extinguished by financial austerity and antipathy towards fashions associated with the Stuarts. For half a century, parks lay under a cloud of cold materialism. Labourers' wages lagged behind prices of wood and agricultural products but, when prices escalated after 1620, wages increased slowly.[10] The rise in wages confronted wealthy landowners with a dilemma. By reducing the number of hands engaged in labour-intensive work in gardens and parks, they would increase the number of those seeking poor relief from poor rates to which landowners themselves made the largest contributions. Parks could be maintained only by increasing returns from woodlands and pasture.

Parks lost in the first half of the seventeenth century

More than twenty parks in Hertfordshire disappeared in the first half of the seventeenth century. Some of these vanished because their owners no longer wanted to hunt deer or visit distant residences. Some were lost through neglect or mismanagement; some were reclaimed for agricultural use; others were cleared for timber sales. Some were destroyed during the Civil War; more were sold after the war to pay debts. Most disparkments were unannounced; few records described the removal of herds of deer or the pulling down of palings. Sir Henry Chauncy recalled that his birthplace, Ardeley Bury, was situated in the middle of an ancient park 'now disparked'.[11] Salisbury Park rapidly passed through the hands of a succession of owners in the early seventeenth century; by 1638, although it was still named as a park, it had ceased to contain deer.[12] When the Bishop of London regained possession of Stortford Park after the Restoration, the palings had been removed.[13] In Hunsdon, three Elizabethan parks were reduced to one. Matthew Bluck, an alderman of the City of London, who purchased two adjoining parks in 1671, made Hunsdon House his residence and disparked Hunsdon Bury in 1684.[14] In a neighbouring parish, Stanstead Bury lost its old park and gained a new one on the north side of the road from Hoddesdon to Sawbridgeworth. Other old parks at Gilston and Knebworth were replaced by new parks on adjoining sites.

In the early seventeenth century some herds of deer suffered large losses through severe winters, overstocking and malnutrition. Parks where trees had been cut down and supplementary feedstuffs were scarce suffered more than others. At Hertingfordbury, which belonged to the Crown, a special commission in 1605 reported that the park contained '205 acres of very hard soil which would keep 150 deer and no more' and, out of the 200 deer kept there, 160 had died in one year.[15] James I enjoyed hunting, having a hunting lodge at Royston[16] and paying frequent visits to his own and his subjects' parks in Hertfordshire. Sir John Spencer also hunted in north Hertfordshire at Barley and Offley. The second Earl of Salisbury purchased Quickswood near Clothall in 1617 and built a hunting lodge, stables and a brewery there.[17] In 1635, the stables housed thirty horses, of which seven were hunters. The Cecils did not keep a park; they hunted in open woods and fields.

Charles I, in contrast to his father, regarded his outlying properties not as hunting grounds but as potential sources of revenue. The royal park at Kings Langley was cleared for cultivation and, in 1652, ten tenant farmers occupied 'land in the park'.[18] The Prince of Wales' park at Berkhamsted was let to Sir Edward Carey, who built a house there in 1611. In 1618, the 700-acre park was enlarged by a further 300 acres. Trees cut from Frith Common were used for palings to enclose the extension.[19] Ten years later, the park was reduced from 1,132 acres to 376 acres, most of the disparked land having been ploughed up. By 1651, it had been reduced again to 253 acres, and after the Restoration 376 acres were recorded as lying within the boundaries of the 'old park'.[20] John Seller's map in 1675 showed no parks at Hertingfordbury, Kings Langley or Berkhamsted.

The increasing demand for food and animal feedstuffs generated by London's growing population exerted a strong pressure on landowners to convert their parks to agricultural use. Parks disappeared from the south of the county, especially south and east of Hertford. As settlements advanced up the Lea valley, the threat of urban marauders, combined with economic incentives to produce food, swept over parks. Along the road to Ware and Cambridge, Theobalds, Cheshunt Park and Rye Park, Stanstead Abbots, had disappeared by the time Seller's map was made in 1675. Ponsbourne Park, north of Cuffley, was mentioned as being disparked in 1640.[21] Other parks in south Hertfordshire disappeared without explanation, except that they lay close to roads from London. Much further from London, in the north-west corner of the county, Pendley Park also disappeared before 1675.

The Civil War and the Interregnum were devastating periods for parks. Many parks were damaged or plundered by armies from both sides, most frequently by parliamentarians, and destruction continued at a few places up to ten years after the fighting stopped. In 1643, Ashridge was overrun by parliamentary troops, who sacked the house and killed the deer.[22] The ardent royalist Lord Arthur Capel was executed in 1649, his estates at Hadham, Cassiobury and Walkern were confiscated and his parks plundered.[23] In 1660, his son regained parks at Hadham and Cassiobury but Walkern Park, which had been well stocked with deer in the early seventeenth century, was no longer shown as a park in 1675.[24] The king's park at Theobalds was broken into[25] and a parliamentary survey in 1650 indicated that the stock of deer had been greatly depleted since 1608; however, the park still contained timber worth £7,259, and 15,608 trees were marked for use by the navy.[26] During the next three years, numerous complaints were made about Londoners pilfering wood, stealing deer and cutting and removing timber trees.[27] Thomas Fuller was shocked by the demolition of the palace in 1651, lamenting that 'the seat of a monarch is now become a little commonwealth; so many entire tenements, like splinters, have flown out of the materials thereof'.[28] The buildings were not, as he alleged, 'taken to the ground'; parts were repaired and lived in after the Restoration.

At Stagenhoe, Tyttenhanger and other places, reconstruction began in the 1650s. At Gorhambury, almost all traces of Francis Bacon's unfinished garden vanished after his death in 1626. When John Aubrey paid a visit in 1656, he lamented that the park was 'now plowed up and spoil'd'.[29] In 1652, a puritan lawyer, Sir Harbottle Grimston, who had married as his second wife a niece of Francis Bacon, bought the house and 1,582 acres of land around Gorhambury for £12,760. The son of a puritan landowner in north-east Essex, he had been a member of the Long Parliament and in 1660 he was chosen as speaker of the House of Commons.[30] During the thirty years or so after the initial purchase, he spent a further £39,000 on seventy purchases, adding another 2,768 acres to the estate.[31] In 1663, he pulled down Verulam House, Bacon's summer house at the Pondyards, and, in the 1670s, started building a new house up the hill on the site of the present mansion.

A long-term consequence of the Civil War was the impoverishment of some landowners, who lost income from rents, borrowed money to buy back their estates and suffered the effects of declining land values. Household expenditure was cut by employing fewer servants and neglecting repairs. Sopwell fell into a ruinous state and in 1669 was one of the purchases made by Sir Harbottle Grimston, who removed materials for alterations at Gorhambury.[32] In the early seventeenth century, Furneux Pelham was too expensive to maintain. Richard Mead bought the property, pulled down the greatest part of the hall, sold the materials and opened the park. In 1677, the property had passed to Felix Calvert, a London brewer and banker, who began to improve the place,[33] and, by the end of the century, Chauncy noted that the park there was 'lately paled and stocked with deer'.[34] The Fanshawe family, who had held Ware Park for three generations and had created a fine garden with elaborate water features, was made destitute by supporting Charles I.[35] In 1668, Viscount Fanshawe was forced to sell the estate to Sir Thomas Byde, a local brewer, who restocked the park.[36] Ashridge, which had been badly damaged during the war, was modernised and the park enlarged and refurbished at great expense in 1668.[37] The Earl of Bridgwater expressed a wish that his posterity would 'enjoy the satisfaction and content' of these costly adornments.

Tree-planting

Much standing timber was cut to raise cash instantly to pay bad debts, resulting in a backlash from contemporaries. Early in the seventeenth century, Arthur Standish complained about the general destruction of woods and called upon landowners to plant new stands of timber.[38] In the Commonwealth period, Walter Blith advocated clearing scrub, breaking up heaths, and sowing clover and sainfoin to increase production of hay and corn; and although he strongly disapproved of royal forests and noblemen's parks, he expressed concern about mounting losses of timber and wood, and recommended 'doubling the growth of wood by a new plantation'.[39] Another republican, Samuel Hartlib, encouraged landowners to increase profits from their estates by 'a universal planting of trees'.[40] In 1664, alarmed by the rapid wastage of the nation's timber resources, John Evelyn wrote *Silva*, a treatise on forestry for the Royal Society that became a leading text on trees and planting. He urged all landowners to arise and plant and restore the depleted stands of timber on their estates, appealing in particular to gentlemen and persons of quality to 'adorn their desmesnes with trees of venerable shade and profitable timber'.[41] In the dedication to an edition published fourteen years later, he claimed that he had succeeded in persuading his countrymen to plant millions of trees.[42]

Leading landowners in Hertfordshire responded by planting in their parks and large estates and began to keep detailed records of tree-planting and woodland management. The Hatfield archives, for instance, record appointments of bailiffs, woodwards and park keepers, who supervised the woods. In the late seventeenth century, wood from the Hatfield estate was sold as fuel for domestic consumption locally and for shipment to London, to supply Hertfordshire maltsters and for charcoal burning, while oak bark was stripped for sale to tanners. Some timber cut on the estate was set aside for repairing buildings, barns, gates and fences, and that for sale was valued by independent surveyors. In 1686, returns from wood and timber amounted to nearly 5 per cent of the total income of the Cecil estates in Hertfordshire.[43] New plantations of trees were also made at Ashridge, Cassiobury and Moor Park. They were visible expressions of the restoration in the landscape.

John Seller's map, 1675
From 1598 to 1675, maps of Hertfordshire had been based on surveys by Saxton and Norden. The restoration of the monarchy, the return of the nobility and gentry and, above all, the revival of trade and industry, created an urgent demand for new surveys which accurately delineated principal roads and waterways and indicated the

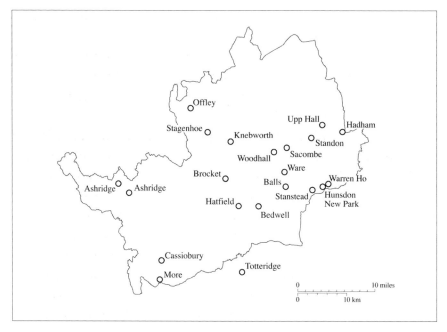

Figure 3.1: Parks in Hertfordshire in 1675. Based on Hertford Shire actually survey'd and delineated, *by John Seller. Full details are listed in Table 3.1. Drawn in the Geography Department, UCL*

correct position and layout of towns, villages and gentlemen's seats. Peter Barber has remarked that Charles II was 'genuinely excited by maps and charts',[44] and mapmakers hoped that the king would patronise a national survey, as Queen Elizabeth had done. He showed an interest in studies of astronomy, geography and hydrography presented by fellows to the Royal Society and formed an important collection of military maps to be housed by the Board of Ordnance in the Tower of London, but his offers of support to map-makers fell short of giving them money. Since neither the Crown nor parliament were willing to grant funds for a national survey, the initiative was taken by private enterprise.

John Seller, son of a cordwainer in Wapping, was apprenticed to a plate printer and admitted to the Merchant Taylors Company in 1654; he later became a liveryman.[45] In 1667, he answered a set of magnetical queries propounded by the Royal Society and at the same time became a member of the Clockmakers Company.[46] He set up in business as a maker of instruments, charts and maps and was appointed Hydrographer to the King, becoming the first English printer to supply mariners' charts; his volume, *The English Pilot* (1671), charting approaches to English harbours, was still used in the nineteenth century.[47] In collaboration with John Oliver, a surveyor, and Richard Palmer, an engraver, Seller undertook to carry out a new survey of all the counties in England.

The survey of Hertfordshire was probably carried out in 1675 and the map was published in 1676.[48] It is not clear who conducted the survey in the field, but Seller was responsible for a cartographic innovation whereby the map was orientated along the prime meridian of St Paul's in London. Degrees, minutes and intervals of 15 seconds were graduated along the bottom margin and a scale of latitude was graduated along the right-hand margin. Compass bearings between landmarks were observed and distances along main roads were measured and recorded. The map was engraved at a scale of approximately 1 in 147,310 or about 0.43 inches to one mile.[49] Donald Hodson considers it more accurate than any previous survey of the county. It certainly contained more information than previous surveys, and woods and parks were newly plotted (Figure 3.1).[50] Following the upheaval and destruction of the Civil War, only twenty-one parks remained, compared with a total of thirty-six shown on Saxton's and Norden's maps.

Parks as formal gardens

After 1670, large parks at Cassiobury, Gilston, Benington and Knebworth were laid out as extensive formal gardens in a Franco-Dutch style. The most spectacular transformation was carried out at Cassiobury Park. In 1661, Arthur Capel, whose father had been executed, was created Earl of Essex by Charles II.[51] In 1672 he was appointed Lord-Lieutenant of Ireland, in which capacity he showed 'prudence in considerably augmenting his Estate, without reproach'.[52] As his fortunes rose, he set about refurbishing the old house. In 1677, he commissioned Hugh May to add a spacious entrance range and a palatial east wing where the king and court might be received.[53] The king did not come, however, and the building was still unfinished when Evelyn paid a visit in 1680. The surroundings of Cassiobury were its glory. Evelyn remarked:

Table 3.1 Parks in Hertfordshire in 1675

Park	Grid Reference	Owner
Ashridge, Lt Gaddesden	984128	John Egerton, 3rd Earl of Bridgwater
Ashridge, Nettleden	008107	John Egerton, 3rd Earl of Bridgwater
Balls, Hertford	335120	Lady Mary Harrison
Bedwell Park, Essendon	277076	Thomas Atkins
Brocket Hall, Hatfield	214130	Sir Thomas Reade Bt
Cassiobury, Watford	095972	Arthur Capel, Earl of Essex
Hadham Hall, Lt Hadham	452227	Arthur Capel, Earl of Essex
Hatfield	236084	James Cecil, 3rd Earl of Salisbury
Hunsdon New Park	412123	Matthew Bluck
Knebworth	231210	Sir William Lytton
More Park, Rickmansworth	075933	Sir John Bucknall
Offley Place	145272	Sir Brockett Spencer
Sacombe	339190	Sir John Gore
Stagenhoe, St Pauls Walden	185227	Sir John Austen Bt
Standon Lordship	392214	Walter, 2nd Lord Aston
Stanstead Park, Stanstead Abbots	410112	Ralph Baesh
Totteridge Park	283942	Richard Griggs
Upp Hall, Braughing	409241	Dorothy Dicer
Ware Park	333144	Sir Thomas Byde
Warren House, Eastwick	425124	Matthew Bluck
Woodhall Park, Watton	318189	Sir John Boteler

Source: *Hertford Shire Actually Survey'd and Delineated by John Seller, Hydrographer to the King* (1676) BL Maps K. Top. 15. 43.

No man has been more industrious than this noble Lord in Planting about his seate, adorn'd with Walkes, Ponds and other rural Elegancies; but the soile is stonie, churlish, and uneven, nor is the water neere enough to the house, tho' a very swift and cleare stream runs within a flight shot from it in the vally.[54]

The earl's gardener, Moses Cook, moved from Hadham Hall in 1669 to superintend the work of laying out the grounds at Cassiobury. To collect ideas for the design, he was sent to view Versailles and other great gardens in France. In 1676, he published *The manner of raising, ordering and improving forrest trees*, which was widely acclaimed and reprinted three times.[55] The book described how an 'avenue', a word introduced into English by Evelyn, was formed by trees taken from the nursery at Hadham Hall.[56] On flat or evenly sloping ground, as at Versailles, a formal layout produced a striking effect but on an undulating surface, as at Cassiobury, the straightness of long avenues would appear distorted. Cook admitted that, in order to correct the irregularity of the terrain at Cassiobury, he was 'forced to cut through one Hill thirty Rod, most of the Hill two foot deep, into a sharp Gravel'.[57] A bird's-eye view of the completed work engraved by Joannes Kip and Leonard Knyff shows a long avenue leading from formal gardens in front of the house to a circular bowling green at the southern end (Figure 3.2).[58] Another long avenue of lime trees, cut through regularly ordered plantations, led east from the entrance front to the Hemel Hempstead road. A *patte d'oie*, or goosefoot, of avenues and rides fanned out from a round point near the public highway. On the western side of the house, where deer grazed, there were fewer trees.

At Gilston and Benington, where parks are not shown on Seller's map, extensive formal gardens were laid out in the later seventeenth

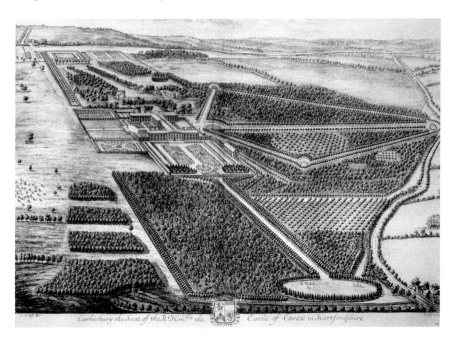

Figure 3.2: Cassiobury Park, seat of the Earl of Essex, 1707. Formal layout of the park illustrated by Joannes Kip and Leonard Knyff in Britannia illustrata, *1707. Reproduced by kind permission of HALS*

century, and are identified as parks on Oliver's map of 1695. A house was built at New Place, Gilston, in the 1570s by Henry Chauncy, great-grandfather of the historian, and enlarged by John Gore about 1640. After the Restoration, John's son Humphrey was knighted and he enclosed a new park here.[59] Chauncy noted that 'he did much to adorn the House with Walk and Gardens and made a pretty Park to the same'.[60] The new park was laid out with avenues and rectilinear plantations. Benington Park, named in *Domesday Book* and maintained until Elizabethan times, was disparked by 1580. In 1614, the place was bought by Sir Julius Caesar, Master of the Rolls, for his son Charles.[61] Julius or Charles Caesar may have been responsible for transforming the surroundings of the house into ornamental grounds, digging a large, square sunken garden 100 yards by 100 yards, with gazebos at three corners and a fountain in the centre.[62]

At Knebworth, the old park fell out of use in the late sixteenth century. After 1641, a new park was created to provide a grand setting for the house. A long avenue of sweet chestnuts was planted along a north-easterly axis from the front of the house and parallel rows of trees extended in a north-westerly direction.[63]

Restoration parks as status symbols
Partly compensating for the twenty-four parks that disappeared from county maps between 1598 and 1675 were nine new parks shown on Seller's map, the creation of which visibly proclaimed rises in family fortunes. Upwardly mobile landowners married into wealthy families, bought land put up for sale by impoverished gentry and by individuals who had no heirs or successors. Hertfordshire, because of its proximity to the capital, was regarded by nouveaux riches as an attractive place for social advancement. In the reign of Charles I, John Belasyse, a Lincolnshire landowner and MP for Thirsk, acquired Sacombe by marrying Jane, daughter and sole heir of a local squire, Sir Robert Boteler of Watton Woodhall. Belasyse raised six regiments for the king, fought at the battles of Edgehill, Newbury and Naseby and, in 1645, was created a baron.[64] After the defeat of the royalists, he suffered 'pecuniary embarrassment' and was forced to sell his property at Sacombe to Sir John Gore.[65] Gore, appointed sheriff in

1654, enlarged the house and enclosed a park. In 1688, Sacombe changed hands again. It was bought by Sir Thomas Rolt, president of the East India Company and Governor of Bombay, who also became sheriff in 1695. Another estate transferred from a local gentry family to a family from London was Upp Hall in Braughing. The newcomer, Robert Dicer, was appointed sheriff in 1659 and created baronet in 1661. About 1695, the new hall and surrounding park were acquired by William Harvey, later elected MP for Essex.[66] Steps up the social ladder from knighthood to baronetcy to peerage or from magistracy to sheriff to deputy lieutenant or to a seat in parliament were accompanied by house-building and park-making.

Few Hertfordshire families succeeded in staying on their ancestral estates for more than three generations. In 1637, when the house and grounds of Balls Park were bought by John Harrison, Farmer of Customs, the property was described as 'now decayed'.[67] Knighted in 1640 and elected MP for Lancaster, Harrison 'built a very fair stately Fabrick of Brick in the middle of a Warren'.[68] During the Civil War, the estate was sequestered, the house stood empty, the gardens and orchard were left untended and the family was made homeless. Harrison recovered the property by paying a £1,000 fine. After the war, a new park replaced the warren and the estate eventually passed to John's son, Richard Harrison, who served the East India Company as Governor of Fort St George.[69] Another estate, Offley Place, was held continuously by the descendants of Sir John Spencer of Althorp through the troubled years of the Civil War; it remained in the hands of the Spencer family for seven generations.[70] The house was improved and a park created by Sir Brockett Spencer in the middle of the seventeenth century.[71] A grander Offley secured a position for the Northamptonshire magnate among the county elite in Hertfordshire. Confiscation and debts led to the decline of some families and the loss of parks but some land that came on the market was bought by rising families who created new parks. Before 1675, more families lost parks than gained; after 1675, there were more winners than losers.

During the last quarter of the seventeenth century successful landowners, who regarded themselves as the leaders of Restoration society, displayed their ascendancy by enlarging their estates, adding

Figure 3.3: Stagenhoe, seat of Sir John Austen, Bart., 1700. Park of a gentry family, drawn by Jan Drapentier for Sir Henry Chauncy, Historical antiquities of Hertfordshire *(London, 1700), p. 414. Reproduced by kind permission of HALS*

new wings to their houses and extending or, in some places, creating new parks. In 1662, Thomas Fuller glorified their contribution to the making of the nation in *The history of the worthies of England*, and at the end of the century Sir Henry Chauncy commemorated the emergence of local worthies in *The historical antiquities of Hertfordshire*. Chauncy was the eldest son of a squire, who married the daughter of a squire and raised a large family. He served as a local magistrate from 1661. In 1680, he became the first recorder of Hertford County Court and, in 1681, he inherited his father's estate at Ardeley Bury and received a knighthood. He then settled down to collecting documents and other materials for writing the first history of his native county. He was a careful scholar, deeply conservative in his outlook, particularly interested in tracing the descent of manors and establishing dynastic connections between landowning families. He was less interested in the origins of the new rich and paid little attention to common folk.[72]

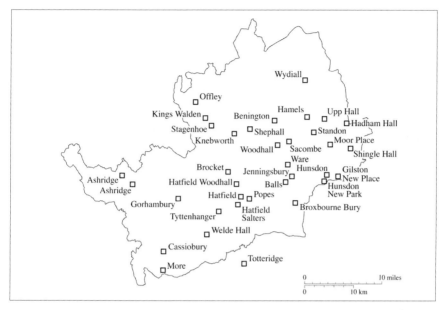

Figure 3.4: Parks in Hertfordshire in 1695. Based on The actual survey of the county of Hertford, *by John Oliver. Full details are listed in Table 3.2. Drawn in the Geography Department, UCL*

Chauncy's work was illustrated by engravings of twenty-seven houses and parks of the leading gentry. The engraver, Jan Drapentier, depicted the unceremonious, rustic activities of local squires — tending their farms, gardens and orchards, riding, shooting and playing bowls — rather than the magnificent mansions of the nobility at Hatfield and Cassiobury. His view of Stagenhoe, for instance, emphasised the lateral spread of the garden, with neat flower beds and orangery on the left hand and a bowling green on the right (Figure 3.3). The precincts of the house were enclosed by a high wall punctuated by railed gates. In the park, huntsmen and a pack of hounds pursued a stag, while a carriage and outrider approached the house along a radial avenue. Tim Mowl remarks that houses and grounds of the gentry did not conform to the latest fashion in design; rather, they incorporated a variety of features added by earlier generations. At many places, pavilions and banqueting houses were raised on platforms to overlook garden walls and capture views into parks and the landscape beyond.[73] To complete the record of gentrification, John Oliver mapped new parks that had not been included on Seller's survey.

Figure 3.5: Parks in the Stort valley in 1675. Detail from John Seller's survey, showing parks at Warren House, Hunsdon New Park and Stansteadbury. © British Library Board — all rights reserved (Maps K.Top.15.43)

John Oliver's map, 1695

After publishing maps of Hertfordshire, Middlesex, Surrey and Kent, John Seller's partnership collapsed and, about 1693, John Oliver decided to produce a new map of Hertfordshire under his own name.[74] Nothing is known about Oliver's early life but in 1687 he declared that he had practised surveying for forty years.[75] He acquired fame as one of four surveyors, alongside Robert Hooke, Peter Mills and Edward Jerman, appointed by the Corporation of the City of London to supervise the reconstruction after the Great Fire. In 1667, he began drawing certified plans of building sites to identify former property owners and demarcate parcels of land required for road widening and other public purposes.[76] Howard Colvin states that 'his surveys were more careful and detailed' than those by the other surveyors.[77] In the course of his work in the City he was engaged by the Mercers Company in 1668 to complete the building of a new hall and chapel; about 1670, he was appointed by the Skinners Company to design their new hall and, in 1675, he was appointed assistant surveyor for the building of the new St Paul's Cathedral, a position he held for the rest of his life. In 1691–5 he supervised the building of Christ's Hospital School for Girls at

Figure 3.6: Parks in the Stort valley in 1695. Detail from John Oliver's survey, showing parks at New Place, Gilston, Hunsdon House and Hunsdon New Park. © British Library Board — all rights reserved (Maps *2855.(24))

Hertford, at a time when he was preparing the new map of the county.

In August 1694, drawings for the Hertfordshire map, carefully corrected, were engraved on two plates at a scale of approximately 1 in 86,800 or about 0.73 inches to a mile.[78] Most topographical features on Oliver's map were copied from those on Seller's map, compiled twenty years earlier. In one important respect, however, Oliver's map was completely revised and brought up to date. The new map showed fourteen more parks than Seller's, and only Bedwell Park, whose name was inscribed, was not represented within palings (Figure 3.4). The additions may have been made partly in response to advance publicity in the *London Gazette*. On 16 August 1694, Oliver announced that 'To make the Map more compleat' he 'would print with it an Alphabetical Table of the Nobility and Gentry of the County, with references to their Seats, provided the due Information' be sent to him before 10 September.[79]

The advertisement was not the sole reason for the increase in the number of parks recorded, however; Oliver also carried out a new field survey of parks. In the Stort valley between Sawbridgeworth and Stanstead Abbot he showed parks at New Place, Gilston, at Hunsdon House, which Seller had named Warren House, west of Eastwick

Table 3.2 Parks in Hertfordshire in 1695

Park	Grid Reference	Owner
Ashridge, Lt Gaddesden	984128	John Egerton, 3rd Earl of Bridgwater
Ashridge, Nettleden	008107	John Egerton, 3rd Earl of Bridgwater
Balls, Hertford	335120	Richard Harrison
Benington Place	310229	Charles Caesar
Brocket Hall, Hatfield	214130	Sir James Reade Bt
Broxbourne Bury, Hoddesdon	353071	Sir Henry Monson Bt
Cassiobury, Watford	095972	Algernon Capel, 2nd Earl of Essex
Gorhambury, St Michael	113080	Sir Samuel Grimston
Hadham Hall, Lt Hadham	452227	Algernon Capel, 2nd Earl of Essex
Hamels, Braughing	376247	Sir Thomas Brograve Bt
Hatfield	236084	James, 3rd Earl of Salisbury
Hatfield, Salters Lodge	237066	James, 3rd Earl of Salisbury
Hatfield Woodhall	235106	James, 3rd Earl of Salisbury
Hunsdon House	425124	Matthew Bluck
Hunsdon New Park	412123	Matthew Bluck
Jenningsbury, Lt Amwell	342119	Giles Dunster
Kings Walden Bury	161235	Rowland Hale
Knebworth	231210	Sir William Lytton
Moor Place, Much Hadham	423187	William Berners
More Park, Rickmansworth	075933	Lord Charles Cornwallis
New Place, Gilston	441129	Sir Humphrey Gore
Offley Place	145272	Sir John Spencer Bt
Popes, Hatfield	259077	Thomas Shatterden
Sacombe	339190	Sir Thomas Rolt
Shephall Bury, Stevenage	256229	George Nodes
Shingle Hall, Sawbridgeworth	469172	Philip Halton
Stagenhoe, St Pauls Walden	185227	Sir John Austen Bt
Standon Lordship	392214	Walter, 2nd Lord Aston
Totteridge Park	283942	Sir Paul Whichcote
Tyttenhanger, Ridge	192047	Sir Thomas Pope Blount Bt
Upp Hall, Braughing	409241	Dorothy Dicer
Ware Park	333144	Sir Thomas Byde
Welde Hall, Aldenham	175011	Thomas Aram
Woodhall Park, Watton	318189	Philip Boteler
Wyddial Hall	373317	James Goulston

Source: John Oliver, *The Actual Survey of the County of Hertford* (London, 1695) BL Maps *2855 (24).

church, and at Hunsdon New Park, west of Hunsdon village. A park north of Stansteadbury marked on Seller's map had disappeared from Oliver's survey (Figures 3.5 and 3.6). A total of thirty-five parks was recorded in Hertfordshire in 1695.

Late seventeenth-century parks

Some parks were newly created in this period, often by old-established families who had prospered and felt confident enough to assert their superiority by enclosing a park. The Nodes, for instance, had been in possession of Shephall Bury since the dissolution of St Albans Abbey. The first George Nodes was Sergeant of the Buckhounds to four Tudor monarchs from Henry VIII to Queen Elizabeth. He died at Shephall in 1564. Succeeding generations, all named George Nodes, kept Shephall Bury in the family,[80] and it was the fifth George Nodes who owned the park that appeared on Oliver's map. Similarly, Richard Hale, a wealthy citizen of London, bought Kings Walden Bury in 1576 and the estate remained in the Hale family until 1884.[81] Succeeding members of the family served as sheriff before the Civil War and in 1663 the family owned a substantial house, assessed for seventeen hearths.[82] Their position in county society was assured in 1669, when William Hale started to enclose the park at Kings Walden.[83] The Brograves, a landed family from Beckenham, Kent, acquired lands in Braughing, Standon and Westmill, and in about 1580 John Brograve built Hamels, a neat brick house, on a dry hill overlooking a prospect to the east. A century later, Sir John Brograve, great-great-grandson of the purchaser, 'enlarg'd his Park and adorned his House with several delicious walks without'.[84] Jan Drapentier's engraving of Hamels shows deer and park pales in the background.

Many new parks, however, were made by newcomers to the county. Richard Goulston, a London lawyer, purchased Wyddial Hall in 1643. After the Civil War, the hall was enlarged and a park created.[85] Richard's son James, a second-generation entrant to the ranks of the gentry, was sheriff in 1684 and inherited the estate in 1686.[86] Again, deer were depicted in Drapentier's engraving of Wyddial. In 1650, Sir Richard Atkins, an eminent London lawyer, acquired Moor Place in Much Hadham. In 1660, he was created a baronet and made a small park at Moor Place.[87] By 1695, the park had passed to William Berners. In 1667, Broxbourne Bury descended by marriage to Sir John Monson, who moved from his estate in Lincolnshire. Three years later he obtained a licence to empark 320 acres.[88] Sir John was admired as 'a Gentleman of brisk Humour' who kept 'a free and bountiful Table, was very hospitable to his Neighbours and very charitable to the Poor'.[89] He fitted easily into the roles of magistrate and deputy lieutenant for the county. His grandson and successor, Sir Henry Monson, baronet and MP, inherited a park stocked with deer at Broxbourne. Popes Park, in Hatfield, was newly enclosed by Thomas Shatterden, who came from Eltham in Kent and was rapidly promoted to sheriff in 1689.[90] Little is known about the making of a park at Welde Hall, Aldenham, or its owner, Thomas Aram. There is also little information about the origins of the new park at Jenningsbury, owned in 1695 by Giles Dunster.

Oliver omitted to depict as parks some places described as parks by Chauncy. Aspenden, for example, had been in the hands of the Freman family since 1607. The Fremans were London merchants, the first serving as lord mayor in 1633, the second elected to parliament and the third, who succeeded to the estate in 1665, becoming an MP for Hertfordshire.[91] Chauncy recounts that the second Ralph Freman had a general insight into architecture and husbandry. During the Civil War he retired from public life and 'made his House neat, his Gardens pleasant, his Grove delicious'. The third Ralph Freman 'cased and adorned his Mannor House with Brick' and improved the gardens.[92] Drapentier illustrated regular plantations of trees, park palings and a herd of deer at Aspenden.[93] At Pishiobury, another park excluded by Oliver, Lady Arabella Wiseman owned a paddock for deer as well as 'a fair bowling green and fair walks extending for about four furlongs'.[94] A further example is Hertingfordbury, which was acquired in 1681 by John Culling. He built 'a very fair house' and laid out neat, formal gardens. After a long period of neglect, the park appears to have been restored and was named 'The Parke' on Drapentier's engraving.[95] In addition to naming parks, Chauncy described improvements at other seats that were not parks: some properties were beautified by the creation of large gardens with parterres, terraces and long avenues.

Three large pleasure grounds were adorned with long avenues that were to persist as features in landscape gardens in the eighteenth century. Moor Park, Rickmansworth, had been formed into a celebrated Renaissance garden in the early seventeenth century.[96] In 1673, Robert Cary, Duke of Monmouth, built a new red-brick house at the top of the hill in the centre of the park. From the house avenues radiated outwards to public roads beyond the park pales.[97] The park was transformed by Charles Bridgeman in the early eighteenth century and later by Capability Brown in the 1750s, but lines of avenues were still represented on Dury and Andrews' map in 1766. At Gorhambury, after the death of Sir Harbottle Grimston in 1685, his son, Sir Samuel Grimston, continued to build and to plant avenues in the park,[98] and when, in the middle of the eighteenth century, Gorhambury was landscaped by Nathaniel Richmond, the avenues were preserved. A third park, at Tring, surrounded by grand baroque gardens, was laid out by Henry Guy, Secretary to the Treasury and Groom of the Bedchamber to Charles II.[99] In furthering his ambition to be created a peer, Guy commissioned Sir Christopher Wren to design an imposing mansion where he might receive the king. Unfortunately Charles II did not pay a visit nor confer a peerage; instead, William III visited Tring Park in 1690. Daniel Defoe reported that the enlargement of the grounds caused:

> an eminent contest between Mr. Guy and the poor of the parish, about his enclosing part of the common to make a park; Mr. Guy presuming upon his power, set up his pales, and took in a large parcel of open land, call'd Wiggington Common; the cottagers and farmers oppos'd it, by their complaints a great while; but finding he went on with his work, and resolv'd to do it, they rose upon him, pull'd down the banks, and forc'd up his pales, and carried away the wood, or set it on a heap and burnt it; and this they did several times, till he was oblig'd to desist; after some time he began again, offering to treat with the people, and to give any equivalent for it: But that not being satisfactory, they mobb'd him again.[100]

In the early eighteenth century the park was newly designed by Charles Bridgeman, who created a north–south axial vista.

Estates and strict settlements

During the seventeenth century many parks disappeared and some new parks were created. Many families lost their estates and new families took their places. Possession of land was insecure and family succession precarious, and almost all landowners welcomed the return of Charles II and looked forward to repairing their property and recovering their fortunes. Above all, they wanted to end the threat of lands being seized and heirs left destitute and, to this end, lawyers devised a system that made it difficult for the state to confiscate or creditors to foreclose on land. By means of strict settlements, owners agreed to pass estates to their eldest surviving son or, in the absence of sons, to ordered successions of kinsfolk. For their part, heirs were bound not to sell the settled or entailed lands. A member of each generation in turn held the property as tenant-for-life. Brides brought dowries to estates on marriage and settlements empowered life tenants to charge jointures in order to provide annuities for surviving widows. Younger sons and daughters might be allotted portions out of settled estates or might be given bequests of personal property. Succession was settled for three generations and family pressure generally pushed it into a fourth generation.[101]

Strict settlement and prudential marriage led to territorial aggrandisement by the largest owners at the expense of the smallest. The system was widely adopted in Hertfordshire and elsewhere between 1660 and 1680.[102] At the end of the century, the Cecils stood at the apex of county society; they held the senior earldom, owned the largest estate, the greatest parks, a palatial house and continued to add to their possessions. Capels and Bridgwaters succeeded in recovering lands lost in the Civil War, enlarged their parks and were granted earldoms. Charles II conferred titles on other families, and the number of parks owned by baronets increased from two on Seller's map to six on Oliver's.

A recurrent problem for the settlement system was that rising dynasties frequently failed to produce male heirs. Eldest sons tended to marry late or not at all, some fathers outlived their children and some owners fathered no legitimate sons. Nevertheless, inheritance continued to be the principal means of transferring estates. In Hertfordshire, between 1660 and 1679 two-thirds of estates were transferred by inheritance; between 1680 and 1699 the proportion rose to four-fifths.[103] In the whole period from 1660 to 1699, about one in four estates transferred by inheritance passed by indirect inheritance to brothers, sisters, uncles, aunts, cousins, nephews, nieces or people related only by marriage.[104] In default of an heir, a few estates were sold.

Minor gentry were under the greatest pressure to sell. Their incomes were squeezed between low rents and heavy taxes.[105] Some avoided sales by marrying heiresses but others were forced to dispose of their estates. Purchasers mostly came from London: courtiers and office holders constituted a diminishing proportion, while lawyers took an increasing share and businessmen, bankers and merchants were the most numerous and wealthiest group of land-seekers in Hertfordshire between 1640 and 1699.[106] Many of the newcomers did not settle. East Indiamen sought homes for retirement and their heirs decided not to stay, military officers moved out when they were recalled for duty and many financiers returned to the City after residing in the country for a few years. The presence of Londoners was remarked upon by Robert Morden:

> this County has an incredible number of Pallaces and fair
> Structures of the Gentry and Nobility. From Totteridge,
> where the County begins, and East Barnet to Ware, are so
> many Beautiful Houses that one may look upon it almost as
> a continual Street. The rich Soil and wholesome Air, and the
> excellency of the County have drawn hither the Wealthiest
> Citizens of London.[107]

An area between Hatfield and Ware was among the first to be occupied by nabobs and bankers.

The influx of newcomers was not large enough to upset the dominance of ancient families in county society. Of estates in Hertfordshire that were transferred between 1660 and 1699, no more than one in five was disposed of by sale and two-thirds of sales were of estates put on the market by recent purchasers or their heirs.[108] Most Londoners were transient owners, birds of passage among the nested colony of native families, and, perhaps unsurprisingly, the turnover of smaller properties was more rapid than of large estates as newcomers replaced minor gentry rather than greater lords. Some married daughters of landed families and moved in when their fathers-in-law died.

In terms of the money spent on laying out formal gardens, planting interminable avenues and employing large numbers of skilled tradesmen and labourers, newcomers were not to be outdone by ancient families. They competed openly in displaying their wealth and aspirations to grandeur. Whether or not they hoped to found landed dynasties, they spent freely on making significant marks on the landscape. For families who followed the path of strict settlement, the long-term prospects of enjoying the beauties of tall trees lining avenues were promised to the second generation and the satisfaction of seeing groves of oaks reach maturity were reserved for third and fourth generations.

Notes

1.   R. Strong, *The Renaissance garden in England* (London, 1979), p.106.

2.   J.J. Antrobus, *Bishops Hatfield: some memories of its past* (Hatfield, 1912), pp.56–7.

3.   W. Temple, *Upon the gardens of Epicurus, or of gardening in the year 1685* (London, 1692), p.126.

4.   Strong, *Renaissance garden*, p.144.

5.   Hertfordshire Gardens Trust and Williamson, *Parks and gardens of west Hertfordshire*, p.11.

6.   P. Henderson, 'Sir Francis Bacon's water gardens at Gorhambury', *Garden History*, 20 (1992), pp.116–31.

7.   Strong, *Renaissance garden*, pp.130–3.

8.   A. Clark (ed.), *'Brief lives', chiefly of contemporaries set down by John Aubrey, between the years 1669 & 1696*, vol. II (Oxford, 1898), pp.79–83.

9.   B. Vickers (ed.), *Francis Bacon: essays or counsels, civil and moral* (London, 2002, first published 1625), 'Of gardens', pp.163–70, quotations from pp.164, 165, 166, 167, 168.

10. Bowden, 'Agricultural prices, farm profits and rents', pp.657–61, 864–5.

11. Chauncy, *Historical antiquities*, vol. I, p.107.

12. Gover, Mawer and Stenton, *Place-names of Hertfordshire*, p.68.

13. *VCH Hertfordshire*, vol. 3, p.297.

14. *VCH Hertfordshire*, vol. 3, p.329.

15. *VCH Hertfordshire*, vol. 3, p.464, citing Duchy of Lancaster, Special Commission (1605), p.674.

16. A. Thomson, 'Progress, retreat and pursuit: James I in Hertfordshire', in D. Jones-Baker (ed.), *Hertfordshire in history: papers presented to Lionel Munby* (Hertfordshire Local History Council, 1991), pp.93–107.

17. C. Dalton, 'The gardens at Quickswood, the hunting lodge of the Earls of Salisbury' in A. Rowe (ed.) *Hertfordshire garden history: a miscellany* (Hatfield, 2007), pp.27–9.

18. Munby, Hertfordshire landscape, p.152; L.M. Munby (ed.) *The history of King's Langley* (King's Langley, 1963), pp.58–9.

19. G.H. Whybrow, *The history of Berkhamsted Common* (London, 1934), p.35.

20. Hertfordshire Garden Trust and Williamson, *Parks and gardens of west Hertfordshire*, p.14.

21. *VCH Hertfordshire*, vol. 3, p.105.

22. H.J. Todd, *The history of the College of Bonhommes at Ashridge* (London, 1823), pp.65–6.

23. Stone and Stone, *An open elite?*, p.120.

24. *VCH Hertfordshire*, vol. 3, p.154.

25. E.S. de Beer (ed.), *The diary of John Evelyn* (Oxford, 2000), vol. 1, pp.54–5; 2, 81, entry for 19 April 1643.

26. D. Lysons, *The environs of London*, vol. 4 (London, 1796), p.38 citing Augmentation Office, 'Survey of Enfield Chase and Theobalds Park' (1650).

27. W. Robinson, *The history and antiquities of Enfield*, vol. 1 (London, 1823), p.197.

28. T. Fuller, *The history of the worthies of England*, P.A. Nutall (ed.), vol. II (New York, 1965, first published 1662), p.38.

29. Clark, *'Brief lives'* by John Aubrey vol. I, 393.

30. C.W. Brooks, 'Sir Harbottle Grimston, second baronet (1603–1685)', in *Oxford Dictionary of National Biography*, vol. 24 (Oxford, 2004), pp.35–38.

31. C. Clay, 'The evolution of landed society after the Restoration', in J. Thirsk (ed.), *The agrarian history of England and Wales. Vol. V 1640–1750. Agrarian change* (Cambridge, 1985), p.185; C. Clay, 'Two families and their estates: the Grimstons and the Cowpers from c.1660 to c.1815', (PhD thesis, Cambridge, 1966).

32. J.C. Rogers, 'The manor and houses at Gorhambury', *St Albans and Hertfordshire Architectural and Archaeological Society Transactions*, New Ser. 4 (1933–5), p.73.

33. *VCH Hertfordshire*, vol. 4, p.102.

34. Chauncy, *Historical antiquities*, vol. I, 286.

35. Strong, *Renaissance garden*, pp.123–4.

36. A. Fea and B. Marshall (eds.), *Memoirs of Lady Fanshawe* (London, 1905), p.230; Stone and Stone, *An open elite?*, p.191.

37. Stone and Stone, *An open elite?*, p.351, citing Huntington Library, Bridgwater MS 8117.

38. A. Standish, *New directions of experience, authorized by the king's most excellent majesty, as may appeare, for the planting of timber and firewood* (London, 1614).

39. W. Blith, *The English improver improved; or the survey of husbandry surveyed* (London 1652).

40. S. Hartlib, *Design for plenty; by a universal planting of trees* (London, 1652).

41. J. Evelyn, *Silva, or a discourse of forest trees and the propagation of timber in his majesty's dominions*, A. Hunter (ed.) (York, 1801, first published 1664), vol. II, Advertisement I, xlix, p.303.

42. Evelyn, *Silva*, 'Dedication to the King' in new edition (1678) p.iv.

43. P.R. Barton, 'Woodland management in the late seventeenth century', *Hertfordshire Archaeology*, 7 (1986), pp.181–200.

44. P. Barber, 'Maps and monarchs in Europe 1550–1800', in R. Oresko, G.C. Gibbs and H.M. Scott (eds.), *Royal and republican sovereignty in early modern Europe* (Cambridge, 1997), p.105.

45. S. Tyacke, *London map-sellers 1660–1720* (Tring, 1978), p.139.

46. L. Worms, 'John Seller (1632–1697)', in *Oxford Dictionary of National Biography* (Oxford, 2004), vol. 49, pp.720–21.

47. Delano-Smith and Kain, *English maps*, pp.156–8.

48. *Hertford Shire actually survey'd and delineated by John Seller, Hydrographer to the King* (1676), British Library (BL) Maps K. Top. 15.43.

49. Hodson, *Printed maps of Hertfordshire*, p.32.

50. D. Hodson, *Four county maps of Hertfordshire* (Stevenage, 1985), p.1.

51. R.L. Greaves, 'Arthur Capel, first Earl of Essex (1632–1683)', in *Oxford Dictionary of National Biography* (Oxford, 2004), vol. 9, pp.976–82.

52. Beer, *Diary of John Evelyn*, vol. 4, p.201.

53. Smith, *English houses*, pp.83–4.

54. Beer, *Diary of John Evelyn*, vol. 4, p.200, entry for 18 April 1680.

55. M. Cook, *The manner of raising, ordering and improving forrest trees; also, how to plant, make, and keep woods, walks, avenues, lawns, hedges, etc.* (London, 1676).

56. 'Avenue' was first used in its present sense in describing an avenue of lime trees at Audley End, Essex, on 1 September 1654 in Beer, *Diary of John Evelyn*, vol. 3,

p.141; Cook was the first to use the word in a book title in 1676 (see n.55, above). A valuable general study is S.M. Couch, 'The practice of avenue planting in the seventeenth and eighteenth centuries', *Garden History*, 20 (1992), pp.173–200.

57. Cook, *Manner of raising trees*, p.21.

58. J. Kip and L. Knyff, *Britannia illustrata, or views of several of the royal palaces as also of the principal seats of the nobility and gentry of Great Britain elegantly engraven* (London, 1707).

59. *VCH Hertfordshire*, vol. 3, p.321 citing Close Roll 9 Wm III part V no. 4; the park pales are depicted in Jan Drapentier's engraving in Chauncy, *Historical antiquities*, vol. I, p.372.

60. Chauncy, *Historical antiquities,* vol. I, p.373.

61. *VCH Hertfordshire*, vol. 3, pp.73–4.

62. Information from Mrs Anne Rowe.

63. Rowe, 'The parks of Knebworth'.

64. G.E.C., *The complete peerage*, vol. 2, pp.89–90.

65. *VCH Hertfordshire*, vol. 3, 137.

66. *VCH Hertfordshire*, vol. 3, 311.

67. *VCH Hertfordshire*, vol. 3, 412 citing Close Roll 13 Chas I.

68. Chauncy, *Historical antiquities*, vol. I, pp.520–1.

69. *VCH Hertfordshire*, vol. 3, p.413.

70. *VCH Hertfordshire*, vol. 3, p.41.

71. Chauncy, *Historical antiquities*, vol. II, p.193; park palings are illustrated in Jan Drapentier's engraving.

72. N. Doggett, 'Sir Henry Chauncy (1632–1719)', in *Oxford Dictionary of National Biography* (Oxford, 2004), vol. 11, p.265.

73. T. Mowl, 'John Drapentier's views of the gentry gardens of Hertfordshire', *Garden History*, 29 (2001), pp.158, 161–2.

74. S. Bendall, *Dictionary of land surveyors and local map-makers of Great Britain and Ireland*. vol. 2. Dictionary (London, 1997), p.386.

75. H.M. Colvin, *A biographical dictionary of English architects 1660–1840* (London, 1954), p.423.

76. London Topographical *Society, Survey of building sites in the City of London after the Great Fire of 1666,* by Peter Mills and John Oliver, 5 vols, (London, 1962–67).

77. Colvin, *Dictionary of English architects*, p.423; one of Oliver's Certificate Surveys is illustrated in Delano-Smith and Kain, *English maps*, p.209.

78. J. Oliver, *The actual survey of the county of Hertford* (London, 1695), BL Maps *2855 (24).

79. Tyacke, *London map-sellers,* p.65; the advertisement appeared in the *London Gazette* on 16 August 1694.

80. *VCH Hertfordshire*, vol. 2, pp.443–4.

81. Smith, *Hertfordshire houses*, p.111.

82. *VCH Hertfordshire*, vol. 3, p.33.

83. A. Rowe, 'Kings Walden Park', unpublished MS (2003) (HALS Herts Gardens Trust 3898), p.1.

84. Chauncy, *Historical antiquities*, vol. I, pp.445–6; A. Rowe, *Garden making and the Freman family; a memoir of Hamels, 1713–1733* (Hertford, 2001), pp.xi–xiii.

85. *Ibid.*, pp.1, 223; *VCH Hertfordshire*, vol. 4, p.116.

86. Smith, *Hertfordshire houses*, p.216.

87. Chauncy, *Historical antiquities*, vol. I, p.316.

88. *VCH Hertfordshire*, vol. 3, p.432; TNA: PRO Warrant Books 1670. 474 (IND 6753).

89. Chauncy, *Historical antiquities*, vol. I, pp.566–7.

90. *VCH Hertfordshire*, vol. 3, p.103; H. C. N. Daniell, 'Popes Manor, Essendon' East Herts. *Archaeological Society Transactions* 7 (1923) pp.148-60.

91. *VCH Hertfordshire*, vol. 4, pp.17–18.

92. Chauncy, *Historical antiquities*, vol. I, pp.244–9.

93. *Ibid.*, vol. I, p.240.

94. *Ibid.*, vol. I, p.348.

95. *Ibid.*, vol. I, p.535.

96. Strong, *Renaissance garden*, pp.141–6.

97. Hertfordshire Gardens Trust and Williamson, *Parks and gardens of west Hertfordshire*, p.21; E. W. Brayley and J. Britton, *The beauties of England and Wales* (London, 1806), vol. 7, p.312.

98. Rogers, 'Gorhambury', pp.78–9.

99. Hertfordshire Garden Trust and Williamson, *Parks and gardens of west Hertfordshire*, p.20; A. Fletcher, 'Tring Park, part I (1680–1800)', *Hertfordshire Gardens Trust Annual Report* 1998–1999, pp.12–15.

100. D. Defoe, *A tour through England and Wales* (London, 1927, first published 1724–26), vol. 2, pp.15–16.

101. Habakkuk, *Marriage, debt and the estates system*, pp.1–49, 77–239.

102. *Ibid.*, p.19.

103. Stone and Stone, *An open elite?*, table 4.6.

104. *Ibid.*, table 3.1.

105. Stone and Stone, 'Country houses', p.75.

106. Stone and Stone, *An open elite?*, table 6.2.

107. R. Morden, *The new description and state of England* (London, 1704), p.71.

108. Stone and Stone, *An open elite?*, tables 5.3, 5.8.

Chapter IV
Early Eighteenth-century Parks

IN 1700, AFTER A CENTURY OF CONFLICT and insecurity, Hertfordshire landowners looked towards a future in which they would enjoy undisturbed possession of their estates and would be able to pass them on to their heirs. Parks remained the most conspicuous status symbols in rural society, but deer were no longer essential components of the image. Park palings came to be viewed, rather, as defences guarding the privacy of isolated residences. Within the pales, landscapes were valued for their ornamental beauty. Few, however, could afford the initial expense of laying out elaborate designs and all but the very rich favoured simpler and less costly schemes. In the long term, some income might be generated by sales of wood and timber and profits from grazing livestock.

In the seventeenth century, two influential thinkers had anticipated a change in landscape taste towards informality and wildness. Henry Wotton had asserted that 'gardens should be irregular', as exemplified in Sir Henry Fanshawe's contrivance of 'a delightful confusion' at Ware Park.[1] Francis Bacon, who owned Gorhambury, disapproved of topiary and intricate patterns formed with coloured gravels. He sought prospects over open country and embraced natural features in his ideal garden. For the heath, which was the third part of his plan, he wished it 'to be framed, as much as may be, to a natural wilderness'.[2] What turned the philosophical objections of Wotton and Bacon into a fundamental rejection of regularity was the idea that regularity, by imposing strict control over nature, represented authoritarianism.

In the early eighteenth century, informality was welcomed in the name of liberty, allowing natural forms to express themselves freely. The Earl of Shaftesbury championed the cause of liberty and nature. 'O GLORIOUS *Nature*! supremely Fair and sovereignly Good!' he rejoiced, 'whose every single Work affords an ampler Scene and is a nobler Spectacle than all that ever Art presented.' For Shaftesbury, a wilderness would 'appear with a Magnificence beyond the formal Mockery of Princely Gardens'.[3] Joseph Addison dreamed of a landscape inhabited by the Goddess of Liberty, not encumbered with fences and inclosures.[4] 'The beauties of the most stately Garden or Palace lie in a narrow compass,' wrote Addison, 'but, in the wide Fields of Nature, the Sight wanders up and down without Confinement.'[5] Alexander Pope echoed these sentiments in *An epistle to the Earl of Burlington*, pleading:

> In all let *Nature* never be forgot.
> Consult the *Genius* of the *Place* in all.[6]

Pope abhorred formal gardens, where

> Grove nods at grove, each Alley has a brother,
> And half the platform just reflects the other.
> The suff'ring eye inverted Nature sees,
> Trees cut to Statues, Statues thick as trees.[7]

The largest landowners in Hertfordshire were slow to respond to the call for a naturalistic style. Leaders of taste, in particular the Cecils, Capels and Egertons, had spent large sums of money on grand and elaborate layouts. Brompton Park and other nurseries had encouraged them to buy large quantities of limes, chestnuts, yews, hornbeams and elms in order to plant long avenues. Moses Cook, gardener to the first Earl of Essex, sold his partnership share in the Brompton Park Nursery in 1689 to Henry Wise, assistant to George London. When Queen Anne came to the throne in 1702 she chose Wise to be royal gardener because he offered to maintain the royal parks and gardens less expensively than George London. Wise adhered strictly to the formal style and his schemes were by no means cheap; he left a vast fortune of over £100,000 when he died in 1738.[8]

Stalwart royalists, including those eager to wage war against Louis XIV, were not persuaded to break up their avenues and plantations for the sake of liberty. Not only were they unsympathetic to the notion of extending freedom to the common people but they disliked untamed nature, which they regarded as rude and unrefined. Not until arable open fields, commons and wild heaths were enclosed and parcelled into regular chequerboards of fields was it appropriate to relax straight lines within the boundaries of parks. A new distinction had to be drawn in the landscape between orderly, cultivated fields and largely empty spaces reserved for the pleasures of solitary owners.

Charles Bridgeman

In Hertfordshire, the first tentative steps towards the new style were taken at six places designed by Charles Bridgeman. Bridgeman was a surveyor by training.[9] He took the place of George London as a partner with Henry Wise in Brompton Park Nursery and shared profits made by the nursery from supplying clients with large quantities of even-aged trees for their avenues. In 1726 he was appointed Royal Gardener in succession to Wise.[10] He was the acknowledged master of the geometric style, creating compositions articulated along strong axial vistas, in which straight canals and rectilinear basins were flanked by long avenues consisting of two or three rows of trees. Bridgeman's schemes were bolder, grander and probably more costly than those devised by his predecessors. His clients, most of whom were newly rich, welcomed his novel concessions to informality. He introduced the sunk fence or ha-ha, opening views from the windows of the house into the park, and extended vistas through the park into the countryside beyond. He also placed arcadian temples and obelisks at vantage points far from the house and drew serpentine walks through dense plantations. Houses were built high on slopes, overlooking both park and open country beyond. In three dimensions, a mantle of trees and grass spread over undulating surfaces looked natural as well as elegant.

Bridgeman's earliest commission in Hertfordshire was at Sacombe Park.[11] The property had been bought in 1688 by Sir Thomas Rolt,

president of the East India Company and Governor of Bombay.[12] Sir
Thomas was succeeded in 1710 by Edward Rolt MP, one of five of
Bridgeman's clients who profited from investments in South Sea
Company stock, selling before the bubble burst. A house designed by
James Gibbs was never built and, between 1715 and 1717,
Bridgeman received payments for preparing plans of the park.[13] The
layout consisted of a long axial vista with a straight canal and octag-
onal basin opening a prospect towards distant countryside. Nathanael
Salmon, author of a new history of Hertfordshire, praised the owner
for adorning the place with:

> most beautiful walks and vistos through the woods... It's hard
> to say whether nature or art be most admirable here. The
> artist seems to have attempted shewing nature to greatest
> advantage. At the end of one walk is a sort of theatrical work,
> shaded by oaks at unequal distances, as they happened to
> grow, such as one would wish represented in a landschape.[14]

Salmon particularly admired the natural beauties of the park and was
the first observer to liken its appearance to a landscape painting.

Tring Park, where a grand Wren mansion was set in a baroque
garden, was inherited in 1708 by William Gore, who, like Edward
Rolt of Sacombe, successfully invested in the South Sea Company and
was elected MP. Bridgeman prepared plans for Tring some time
between 1711 and 1725. Classical temples, an obelisk in the woods,
a pavilion overlooking a bowling green and a pyramid at the southern end of Bridgeman's grand axial vista were designed by James
Gibbs.[15] The main feature of Bridgeman's scheme was a long canal to
the south of the house, flanked by rows of yews and elms. To the
north, a long avenue stretched beyond Market Street. The long
north–south axis designed by Bridgeman lay across the east–west
range of ornate gardens laid out in the late seventeenth century for
Henry Guy. A bird's eye view engraved for *Vitruvius Britannicus* illustrated the intersection of the two designs (Figure 4.1). In 1724, a
visitor to Tring remarked that 'the gardens are so rich that here are
always 9 men and often 4 boys more to keep them'.[16] The enclosing

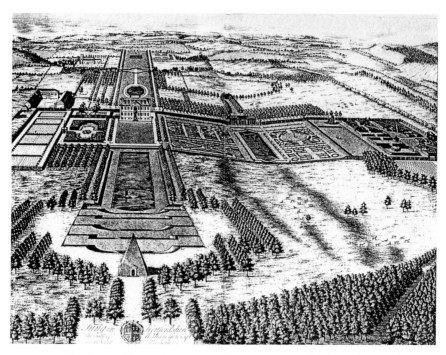

Figure 4.1: View of Tring Park, seat of William Gore, 1739. Charles Bridgeman's long north–south axial vista crossed the east–west layout of late seventeenth-century gardens. Engraving by John Rocque in Vitruvius Britannicus *(1739), vol. IV, pls 104–5. Photograph by Matt Prince*

of 300 acres to enlarge the park for 300 head of deer was achieved after a long struggle with the commoners.[17]

The most extravagant of Bridgeman's Hertfordshire commissions was Moor Park.[18] The money to purchase the estate from the Duchess of Monmouth, largely to rebuild and decorate the mansion and to carry out Bridgeman's grand design all came from speculation in the South Sea Company; Benjamin Styles had received inside information from his brother-in-law warning him to sell his stock before the crash.[19] Salmon reported that 'Mr Styles is making the place most magnificent'. In 1725, a ridge had already been cut through to open a 'visto' towards Watford,[20] and the prodigality of lowering a hill some thirty feet at a huge cost drew Pope's scorn:

Or cut wide views through Mountains to the Plain,
You'll wish your hill or shelter'd seat again.[21]

Figure 4.2: A perspective view of the bowling green at Gobions, a seat of Sir Jeremy Sambrooke, Bart., 1748. The players relaxed in a formal setting. From an engraving published by John Tinney, March 1748. © British Library Board — all rights reserved (Maps K.Top.15.64d)

Undeterred by considerations of expense or fears of exposure to high winds, Styles planned to excavate a second opening through the hill that obstructed the view towards Uxbridge. The main feature of Bridgeman's layout was a broad axial vista along which a canal and an octagonal basin were aligned. A *patte d'oie* of three avenues radiated from the north-west side of the house.[22]

Little is known about Bridgeman's work at Gobions, North Mimms. His client, Sir Jeremy Sambrooke, was another investor in the South Sea Company who made a profit from a timely sale of his stock. Like other clients he also commissioned James Gibbs to build a new house. It is not certain, however, whether Gibbs designed the sham medieval arch, the only building that remains standing on the site.[23] In the early nineteenth century, the owner of neighbouring Brookmans Park bought the estate; the house was pulled down and Bridgeman's layout was abandoned; a wood covering about a hundred acres still contains vestiges of banks, ditches, an ornamental canal and trees planted in the eighteenth century. Contemporary visitors were full of praise for Gobions. Defoe remarked on the 'great beauty' of the place and George Bickham described it as 'a sensible Resemblance in Miniature of Stow', the celebrated landscape park in north Buckinghamshire.[24] In 1732, Queen Caroline with the three eldest princesses came to view Sambrooke's 'fine gardens, waterworks and his collection of curiosities' (Figure 4.2).[25] A delightful view of ladies and gentlemen playing bowls at Gobions was published in 1748.

Briggens was yet another park improved out of the proceeds of speculation in the South Sea Company. Its owner, Robert Chester, was a goldsmith and traded with the West Indies as well as being a director of the South Sea Company. He enclosed a park at Briggens in 1720. Salmon observed the situation of the mansion, standing:

> upon a beautiful hill, overlooking the meadows, the river
> Stort and part of Essex from the back front; from the other,
> it hath a prospect over a great part of the county, and is seen
> from Cheshunt Common. The avenue to it hath at the
> entrance a large basin, through which a small stream runs
> and a graceful plantation of trees with a variety of slopes
> adorned with statues.[26]

Bridgeman was paid for obtaining trees for this site from Brompton Park Nursery.[27] He may have offered advice on the layout of the park but no plans by him have survived.

Brocket Hall stood within a park enclosed in the sixteenth century. Two unsigned plans, dating from 1731–8, may have been drawn by Bridgeman; certainly, the owner, Thomas Winnington paid forty guineas to Bridgeman's widow in 1739. Unlike most of Bridgeman's clients, Winnington came from a family of country squires who owned land in Worcestershire. He had been brought up in a Tory household but, when elected MP, he supported Robert Walpole and won promotion to paymaster general. He came into possession of Brocket by marrying Love, daughter of Sir James Reade and coheir of her grandfather, Sir John Reade, the third baronet.[28] Brocket Park, bounded on the west by the Great North Road, was conveniently situated for travel to Westminster.

Bridgeman may have been consulted at Cassiobury, continuing an association with Brompton Park Nursery initiated by Moses Cook, gardener to the first Earl of Essex.[29] Long avenues were planted in the early eighteenth century in the Upper Park, to the west of the river Gade, and straight rides converging on *ronds points* were cut through Whippendell Woods in the manner of Bridgeman. The beauty of these woods was singled out for praise by Stephen Switzer, a leading exponent of the new informality.[30] Perhaps as a mark of appreciation, the third Earl of Essex acquired a bust of Bridgeman which was displayed in the house.[31] A designer who followed the style of Bridgeman, Thomas Wright of Durham (1711–1786), came to Cassiobury in the 1740s and may have designed whimsical garden buildings there.[32]

Beechwood was another park improved in the early eighteenth century in a style characteristic of Bridgeman. A long avenue to the south and east and rectilinear blocks of trees to the east were not aligned on the house, but wildernesses on either side of the north front framed an axial vista.[33] Salmon described Beechwood as 'a well built delightful seat, on a rising ground, in the middle of a park'.[34]

Deer parks

Of the parks transformed by Bridgeman, Tring, Brocket and Cassiobury almost certainly had herds of deer. It is less certain that Sacombe, Moor Park or Gobions did so and unlikely that deer were kept at Briggens. No inventory of deer in the county exists, but two foreign visitors remarked on the prevalence of deer-keeping. In 1728, Cesar de Saussure observed that 'most country houses have parks and rabbit warrens. These parks are surrounded by walls or palings of oak, and contain woods, fine trees, bushes, meadows, some cultivated lands, and always a pond or stream.' Among the 'magnificent properties belonging to noblemen, wealthy gentlemen and merchants' in Hertfordshire he considered that the finest were Moor Park, Hatfield, Cassiobury and Tewin House.[35] He was surprised at the large numbers of animals kept and their good condition. He also noted that 'A deer park, not too distant from London, brings in a very good revenue, for a haunch or quarter of this venison is sold for half a guinea, and sometimes even for twelve and fifteen shillings.'[36] Not only were deer valued as privately owned, domesticated livestock, it was no longer thought improper to sell them.

In 1748, the Finnish botanist Pehr Kalm came to England to study farming practices and record the flora of the Chiltern Hills. His first impression of the countryside between Hemel Hempstead and Little Gaddesden was that 'ploughland, meadow, orchard, park and garden as well as some of the grazing were all enclosed with hedges of various kinds of deciduous shrub'. On the northern side of the hills, he noted 'grazing lands and parks were much more frequent'.[37] During his three-week stay at Little Gaddesden, Kalm visited the Duke of Bridgwater's park at Ashridge, where he was informed that over a thousand deer were kept, and observed that deer had eaten all the bark off fresh young beech, ash and hawthorns which had been felled: 'Of all the trees the ash was most damaged by them and the most gnawed'.[38] In summer, the deer subsisted on grazing in the park but in winter they were fed hay that was stored in barns built for this purpose. Kalm, like de Saussure, remarked on the sale of meat, buck-skin, doeskin and horns, the latter in great demand for knife handles as well as being valued for medicinal use.

Game laws

The apparently peaceful glades of early eighteenth-century sylvan landscapes held hidden terrors for many park owners and their keep-ers. Enclosure of commons deprived the rural poor of grazing for their cows, firewood for their hearths, occasional rabbits for their pots and seasonal pickings of nuts and fruit. Denied access to these accustomed means of supplementing meagre diets, some cottagers and also aggrieved farmers and craftsmen were emboldened to break into the preserves of the gentry and help themselves to wood, deer and other wild animals. After the insecurity and disorders of the early sev-enteenth century, landowners determined that not only deer but also hares, partridges, pheasants and other game should be strictly reserved for their own exclusive enjoyment. The Game Act of 1671 decreed that game could only be taken by possessors of freehold prop-erty worth at least £100 per year or by leaseholders whose property was worth more than £150 per year. The act restricted access to game to the richest owners of land. Tradesmen and professional people, however wealthy and respected they might be, were forbidden to hunt.[39] By isolating a privileged few from the rest of the population, the act provoked violence as well as disobedience.

Some landowners, who wished to placate their neighbours or win votes in local elections, issued indulgences permitting unqualified people to hunt on their land. Other landowners, acting as magistrates, found it difficult to enforce the law. People were unwilling to identify and apprehend poachers. From 1671 to 1723 a dozen new acts were passed, stopping indulgences, increasing penalties, widening the scope of offences, prohibiting the sale of game and giving powers of arrest to keepers. An effect of these measures was to encourage poachers to join armed gangs and disguise themselves by blacking their faces. In 1721, two keepers were killed and several others were wounded in encounters with gangs in royal forests and private parks in Berkshire and Hampshire. Violent affrays occurred in other parts of England, including the district around Enfield Chase extending into south Hertfordshire, where timber was cut down and deer taken. The Black Act of 1723 was intended to prevent further attacks on keepers and park owners, and created some fifty new capital offences that went far beyond protecting deer and other game. It imposed the death penalty for merely appearing in the neighbourhood of a game reserve armed and with a blackened face. Other capital offences included maiming cattle, draining fish ponds, and setting fire to houses, barns and haystacks.[40] In the opinion of a lawyer, 'the act constituted in itself a complete and extremely severe criminal code'.[41] Subsequent legal judgements extended the scope of the act and inaugurated a brutal regime of punishing the poor, the weak and the discontented. Systematic oppression failed to improve the security of owners and keepers and did nothing to enhance the amenity of parks.

John Warburton's map, 1725

The early eighteenth-century chroniclers of Hertfordshire society extolled the virtues of ancient lineages, cherished the descent of manors and revered aristocratic privileges. Sir Henry Chauncy was proud of his connections with other gentry families throughout the county. Chauncy was followed as antiquary and historian by a rector's son, Nathanael Salmon, who entered Corpus Christi College,

Cambridge, in 1690 at the age of 15 and graduated as bachelor of laws in 1695.[42] He took up his father's profession as curate of Westmill. On appointment, he swore the statutory oath of allegiance to William III, but in 1702 he refused to pledge himself to Queen Anne, because the law now required him also to abjure James II's son. This was more than a defender of the principle of legitimate succession could swallow. Debarred from a living in the church, Salmon turned his mind to the practice of medicine, first at St Ives in Huntingdonshire and then at Bishop's Stortford. In 1710 he was admitted as an extra-licentiate of the College of Physicians. He later earned what he could as a writer.[43] In style and content, his *History of Hertfordshire* was closely modelled on Chauncy's work, drawing on material left unpublished by Chauncy, as well as incorporating fresh research. The book addressed a readership among the Tory gentry and the clergy. Salmon displayed his convictions in describing 'the purgatory' of the 'rebellion' and the sufferings of noble families at the hands of 'the scum of the nation'.[44] His descriptions of landscapes were freshly drawn from personal observations but he avoided visiting some places held by descendants of notorious parliamentarians.

Like Chauncy and Salmon, John Warburton (1682–1759) was a genealogist and antiquary, who styled himself 'Esquire' and traced his descent from an Elizabethan knight.[45] In most other respects, he differed from the two historians. His family possessed no landed estate and he did not attend university. He was born at Bury in Lancashire and his sole interest in Hertfordshire lay in making a map of the county. Warburton was first employed by the Inland Revenue. In 1708, while serving as a customs officer at Cockermouth, Cumberland, he entered details of surveys he had not made in his register. For this offence he was demoted and posted to Newcastle. He subsequently moved to Darlington, Hartlepool and Hexham. In 1715, he acted as a government informer in north-east England during the Jacobite rising and afterwards assisted at an inquiry into forfeited estates. In 1716, he was promoted to the rank of Collector at Richmond in Yorkshire, but two years later he was demoted for drunkenness and sent to Wakefield. Shortly after this he resigned from the Inland Revenue and began preparing a map of Yorkshire. In this

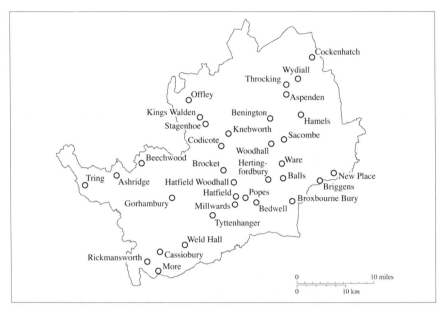

Figure 4.3: Parks in Hertfordshire in 1725. Based on A new and correct map of Middlesex, Essex and Hertfordshire actually surveyed by John Warburton, Esq., Somerset Herald and F.R.S., Joseph Bland and Payler Smith. *Full details of the parks are listed in Table 4.1. Drawn in the* Geography Department, UCL

enterprise, he gained the patronage of Ralph Thoresby, a wealthy Leeds cloth merchant.[46] The map was published in 1720.

The year 1720 was a turning point in Warburton's life. In March 1719 he had been admitted as a Fellow of the Royal Society and in January 1720 he was elected Fellow of the Society of Antiquaries. In June 1720 he was appointed Somerset Herald because, it was alleged, he had 'rendered some service to the government in helping to secure the conviction of some of those who had taken part in the rebellion of 1715'.[47] Warburton was shunned by the other heralds and in particular by Garter King of Arms, John Anstis, a high Tory, diligent scholar and stickler for etiquette. Anstis' position as head of the College had been seriously compromised by his arrest in 1715 on suspicion of supporting the Jacobite uprising in Cornwall.[48] Although charges of treason were dropped, Anstis was not reinstated as Garter King of Arms until 1718. His later career was embittered by personal quarrels and legal disputes. Warburton inflamed Anstis' hostility by neglecting his duties and embarking on a project to produce a series of maps covering England and Wales, starting with a map of the three counties of Middlesex (including the City of London), Essex and Hertfordshire. He engaged as assistants Joseph Bland and Payler Smith, who had carried out field surveys for the Yorkshire map.

In October 1720, a draft, based on the prospectus for the Yorkshire map, was amended to serve as proposals for the new survey of Middlesex, Essex and Hertfordshire. A year later, a revised version of the proposals was sent to the nobility, gentry and other worthy persons, appealing for subscriptions. As a special offer to subscribers, Warburton proposed that 'on the margins of each map will be placed coats of arms of the nobility and gentry, all engraved in their proper colours'.[49] The basic subscription was ten shillings and gentlemen entitled to arms were charged a supplementary fee of one guinea for examining documentary records and engraving. The field survey began in 1721 and was completed in November 1723,[50] and the engraving and printing of six sheets at a scale of approximately 1 in 94,530 or about 0.67 inches to one mile was completed in early 1725 (Figure 4.3).

In April 1725, the College of Arms assembled in chapter announced that in armorial decorations of maps published by Mr Warburton:

> there are not only several Falsities committed by ascribing Arms to Persons who have no Right to them, but notorious Mistakes also in the Bearings and Hatchings of Metal and Colours of the Arms of Gentlemen who have a Right. That he hath frequently been admonished by the King's Heralds and Pursuivants, in their publick Chapters to desist from publishing of Arms without a proper Authority for so doing. And furthermore, the Kings of Arms think convenient to notify that they will speedily take legall Methods to prosecute such Persons as have, or shall continue to usurp Coats of Arms and Crests, to which they have no Right.[51]

Warburton ignored the threat of legal action and in August 1725 reported that copies of the map had been delivered to subscribers,

Table 4.1 Parks in Hertfordshire in 1725

Park	Grid Reference	Owner
Ashridge, Lt Gaddesden	994121	Scroop Egerton, 1st Duke of Bridgwater
Aspenden	352284	Ralph Freman
Balls Park, Hertford	335120	Edward Harrison
Bedwell Park, Essendon	277076	Samuel Whitbread
Beechwood, Flamstead	045144	Sir Thomas Sebright Bt
Benington Place	310229	Sir Charles Caesar
Briggens, Hunsdon	413112	Robert Chester
Brocket, Hatfield	214130	Sir Thomas Winnington
Broxbourne Bury, Hoddesdon	353071	Sir John Monson Bt
Cassiobury, Watford	095972	William Capel, 3rd Earl of Essex
Cockenhatch, Barkway	396361	Edward Chester
Codicote Bury	220187	James Biss
Gorhambury, St Michael	113080	William, 1st Viscount Grimston
Hamels, Braughing	376247	Ralph Freman
Hatfield	236084	James, 5th Earl of Salisbury
Hatfield Millwards	236065	James, 5th Earl of Salisbury
Hatfield Wood Hall, Welwyn	235106	Thomas Shallcross
Hertingfordbury Park	310121	Elizabeth Culling
Kings Walden Bury	161235	Paggen Hale
Knebworth	231210	William Robinson (Lytton)
More Park, Rickmansworth	075933	Benjamin Styles
New Place, Gilston	441129	William Plumer
Offley Place	145272	Sir Henry Penrice Bt
Popes, Hatfield	259077	David Mitchell
Rickmansworth Park	057954	Temple Whitfield
Sacombe Bury	339190	Edward Rolt
Stagenhoe, St Pauls Walden	185227	Robert Heysham
Throcking House	338300	Robert Elwes
Tring House	926111	William Gore
Tyttenhanger, Ridge	192047	Sir Thomas Pope Blount Bt
Ware Park	333144	Thomas Plumer Byde
Weld Hall, Aldenham	175011	Thomas Aram
Woodhall Park, Watton	318189	John Boteler
Wydiall Hall	373317	Richard Goulston

Sources: John Warburton, *A new and correct map of Middlesex, Essex and Hertfordshire actually surveyed by John Warburton, Esq., Somerset Herald and F.R.S., Joseph Bland and Payler Smith, Gent.* (London, 1725) BL Maps C.29.f.6. Names of owners have mostly been taken from Warburton, *Proposals for publishing by subscription a new, large and most correct map of London, Middlesex, Essex and Hertfordshire* (London, 1721), *Victorian County History, Hertfordshire*, and Nathanael Salmon, *The history of Hertfordshire* (London, 1728).

Figure 4.4: Parks in the Stort valley in 1725. New Place, Gilston, was the only park to be depicted by palings on John Warburton's map. Hunsdon House, Briggens and Stanstead Bury were represented as seats. By courtesy of the MacLean Collection

adding that four eminent astronomers and mathematicians had certified that his survey had been 'very carefully and accurately performed'.[52]

A close examination of its features confirms that in the representation of parks, seats, roads and settlements, Warburton's map compares favourably with Oliver's map of 1695 (Figures 4.4 and 4.5). Warburton's delineation of parks, seats and roads in the Stort valley was based on a new and detailed survey. In a section further north, Hamels and Wydiall parks were positioned in relation to Ermine Street more accurately than on Oliver's map. In these two localities, Warburton depicted fewer enclosed parks than Oliver.

In defiance of the warning by the College of Arms, the border of the Hertfordshire map was decorated with the arms of 180 families arranged alphabetically, from Allington to Wynne, and numbered (Figure 4.6).[53] The seats of the named families were located within squares on the map. Thus '78. Viscount Grimston' was located in square H5 on the map, '78' being inscribed against 'Gorhambury', west of St Albans. The families named by Warburton correspond with the names of families occupying those seats about 1725, as recorded in the *Victoria County History*, and all but three of the thirty-four parks

*Figure 4.5: Parks along Ermine Street in 1725. Hamels and Wyddial parks were correctly
sited in relation to Ermine Street. Hadham Hall, Uphall and Stondon Lordship were
represented as seats on John Warburton's map. By courtesy of the MacLean Collection*

depicted on the map were principal residences of armigers. Parks at
Aspenden and New Place were owned by families who had coats of
arms but lived elsewhere: Aspenden was held by Ralph Freman of
Hamels and New Place was owned by William Plumer who lived at
Blakesware, Wareside. Weld Hall, owned by Thomas Aram, was the
only park not held by a family bearing a coat of arms. The seats of

several leading families were not in fact situated in parks: the Duke of Leeds' residence at North Mymms Place, Earl Cowper's Cole Green, Lord Aston's Standon Lordship and Sir Charles Buck's Grove at Watford were among places not represented as parks on the 1725 map.

Sales to non-subscribers of the large map, which covered three counties, were disappointing. In 1726, maps of separate counties on single sheets, at a reduced scale of approximately 1 in 147,310 or about 0.43 inches to one mile, suitable for keeping in portfolios, were engraved and published.[54] The margins of the smaller map were not decorated with coats of arms. The intended surveys of the remaining counties were not carried out.

Twenty years later, Warburton had sunk deeply in debt. To earn some money, he advertised a new edition of the large-scale map of Middlesex, including the City of London.[55] The borders of this map were to be surrounded by coats of arms of over 500 families. The College of Arms reacted swiftly to forbid publication of the offending armorial bearings. On 20 February 1748, the Earl Marshal issued a warrant commanding Warburton to prove the right of each person to the arms displayed on the map and not to sell any copies until one of the Kings of Arms was satisfied with the proofs submitted. Warburton responded by appealing over the heads of the Kings of Arms to the arbitration 'of the impartial Publick, on whom I chiefly depend'.[56] He boldly asserted that London merchants were no less honourable and as fully entitled to respect as other free and independent persons. He also claimed, without offering relevant statistics, that 'citizens of London consist chiefly of descendants from the younger sons of the best families in the kingdom'.[57]

In 1749, a new edition of the Hertfordshire map was published at the original scale of approximately 1 in 94,530 or about 0.67 inches to a mile. It seems to have been printed from plates engraved in 1723–5 with heraldic borders clipped off.[58] The parks shown on the 1749 map are the same as those shown in 1725, with the sole addition of a small park at Cole Green. It is also worth remarking that Throcking Park is included in the 1749 edition, although the manor house had been pulled down in 1744 as a result of a family quarrel. Briggens, a new park laid out by Charles Bridgeman in a fashionable

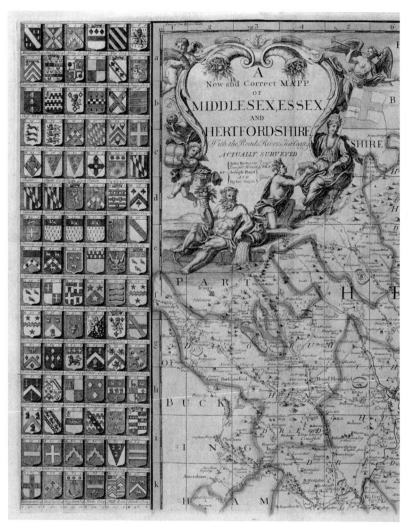

*Figure 4.6: Coats of arms decorating the margin of John Warburton's map of Hertfordshire,
1725. As Somerset Herald, Warburton appealed for subscriptions from the nobility, gentry
and other worthy persons by displaying their coats of arms.
By courtesy of the MacLean Collection*

open style, is depicted as having a row of palings on the north side but
no enclosure on its west or east boundaries.

Warburton adhered strictly to the convention of representing
parks as fenced enclosures; unfenced pleasure grounds of city merchants were not regarded as proper parks. Jeremy Sambrooke's much
admired Gobions, Sir Thomas Clarke's Brickendonbury, William

Gardiner's Pishiobury, Sir John Garrard's Lamer and Sir William Leman's Nyn Hall were not shown as parks. For all his pleading on behalf of wealthy newcomers from the City, Warburton was extremely conservative in defining parks.

Parks shown on Warburton's map

Warburton's map recorded in 1725 one park fewer than Oliver's map of 1695, the losses almost balancing the gains. Of the total of thirty-five parks represented in 1695, eleven did not appear in 1725, and another ten that had not appeared in 1695 were newly shown in 1725. Of the eleven lost parks, two shown at Ashridge in 1695 were consolidated into one large park on the 1725 map. Totteridge Park ceased to be a park when it was bought in 1720 by James Brydges, Duke of Chandos, being swallowed in the extensive estate surrounding his ostentatious residence at Cannons, near Edgware. Upp Hall passed into the hands of William Harvey, MP for Essex, who spent much time away from Hertfordshire at Chigwell and Westminster. Hadham Hall was owned by the Earl of Essex, whose seat and park were at Cassiobury. Jenningsbury, Moor Place, Shephall Bury, Hunsdon House and Standon Lordship were seats of families for whom Warburton engraved coats of arms but did not delineate parks. Shingle Hall disappeared entirely. It was neither a park nor the seat of a family bearing arms.

Of the ten parks that were shown in 1725 but had not been recorded in 1695, Aspenden Hall was a second park belonging to the Freman family. From 1716 to 1729, Aspenden supplied seeds and young trees for improvements to Ralph Freman's principal residence at Hamels.[59] At Aspenden itself, a long avenue of limes planted in 1728, signified its enhanced status as an ornamental park. The owner of Hertingfordbury was not recorded as an armiger, but the house was of long standing, having been built by John Culling between 1681 and 1687, and Jan Drapentier illustrated a 'Parke' there a few years later.[60]

Bedwell Park, Beechwood, Cockenhatch, Codicote Bury, Rickmansworth Park, Throcking House and Tring Park all belonged to families for whom Warburton engraved coats of arms and all but Throcking had houses rebuilt or extended in the early eighteenth century.[61] It is not clear why Bedwell Park was omitted from Oliver's map.

It was shown as a park on Seller's map in 1675, when it belonged to a family who had occupied it continuously since 1651, and Chauncy noted that the then owner, Thomas Atkins JP, had 'much adorned this seat with pleasant gardens'.[62] In 1725, the place was owned by Samuel Whitbread, the brewer.[63] Beechwood was a spacious park improved in the early eighteenth century in the manner of Bridgeman. Cockenhatch had been in the hands of the Chester family since 1540, following the dissolution of Royston Priory. The manor house was rebuilt by Edward Chester in 1716.[64] An estate survey in 1728 showed the park laid out with intersecting avenues and a long canal, as it was before its sale to Admiral Sir John Jennings, owner of neighbouring Newsells.[65] Codicote Bury passed through many hands from the dissolution of St Albans Abbey until it was bought by George Poyner, citizen and merchant of London. Chauncy reported that Poyner 'built a fair house with convenient stables and outhouses'.[66] In 1725, a small park at Codicote was occupied by James Biss, a relative of Poyner. Rickmansworth Park was probably enclosed by Temple Whitfield just before Warburton made his survey.[67] Throcking appears to have remained emparked after Robert Elwes the younger pulled down a large new mansion in order to prevent his brother's heir from coming into possession of it.[68] At Tring Park, Bridgeman completed the new layout at the time Warburton was preparing his map.

Parks enlarged and beautified in the early eighteenth century

Few of the improvements made to parks in Hertfordshire in the early eighteenth century moved towards the natural informality advocated by Addison. Hamels was exceptional in enhancing the apparent height of natural slopes by the judicious planting of silver firs, spruce and Scots pine. Near the house, Ralph Freman laid out a formal garden, including broad avenues, ornamental canals and statuary, but further away he planted a wilderness threaded with serpentine walks. Planting was started in 1713 and continued for more than twenty years. A bird's eye view depicted by Badeslade in 1722 shows an extensive deer park surrounding the formal layout (Figure 4.7).[69] The principal axis of the new design lay to the south of the house, from the centre to the left of the engraving. A first vista led from a terrace

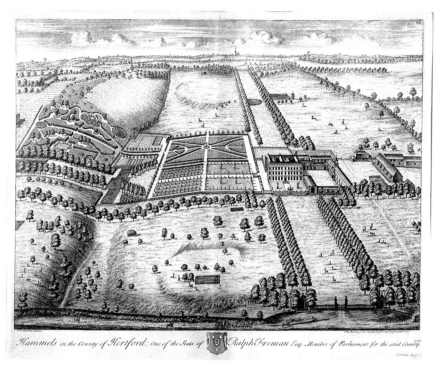

Figure 4.7: View of Hamels, a seat of Ralph Freman, 1722. An informal wilderness was situated at a distance from the house on the left of the view. Drawn by Thomas Badeslade, engraved by T. Harris, 1722. Reproduced by kind permission of HALS (BRAU/30)

down through gardens and across an ornamental canal at the bottom of a bourne. Another vista aligned north–south traversed a shrubbery and a kitchen garden, leading the eye uphill to an informal wilderness. The gardens were surrounded by a deer park which was crossed by a long east–west avenue from Ermine Street to Great Munden church on the horizon.

Also improved in this period was Balls Park, described by Salmon as 'this beautiful seat', which Edward Harrison 'greatly augmented and improved and the land about laid into a park'.[70] Harrison had amassed a fortune in India, rising from captain of East Indiamen to governor of Madras. He returned home in 1717, was appointed director and later chairman of the East India Company and elected Whig MP for Weymouth and then for Hertford and, from 1726 to his death in 1732, he held office as postmaster-general.[71] The expansion of the park was mostly carried out after 1722.

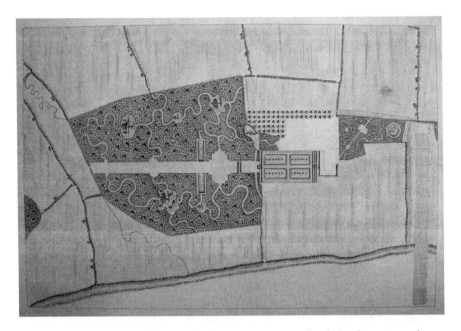

*Figure 4.8: Plan of Kendal Hall, Aldenham, c.1740. An undated plan for a new park,
represented a large area of informal wilderness. The plan was probably drawn when William
Jephson was building the house. Reproduced by kind permission of HALS (D/EB 1622 P3)*

The park at St Paul's Walden Bury was formed in the 1720s, just
too late to be shown on Warburton's map. Edward Gilbert, a City
merchant, bought the property and began building a compact
Palladian house. He died in 1724 and his son, Edward Gilbert junior,
who lived until 1762, completed the building and laid out the grounds
in an essentially formal style.[72] At the far end of a broad lawn in front
of the house, he placed a *patte d'oie*, from which stretched a long
central alley and two diverging alleys, each lined with clipped beech
hedges. The vistas were terminated by a statue, a temple and the
tower of the parish church. The ground between the alleys was thinly
planted with oaks, Scots pine and other trees.[73]

At about this time, the delightful natural declivities of the Mimram
valley were being discovered. Tewin House, which had been purchased
in 1690 by William Gore, who made 'a fair Addition' to the house,[74]
was bought in 1715 by General Joseph Sabine, who had fought
bravely with the Duke of Marlborough in Flanders and later commanded the British army in Scotland, following the Jacobite rising.[75]
Sabine built a completely new house at great expense between 1716

and 1718.[76] At neighbouring Tewin Water, James Fleet, 'a gentleman of Great Fortune', repaired and beautified the capital messuage.[77] Fleet was engaged in planting when he was appointed sheriff in 1718.[78] Both these properties were acquired later by the Cowper family.

The Golden Parsonage at Great Gaddesden was a large house set within extensive gardens, but it possessed no deer park. The Halsey family had owned the place since the dissolution of the monasteries and had prospered since the mid-seventeenth century. Sir John Halsey had been master of chancery and his heir Thomas was sheriff in 1679 and MP between 1685 and 1713.[79] An estate map drawn in 1717, two years after Thomas's death, shows the house surrounded by rectangular enclosures bordered with trees. The main gardens lay to the south and east of the house. Beyond the gardens, an area of woodland called 'The Grove' was probably designed as a wilderness.[80] Henshaw Halsey rebuilt the house and probably transformed the gardens. A half-mile-long avenue, not aligned on the house, pointed to the south-west. The girths of the lime trees suggest that the avenue was planted about 1720.[81]

In about 1740, Kendals Hall, Aldenham, was depicted on a remarkable estate plan (Figure 4.8). The plan shows a large garden, articulated along an axial vista, extending north of the house. In front of the house lay rectangular gardens, and on either side of the axial vista lay wildernesses, threaded with winding paths and small openings planted with specimen trees.[82] Stumps of sweet chestnuts and hornbeams suggest that the wildernesses may have been formed out of an earlier coppiced wood. William Jephson, a London wine merchant, who purchased the estate in 1739, probably designed the garden in the manner of Stephen Switzer.[83]

Much attention was paid to the management of woods and grass but avenues still prevailed. Many landowners preferred to make their mark on the landscape in the grand manner. In 1703, Thomas Clarke inherited Brickendonbury from his father, who had been a mercer and lord mayor of London.[84] Clarke's niece and heir married Thomas Morgan, a Welsh squire and MP. After Clarke died in 1754, Morgan and his wife built a new house surrounded by woods and planted a mile-long avenue that stretched to the outskirts of Hertford. Morgan's Walk at Brickendonbury was one of the last and longest axial vistas in Hertfordshire.[85]

Stately avenues, straight canals and formal flower beds were still being laid out in the middle of the eighteenth century, many years after parks in other parts of England had been transformed by William Kent into Arcadian landscapes, resembling scenes painted by Claude Lorrain. No Hertfordshire landowner invited Kent to perform his magic on their domain. Even the novelties of Gobions could not rival the charms of such fashionable showplaces as Stowe, Houghton or Chiswick. Tim Richardson mentions Hamels, Tring and St Pauls Walden Bury as places in Hertfordshire where informal landscapes were created in the early eighteenth century. These parks exhibited a greater variety of features than the baroque gardens which preceded them. Within rectilinear plantations, different kinds of trees were planted and serpentine walks or 'wiggles' twisted and turned through the trees. Densely planted, shaded areas with romantic grottos alternated with sunlit expanses of grass and vistas that looked across farmland towards church towers or monuments.[86] In the course of half a century, nature itself had softened the rectilinear outline of plantations at Cassiobury Park (Figure 4.9). John Wooton's painting represented the view towards the house as an informal landscape. In Hertfordshire, 'the twilight of imperfect essays' described by Horace Walpole,[87] lasted until the middle of the eighteenth century, before the clear light of landscape gardening shone on open plains and calm stretches of water in the second half of the century.

Landowners and parks

In the early eighteenth century, lords and gentlemen who owned parks in Hertfordshire ruled the county but not the nation. In 1704, Daniel Defoe reported that 'The Gentlemen of the Royston Club settle all the affairs of the county and carry all before them'; the club met on the first Thursday every month.[88] They appointed magistrates and sheriffs, they exercised the gift of livings in the church and they also selected candidates for election to parliament. Since the introduction of land tax in 1691, they paid a larger share of direct taxation than other taxpayers. They paid for Marlborough's victories over Louis XIV and for naval wars that defended Britain's overseas trade and colonial empire. Regardless of their eminence in county society, the largest landowners

Figure 4.9: View of Cassiobury Park, c.1748. The painting by John Wootton was composed in the style of a classical scene depicted by Claude Lorrain. It was a complete contrast to the strict formality of the late seventeenth-century layout. In the foreground, a house party, from left to right, included Lady Clarendon; Lady Mary Forbes; Dr Johnson, Bishop of Worcester; William, the fourth Earl of Essex, mounted on a pony; Lady Caroline Egerton, sister of the young Duke of Bridgwater, who was running towards her; Lady Anne Capel; and Lady Diana Capel, attended by a servant on horseback. Across the River Gade, in the middle distance, mature trees were grouped informally and, in the background, the west front of Cassiobury House emerged from dense plantations of hardwoods. By courtesy of Watford Museum Collection

were excluded from successive national governments which, for half a century after 1714, were led by different factions of Whigs. The owner of Ashridge, John Egerton, fourth Earl of Bridgwater, held office briefly as President of the Board of Trade (1696–9) and First Lord of the Admiralty (1699–1701), but succeeding Egertons were out of government for the rest of the eighteenth century.[89] William, the first Earl Cowper, of Cole Green, was Lord Chancellor from 1714 to 1718 but his descendants did not enter the judiciary or obtain ministerial positions; rather, they spent their time improving their lands and buying neighbouring properties in the Mimram valley. The Cecils at Hatfield, who had been at the centre of government under Queen Elizabeth and James I, remained out of office from 1612 to 1783.[90] The Capels at Cassiobury, as staunch Tories with Jacobite leanings, were regarded with suspicion by those in power. These families were outside the favoured circle of Whigs who dispensed patronage and promoted the arts. Their influence was confined to county affairs. As exceptions, two ambitious MPs, Thomas Winnington at Brocket and Edward Harrison at Balls Park, came to live in Hertfordshire to be within easy reach of Westminster. They were both appointed to senior positions in Robert Walpole's government. Other wealthy newcomers from London who bought land in Hertfordshire were content to accept small tokens of respect as rewards for joining the squirearchy. The 'monied interest' settled for a quiet life and made no attempt to use their wealth to supplant the established order.

It was difficult for landowners to make changes in the landscape while returns from agricultural land remained depressed. Grain prices stayed low, the price of wheat falling more often than rising in the century before 1750.[91] Farmers and landowners made strenuous efforts to use land more efficiently and crop yields were gradually increased. Studies of probate inventories in Hertfordshire indicate that from the late seventeenth to the early eighteenth century bare fallows were greatly reduced, the area being sown instead with grass seeds; clover and sainfoin increased, rye declined dramatically, the area under wheat decreased a little and barley was grown more widely.[92] In south-west Hertfordshire, arable land on heavy soils was laid down to grass to be mown for hay to supply an expanding market in the greater London region, to provide grazing for sheep, cattle and horses and to support a dairy industry producing butter.[93] In the 1720s, Daniel Defoe reported that two foreign gentlemen passing across Bushey Heath, looking down into the vale of St Albans, 'were surprised at the beauty of this prospect' and one of them remarked that 'England was not like other countries, but it was all a planted garden'.[94] The patchwork of small, deeply hedged fields was the work of many independent farmers but, during the early eighteenth century, only the largest landowners had sufficient resources to invest in improvements and many small owners were forced to sell their holdings.

Christopher Clay has calculated that the area of land held by estates of over 10,000 acres increased between 1660 and 1750, while the number of landowners in possession of fewer than 300 acres decreased.[95] Although agriculture remained depressed, the price of land rose steadily after 1710.[96] Purchasers were mainly large proprietors adding to their estates and wealthy newcomers investing in land as a security, the type of landowner who could afford to commission trained book-keepers and valuers to manage their estates efficiently. Clay has examined the process of territorial aggrandisement with reference to two Hertfordshire estates: that of the Grimstons at Gorhambury and of the Cowpers at Cole Green.

The core of the Gorhambury estate was acquired by Sir Harbottle Grimston between 1652 and 1683. Almost all acquisitions lay within four miles of his seat. The Grimstons added to their fortunes by marrying heiresses: Sir Harbottle married a niece and heiress of Francis Bacon, who owned the original estate. Harbottle's son, Sir Samuel, outlived his wife and children and passed on huge debts to his successor, a nephew, William Luckyn, who changed his name to Grimston. In 1706, William married Jane Cook, daughter of a wealthy London wax chandler. Her marriage portion helped to reduce the outstanding debts but William was obliged to cut all mature oaks, screens of elms and other fine timber in the park. In 1719, when the finances of the estate were no longer precarious, William was created Viscount Grimston.[97]

At Cole Green in 1721, William, first Earl Cowper, the Lord Chancellor, was able to buy many small properties in the Mimram valley from Robert Middleton of Chirk Castle, Denbighshire, who had married the daughter and heiress of Sir John Reade of Brocket Hall. While Middleton used Cowper's money to buy land near his Welsh seat, the second and third earls Cowper purchased copyhold land in half a dozen Hertfordshire manors and so became tenants of the Earl of Salisbury. The third earl spent most of his life in Florence, where he married and raised a family. In 1754, he inherited from his uncle, the Earl of Grantham, over £100,000. With savings made from living abroad and his inherited wealth he bought estates adjoining Cole Green, at Tewin, Panshanger and Hertingfordbury.[98] Figure 4.10 indicates that by 1769 the estate held a commanding position in the Mimram valley between Hertingfordbury and Tewin, and possessed two outlying portions of land between Welwyn and Hatfield. The methods of building up these estates were to obtain sums of money from marriage settlements or windfall bequests, to consolidate acquisitions adjoining the principal seat, to dispose of outlying properties

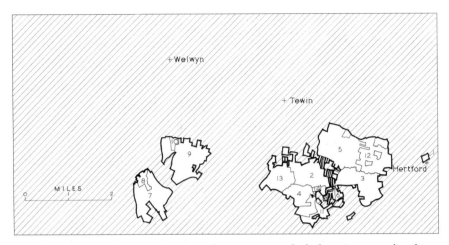

Figure 4.10: Earl Cowper's estate, 1769. The estate consisted of a large area extending from Hertingfordbury to Tewin and smaller areas near Hatfield. Compiled from surveys by William Smith, agent to the third and fourth earls Cowper (HALS DE/P). Drawn in the Geography Department, UCL

by sale or exchange and to acquire copyhold tenures with a view to buying the freeholds. When a minor inherited an estate, guardians or the Court of Wards collected rents and paid running expenses and the accumulated balance was passed to the heir on coming of age. This sum might be used for buying land or investing in improvements. The wealth of the Cowper family was replenished by the third earl living abroad for fifty years, spending little of his income at Cole Green.[99] His successor, George Augustus Nassau Clavering Cowper, the fourth earl, inherited as a minor and died at the early age of 22. The estate and its accumulated revenues then passed to the fifth earl, who possessed ample means to lay out a large new park at Panshanger.

The objects of estate management in early eighteenth-century Hertfordshire were to find reliable tenants who would pay their rents regularly, to encourage farmers to improve the quality of their grass-lands, to eliminate fallows and to reclaim wastes. Owners themselves aimed to take in hand larger areas to raise trees for timber, to lay down more grass to make hay, to breed and feed horses, cattle and sheep and to appropriate and enclose heaths and common wastes.[100] Large landowners were more successful in achieving these objectives than small proprietors because they employed professional staff to draw up contracts and tenancy agreements, keep full and accurate accounts of income, expenditure and capital transactions, survey farms and fields, and prepare plans and specifications for buildings and drainage works. Large estates were beginning to be managed as commercial enterprises whose executives had vested interests in making them profitable. An influx of merchants, bankers and brewers among the Hertfordshire gentry played an important part in raising standards of financial management.

During the early eighteenth century, the land market in Hertfordshire was brisk. Estates or parcels of land that failed to produce sufficient income to meet recurrent expenditure, including land tax, tithes and poor rates, were put on sale. In Hertfordshire, the turnover of properties was more rapid than in most other parts of England. First-time buyers and heirs of first-time buyers were more numerous than in other counties and they were also the most frequent sellers of land.[101] In 1733, Wormleybury was bought by John Deane who had made two fortunes and lost one in India. Immediately, he pulled down the old Tudor house and started to build a large new mansion. A year later, Deane was appointed sheriff and was spending far beyond his means on building and entertaining. At the end of 1734, he was forced to sell a neighbouring property and then to mortgage the newly built Wormleybury. By 1739 he was bankrupt and departed to work as a tapster in a London tavern.[102] Overspending on building and laying out grounds was rarely so serious as to cause the fall of an estate. Even Wormleybury and its park were restored by another nabob a few years later.

Other extravagances consumed some large fortunes. A few families were ruined by gambling, while others fell victim to political ambitions. Charles Caesar, who inherited Benington Place from his father in 1694, demolished the old house and built a spacious new mansion. Before he moved in, the mansion burnt to the ground and he went to live in a small house on the estate. His wife, Mary, daughter of Ralph Freman of Aspenden, was a garden designer, and built and decorated a grotto and tended the plants. As a Tory who sympathised with Jacobites, Caesar spent the rest of his life and the remainder of his fortune fighting parliamentary elections. He first stood for the borough of Hertford in 1701 and fought six later elections before winning two ruinously expensive contests for the county seat in 1728 and 1736. He died insolvent and broken-hearted in 1741, leaving debts so large 'that all he possessed was forced to be sold'.[103] All was not yet lost. Caesar's son, Charles the younger, married an heiress and came into possession of another estate, Bayford Place. Sadly, the couple had no son and, on his death, Bayford Place had to be sold so that the proceeds could be divided between their two daughters.

One of the most frequent causes for breaking up estates was the failure of owners to leave sons to succeed them. Demographic failure was particularly severe in the early eighteenth century. Lawrence and Jeanne Stone have analysed 2,312 transfers of large country houses in Hertfordshire (1,108 transfers), Northamptonshire (855) and Northumberland (349) from 1540 to 1880. Transfers by inheritance, by sale and by other means have been analysed for ten-year periods and demographic characteristics of owners have also been analysed. The most prolonged crisis for intergenerational succession occurred between 1700 and 1749, when as many as 43 per cent of owners died leaving no surviving son. During that period, no fewer than 16 per cent of owners never married, deliberately denying themselves all hope of having legitimate heirs. Many married late: the average age of landowning husbands was 26 years and 19 per cent of marriages were childless. In a further 8 per cent of families, sons died before their fathers.[104] Infant mortality remained high and deaths from smallpox rose during the first half of the eighteenth century.

Daughters who married aristocrats were expected to bring large dowries and younger sons generally required costly educations. The optimum size of family for a landowner was one healthy son. It is per-haps unsurprising in the light of this that the largest estates belonged to families that succeeded in producing male heirs for at least three generations. The Cecils, Capels, Egertons and, after a faltering start, the Grimstons all passed their lands and titles directly from fathers to sons, from paternal grandfathers to grandsons or from fathers to only daughters, whose husbands became owners on marriage.

Most estates without male heirs passed by indirect inheritance to a brother or a brother's son, but some had to be sold in order to pro-vide for surviving widows and daughters. The percentage of all properties in the Stones' sample that were transferred by indirect inheritance rose from about 11 per cent in 1670 to about 34 per cent in 1770. During the same period, the percentage of all properties disposed of by sale fluctuated from about 17 per cent to about 12 per cent.[105] In Hertfordshire, families owning small estates were much more likely to become extinct than families owning large properties.

The struggle for survival among the long-established families of Hertfordshire's gentry and the political orientation of the most influential aristocrats help to account for the reluctance of the leaders of fashion to transform their parks in the naturalistic manner approved by Addison and Pope. The tastes of wealthy newcomers from the City of London and Westminster were not constrained by penury and not dictated by Tory principles, but the new rich readily adopted the formal style prevailing in the county. Nabobs and bankers considered Hertfordshire a safe place to live and invest part of their fortunes. Defoe described how the tradesmen of England searched assiduously for 'the coats of arms of their ancestors in order to paint them upon their coaches' and 'carve them upon the pediments of their new mansions'.[106] A stiff, rather old-fashioned grandeur appealed to them more than a libertarian embrace of untamed nature. Even Whig MPs, including Edward Harrison at Balls Park and Thomas Morgan at Brickendonbury, who found it convenient to live within half a day's journey from Westminster, shunned the new fashion. Admittance to the county elite imposed its own cultural values on newcomers. They were expected to entertain their neighbours, go to church regularly, take part in wedding celebrations, pay their respects at funerals, attend local race meetings, share the deliberations of quarter sessions and, if they were ambitious, they were expected to take a serious interest in building and making parks.

Notes

1. H. Wotton, *The elements of architecture* (London, 1624).
2. F. Bacon, 'Of gardens' (1625).
3. A.A. Cooper (3rd Earl of Shaftesbury), *The moralists: a philosophic rhapsody* (London, 1709).

4.   J. Addison, *The Tatler*, 161 (18–20 April 1710).

5.   J. Addison, *The Spectator*, 414 (25 June 1712).

6.   A. Pope, 'Of the use of riches.' *Epistle IV, to Richard Boyle, Earl of Burlington* (1731).

7.   *Ibid.*

8.   D. Green, *Gardener to Queen Anne. Henry Wise (1653–1738) and the formal garden* (Oxford, 1956), pp.4, 7, 54–6, 163.

9.   P. Willis, *Charles Bridgeman and the English landscape garden* (Jesmond, 2001), pp.26–43.

10. Green, *Gardener to Queen Anne*, pp.148–50.

11. Willis, *Bridgeman*, p.60.

12. *VCH Hertfordshire*, vol. 3, p.137.

13. Willis, *Bridgeman*, p.433.

14. Salmon, *History of Hertfordshire*, p.225.

15. Colvin, *English architects*, p.235.

16. Yorkshire Archaeological Society Ms328, cited in Hertfordshire Garden Trust and Williamson, *Parks and gardens of west Hertfordshire*, pp.20–1.

17. Defoe, *Tour*, vol. 2, p.15 ; M. Rothschild, *The Rothschild gardens* (Stroud, 1996); R.W. Bushaway, 'Rite, legitimation and community', in B. Stapleton (ed.), *Conflict and community in southern England* (Stroud, 1992), pp.110–34.

18. Hertfordshire Gardens Trust and Williamson, *Parks and gardens of west Hertfordshire*, p.28.

19. H.A. Armitage, *A history of Moor Park* (London, 1964), p.17.

20. Salmon, *History of Hertfordshire*, p.110.

21. Pope, 'Of riches'.

22. Willis, *Bridgeman*, p.62, pl. 51a.

23. B. Jones, *Follies and grottoes* (London, 1953), p.345.

24. Defoe, Tour, vol. 2, p.184; G. Bickham, *The beauties of Stow* (London, 1750), pp.66–7.

25. *Gentleman's Magazine*, 19 July 1732, cited in A. Jones (ed.), *Hertfordshire 1731–1800, as recorded in the Gentleman's Magazine* (Hertford, 1993), p.2.

26. Salmon, *History of Hertfordshire*, p.253.

27. Willis, *Bridgeman*, pp.59, 62, 128; A. Skelton, 'The development of the Briggens estate, Hunsdon, since 1720', *Hertfordshire Archaeology*, 12 (1994–6), pp.111–28.

28. R. Sedgwick, *The history of parliament: the House of Commons 1715–1754* (London, 1970), vol. II, p.550.

29. Hertfordshire Gardens Trust and Williamson, *Parks and gardens in west Hertfordshire*, p.32.

30. S. Switzer, *Ichnographia rustica* (London, 1718).

31. H. Poole, 'Social life at Cassiobury', in S. Poole (ed.), *A fair and large house at Cassiobury Park 1546–1927* (Watford, 1985), p.44.

32. E. Harris (ed.), *Thomas Wright: arbours and grottos* (London, 1979).

33. Hertfordshire Gardens Trust and Williamson, *Parks and gardens in west Hertfordshire*, pp.29–30.

34. Salmon, *History of Hertfordshire*, p.142.

35. C. de Saussure (ed. and trans. by Madame van Muyden), *A foreign view of England in the reigns of George I and George II: letters to his family* (London, 1902), pp.307–8.

36. *Ibid.*, pp.308–9.

37. W.R. Mead, *Pehr Kalm: a Finnish visitor to the Chilterns in 1748* (Aston Clinton, 2003), pp.35, 37.

38. *Ibid.*, p.61.

39. P.B. Munsche, *Gentlemen and poachers: the English game laws 1671–1831* (Cambridge, 1981), pp.15–17.

40. E.P. Thompson, *Whigs and hunters: the origin of the Black Act* (London, 1975), pp.21–3.

41. L. Radzinowicz, *A history of English criminal law and its administration from 1750* (London, 1948), vol. I, p.77.

42. S.G. Doree, 'Nathaniel Salmon: Hertfordshire's neglected historian', in D. Jones-Baker (ed.), *Hertfordshire in history: papers presented to Lionel Munby* (Hertfordshire Local History Council, 1991), pp.205–22.

43. W.R. Powell, 'Salmon, Nathanael (1675–1742)', in *Oxford Dictionary of National Biography*, vol. 48, p.731.

44. Salmon, *History of Hertfordshire*, pp.41, 337.

45. T. Woodcock, 'John Warburton (1682–1759)', in *Oxford Dictionary of National Biography*, vol. 57, pp.260–1.

46. W.B. Crump, 'The genesis of Warburton's "Map of Yorkshire" 1720', *Thoresby Society Miscellanea*, 28 (1928), pp.385–404.

47. A. Wagner, *Heralds of England: a history of the office and College of Arms* (London, 1967), p.384.

48. S. Handley, 'John Anstis (1669–1744)', in *Oxford Dictionary of National Biography*, vol. 2, pp.278–80.

49. J. Warburton, *Proposals for publishing by subscription a new, large, beautiful and most correct map of London, Middlesex, Essex and Hertfordshire (and the rest of the counties in England and Wales) by actual survey and dimensuration, with the coats of arms and seats of the nobility and gentry, as in those of Yorkshire and Northumberland already published by John Warburton, Esq., Somerset Herald of Arms and F.R.S.* (London, 1721), p.2.

50.   D. Hodson, 'John Warburton 1716–25 and 1749', in D. Hodson (ed.),
      County atlases of the British Isles published after 1703 (Tewin, 1984), vol. I,
      p.174.

51.   *Ibid.*, vol. I, p.175, quoting *Daily Post*, 9 April 1725.

52.   *Ibid.*, vol. I, p.175, quoting *London Journal*, 14 August 1725.

53.   *A new and correct map of Middlesex, Essex, and Hertfordshire actually
      surveyed by John Warburton, Esq., Somerset Herald and F. R..S., Joseph
      Bland and Payler Smith, Gent.* (London, 1725) (British Library (BL) Maps
      C.29.f.6).

54.   *The counties of Essex, Middlesex and Hertfordshire actually survey'd by
      several hands* (London, 1726) (BL Maps K. Top.VI.69).

55.   Hodson, 'John Warburton', p.176, quoting *General Advertiser*, 20 January
      1748.

56.   J. Warburton, *London and Middlesex illustrated by a true and explicit
      Account of the Names, Residence, Genealogy and Coat Armour of the
      Nobility, Principal Merchants and other Eminent Families trading within the
      Precincts of this most opulent City and County, All Blazon'd in their proper
      Colours* (London, 1749), pp.i , ii.

57.   *Ibid.*, p.iv.

58.   *To the nobility and gentry of Hertfordshire, subscribers to this work, this map
      is most humbly dedicated, by their oblig'd servant John Warburton Somerset*
      (London, 1749) (BL Maps * 2855.(6)).

59.   Rowe, *Garden making*, p.xlv.

60.   Chauncy, *Historical antiquities*, vol. I, p.535.

61.   Smith, *Hertfordshire houses*, pp.24, 50, 52, 54, 56, 147, 192.

62.   Chauncy, *Historical antiquities*, vol. I, p.544.

63.   *VCH Hertfordshire*, vol. 3, pp.460–1.

64.   Smith, *Hertfordshire houses*, p.24.

65.   HALS D/ERy P1.

66.   Chauncy, *Historical antiquities*, vol. II, p.408.

67.   *VCH Hertfordshire*, vol. 2, p.374.

68.   *VCH Hertfordshire*, vol. 4, p.113.

69.   Rowe, *Garden making*, p.xlii–liv, 1–48; A. Rowe, 'Country house chameleon:
      the story of Hamels Mansion', *Hertfordshire's Past*, 43:4 (1998), pp.44–54.

70.   Salmon, *History of Hertfordshire* 41.

71.   Sedgwick, *History of parliament*, vol. II, p.113.

72.   *VCH Hertfordshire*, vol. 2, p.405; Jones, *Hertfordshire in the Gentleman's
      Magazine*, pp.132–3.

73.   C. Hussey, *English gardens and landscapes 1700–1750* (London, 1967),
      pp.84–8.

74. Chauncy, *Historical antiquities*, vol. I, p.541.

75. J. Spain, 'Joseph Sabine (1661–1739)', in *Oxford Dictionary of National Biography*, vol. 48, pp.515–16.

76. W. Branch Johnson (ed.), *Memorandoms for... the diary between 1798 and 1810 of John Carrington, farmer, chief constable, tax assessor, surveyor of highways and overseer of the poor of Bramfield in Hertfordshire* (Chichester, 1973), p.145.

77. *Ibid.*, p.23.

78. *VCH Hertfordshire*, vol. 3, p.481.

79. B.D. Henning, *The history of parliament: the House of Commons 1660–1690* (London, 1983), pp.468–9.

80. 'A draught of the estate of Henshaw Halsey, Esq., 1717' (HALS 15595).

81. N. Doggett and J. Hunn, 'Excavations at Golden Parsonage, Gaddesden Row', *Hertfordshire's Past*, 13 (1982), pp.30–3; Hertfordshire Gardens Trust and Williamson, *Parks and gardens in west Hertfordshire*, pp.32–6.

82. Hertfordshire Gardens Trust and Williamson, *Parks and gardens in west Hertfordshire*, pp.36–7; Plan of Kendals Hall, Aldenham, c.1740 (HALS D/EB 1622 P3).

83. D. Wratten, The book of Radlett and Aldenham (Buckingham, 1990), p.31; Switzer, *Ichnographia rustica*.

84. *VCH Hertfordshire*, vol. 3, p.410.

85. Hertfordshire Gardens Trust and R. Bisgrove, *Hertfordshire gardens on Ermine Street* (Abbots Langley, 1996), p.10; Stone and Stone, *An open elite?*, p.157.

86. T. Richardson, *The Arcadian friends: inventing the English landscape garden* (London, 2007), pp.67, 74-5, 336-9.

87. H. Walpole, *The history of modern taste in gardening* (London, 1780), p.43.

88. Historical Manuscripts Commission, *The manuscripts of his Grace the Duke of Portland at Welbeck Abbey* (London, 1897), vol. 4, pp.153–4 cited in J. Hoppit, *A land of liberty? England 1689–1727* (Oxford, 2000), p. 379.

89. G.E.C., *The complete peerage*, vol. II, p.313.

90. D. Warrand (ed.), *Hertfordshire families* (London, 1907), pp.114–23.

91. Bowden, 'Agricultural prices, wages, farm profits and rents', pp.1, 6, 22, 23, 61 and Statistical Appendix, pp.814–70.

92. M. Overton, *Agricultural revolution in England. The transformation of the agrarian economy 1500–1850* (Cambridge, 1996), pp.77, 78, 93, 94, 103, 108.

93. Longman, *A corner of England's garden*, pp.28–53, 76–80.

94. Defoe, *Tour*, vol. 2, pp.8–9.

95. Clay, 'Evolution of landed society', pp.163, 170–1.

96. *Ibid.*, p.176.

97. *Ibid.*, pp.185, 194, 208, based on Clay, 'The Grimstons and the Cowpers'; Rogers, 'Gorhambury', pp.78–85.

98. Clay, 'Evolution of landed society', pp.196, 197, 207; Clay, 'The Grimstons and the Cowpers', pp.260–3, 284–7.

99. Branch Johnson, *Memorandoms for the diary of John Carrington*, pp.24, 37.

100. W. Ellis, *Chiltern and Vale farming explained, according to the latest improvements necessary for all landlords and tenants of either ploughed-grass or wood-grounds* (London, 1733); Mead, Pehr Kalm, pp.34–81; Switzer, *Ichnographia rustica.*

101. Stone and Stone, *Open elite?*, pp.160–1.

102. *Ibid.*, p.166.

103. *Ibid.*, p.158, quoting J. Burke, *The commoners of Great Britain* (1835), vol. II, p.21; L. Munby, 'Charles Caesar (1673–1741)', in *Oxford Dictionary of National Biography*, vol. 9, pp.434–5.

104. Stone and Stone, *Open elite?*, p.157, tables 3.2, 3.3.

105. *Ibid.*, table 4.1.

106. D. Defoe, *The complete English tradesman* (London, 1726), p.377.

Chapter V
Late Eighteenth-century Parks

AROUND THE MIDDLE OF THE EIGHTEENTH CENTURY the confidence and fortunes of Hertfordshire landowners improved. After 1750, a higher proportion of aristocrats married and had children who survived to adulthood; agricultural production increased and rents rose; profits from home farms and returns from wood and timber sales also increased. Above all, landowners, supported by commercially oriented tenants, corn merchants, maltsters, brewers and bankers, dominated local politics. They were able to secure the passage of enclosure acts, and enjoyed a largely free hand in diverting highways and prosecuting poachers. Big spenders had the means and incentives to realise the visions of Shaftesbury, Addison and Pope and put into practice new ideas expounded by Hogarth and Burke.[1] In Hertfordshire, the golden age of landscape gardening opened with the arrival of Capability Brown at Beechwood in 1753. The advance of the naturalistic style was chronicled and publicised by Horace Walpole, Thomas Whateley and other commentators, and the fashion spread rapidly from enthusiastic patrons to eager imitators.

Capability Brown

As head gardener at Stowe, England's most celebrated landscape garden, Lancelot Brown perfected his distinctive style of laying out grounds. He removed walls and fences and smoothed terraces bounding gardens. His sunk fences were better hidden than those designed by Bridgeman, and grass that was mown on the garden side of a sunk fence merged imperceptibly into grass that was grazed in the park, forming extensive sweeps of shaven turf. He was unrivalled in damming streams to form lakes whose surfaces reflected the profiles of houses. He raised the apparent height of slopes by planting circular clumps of trees on their summits, and by judicious planting he opened vistas down valleys and closed views of unattractive features. He was not only a creative genius, but a tireless worker and a person of great natural charm. In 1751, after ten years at Stowe, he moved to Hammersmith and set up as an independent landscape gardener.[2]

Brown's first commission in Hertfordshire came in 1753. Brown was invited by Sir John Sebright to survey the grounds at Beechwood and draw plans for breaking up rectilinear outlines of plantations made about a quarter of a century earlier. He thinned dense blocks of trees to the north of the house but left a number of closely planted clumps among the clearings. Other areas of woodland were moulded into rounded shapes and some new clumps were planted in the southeast quadrant of the park. To the south, a Bridgemanic avenue, flanked by double lines of beeches, was spared. Brown also submitted plans for an ice-house and a gothick bath-house, but these appear not to have been built. Further changes were made at Beechwood in the period 1772–84, when large sums were paid every spring to the nurseryman, John Davenport.[3] Not only was the park producing much profitable beech and oak timber, it was also growing a variety of conifers, distinctly new species in the flora of Hertfordshire. In 1804, Arthur Young noted:

> I have rarely seen finer trees than at … Beechwood: it has
> the name in strict propriety, for the number of stately
> beeches is great; but the soil agrees with all sorts of trees: the
> cedars are immense; the oak very large; the ash straight and
> beautiful; the larch, spruce, and Scotch fir equally fine, but
> the beech uncommon.[4]

In 1754, Brown began to modernise Bridgeman's magnificent garden at Moor Park. Its new owner was the naval hero Admiral Lord Anson, who had captured Spanish ships carrying bullion from their

Figure 5.1: View from Moor Park towards Rickmansworth, c.1765–7. One of three paintings by Richard Wilson, commissioned by Sir Lawrence Dundas. From a position near the western boundary of the park, Wilson portrayed four labourers and their dog resting from the task of setting up park palings. Beyond the park, the prospect took in the church and village of Rickmansworth in the middle distance and extended towards the neighbouring county of Buckinghamshire on the horizon. By courtesy of the Marquess of Zetland — private collection. Photograph: Photographic Survey, Courtauld Institute of Art

South American colonies and had sailed around the world, returning with treasure worth £500,000. The transformation of the landscape here was far less radical than those carried out by Brown on many later occasions, and opinions of its success were varied. Horace Walpole, who saw the place in 1760, while alterations were being carried out, reported: 'I was not much struck with it, after all the miracles I had heard that Brown had performed there. He has undulated the horizon in so many artificial molehills, that it is full as unnatural as if it was drawn with a rule and compasses.'[5] A more favourable view of the earthworks, however, was taken by Thomas Whateley, who visited the park in 1770. He observed that the northern edge of Bridgeman's vista looking east towards Watford had originally formed:

the flat edge of a descent, a harsh, offensive termination; but it is now broken by several hillocks, not diminutive in size and [made] considerable by the fine clumps which distinguish them. They do more than conceal the sharpness of the edge; they convert a deformity into a beauty and greatly contribute to the embellishment of this most lovely scene.[6]

Brown's associate, Nathaniel Richmond, supervised work at the site and Brown made regular payments to him from 1754 to 1759. In 1763, Anson died and the property was bought for £25,000 by the fabulously rich army contractor Sir Lawrence Dundas. He paid out a great deal more money making further alterations.[7] Between 1765 and 1767, Richard Wilson painted three views of Moor Park for Sir Lawrence: one looked over a broad expanse of grass framed by informal masses of trees towards the Palladian mansion on the skyline; another was a prospect across the vale of St Albans towards low-lying Cassiobury, in the distance; and the third was a view looking west towards Rickmansworth. The third view, Figure 5.1, was unusual in representing a park being enclosed. It showed labourers reclining on the grass eating lunch; the partially finished fence stood on their left, and pales lying in the foreground and leaning against a tree to the right were ready to be set up. Anson's elegant Ionic Temple of the Four Winds was destroyed in a storm in 1930 but a tea pavilion designed by Robert Adam survived to become a suburban house.[8]

A few years after planning improvements at Beechwood and Moor Park, Brown was commissioned by Francis, the third Duke of Bridgwater — the 'Canal Duke' — to design the landscape at Ashridge as a setting for a new house being built by Henry Holland senior. Brown made several visits in 1759 and focused his attention on the planting of beeches along the flanks of the Golden Valley, east of the house. He also left some informal clumps to the north by thinning existing woods. Before 1768, he had been paid at least £3,000.[9]

In a letter dated 31 October 1755, Spencer Cowper, Dean of Durham, wrote to his brother, the second Earl Cowper at Cole Green, expressing the hope that 'Mr Brown and you may still go on with yr scheme for beautifying' the place,[10] and entries in the estate ledgers record that between 1755 and 1764, Brown received £618 for unspecified work in the park and gardens.[11] Dury and Andrews' map of 1766 showed the park as bounded by a roughly circular line of palings at the centre of which stood a small new house, its precincts bounded to the south and east by a sunk fence. A long avenue extended from the south side beyond the park boundary to Holy Well by the river Lea. The front of the house faced east, with a broad vista towards the village of Hertingfordbury. To the west lay informal plantations and a winding approach drive. All of Brown's landscape, together with the house, were swept away in 1801, when Repton incorporated Cole Green Park into the grounds of Panshanger.

Brown's early commissions in Hertfordshire lacked the gently curving sheets of water that formed centrepieces in his later designs and became his most distinctive signature. Creating a serpentine lake was the main objective when Brown prepared a plan for David Barclay at Youngsbury in 1770. Brown remarked that 'nature had do[ne] so much, little was wanting, but enlarging the river'. Dotted lines on the plan indicated where the river Rib was to be widened into a stretch of water, with graceful, sinuous outlines, while the grounds were planted with many informal clumps of trees.[12] In 1796, the park was bought by Daniel Giles, who came to the City of London from Caen in Normandy and rose to be governor of the Bank of England. Giles's successors had interests in India.[13]

In 1771–3, Brown was paid over £1,100 by John Willes for work at Digswell. A serpentine lake was formed by damming the river Mimram, and Monk's Walk, a winding path, was drawn through new plantations. Welwyn Garden City has extended over most of the park, but a few eighteenth-century trees remain.[14]

Among places attributed to Brown on stylistic grounds is Dyrham Park, where a Brownian lake still exists and a triumphal arch and many trees planted by General George Keppel are still standing.[15] It is not clear who designed the landscape at Kimpton Hoo for Thomas Brand. Roger Turner notes that Brown submitted a drawing for a bridge and received £150 in 1758, but the bridge was built to a later design by Sir William Chambers. Chambers was responsible for altering the house and he also designed a gateway and other buildings for the new landscape garden.[16] English Heritage reports that Brown not only prepared a drawing for the bridge but made other proposals which were carried out. The forming of the Mimram into a broad stretch of ornamental water was characteristic of Brown's style, as was the line of the drive approaching the house in a broad arc.[17] Dury and Andrews' map shows the precincts of the house, closely planted with shrubs and trees and surrounded on all sides by an open park sweeping down to the banks of the lake. Porters, where Admiral Lord Howe took up residence in 1772, is another park possibly designed by Brown. In 1773, to make the ground ready for landscaping, Lord Howe obtained permission to divert a public highway and two footpaths around the park pales.[18] A visit by Brown is mentioned in Lord Howe's correspondence.[19]

A more doubtful attribution to Brown is made by Cussans in connection with Pishiobury.[20] Jeremiah Milles enlarged the house from plans by James Wyatt in 1782 and Cussans claims that 'there were three magnificent avenues leading from the high road to the mansion, two of which were entirely removed, and the continuity of the third destroyed by Mr Milles on the advice of Capability Brown, who also superintended the construction of a piece of ornamental water'.[21] A long, narrow serpentine lake looks like Brown's work but a straight axial vista and Oak Walk are not in his style. Some later topographers were inclined to give Brown credit for landscaping places that displayed Brownian features or had connections with Brown's clientele, whilst other places were landscaped by Brown's associates or by his contemporaries in a fashionable mid-eighteenth-century idiom.

Nathaniel Richmond

At Moor Park, Brown entrusted the carrying-out of his plans to his associate, Nathaniel Richmond, who was nine years his junior and died a year after Brown in 1784. During the 1750s, Richmond lived at Rickmansworth, where three of his children were born, all of whom died in infancy. In 1760, he set up an independent practice and established a nursery in Marylebone;[22] during the years that followed, he was to advise on various sites throughout Hertfordshire.

In August 1764, he made his first visit to Hitchin to advise John Radcliffe on the layout of Priory Park. Work began in 1768 and from then until 1773, when activities reached a height, Richmond visited the site nearly every month. The park was enlarged to about 100 acres by enclosing part of Hitchin's arable open fields. Most of the trees planted were limes and horse chestnuts; some sycamore and Norway maple were propagated from seed. An ornamental lake was formed by damming the river Hiz under a rustic bridge faced with flints. The house was approached by a long drive, which curved around the edge of the park from an entrance on Gosmore Road.[23]

While work continued at Hitchin, Richmond received payments for two other commissions, one in north-west, another in north-east Hertfordshire. At Tring Grove, he designed a naturalistic landscape for John Seare, for which he was paid £31 in 1764.[24] The park contained a walled kitchen garden and a scatter of trees, probably supplied by Richmond's nursery. The peace and quiet of this rural retreat was disrupted about forty years later by the digging of the Grand Junction Canal. Richard Cox, occupier of Aspenden Hall, paid Richmond a total of £121 18s for unspecified work in the three years 1766, 1767 and 1768. Cox was a City businessman who made money as an agent for the army and wished to transform his park into a fashionable informal landscape.[25]

Richmond was also called upon to work at Sacombe Park, where, in the early eighteenth century, Bridgeman had created a magnificent layout on a large scale. In 1762, the estate passed by marriage from the Rolt family to Timothy Caswall, MP for Hertford. Caswall invited Richmond to transform the formal layout into a naturalistic landscape by rounding Bridgeman's large triangle of woodland to form what was called 'The Clump'. Three fenced paddocks were crossed by an intricate labyrinth of serpentine drives and walks, while scattered trees were planted over much of the surface and an irregular screen of trees was planted on the south-eastern edge of the park.[26] Unfortunately, many old trees were blown down in a freak storm in July 1786.[27]

Similar work proceeded at Gorhambury, inherited in 1756 by James, the second Viscount Grimston, who decided to modernise the park. During the 1760s, Richmond pulled down 'gloomy' walls enclosing the kitchen garden and outer courts, laid out a new entrance drive and planted blocks of closely spaced trees among more openly wooded pastures.[28] Richmond may have continued to work at Gorhambury after the third viscount inherited the estate in 1773. By the end of the eighteenth century, the park was producing much valuable oak timber.[29]

Richmond also laid out the grounds at Lamer House. In 1761, Sir Benet Garrard partly demolished the old family residence and built a compact new house at the top of a hill, commanding extensive views. In order to supply the house and a water closet on the ground floor, an elaborate water-pumping system was designed.[30] Sir Benet died without issue in 1767, leaving the property to his 12-year-old cousin, Charles Drake, who changed his name to Garrard, attended Westminster School and Brasenose College, Oxford, and made a short tour of France before taking up residence at Lamer in 1780. Richmond, who had worked for Charles's father at Shardeloes in Buckinghamshire, was invited to open a vista in front of the house by cutting down many trees and clearing undergrowth. He also laid down a new drive, curving up the slope as it approached the side of the house. A summer house was decorated with knapped flints in the same style as the rustic bridge at Hitchin Priory. Drake paid the last bill to Richmond's widow in 1784. In 1790, Repton paid his first visit to Lamer and finished the landscaping.[31]

In a shorter span of time than Brown, Richmond contributed at least as much to the landscaping of Hertfordshire. He reached the furthest extremities of the county and carried out extensive clearing at Gorhambury and Lamer.

Richard Woods

Another contemporary of Brown and Richmond, Richard Woods was probably born a year after Brown, in 1716, and died ten years after him, in 1793. Nothing is known of Woods' activities until 1751, when he bought a small parcel of copyhold land at Chertsey in Surrey, just over a mile from Philip Southcote's Woburn Farm. Woods was deeply influenced by Southcote's planting of conifers and design of colourful, flowery walks, and it may have been Southcote, who was

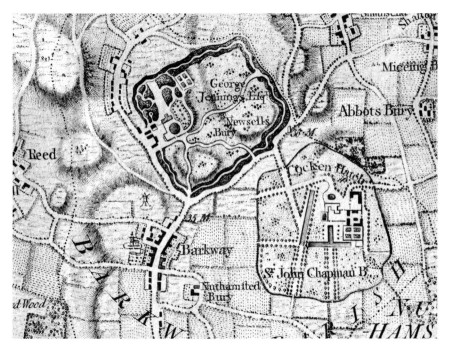

Figure 5.2: Newsells Bury and Cocken Hatch in 1766. Newsells Bury, laid out by Richard Woods for George Jennings, was represented without palings on Dury and Andrews' Topographical map of Hartford-Shire. It was the largest pleasure ground in the county. Neighbouring Cockenhatch, owned by Sir John Chapman, Bart., was laid out in a formal manner and enclosed by palings. Photograph by Matt Prince

born in Essex, that introduced Woods to Lord Petre, his friend and fellow Catholic. In 1768, Woods moved to North Ockendon Hall, where he built up a practice, mainly in Essex and other parts of southeast England. In 1783, he married and settled at Ingrave, on the Petre estate. He continued to work there until his death ten years later.[32]

In November 1763, Woods stayed at George Jennings' seat at Newsells. No record of his plans for the grounds has survived, but the map drawn by Dury and Andrews depicts a greatly exaggerated area of pleasure grounds, encircled by a belt plantation through which a long, winding path was conducted (Figure 5.2). An accurate plan of the estate surveyed in 1788 and an accompanying book of reference indicated an ice-house, a grotto and a great variety of shrubs that had been planted.[33] Within the belt, the landscape was embellished with clumps and irregular groves. A collection of drawings and plans belonging to Jennings' son-in-law and successor, John Peachey, included designs for hothouses, a greenhouse and a gothick lodge that might have been drawn by Woods.

Brocket Park, seat of Peniston Lamb, first Lord Melbourne, was Woods' finest masterpiece; trees, grass and water were placed in exactly the right positions in relation to the house, on the rounded slopes of the valley. Woods first visited the place in December 1770, the year James Paine finished building the finely proportioned red-brick mansion, which was to stand proudly overlooking a lake that Woods created by widening the river Lea. A cascade was partly con-cealed beneath a new bridge designed by Paine. The disposition of trees on the slopes flanking and above the house were not greatly altered, but Woods removed hedges and copses on the meadows on low ground in front of the house, beyond the lake, clearing the fore-ground of the view. Privacy was protected by a mile-long, high brick wall, shutting out the North Road. Woods paid regular visits to the place while work progressed, advising on the siting of a new kitchen garden, pinery, shrubbery and the building of a new dairy and hot-house. In 1771, Arthur Young noted that Brocket Park was 'extremely worth seeing. It contains a fine variety of ground, many hills that com-mand noble prospects, and winding hollows very picturesque; the water is large, much of it finely traced, and of a beautiful colour.'[34] At the end of the century, as the landscape approached maturity, Woods' accomplishment was celebrated in words and painting: William Angus praised the beauty of Woods' layout and illustrated it with an engrav-ing from a sketch by Paul Sandby.[35] In the late 1930s, Lord David Cecil was captivated by what he described as 'that perfect example of the smaller country house of the period, with its rosy, grey-pilastered façade, its charming park, where, backed by woods, the turf sweeps down to a stream spanned by a graceful bridge of cut stone.'[36]

Brown, Richmond and Woods transformed old-established parks into open landscapes at Ashridge, Beechwood, Gorhambury, Sacombe and Brocket. Views towards houses were opened from the park and views from houses were extended across large expanses of parkland. Enclosed gardens were hidden from view, reversing the earlier practice of hiding serpentine walks within secluded wildernesses.

Brown retained avenues at Beechwood, Moor Park and Cole Green, while Richmond and Woods created new landscapes, dispensing entirely with formal elements.

Other landscape parks

Following the lead set by Capability Brown, Nathaniel Richmond, Richard Woods and their patrons, other aspiring landowners sought advice from professional designers or embarked on schemes of their own contrivance. Some owners built new houses and laid out grounds to match; others opened broad prospects and modernised old houses to fit the new surroundings. The acquisition of estates, the building of houses and the laying out of grounds were pursued most actively in south Hertfordshire, along roads leading to London, and in areas of natural beauty.

Soon after acquiring a small estate adjoining Cassiobury, the large territory owned by his father-in-law, Thomas Villiers, Lord Hyde, later Earl of Clarendon, started to rebuild The Grove in 1754–61. A broad sweep of lawn stretched down to the river Gade, which was formed into a lake and spanned by a classical bridge. On the opposite side of the river, to the east, the upper slopes were crowned by a belt plantation screening the park boundary along the line of the Hempstead Road. A large walled garden was situated to the north-east of the house and an extensive pleasure ground lay to the north.[37] The house was enlarged about 1780, to a design by Sir Robert Taylor,[38] and during the late eighteenth century the park was adorned with an extraordinary miscellany of eye-catchers, including a Temple of Pan, a Praeneste or Temple of Fortune, a mausoleum, a 'Scotch Hut', about which a poem was written in 1779, a Tuscan Seat, a Rustic Seat, Druidical Seats, a ruined tower, a pyramid and an ornamental Hoggery. These buildings were described by Daniel Webb in 1810 and sketched by Thomas Baskerville.[39]

In 1757, Bayfordbury Farm was bought by Sir William Baker, a rich merchant, alderman of the City of London for thirty years and prominent whig MP. He immediately set about building a new house, designed by Robert Mylne, at the top of a hill. By 1762, the house was completed and the park enclosed.[40] In 1763, the work of laying out the grounds began. On either side of the house, yew trees and two

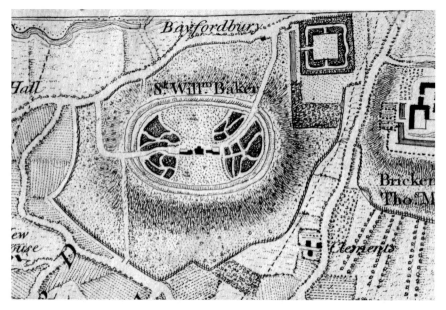

Figure 5.3: Ha-ha at Bayfordbury in 1766. Sir William Baker's new house and garden with lawn and shrubberies were surrounded by a ha-ha. The park and water garden lay outside the sunk fence and were enclosed by palings. Detail from Dury and Andrews' Topographical map of Hartford-Shire. *Photograph by Matt Prince*

large shrubberies were planted. In 1765, ten Cedars of Lebanon, which grew to dominate the skyline, were planted and the whole garden area was encircled by a sunk fence (Figure 5.3), while other sunk fences opened vistas from the park to the pastoral countryside. Up to 1767, the planting operations were directed to the formation of a dense belt of conifers around the park, after which several ornamental clumps were placed on the slopes of lawns at the back and front of the house. The years 1773 and 1774 were spent planting large numbers of oaks on the south side of the park, filling the background with stands of profitable timber and also screening the village of Bayford. In succeeding years a great collection of native and exotic trees was formed.[41] Four generations of the Baker family were assiduous plant collectors and details of all trees planted between 1759 and 1869 were entered in a record book.

Oxhey Place was occupied in the mid-eighteenth century by John Askell Bucknall, a member of a family of London brewers. The well-wooded grounds were enlarged in an informal manner and a vista was opened westward into the valley of a small stream. In 1799, Sir William Bucknall demolished the mansion and abandoned the park.[42]

Langleybury was one of many small seats surrounded by a miniature landscape garden that was formed in the late eighteenth century. A villa residence, boldly sited on rising ground above the Gade valley, had been built in the 1720s by Robert Raymond, who rose to eminence as Lord Chief Justice from 1724 to 1732. No park is represented on Dury and Andrews' map, but in the late 1790s H.G. Oldfield drew the house facing open parkland, approached by a curving drive emerging from a wooded foreground. The Ordnance Survey drawing, made about 1810, shows a park occupying about forty acres to the east of the house. Behind the house, to the west, lay the home farm, whose yards and barns were concealed from view. The Hertfordshire Gardens Trust remarks that 'Langleybury is an intriguing site: the house, although a building of some pretensions, was still closely associated with the service buildings, yards and enclosures of a working farm, and the park was limited in size. Yet clearly the overall layout of the site was carefully considered.'[43] It was a *ferme ornée*, an ornamental farm, whose French name was imported into England and first described by Stephen Switzer.[44]

The planting of clumps and belts, laying down of expanses of grass and construction of curving approach drives were not beyond the means of possessors of modest fortunes. Creating artificial lakes and building imposing mansions were more expensive pursuits, but even these were not prohibitive. The most difficult tasks for those seeking to establish gentlemen's seats were the acquisition of vacant estates, marriages to landed heiresses and selection for public offices. A small number achieved these objectives and the cumulative results of their efforts were evident to travellers from the mid-eighteenth century onwards. As visitors journeyed through the county, they observed new parks, pleasure grounds and elegant villas on either side of the main roads.

By 1766, Hertfordshire had begun to catch up with Middlesex and Surrey as a fashionably landscaped county, but it was still not the most favoured destination for tourists seeking beautiful examples of modern gardening. Thomas Whateley reserved his praise for only one Hertfordshire landscape, at Moor Park.[45] William Watts' album of engravings included a single example from Hertfordshire, Hatfield

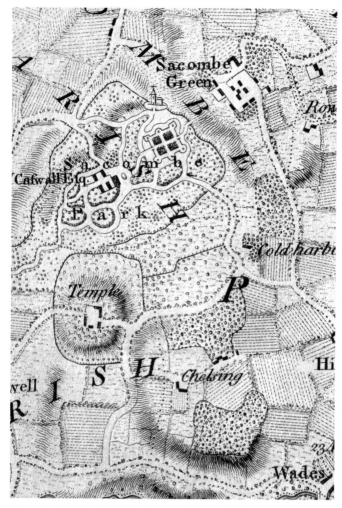

Figure 5.4: Sacombe Park in 1766. The surveyor delineated three lines of palings, including an enclosure around the Temple, suggesting that the park had been extended and divided into paddocks. Detail from Dury and Andrews' Topographical map of Hartford-Shire. *Photograph by Matt Prince*

House, where the removal of walls surrounding the house was welcomed as 'an improvement which has enabled us to give a view of this celebrated place'.[46] Appreciation of the changing face of the countryside was boosted at this time by an outstanding early example of a new county map, that by Dury and Andrews; this was one of twenty-five such maps, covering about 65 per cent of England, that were published between 1765 and 1780.[47]

Andrew Dury and John Andrews' map of 1766

The map of Hertfordshire by Dury and Andrews, based on a new survey, was engraved on nine sheets at a scale of approximately 1 in 32,490 or about 1.95 inches to a mile. It was drawn at a larger scale than earlier county maps and was significantly more accurate in its representation of landscape features. Little is known about the conduct of the survey. Donald Hodson states that John Andrews surveyed the western part of the county, west of the North Road from Chipping Barnet, while Andrew Dury was responsible for organising the survey to the east of that line. Dury, a London bookseller, who had published an atlas of the world and maps of North America, probably paid the largest share of the costs of engraving and publishing, and employed assistants to carry out the field survey in the east of the county.[48]

The map is more richly detailed than most county maps published before that time. It shows no fewer than seven categories of land use: woodland; parkland; heathland or commons; marshland; pasture or

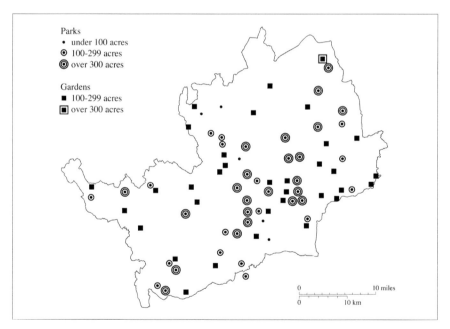

Figure 5.5: Parks and gardens in Hertfordshire in 1766. Forty-five parks enclosed by palings were differentiated from thirty-four unenclosed gardens and pleasure grounds over 100 acres in size. Based on Dury and Andrews' Topographical map of Hartford-Shire. Full details of the parks and gardens are listed in Tables 5.1 and 5.2. Drawn in the Geography Department, UCL

Table 5.1 Parks in Hertfordshire in 1766

Park	Grid Reference	Owner	Acres
Albury Hall	425252	John Calvert	270
Ashridge, Lt Gaddesden	994121	John Egerton, 2nd Earl of Bridgwater	700
Balls Park, Hertford	335120	Audrey, Lady Harrison Townshend	470
Bayfordbury	316104	Sir William Baker	500
Beechwood, Flamstead	045144	Sir John Sebright, Bt	240
Benington Park	310229	John Cheshire	400
Brickendon Bury	330105	Thomas Morgan	530
Brocket Hall, Hatfield	214130	Sir Matthew Lamb	490
Broxbourne Bury	353071	Lord Monson	250
Bury Park, Rickmansworth	059942	Henry Whitfield	150
Camfield Place, Essendon	268069	John Brown	90
Cassiobury, Watford	095972	William Capel, 4th Earl of Essex	810
Cockenhatch, Barkway	396361	Sir John Chapman, Bt	560
Codicote Bury	220187	George Poyner Bisse	50
Cole Green Park, Hertingfordbury	278124	George, 3rd Earl Cowper	370
Dyrham Park, Borehamwood	223985	General George Keppel	200
Gorhambury, St Michael	113080	James, 2nd Viscount Grimston	430
Grove Park, Sarratt	081987	Thomas Villiers, Lord Hyde	200
Hamels, Braughing	376247	Rev. Ralph Freman	450
Hatfield	236084	James Cecil, 6th Earl of Salisbury	830
Hatfield, Millwards	236065	James Cecil, 6th Earl of Salisbury	430
Hatfield Woodhall, Welwyn	235106	Thomas Hutchinson	340
Hitchin Priory	184286	John Radcliffe	30
Kings Walden Bury	161235	William Hale	180
Knebworth	231210	Mrs Lytton	430
Lockleys, Welwyn	237159	Charles Gardener	330
Moor Park, Rickmansworth	075933	Sir Lawrence Dundas	450
Moor Place, Much Hadham	423187	James Gordon	280
New Place, Gilston	441129	William Plumer	290
North Mymms Place	217042	Thomas Osborne, 4th Duke of Leeds	420
Nyn Hall, Northaw	279031	John Grainger Leman	80
Offley Place	145272	Sir Thomas Salusbury	90
Pelham Hall, Furneux Pelham	427279	Nicholas Calvert	300
Popes, Hatfield	259077	Sir Benjamin Trueman	180
Porters, Shenley	182008	Rev. Dr Jubb	180
Sacombe	339190	Timothy Caswall	620
St Pauls Walden Bury	187216	Mrs Mary Bowes	100

continued

Table 5.1 Parks in Hertfordshire in 1766 *continued*

Park	Grid Reference	Owner	Acres
Stagenhoe, St Pauls Walden	185227	Giles Thornton Heysham	250
Tewin Water	255145	Lady Elizabeth Cathcart	200
Totteridge Park	233942	William Lee	100
Tring Park	926111	Charles Gore	290
Tyttenhanger	192047	Henry Yorke	250
Ware Park	333144	Thomas Plumer Byde	320
Woodhall Park, Watton	318189	John Boteler	480
Wyddial Hall	373317	Richard Goulston	330

Sources: A. Dury and J. Andrews, *A topographical map of Hartford-shire, from an actual survey* (1766). Almost all names of owners are transcribed from the map itself. Additional names have been taken from Arthur Jones (ed.), *Hertfordshire 1731–1800 as recorded in The Gentleman's Magazine* (Hatfield, 1993).

meadowland; arable land; and kitchen gardens. It distinguishes three types of roads: those enclosed on both sides by hedges; those enclosed on one side only; and open roads. It also identifies villages, towns, bridges, churches, windmills and watermills.[49] Dury and Andrews followed the same conventions of estate and garden surveying displayed in John Rocque's highly praised map of Berkshire (1761). Rocque had come to mapmaking as a 'dessinateur des jardins', and demonstrated how to represent different styles of ornamental layout on a small-scale map.[50] Dury and Andrews thus depicted the size, shape and layout of parks, gardens and pleasure grounds in minute detail: parks encompassed by palings were differentiated from ornamental grounds surrounded by belt plantations or lines of trees. The contrast is exemplified by the empaled boundary of Cockenhatch Park and neighbouring Newsells Bury, surrounded by a belt plantation through which a serpentine walk threaded its way. At Bayfordbury, the engraver clearly delineated a sunk fence encircling the house and garden illustrated in Figure 5.3. Sacombe Park (Figure 5.4), Moor Place and Ashridge were enclosed by more than one line of palings, as if areas of parkland had been enlarged or reduced in the past. In the Stort valley, Briggens and Pishiobury were bounded partly by park pales and partly by ends of avenues. For the purpose of the present survey, these open-ended parks are classified as gardens. To assist in making comparisons with earlier cartographic representations of

Table 5.2 Gardens over 100 acres in Hertfordshire in 1766

Park	Grid Reference	Owner	Acres
Aspenden Hall	352284	Richard Cox	140
Ayot St Lawrence	195170	Lionel Lyde	100
Bedwell Park	277076	Samuel Whitbread	190
Berkhamsted Place	991088	Robert Hucks	100
Blakesware, Ware	405163	William Plumer	180
Briggens, Hunsdon	412112	Thomas Blackmore	130
Chesfield Lodge, Graveley	246275	Lawndey Sparhawk	150
Childwickbury, St Michaels	139102	Caleb Lomax	150
Gobions, North Mymms	252039	Mrs Sambrooke	150
Golden Parsonage, Gt Gaddesden	051126	Thomas Halsey	180
Goldings, Waterford	311143	Lady St John	170
Gt Hyde Hall, Sawbridgeworth	496154	Sir Conyers Jocelyn, Bt	200
Hadham Hall, Lt Hadham	452227	William Capel, 4th Earl of Essex	190
Hertingfordbury	310121	Maj. Gen.William Cowper	200
Hoo, Kimpton	187195	Thomas Brand	220
Hunsdon House	420127	Nicholas Calvert	140
Kendalls Hall, Aldenham	173982	William Gibson	180
Lamers, Wheathamstead	181160	Sir Benet Garrard	180
Lt Offley House	130285	Sir Thomas Shawsbury	180
Marden Hill, Tewin	279140	Richard Warren	140
Newsells, Barkway	386367	George Jennings	540
Oxhey Place	114933	John Askell Bucknall	190
Pishiobury, Sawbridgeworth	480134	Edward Gardiner	250
Putteridge Bury, Lilley	118245	Sir Benjamin Rowlins	110
Quickswood, Clothall	275328	James Cecil, 6th Earl Salisbury	200
Rothamsted, Harpenden	125131	John Bennet	120
Roxford, Hertingfordbury	303104	Nathaniel Bracy	200
Russells Farm, Watford	091995	Lady Diana Capel	150
St Margarets Manor, Stanstead	380117	Bibye Lake	100
Standon Lordship	392214	Lord Aston	100
Tring Grove	925134	John Seare	110
Westbrook Hay, Bovingdon	025054	Lomax Ryder	130
Wormley Bury	355059	Sir Abraham Hume	100
Youngsbury, Standon	378179	William Buckle	150

Source: A. Dury and J. Andrews, *A topographical map of Hartford-shire, from an actual survey* (1766). Almost all names of owners have been transcribed from the face of the map.

parks, two lists have been compiled: the first includes all parks of whatever size, enclosed by palings, of which there were forty-five; the second lists gardens and ornamental grounds over 100 acres in extent, which were thirty-four in number (Figure 5.5).

All parks depicted on Warburton's map of 1725, with the exception of Throcking and Weld Hall, Aldenham, were shown by Dury and Andrews; twenty-eight of them were shown as empaled parks and Aspenden, Bedwell Park, Briggens and Hertingfordbury were shown as large gardens. Many places had changed hands between 1725 and 1766: of the thirty-two places which appeared on the two maps, thirteen bore different family names on the later map. It is not surprising that the map drawn by Dury and Andrews — at nearly three times the scale of the earlier map — recorded a greater number of parks and large gardens, but documentary evidence indicates that at least some of the nineteen additional parks and twenty-nine additional large gardens were newly created between 1725 and 1766. Landscaping also led to an expansion in area as well as in the number of parks and large gardens. Characteristically, the new landscapes were settings for new houses, built on higher ground. Many were sited along roads leading to London.

Dury and Andrews presented parks and large gardens as conspicuous symbols of power and patronage. Owners of parks were named on the map: the Earl of Salisbury was named as possessor of two parks at Hatfield and a hunting lodge at Quickswood near Clothall; the Earl of Essex resided at Cassiobury Park and also held a large garden at Hadham Hall, while his aunt, Lady Diana Capel, lived at Russells Farm, on the opposite side of the Hempstead Road from Cassiobury and his son-in-law, Lord Hyde, occupied Grove Park, to the north of Cassiobury. Earl Cowper's park was at Cole Green, while his cousin, Major-General William Cowper, occupied a large garden at Hertingfordbury. Brewer and financier Nicholas Calvert owned a park at Furneux Pelham and extensive ornamental grounds at Hunsdon House; his cousin, John Calvert, owned a park at Albury and other relatives, Ben Calvert and Peter Calvert, had seats with small gardens. Members of two other brewing and banking families, William Plumer and Thomas Plumer Byde, each held an enclosed park and also a large garden at a different site. By naming their owners, the mapmakers added to the aura of privilege that emanated from parks and pleasure grounds.

Perhaps for similar reasons, the map exaggerated the area of many large gardens and enclosed parks. A comparison of measurements of thirty large gardens shown on Dury and Andrews' map with their equivalents on the first edition Ordnance Survey drawings shows that eighteen were larger on the 1766 map than in 1799–1812, four were about the same size, and only four were smaller (eight were not represented on the later survey). Of forty-five enclosed parks, twenty-two were larger on the 1766 map than in 1799–1812, eight were about the same size, eleven were smaller and four were not comparable. In an exceptional instance, Dury and Andrews reduced the true size of an important park. On their map, Ashridge Park measures 700 acres, and adjoining woodlands to the north, within the boundaries of Hertfordshire, measure about 310 acres. A large-scale estate survey of the park, dated four years earlier, recorded its area as 1,007 acres, with adjoining woodlands to the north, extending into Buckinghamshire, covering an additional 695 acres.[51] On the first edition one-inch Ordnance Survey map, Ashridge Park measured 1,080 acres. Areas of medium-sized parks and gardens were more exaggerated than the areas of the largest parks.

The pattern of woods, groves and scattered trees on a carpet of grass gave a park-like appearance to large areas of the county, as represented by Dury and Andrews. A nearly continuous ribbon of parkland followed the Mimram valley from Lockleys through Digswell, Tewin, Marden Hill and Cole Green to Hertingfordbury. In the Lea valley, parkland extended from Brocket through Hatfield Woodhall to Hatfield Home Park and, further downstream, from Bayfordbury, through Brickendon Bury to Balls Park. In the Gade valley, a cluster of parks to the north of Watford, centred on The Grove and Cassiobury, gave the landscape a sylvan aspect.

Parks and pastoral husbandry

Parks offered not only pretty prospects to be viewed from the windows of mansions but afforded valuable sources of income for their owners. The two basic elements of parkland scenery, grass and trees, were grown for profit as well as for pleasure. Arthur Young noted that the 'quantity of grassland in the county is extremely small' and that much of it was 'kept artificially productive' at whatever cost, 'wherever the residence of a gentleman is found'.[52] Some grazing of lawns and pastures was managed directly by the home farm and some was leased to local farmers. Brocket Park gained a small advantage from the droving traffic that passed along the North Road by charging drovers and wagonners for accommodating flocks and wagon teams overnight.[53] Parkland grass required heavy stocking during the summer but cattle needed to be removed before autumn rains to avoid the turf being broken into bare, muddy patches. In order to control the intensity of grazing, livestock needed to be fenced in and fences or hedges had to be positioned so as to keep vistas open. Plantations were contrived to disguise subdivisions and when parks were expanded sections of earlier belts were retained to form separate paddocks without intruding into open landscapes.

Aristocratic owners took a special interest in the selective breeding of horses, hounds, sheep and cattle. Lord Grimston's farm at Gorhambury raised a flock of improved South Down sheep and the owner shared information on managing the breed with his tenants. Other leading landowners who bred South Downs and crossed them with new Leicesters included the Duke of Bridgwater, the earls of Essex and Clarendon, Sir John Sebright, Colonel Dorrien of Haresfoot, Mr Hale of Kings Walden, Mr Calvert of Albury, Mr Byde of Ware Park and Mr Casamajor of Potterells; all of them were the possessors of large parks and pleasure grounds. At Hatfield, the Marchioness of Salisbury kept 150 wild hogs in the park and fed them on lettuces. At The Grove, the Earl of Clarendon selected eighteen of the weaker deer from his herd of 350, provided them with winter feed, sheltered them in a small yard and sold them at a profit the following spring.[54] By selling haunches of venison, this noble lord openly offended against a law passed in 1755 forbidding the sale of game.[55]

During the late eighteenth century, Hatfield and a few other home farms experimented with new crops and different methods of cultivating arable land within the boundaries of parks. For most owners, however, grass remained the preferred surface cover. Grass lay open

Figure 5.6: The Milbanke and Melbourne families, 1769–70. This painting by George Stubbs celebrates the union of the two families. On the right, on his horse, was Sir Peniston Lamb (later Lord Melbourne), owner of Brocket Hall. On the left, in a park phaeton, sat his 16- or 17-year-old bride, Elizabeth Milbanke. Her father, Sir Ralph, a Yorkshire squire, stood next to her, while her brother posed casually in the centre. Reproduced by permission of the National Gallery

for riding, walking and other pastimes. In parks, landowners perfected the skills of horsemanship, bred the finest thoroughbreds and built commodious stables. Riding horses were highly esteemed, as witnessed by owners' meticulously kept stud books and the remarkably sensitive portraits of horses belonging to the aristocracy painted by George Stubbs (Figure 5.6).

Parks and forestry

Adoption of an informal style of landscape gardening resulted in the replacement of deer by sheep, cattle and horses. An ideal landscape was visualised as an ancient deer park but, in practice, the keeping of animals that browsed on leaves and tender shoots and stripped bark from saplings was incompatible with planting trees and growing timber. The efficient management of timber resources and profitable utilisation of grazing land required a change from deer to farm stock.

At the same time, sporting pursuits changed from hunting deer to fowling, netting or hawking game birds and hunting foxes, natural predators of ground-nesting birds. Guns and lead shot for shooting birds were introduced at the end of the eighteenth century,[56] and the preservation of pheasants in their preferred woodland habitat greatly increased the number of birds for shooting. Where wooded groves were lacking, they had to be planted: during the late eighteenth century, the provision of pheasant cover was 'a major factor in the general upsurge in tree-planting in England'.[57] Measures to protect game underlined the exclusive private ownership of woods where pheasants were raised, finally extinguishing rights claimed by commoners to enter parks and take firewood freely.

Wood and timber were the largest generators of income for parks and returns increased as the century progressed. After 1750, forestry expanded significantly in response to the rising price of oak timber, led by demand from the Royal Navy and encouraged by patriotic treatises and awards of medals annually by the Society for the Encouragement of Arts.[58] Free-growing oaks in parks produced crooked timber, curved pieces and knee joints highly prized by ship-builders. Oaks, beeches and elms planted in the middle years of the eighteenth century were beginning to yield marketable timber during a peak of demand in the Napoleonic wars, and a few owners took advantage of high prices to pay debts or raise money for building. When George Caswall inherited Sacombe from his father in 1802 he decided to sell trees, some of which had been planted by Bridgeman and Richmond, in order to build a grand new house. John Carrington recorded in his diary that in April and May 1803 no fewer than 1,732 trees were cut down by 140 men in 'the Great Fall of Timber'.[59] The sale of timber, bark and tops fetched £8,016. Storms, however, inflicted the greatest losses on stands of slow-growing timber and the incidence of damaging winds was random. At Sacombe many tall trees were blown down by a whirlwind in 1786, and the park was severely hit again by a tremendous gale that struck south Hertfordshire in November 1795, which also tore up or shivered to pieces 250 of the finest oaks in Cassiobury Park and caused damage estimated at £500 to timber in Hatfield Park.[60]

Most owners prudently conserved stocks of valuable timber, cutting it sparingly and replacing it with new plantations on a regular schedule; such care was worthwhile, as estate accounts indicate how sales of wood and timber increased in value. Brocket Park was stocked with much uneven-aged timber in 1746, when it was bought by Matthew Lamb, a wealthy lawyer. Lamb started building the present house and altering the landscape. After he died in 1768, his son, Peniston Lamb, Lord Melbourne, called in Richard Woods and continued the work. Brocket Hall estate accounts cover the years 1773–8, 1780–1821 and 1837–45[61] and contain details of receipts from the sale of wood and timber and expenditure on labour in the pleasure grounds, kitchen garden and shrubbery. In the first six-year period, during which planting and landscaping were in progress, wood and timber sales amounted to £491 14s 9d, and bills for outdoor labour totalled £2,098 16s 11d. A lofty deciduous cypress, *Taxodium distichum*, as well as cedars from Barnet, orange trees from Northamptonshire and a large quantity of planes, were planted and about £20 a year was spent on seeds, shrubs and sundry plants. From 1780 to 1821, almost exactly £200 was spent each year on labour in the pleasure grounds and gardens. Receipts from sales of wood and timber increased steadily from an average of less than £100 a year between 1780 and 1794 to about £200 a year from 1795 to 1804. In 1805 sales reached £775 6s 7d and in 1810 they rocketed to £1,157 15s 10d.

The significant feature of the wood and timber sales at Brocket is that while there were large variations from year to year, the average for ten-year periods moved steadily upwards, regardless of changes in the value of the pound or fluctuations in agricultural rents. In the second decade of the nineteenth century, wood and timber earned on average £415 a year; in the last series of accounts for 1837 to 1845, the average rose to £483 a year. Annual plantings made between 1793 and 1823 were both extensive and varied, consisting of large numbers of beech, oak, hornbeam and sweet chestnut, as well as Scots pine and larch. Before 1820, the accounts record sales mainly of oak, ash, elm and beech. In 1821, 'fir', meaning Scots pine, was mentioned for the first time. The revenue from forestry was sufficient to pay for the upkeep of the park and gardens and defray most of Lord Melbourne's household expenses. Even casual profits from the trimmings and lopped wood, sold at an annual wood feast, more than covered the expenses of a gamekeeper and a rat and mole catcher.

At Beechwood Park, in contrast, receipts from sales of timber and firewood barely exceeded the cost of labour in the grounds. From 1750 to 1775, annual receipts from timber never fell below £86 5s 3d, and from firewood they were never lower than £93 4s 9d. In one year, they rose to £320 1s 6d and £235 1s 6d respectively. During the same period, wages bills remained steady, at about £200 a year.[62]

Both Brocket and Beechwood were large estates, of 800 and 700 acres respectively. On the smaller, 200-acre, estate of Thomas Halsey at Gaddesden Place, receipts from wood and timber sales in 1788 were about £180 and labour expenses were £52 10s.[63] By 1804–7, a gamekeeper and four gardeners were permanently employed and temporary labour was hired for felling and planting trees.[64]

At Knebworth in 1768, income from a large estate, including a 430-acre park, totalled £4,000, and was derived from three sources: rent from tenant farmers, £2,900; sales of wood and timber, £1,000; game and shooting rights, £100. Expenses amounted to £1,500 for running the house, £650 for the garden and £330 for the upkeep of the stables.[65]

Important conclusions may be drawn from these records. First, the maintenance of landscape gardens was amply repaid by sales of timber, except in years when expenditures on building and landscaping were particularly heavy, with large estates receiving higher rates of return from forestry than small estates. Second, it is clear that planting and felling proceeded in tandem year after year, under the direction of a succession of owners and their agents. On estates where succession was settled for three generations, it was advantageous to grow slow-maturing hardwoods, especially oak, beech and elm. Owners of unsettled estates preferred to plant quick-growing trees, including pine and larch, to make an early visual impression. Third, the role of landscape designers was to modify plans for future planting rather than lay out grounds afresh. In old parks, designers were restrained from cutting down avenues or single noble trees. The leading landscape gardener at the end of the eighteenth century, Humphry Repton, spent much of his time continuing or suggesting minor alterations to work begun by his predecessors.

Humphry Repton

Humphry Repton was 36 years old in 1788, when he printed a trade card announcing his new vocation as 'landscape gardener' and set out to fill a gap left by the death of Capability Brown five years earlier. His aim was high but his practice was to encounter threats and challenges unknown in Brown's lifetime. The continent of Europe was to be convulsed by the French Revolution and the march of Napoleon's armies to overthrow ancient monarchies and abolish aristocracies. In Britain, whig landowners held power as firmly as ever at all levels of government, but threats of revolution and invasion could not be lightly dismissed. Despite these fears, in Hertfordshire, merchants, professional people and a few manufacturers gained enormous fortunes and were spending some of their money buying land, building fine houses and laying out pleasure grounds. In a career spanning thirty years, Repton received more than twice as many commissions as Brown, but he died a poor and disappointed man. His earnings in 1802 were half those received in 1799, partly because the old-established families for whom he worked were hard-pressed by wartime taxation and could no longer afford big changes.[66] For new clients, he was called upon to design new layouts not always to his liking. In Hertfordshire, he was consulted at seventeen places, mostly by new owners.[67]

Repton first visited Lamer in 1790 and in 1792 submitted his proposals in a Red Book, so-called because it was bound in red morocco. The book contained watercolour sketches with overlays, or slides, showing the landscape before proposed alterations were carried out. The underlying sketches showed Repton's vision of the landscape after improvement. In the Red Book for Lamer he praised the work of Richmond, who had been engaged there a few years earlier, and recommended continuing planting on the lawn and small changes to the approaches.[68]

At several places, including Little Court, Buntingford and Wyddial Hall, little or nothing came of Repton's visits. At Little

Court, no improvements were carried out before Richard Spurrier's early death two years later. The property was then sold.[69] In 1790, Repton also visited a neighbouring estate, Wyddial Hall, seat of John Ellis, a whig MP. Again, no details of his proposals have survived.

Before 1794, Repton advised Samuel Gaussen, a wealthy London merchant, governor of the Bank of England, director of the East India Company and MP, to break the lines of an avenue at his newly acquired Brookmans Park. At the same time, he was invited to improve Offley Place. His client there was 70-year-old Lady Salusbury, widow of a judge of the High Court of the Admiralty, for whom he had laid out the grounds of a suburban villa at Brondesbury in Middlesex. Repton's view of the house and mausoleum at Offley was published in Peacock's *The Polite Repository* in May 1795.[70] The Grove, seat of the Earl of Clarendon, was another place illustrated in *The Polite Repository* in November 1798, although there was no indication as to what improvements were recommended.

In 1799, Repton embarked on his most ambitious scheme in Hertfordshire. It was for Peter Leopold Louis Francis Nassau Clavering Cowper, the fifth Earl Cowper. The 21-year-old earl had just inherited a large estate, including lands in Digswell, Tewin, Cole Green and Panshanger in the Mimram valley, together with a large sum of money which had accumulated while his father had lived in Italy and during his own long minority. Repton was invited to make a comprehensive plan for improving the landscape. In May 1799, he first visited Tewin Water, then occupied by Henry Cowper, a cousin of the earl. The Red Book, submitted two months later, outlined his proposal to unite 'the whole of the beautiful valley from Welwyn to Hertford' into a continuous landscape garden, giving each park 'a degree of extent and consequence which it could not boast exclusive of the others, and while each possesses its independent privacy and seclusion, their united lawns will, by extending thro' the whole valley enrich the general face of the country.'[71] The river was widened into a small lake, the drive was hidden by a screen of trees, footpaths within the park were closed and trees were planted on high ground to the east and south of the house.[72]

In June 1799, he paid his first visit to Panshanger and saw that an ideal position for a new mansion would be on the gentle slope of the

Figure 5.7: Humphry Repton's view of Panshanger, 1800. Repton's Red Book *illustrated his proposal for improving the landscape within the newly enclosed park, including the broadening of the River Mimram into an ornamental lake. From H. Repton, 'Panshanger Red Book', 1800, Plate II. By kind permission of HALS (D/EP/P21A)*

valley, north of the river.[73] The river flowed south in a broad bend that was to be ponded into an imposing lake (Figure 5.7), excavations for which were started immediately. By August, eighty men were at work and, the following month, as they dug deeper, 110 were employed. In 1800, a boat house and a small island were constructed to conceal the dam. A little further downstream, a second dam was fashioned into a cascade which held back the main body of water. Upstream, a third stretch of water was formed behind a weir over which a carriage bridge was built. The upper lake served as a reservoir from which water was to be pumped to the house, about ninety feet higher up. The cost of creating thirteen acres of ornamental water was over £2,000.[74] A site for the new house was decided upon in February 1800, when Repton delivered his Red Book, together with plans and elevations for the house, drawn in collaboration with his son, John Adey Repton.[75]

Before building started, the earl applied to Hertford Quarter Sessions for permission to divert six miles of highways, public roads and footpaths. In November 1800, permission was granted to stop up the main road from Welwyn to Hertford, which previously passed within a few yards of the old mansion. In addition, all minor roads leading into it were sealed off, the road from Cole Green to Tewin was closed and many footpaths crossing former open fields were eliminated. New main roads made detours around the perimeter of the park and the old roads were adopted as private carriageways leading to the site of the new house. This arrangement gave the desired impression that the most important roads led directly to the mansion and public highways were less important branch-roads. To heighten the illusion, ostentatious entrance lodges were built at Cole Green and Poplars Green and wide approaches were planted with chestnuts and beeches. In the winter of 1800/1, three miles of public road were built at a cost of almost £800. After that, several miles of palings were erected around the newly enlarged park.

To extend and consolidate his property, the earl purchased nearly a square mile of land adjoining the original Panshanger estate. In 1800, he paid the Marquis of Downshire £11,500, considerably more than the estimated value, for the Sele estate. Even more extravagant

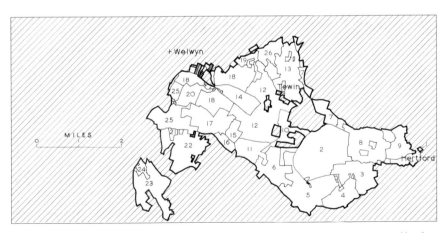

Figure 5.8: Panshanger estate in 1809. The estate consisted of a continuous tract of land between Welwyn and Hertingfordbury. The outline of Panshanger Park, designed by Humphry Repton, is located at 2 on the map; Tewin Water is located at 14. Based on 'Survey of Earl Cowper's estates in Hertfordshire', by Edward Johnson (HALS DE/P/P33). Drawn in the Geography Department, UCL

was the price of 30,000 guineas paid for Tewin House estate in 1803. These purchases gave the earl control over almost all land in the parishes of Hertingfordbury, St Andrew's Hertford and, with the exception of Richard Flower's estate at Marden Hill, of Tewin as well. Figure 5.8, based on a detailed survey by Edward Johnson, represents the consolidation of the estate up to 1809.[76] By far the most important acquisition in Hertingfordbury was effected by the partition of the common fields under the enclosure act of 1801. The earl was awarded four-fifths of the land involved, and secured as his share all the former open fields adjacent to his estate, including 120 acres of land which had previously separated Cole Green Park from Panshanger. This area was converted to parkland, uniting the two parks within the same boundary.

When the old mansion at Cole Green was pulled down in late 1801, no orders had been given to start building a new house at Panshanger. Little progress was made until the earl married Mary Lamb, daughter of Lord Melbourne, in 1805. At this time, a fresh architect, William Atkinson, modified Repton's designs and supervised the construction of the large gothick house from 1806 until it was completed in 1809.

The genius of Repton's landscape design was its simplicity and flexibility. The simple, basic elements were three large sheets of water and a new outer boundary, both quickly put in place. Flexibility was provided by the large amount of space available for almost indefinite expansion of the planted area, which enabled successive owners to continue the work of landscaping for the next hundred years within guidelines laid down in 1800. Land between the kitchen garden and the road was planted first, followed by land between the house and the lake. Plantations continued on the southern edge of the lake, and were extended to conceal approaches from Hertford and from Cole Green and then to form miles of belt plantations. Planting continued after Repton's death in 1818 and that of the earl in 1837, and was still proceeding as late as 1913. Nikolaus Pevsner described views seen through the mature plantations down the valley as 'superb, one of Repton's most perfect scenes'.[77] In 1953, the house was pulled down and, later, a new main road was cut diagonally across the park. The

Figure 5.9: View of the south-west front of Cassiobury House, 1815. Here, John Chessel Buckler depicted the new gothick facade designed by James Wyatt. The gardens were separated from the deer park by a low wall; the family and visitors strolled in the park. By courtesy of Watford Museum Collection. Photograph: Photographic Survey, Courtauld Institute of Art

estate was bought by gravel diggers who agreed to preserve the Broad Water and its islands as wildlife habitats.

At Cassiobury, a large gothick house was built by James Wyatt in 1800 for the fifth Earl of Essex (Figure 5.9). In 1801, Repton recommended thinning the avenues and glades 'to open some large areas within the woods, and so produce a spacious internal lawn of intricate shape and irregular surface'.[78] He retained a straight gravel walk leading to the front of the house and widened the river Gade into a lake. The opening of the Grand Junction Canal in 1805 introduced a new feature in the landscape,[79] and, in response, ornate rustic cottages were built for the carpenter and the gamekeeper between the house and the canal, as well as a large cottage in the style of a Swiss chalet, which housed the groom and his family on the ground floor and provided accommodation for visitors on the balconied upper floor (Figure 5.10).[80] Boatmen and horsemen on the canal were kept under constant surveillance by the earl's watchmen as they entered and left the park.

Figure 5.10: Swiss Cottage, Cassiobury Park, undated. A Swiss Cottage and other rustic cottages were built by workmen on the estate, from timber grown and cut in the park. This picturesque scene was sketched by James Baker Pyne in the early nineteenth century. By courtesy of the Watford Museum Collection

Between 1802 and 1804, Repton received five commissions for small places in west Hertfordshire. It is uncertain what he did for J. Abbot Green at Marchmont House, Hemel Hempstead. For George Stainforth, he sketched new views of Wood Hill, Hatfield. For Matthew Towgood at New Barns, Sopwell, he recommended that land in front of the house be laid down to grass and planted with scattered trees and that a new approach drive from the north and lodges, should be constructed. He proposed making an opening in the line of trees obstructing views to the south of the house, and forming a curving fish pond in place of an existing canal. All these proposals were carried out, although the fish pond is now dry and has been partly filled in.[81] New Barns is now Sopwell House Hotel and most of the park was acquired by Verulam Golf Club. Repton and his son, John Adey, were consulted by William Towgood on designs for both house and grounds at Organ Hall, Aldenham. At Wall Hall, also in Aldenham, Repton was called upon by George Thellusson, East India Company director, City banker and MP, to transform a farm into pleasure grounds for a new house. A broad walk, gothick arch and ornamental planting date from this period.[82] The estate has since been taken for residential development.

In 1808, Repton visited two places in east Hertfordshire. For attending Sir Culling Smith at Bedwell Park, Essendon, he received twenty guineas. At Haileybury, he prepared a report, sketches and plans for laying out the grounds of the new East India College, which involved the creation of two curving stretches of water by reshaping three rectangular brick pits, and the planting of rose borders and a rosebank.[83]

Repton's last work in Hertfordshire was at Ashridge. He paid his first visit there in 1813 to advise how the new house, a giant gothick pile designed by James and Jeffry Wyatt, might be assimilated within the venerable 1000-acre park. He decided not to transform the wider landscape, which he found so flat and uninteresting that it hardly seemed to justify expensive improvement, and, apart from suggesting that a plantation of eight acres would hide part of the naked lawn in front of the house, he confined his 'views within the narrow circle of the garden'. The fourteen acres to be set out as gardens were bounded on both sides by straight lines of lofty trees: on the east, by a lime walk; on the west, by a line of elms. The ground itself was divided into two parts: a bowling green or lawn on the east, and an assemblage of gothick gardens on the west, of which he was particularly proud. The atmosphere of these gardens was inspired by Repton's feelings towards the monastic foundations of Ashridge. The Monks' Garden, with its closely clipped low box hedges, its fragrant herbs and shrubs and its canopied well cover, was encompassed on two sides by a cloister. The Rosarium, a perfect circle enclosed by a yew hedge, possessed an air of solitude and peace. In addition to these features were an arboretum of exotic trees, a magnolia and American garden planted with conifers, a small mount garden and a dell in which there was a grotto and a rock garden. Repton came to regard this project as the favourite 'child of my old age and declining powers'.[84] The ensemble reflected the new tastes of the nineteenth century, rather than those which had gone before.

In the present landscape, traces of Repton's work are few and far between. His presence is recalled, here and there, by a haunting reflection of a gothick mansion in a lake, a surprising glimpse of a vista and, on the skyline, by an informal group of ancient oaks or a solitary clump of beeches. Large houses at which he worked have been demolished at Lamer, Brookmans Park, Panshanger, Cassiobury, Wall Hall, Organ Hall, Wood Hill, Marchmont House and Bedwell, but among surviving relics are an elegant carriage bridge and curving approach drive at The Grove and free-standing oaks and aged limes at Cassiobury. Some features of his gardens have been faithfully reconstructed at Ashridge.

Repton is better remembered for his visions of idyllic landscapes rendered in hundreds of attractive watercolour sketches of sunlit scenes and also for his theories set out in three handsomely illustrated volumes.[85] In 1806, he published an unillustrated history of gardening, bringing up to date his criticisms of Richard Payne Knight's *An analytical inquiry into the principles of taste*, published in the previous year.

The Picturesque controversy

Repton planned to publish *Sketches and hints on landscape gardening* in 1794 but its appearance was delayed by a year because he demanded the plates be re-engraved and additional sections be inserted as rejoinders to a concerted attack on his work by two Herefordshire squires, Richard Payne Knight in *The landscape: a didactic poem*, and Uvedale Price in *An essay on the picturesque*. Both these manifestoes were published in 1794 and were all the more wounding because they were totally unexpected; early in his career, Repton had sought advice in a friendly manner from Knight and Price when designing places close to their estates in Herefordshire.

The dispute between them arose from differing perceptions of ideal landscapes. Brown and Repton aimed to enhance natural beauty by rounding surfaces, softening edges, smoothing irregularities, forming streams into calm lakes and composing views framed by masses of trees on either side. Price and Knight created picturesque scenes by displaying rocky cliffs, rough vegetation, swirling streams, tumbling waterfalls, mouldering ruins, rutted lanes and the sight of men and women labouring in the fields.

Repton claimed that 'appropriation', a device which marked the full extent of a landowner's possessions, was 'one of the leading principles' of landscape gardening.[86] Knight, on the other hand, strongly objected to the parading of monuments, eyecatchers, entrance lodges, servants' cottages built to copybook patterns and coats of arms emblazoned on almshouses, inn signs and milestones on roads passing by estates.[87] Repton's reputation for appropriating milestones was caricatured in 'Marmaduke Milestone', who appeared as the landscape gardener in the satire *Headlong Hall*, by Thomas Love Peacock,[88] in which a lengthy discussion was conducted between Mr Milestone, Squire Headlong and his two daughters concerning the merits and defects of the picturesque and the beautiful.

The objection to appropriation raised another question: how far was beauty compatible with utility? Repton thought that appreciation of beauty in a park should be untainted by considerations of profit. In particular, he insisted that parkland and farmland 'must be distinct objects and ought never to be brought together in the same point of view'.[89] Price and Knight were not alone in embracing a Virgilian ideal that celebrated the skill of the cultivator in making the earth bear fruit, and they admired the patience of the forester in raising noble trees. William Marshall, a contemporary of Repton, insisted that landscapes be useful and valuable as well as beautiful, asserting that:

> trees, in general, are capable of producing an ornamental
> effect; and there is no tree which may not be said to be more
> or less useful. But their difference in point of value, when
> arrived at maturity, is incomparable; and it would be the
> height of folly to plant a tree whose characteristic is
> principally ornamental, when another, which is more useful
> and equally ornamental, may be planted in its stead.[90]

In practice, Repton was careful to save growing timber. He recommended judicious thinning of dense stands and occasionally advised cutting one or two mature trees but avoided clear felling. Price's treatment of trees was very similar to Repton's. Probably the one and only intervention Price made in shaping the Hertfordshire landscape was at Cassiobury in September 1824. He spent two days there as guest of the Earl of Essex, directing the clearing of thorns and ash seedlings from a neglected dell surrounded by fine old cedars of Lebanon, junipers, laurels and other exotic trees. He remarked on this clearance that, although he was 'professionally picturesque', he was 'very much of a tree-monger'.[91]

In other respects, Repton's views were closer to those of Price and Knight than to Brown's. Repton approved Brown's method of forming serpentine stretches of water and opening extensive prospects, but, unlike Brown, he agreed with Price in objecting to clumps. He thought that more natural groupings of trees might be achieved by planting single trees in front of dense masses, and had learned from experience that it was necessary to plant thickly at first and to thin later. He recommended planting fast-growing conifers as nurse trees to provide shelter for new plantations and advised putting up fences to prevent animals from browsing. As soon as clumps were established, the fences should be removed, conifers cut down and outlines broken by thinning trees at the edges. Both Price and Repton disliked belt plantations and especially walks leading through them. Price complained that a perimeter walk

> has all the sameness and formality of an avenue... without
> any of its simple grandeur, for though in an avenue you see
> the same objects from beginning to end, and in a belt a new
> set every twenty yards, yet each successive part of this
> insipid circle is so like the preceding, that though really
> different, the difference is scarcely felt.[92]

Repton, however, urged the necessity for separating parkland from adjoining farmland and regarded a plantation as the most natural means of hiding park pales. To make a belt intricate and varied he advocated following the form of the ground, varying its width and diverting a path to emerge in places where the walker might enjoy a view of distant prospects.

Repton also disapproved of the bareness of Brown's shaven lawns and the levelling of banks sloping down to the water's edge. He frequently planted trees on the banks of lakes and recommended that cattle or sheep be deployed to enliven broad swathes of grass. He agreed with Price that the vastness of a prospect across an extensive lawn did not impress the viewer with the magnificence of a place, and thought a house ought not to be seen at so great a distance that it appeared smaller than it really was. A distant view of a house could be avoided by planning an appropriate route for an approach drive: where possible, a drive was drawn to continue the line of a public highway and the public road was deflected at an angle away from the drive; the house was kept out of sight until the last few yards.

Price and Repton both preferred buildings in the gothick style; Repton because the vertical emphasis of a gothick facade contrasted sharply with round-headed trees, Price because the gothick idiom suggested ancestral connections with an old manor house, castle or abbey. Repton also differed from Brown in restoring flower gardens, terraces and gravel walks in front of a house. He believed 'symmetry is allowable, and indeed necessary, at or near the front of a regular building'.[93]

The Picturesque controversy was more spin than substance, more about words than deeds. The ideas of the contenders were closer than their caustic rhetoric implied, but they remained apart geographically. Stephen Daniels observes that an 'understated, latent source of picturesque power in Price's and Knight's writings is located in the history of Herefordshire as a border country between England and Wales'.[94] In practice, the Picturesque was an appropriate mode for perceiving landscapes in highland Britain.[95] In Hertfordshire, by contrast, Price's and Knight's ideas were not directly applicable, but they influenced the design of buildings, the revival of gardens and the modification of plantations. Repton himself endorsed and proposed these changes.

The Picturesque had little immediate impact on the appreciation of landscape by topographers and guide-book writers. When Hertfordshire was illustrated and described in Edward Brayley and John Britton's *The beauties of England and Wales* in 1808, the prevailing taste was that of Bridgeman and Brown rather than the Picturesque. Places singled out for special praise included Gorhambury, where 'the surface is agreeably diversified; and scenery composes some good landscapes; to which the contiguity of Pre Wood gives additional interest'.[96] In utilitarian terms, it was noted that the park and grounds at

Gorhambury were well-stocked with fine timber, particularly beech, oak and elm, and 'a considerable quantity' of fine deer were kept. Tring Park was described as 'pleasantly varied by bold swells and command-ing eminences', and the beech timber was 'particularly luxuriant'. Beechwood also stood in 'a delightful and well-wooded park, particu-larly abounding in fine beech'. The owner was renowned for his agricultural improvements. Brayley and Britton were most impressed with Watton Woodhall, described as a 'beautiful seat' occupying 'one of the finest situations in the county', the mansion 'standing on an emi-nence in a large park, nobly diversified by hill and vale, and watered by several small streams which flow into the river Beane'. Here again, 'the woods are extensive and many of the trees are of great magnitude and luxuriant growth'. Wormley Bury had an unusual feature indicative of mid-eighteenth-century Chinoiserie. The grounds were described as 'pleasant, though not extensive; and their beauty is much increased by a sheet of water, over which is a Chinese bridge'. The owner of Wormley Bury, Sir Abraham Hume, had been a director of the East India Company and set about cultivating many rare plants from India and the Far East. He designed a stove to keep the temperature of his hot houses constantly warm.[97] Among the most favoured places was Brocket, whose park and grounds were acknowledged to be 'very beau-tiful; and the scenery is much enriched by the river Lea which flows through the park and has been formed into a spacious sheet of water'. In Brayley and Britton's descriptions, sloping ground, extensive woods and sheets of water were the most attractive features. They also sub-scribed to the view that the size of an estate and the value of its beeches, oaks and elms added to its prestige. They relished the sight of conspic-uous expenditure, unshadowed by any prospect of short-term gain, and contemporary maps convey similar messages. Ordnance Survey maps, on the other hand, provide the first accurate measurements of the size of parks and precise delineations of their contents.

The Ordnance Survey's two-inch drawings, 1799–1812

Under the threat of an invasion from France, the government set up the Ordnance Survey in 1791 to carry out a trigonometrical survey of the whole of Britain, beginning with the Channel coast. The survey-

Figure 5.11: Kings Walden Bury, Stagenhoe Park and St Pauls Walden Bury in 1810. The representation of a formal layout at St Pauls Walden Bury contrasts with the treatment of naturalistic parkland at Stagenhoe and Kings Walden. Detail from Ordnance Survey two-inch drawings in 1810. © British Library Board — all rights reserved (Maps OSD. 148)

ors arrived in south-east Hertfordshire in 1799 and departed from the north-west of the county in 1812, the survey itself being conducted by teams of Royal Military Surveyors under the command of Lt. Col. William Mudge of the Royal Artillery. Charles Budgen, a senior surveyor with nearly twenty years' military service, William Hyett, who had served for twelve years, Charles Verron, Henry Boyce and one or two other surveyors transcribed the field notes from Hertfordshire. Drawings were prepared at a scale of 1 in 31,680 or two inches to a mile in the Drawing Room at the Tower of London and, from the drawings, plates were engraved at a reduced scale of 1 in 63,360 or one inch to a mile. Sheets of the Old Series one-inch map covering Hertfordshire were published between 1805 and 1834. Top priority was given to accuracy in measuring distances on the ground and orientating objects correctly within the trigonometrical framework.

Microfiche copies of the original drawings have been inspected in the map room at the British Library.[98] They are exquisite works of art,

executed with great precision and delicacy. Hill features were delineated by hachuring to represent slopes. Minor roads, bridges and
prominent landmarks, such as churches and windmills, received special attention because they were important in conducting military
operations. Parks were also surveyed in detail. Boundaries were represented by neatly drawn palings or by bold lines. On the drawings,
parkland was indicated by closely dotted stipple or was tinted green;
on engraved maps, it was shown as fine stipple.[99] All stippled areas of
parkland were more than fifteen acres in extent. Unlike Dury and
Andrews, the Ordnance surveyors did not plot sunk fences, but they
indicated lines of avenues and drives, positions of clumps, single trees,
lodges, stables and other buildings, and the extent of lakes and walled
gardens (Figure 5.11). Single trees were drawn as round-headed on a
short stem, standing on 'a faint horizontal line' to the right of the tree,
'representing the shade which it casts'.[100] In a few places, spiky-topped
conifers were differentiated from bushy-topped hardwoods. Grounds
recently planted were not represented as parkland until trees had

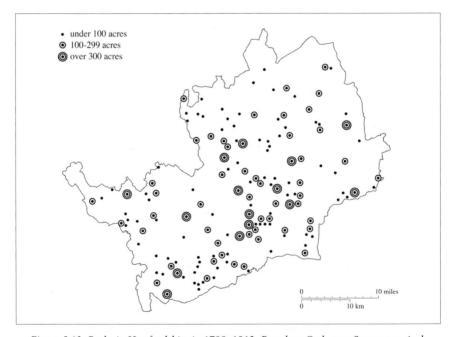

*Figure 5.12: Parks in Hertfordshire in 1799–1812. Based on Ordnance Survey two-inch
drawings, 1799–1812. Full details of parks are listed in Table 5.3. Drawn in the Geography
Department, UCL*

reached a height of twelve feet. Little Court in Buntingford, visited by Repton in 1790, was not named or stippled as parkland on the survey carried out in 1800, but neighbouring Wyddial Hall, an old park, which was visited by Repton at the same time, was duly recorded. At Nyn Hall, Northaw, the old park disappeared and, in its place, the surveyor noted 'now inclosing'. At Hertingfordbury, the surveyor noted in 1799 'house now pulling down', although demolition was not completed until 1816. At Pendley, near Tring, an eighty-acre park restored by Richard Bard Harcourt was recorded by the field surveyors in 1812. Subsequently, the house was pulled down and the abandoned park was omitted from the one-inch map published in 1822. At Welwyn, the original surveyor recorded the name 'St John's Lodge' but the modern name of 'Danesbury' was inscribed on the published map. The field survey also noted the name 'Tallymores', a place in Cuffley, later known as 'Tolmers'. The total number of places stippled as parkland on the drawings was 153, of which 88 were under 100 acres in size (Figure 5.12).

The surveyors distinguished 51 parks enclosed by palings from 102 other stippled parkland areas, outlined by continuous lines.[101] Of the 51 empaled parks, 32 had been represented in the same manner by Dury and Andrews. Most of these were large, old parks, including the largest in Hertfordshire. Some large parks, such as Brickendon Bury, Hamels, Pelham Hall and Tyttenhanger, had shrunk in size since 1766 and lost all or parts of their enclosing fences. Rickmansworth Park, Grove Park and New Place, Gilston, had expanded and been transformed into spacious fashionable pleasure grounds.

Only 13 parks, covering a total of 860 acres, were under 100 acres but over 15 acres in size, whereas 75 gardens and pleasure grounds, covering 3,835 acres, were in the 15- to 100-acre range. Many new suburban villas, surrounded by small areas of parkland, appeared in the closing decade of the eighteenth century. They were mostly concentrated south of the Vale of St Albans and along new turnpike roads leading to the City and Westminster. The line of the Sparrows Herne Turnpike, following the Bulbourne, Gade and Colne, attracted many new residents. In 1808, on the summer schedule for coaches, Tring could be reached in 5½ hours from London by way of

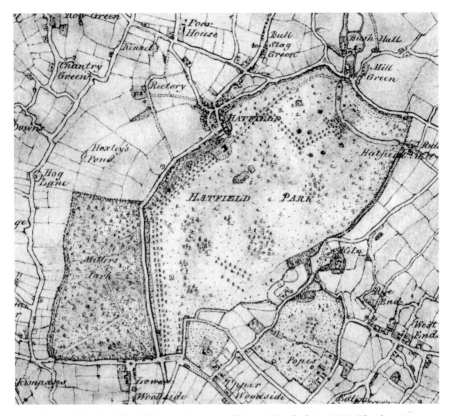

Figure 5.13: Hatfield, Millwards, Popes and Upper Woodside in 1805. The drawings indicated different densities of tree cover in neighbouring parks. Detail from Ordnance Survey two-inch drawings in 1805. © British Library Board — all rights reserved (Maps OSD 149)

Edgware and Sparrows Herne on Bushey Heath. A journey by mail coach down the Great North Road from London to Stevenage took over four hours; along Ermine Street, the road to Cambridge, a journey to Royston took five hours; and on Watling Street, the road to Holyhead, it took three hours to reach St Albans.[102] Since 1750, journey times had been halved, the number of scheduled coach services had doubled and fares had risen considerably. Even before turnpike road surfaces were macadamised in about 1820, the volume of traffic on roads from the capital increased rapidly.

Allowing for differences in the accuracy of the two surveys and, on the Ordnance Surveyors' drawings, a difficulty in measuring areas

continued on p139

Table 5.3 Parks in Hertfordshire in 1799–1812

Park	Grid Reference	Owner	Acres
Albury Hall	427254	John Calvert	360
Aldenham House	168965	Robert Hucks	80
Aldenham Lodge, Radlett	167004	Sophia, Baroness Howe	60
Almshoe Bury	206253	Sir Robert Salusbury Bt	30
Ardeley Bury	301271	Augustus Frederick Spence	160
Ash Park, Bovingdon	020030	Nathaniel Snell	80
Ashlyns Hall, Berkhamsted	991067	James Smith	90
Ashridge Park, Lt Gaddesden	995122	John Egerton 7th Earl Bridgwater	1080
Aspenden	352284	Charles Boldero	170
Aston Bury	276217	John Bagot	20
Aston Place	271225	Edmund Darby	50
Ayot St Lawrence Place	195170	Samuel Lyde	90
Baldock Place House	243337	Edward Hampson	40
Balls Park, Hertford	335120	Lord John Townshend	160
Bayfordbury	315104	William Baker	310
Bedwell Park, Essendon	276076	Sir Culling Smith	200
Beechwood, Flamstead	045144	Sir John Saunders Sebright, Bt	400
Benington Lordship	297236	John Chesshyre	20
Benington Place	312235	Thomas Bullock	120
Berkhamsted Hall	998074	Augustus Pechell	60
Berkhamsted Place	991088	John Roper	90
Birds Place, Essendon	273079	Capt. Robert Clitherow	40
Blakesware, Ware	405163	William Plumer MP	20
Bragbury End, Aston	270209	William Manfield	55
Bramfield Bury	285154	Charles Bourchier	20
Brickendon Bury	330105	Charles Morgan	200
Briggens, Hunsdon	412112	Thomas Blackmore	60
Broadfield House, Cottered	324310	Rev. Thomas Sisson	80
Brocket, Hatfield	214130	Peniston Lamb, Viscount Melbourne	530
Brookmans Park, North Mimms	253048	Samuel Robert Gaussen MP	270
Broxbourne Bury	353072	Jacob Bosanquet	220
Bush Hall, Hatfield	239100	William Thomas Sandiford	40
Bushey Grove	130975	David Haliburton	15
Bushey Hall	136951	William Smith	40
Bushey Manor	129955	Robert Capper	25
Bygrave Park	264360	James Cecil, Marquess of Salisbury	30
Callipers, Chipperfield	051008		20

continued over

Table 5.3 Parks in Hertfordshire in 1799–1812 *continued*

Park	Grid Reference	Owner	Acres
Camfield Place, Essendon	268069	Rev. William Browne	80
Cassiobury, Watford	095972	George Capel, 5th Earl of Essex	880
Chesfield, Graveley	247275	William Parkins	110
Cheshunt House	345027	John Shaw	50
Cheshunt Nunnery	369040	Thomas Artemidorus Russell	80
Cheshunt Park	347045	Oliver Cromwell	30
Childwick Bury, St Michael	140102	Joshua Lomax	120
Clay Hall, Walkern	305250	William Gosling	50
Clothall Bury	281321	James Cecil, Marquess of Salisbury	50
Codicote Lodge	214183	Hon. Thomas Brand of Kimpton Hoo	50
Cokenhatch, Barkway	396361	Sir Francis Willes	80
Coles Park, Westmill	368260	Thomas Greg	70
Colney House, London Colney	173030	George King, 3rd Earl of Kingston	120
Danesbury, Welwyn	229169	Gen. Cornelius Cuyler	120
Digswell House, Welwyn	250151	Peter Leopold, 5th Earl Cowper	130
Digswell Rectory, Welwyn	239149	Rev. John James Watson	30
Dyrham Park, Ridge	223985	John Trotter	150
Edge Grove, Aldenham	144989	Sir John Nicholl	90
Essendon Lodge	274079	John Hodgson	70
Gaddesden Hoo, Gt Gaddesden	033124	Henry Green	70
Gaddesden Place, Gt Gaddesden	038111	Joseph Thompson Halsey MP	70
Gadebridge, Hemel Hempstead	049081	Christopher Thomas Tower	120
Gobions, North Mimms	252039	Thomas Holmes Hunter	170
Golden Parsonage, Gt Gaddesden	051126	Rev. George Nugent	160
Goldings, Waterford	311143	Richard Emmott	30
Gorhambury, St Michael	113080	James, 3rd Viscount Grimston	360
Grove Park, Sarratt	082988	Thomas Villiers, 2nd Earl Clarendon	250
Hacksters End, Berkhamsted	018073	John Field	50
Hadham Hall, Lt Hadham	452227	John Scott	20
Hamels, Braughing	376247	Catherine Mellish	270
Haresfoot, Northchurch	985062	Thomas Dorrien	200
Hatfield	236084	James Cecil, Marquess of Salisbury	1010
Hertford Castle	324125	Nicolson Calvert MP	40
Hertingfordbury	310121	Samuel Baker	70
Hexton House	108306	William Young	140
High Cannons, Ridge	209990	Henry Bonham	140
High Down, Pirton	144305	Emilius Henry Delme Radcliffe	20

continued

Table 5.3 Parks in Hertfordshire in 1799–1812 *continued*

Park	Grid Reference	Owner	Acres
Hilfield Lodge, Aldenham	153963	Hon. George Villiers	140
Hitchin Priory	184286	Emilius Henry Delme Radcliffe	60
Hoo, Kimpton	187195	Hon. Thomas Brand	440
Hook, Northaw	279014		60
Hunsdon Grange	418130	Walter Calvert	70
Hunsdon House	420127	Nicolson Calvert MP	60
Hyde Hall, Sawbridgeworth	496154	Robert Jocelyn, Earl of Roden	200
Ippolitts	197269	Sir Robert Salusbury Bt	50
Julians, Rushden	307326	Adolphus Meetkerke	230
Kendalls Hall, Aldenham	173982	William Phillimore	90
Kings Walden Bury	161235	George William Hale	220
Kitwells, Radlett	191994	Dorothea Tuite	80
Knebworth	231210	Richard Warburton Lytton	410
Knights Hall, Westmill	371256	Thomas Greg	50
Lamers, Wheathamstead	181160	Sir Charles Drake Garrard	200
Langleybury, Abbots Langley	077001	Rev. Sir Edmund Filmer Bt	40
Laurel Lodge, Lt Bushey	146946	Mr Isherwood	20
Lilley Lodge	112278	William Sowerby	60
Lilley Park	114263	John Sowerby	50
Lockleys, Welwyn	237159	John Mackenzie	100
Lower Woodside, Hatfield	247063	William Franks	20
Marchmont House, Hemel Hempstead	053085	J. Abbot Green	60
Marden Hill, Tewin	279140	Robert Macky	60
Markyate Cell	057174	Joseph Howell	90
Marshalswick, Sandridge	163085	George Sullivan Marten	30
Merry Hill House, Bushey	138942	Robert Hucks	15
Micklefield Hall, Rickmansworth	053974	Emmott Skidmore	80
Millwards Park, Hatfield	236065	James Cecil, Marquess of Salisbury	320
Moor Park, Rickmansworth	075933	Robert Williams MP	550
Moor Place, Much Hadham	423187	William Lushington	150
Much Wymondley Priory	218279	Shute Barrington, Bishop of Durham	25
Munden House, Gt Munden	136003	William Baker	30
Nascot Farm, Watford	106968	William Smith	40
New Barns, St Stephens	156054	Matthew Towgood	100
New Organ Hall, Radlett	167997	William Towgood	210
New Place, Gilston	441129	William Plumer MP	410
Newsells, Barkway	386367	Hon. John Peachey	120

continued over

Table 5.3 Parks in Hertfordshire in 1799–1812 *continued*

Park	Grid Reference	Owner	Acres
Node, Codicote	217202		60
North Mymms Park	217042	Henry Browne	570
Offley Place	145272	Sir Robert Salusbury Bt	90
Offley Vicarage	137277	Rev. Lynch Burroughs	40
Panshanger, Hertingfordbury	290132	Peter Leopold, 5th Earl Cowper	810
Pelham Hall, Furneux Pelham	427279	Nicolson Calvert MP	70
Pendley, Tring	943118	Richard Bard Harcourt	80
Pishiobury, Sawbridgeworth	480134	Mrs Rose Milles	90
Ponsbourne, Hatfield	304054	Stephen Sulivan	170
Popes, Hatfield	259077	Rebecca Assheton	150
Porters, Shenley	182008	Louisa Catherine, Marchioness Sligo	280
Potterells, North Mimms	236046	Justinian Casamajor	160
Putteridge Bury, Lilley	118245	John Sowerby	200
Red Heath House, Croxley	066971	John Finch	30
Rickmansworth Park	057955	Henry Fotherley Whitfield	150
Rothamsted, Harpenden	125131	John Bennet Lawes	80
Russells Farm, Watford	091995	George Capel, 5th Earl of Essex	70
Sacombe Park	339190	George Caswall	210
St Pauls Walden Bury	187217	George Bowes, Earl of Strathmore	110
Serge Hill House, Bedmond	107042		30
Shenley Hill	194010	Charles Arnold	50
Shephall Bury, Stevenage	256229	Michael Heathcote	40
Stagenhoe, St Pauls Walden	185227	Robert Thornton Heysham	100
Stocks House, Aldbury	966133	William Hayton	40
Temple Dinsley, Preston	181248	Joseph Darton	30
Tewin Water	255145	Hon. Henry Cowper	210
Theobalds, Cheshunt	345011	Sir George Beeston Prescott Bt	250
Tolmers, Cuffley	303048	Robert Taylor	60
Totteridge Park	233942	Edward Arrowsmith	80
Tring Park	926111	Sir Drummond Smith Bt	240
Tyttenhanger, Ridge	192047	Philip Yorke, Earl of Hardwicke	90
Upper Woodside, Hatfield	250069	John Church	50
Walkern Rectory	292267	Rev. Benjamin Heath	30
Wall Hall, Aldenham	138995	George Woodford Thellusson	70
Ware Park	333144	Thomas Hope Byde	250
Westbrook Hay, Bovingdon	026054	Mrs Mary Ryder	150
Woodhall, Watton	318189	Samuel Smith MP	420

continued

Table 5.3 Parks in Hertfordshire in 1799–1812 *continued*

Park	Grid Reference	Owner	Acres
Wood End, Hatfield	266058	George Stainforth	50
Woolmers Park, Hertingfordbury	286103	Marquis of Stafford	140
Wormley Bury	355059	Sir Abraham Hume Bt	100
Wyddial	373317	John Thomas Ellis	140
Youngsbury, Standon	378179	Daniel Giles	70

Sources: The areas of parks are measured from Ordnance Survey, two-inch drawings for first edition one-inch map of England and Wales. The drawings for Hertfordshire were prepared in 1799–1812. Most names of owners are taken from a list of certificates for killing game, from a register of gamekeepers and from a list of justices of the peace in William Le Hardy and Geoffrey L. Reckitt (eds.), *Calendar to the sessions books 1799 to 1833*, Hertfordshire County Records, vol. 9 (Hertford, 1939), pp.537–669. Additional names are taken from the *Victoria County History* for Hertfordshire; from G.E.C., *The complete peerage of England, Scotland and Ireland* (London, 1912), from R.G. Thorne, *House of Commons 1790–1820* (London, 1986), and from *Poll for Knights of the Shire for the County of Hertford*, 11–12 February 1805.

continued from p134

of parkland where belt plantations lay adjacent to other tracts of woodland, a rough comparison may be made between areas of parks and grounds over 100 acres in 1766 and 1799–1812. In 1766, the total area of parks over 100 acres was 14,600 acres and the total area of pleasure grounds and gardens over 100 acres was 5,720 acres, making a grand total of 20,320 acres. In 1799–1812, the comparable areas were 12,560 acres of parks over 100 acres and 4,680 acres of pleasure grounds and gardens over 100 acres, making a grand total of 17,240 acres. Large parks shrank slightly in the course of those forty years and the total area occupied by large parks, gardens and pleasure grounds appears to have decreased by approximately 15 per cent.

In about 1805, the size of parks almost exactly matched the order of precedence among the nobility and gentry. The largest park was 1080-acre Ashridge, property of the seventh Earl of Bridgwater, cousin and heir to the 'Canal Duke'. Hatfield, the only other park in Hertfordshire to exceed 1000 acres, belonged to the first Marquess of Salisbury, who also owned the adjoining 320-acre Millwards Park (Figure 5.13). The third-largest park, 880-acre Cassiobury, belonged to the fifth Earl of Essex. He and his cousin owned two neighbouring parks. Merged into the 810 acres of Panshanger was Cole Green Park, former seat of the Cowpers. The fifth Earl Cowper also owned

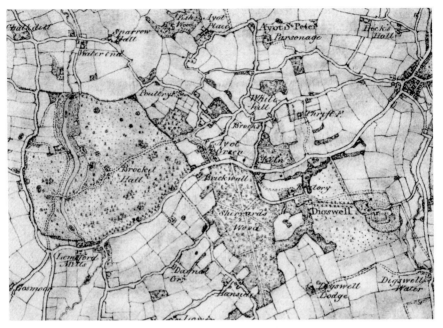

Figure 5.14: Brocket Hall, Sherrards Wood, Digswell Rectory and Digswell House in 1805.
The surveyors differentiated between fenced and unfenced parks. Detail from Ordnance
Survey two-inch drawings in 1805 © British Library Board — all rights reserved
(Maps OSD.149)

Digswell House and leased Tewin Water to his cousin. North Mymms
Park (570 acres) was purchased from the Duke of Leeds by Henry
Browne, appointed sheriff in 1803. Moor Park (550 acres) passed
from army contractor Sir Lawrence Dundas, through the hands of
Thomas Bates Rous, a director of the East India Company found
guilty of bribery, to another director of the company and shipowner,
Robert Williams MP. Brocket (530 acres) was owned by Peniston
Lamb, created Viscount Melbourne, and was the birthplace of his son
and heir, William Lamb, future prime minister (Figure 5.14). Kimpton
Hoo, owned by Hon. Thomas Brand, Watton Woodhall, owned
by Samuel Smith MP, Knebworth, owned by Richard Warburton
Lytton, New Place, Gilston, owned by William Plumer MP, and
Beechwood, owned by Sir John Sebright, were each over 400 acres in
extent. In the 300-acre range were Viscount Grimston's Gorhambury,
John Calvert's Albury Hall and William Baker's Bayfordbury. Size of
park, size of house and size of landed estate corresponded almost

exactly to an owner's position in the social hierarchy. Parks were ranged in order of rank from possessions of a marquess, through those of peers, baronets and knights, to those of local magistrates, gentlemen farmers, city merchants, naval officers and clergymen. Parks and gardens below 100 acres in size were occupied by many different kinds of people.

Unlike earlier surveys, the Ordnance Survey was not directly dependent on private patronage. It issued no subscription list and the surveyors did not record names of owners of parks on their drawings. Owners have been identified from other contemporary sources. Taking 1805 as a date when all but the far north of the county had been surveyed, the fullest sources for names of proprietors are a register of certificates for killing game and a register of gamekeepers, in which not only the names but also the addresses of certificate holders are recorded. A list of justices of the peace for the county contains names but no addresses. Additional names and addresses have been identified from a poll book for the election of a member of parliament for the county.[103] Other names have been gathered from county histories, topographies and biographical notes on peers and members of parliament. At some places, the resident was not the owner but a lessee or grace and favour occupier. At other places, it was not clear whether the holder of the title of lord of the manor was the person who lived in the manor house or principal seat.

The multiplication of parks in the late eighteenth century was associated with improvements in main roads leading to London. The surveyors' drawings show parkland lining roads but they also show how little of the county had been urbanised. Most of Hertfordshire remained deeply rural, with extensive areas of woodland interspersed with tracts of arable and pasture. Many settlements were very small. The largest town, Watford, counted no more than 3,530 inhabitants in 1801, and only ten other places had more than 2,000 people.[104] While the area of heaths and commons had diminished since 1766, the sight of gypsies huddled around camp fires on No Man's Land Common near St Albans added a picturesque touch to the scene. Agrarian landscapes in 1800 would have been characterised by J.M.W. Turner as 'elegant pastoral', as distinct from merely 'pastoral'.[105] They were calm and peaceful, with slow-moving streams and expanses of meadowland studded with fine trees, and were grazed by free-ranging domestic animals. They looked like parkland and reflected the tastes of gentlemanly owners.

Parks and landownership

By the end of the eighteenth century, the application of strict family settlements to a majority of large landed estates in Hertfordshire greatly restricted the amount of land available for sale on the open market. Established families acquired estates mostly by inheritance or marriage; newcomers paid scarcity prices for a few remaining properties. Between 1760 and 1820 city merchants, government contractors, members of parliament, nabobs returning from India, sugar planters, brewers, admirals, generals and clergymen scrambled to buy small estates with spacious grounds. An attractive place of this type was High Cannons, near Shenley, described in a sale catalogue in 1800 as 'a modern, regular square building, seated in the centre of its own grounds, which wear the appearance of a neat park, with a double entrance from the roads by handsome lodges and extensive drives through the grounds'. The grounds, including stables for fourteen horses, four coach houses and a home farm, covered 315 acres.[106] The house had been enlarged in 1773 by a wealthy Cornishman, Robert Trefusis, and further modernised in 1778 by Justinian Casamajor, a planter from Antigua. Before the end of the century, it had again passed briefly through the hands of two MPs.

Many newcomers spent large sums of money on the initial purchase of a property, then spent more on building and laying out the grounds. Some failed to complete improvements, some incurred huge debts, others left no heir. For one reason or another, newcomers were likely to be transient purchaser-sellers. Among the most fleeting newcomers were men who brought back vast fortunes from India. Kate Harwood has identified twenty-one company men, including nine directors, who acquired seats in Hertfordshire.[107] None were richer than two nabobs who bought and sold Watton Woodhall. The first, Thomas Rumbold, served as a captain in Clive's victorious campaign from 1754 to 1757, transferred to the civil service as collector of land revenue in Bihar, privately engaged in building ships and trading in salt and obtained a seat on the Bengal council. Laden with treasure, he returned to England in 1769. One year later, he was elected MP for New Shoreham and married the daughter of a bishop. In 1778, at the age of 42, he paid £85,000 for Watton Woodhall, a ruinous old house on a small estate. He went back to India in 1778 as governor of Madras and resigned less than three years later on grounds of ill health. On returning to England with a second fortune, he had to fend off a parliamentary enquiry into allegations of corruption.[108] He cleared his name, was created a baronet, built a large mansion, expanded the park and planted thousands of trees. He died insolvent at Watton in 1791. In 1794, his trustees sold the property to Paul Benfield for the enormous sum of £150,000. Like Rumbold, Benfield had made a fortune as an official in the East India Company while privately conducting business as a banker and money lender. Like Rumbold too, he had to defend himself against charges of financial impropriety, but his downfall was caused by gross extravagance and the failure of a banking venture in England. In 1799, he was declared bankrupt; he died in abject poverty in Paris in 1810.[109]

One of the cleverest and most energetic directors and chairmen of the East India Company, Laurence Sulivan, handled remittances on behalf of sea captains in Bombay and later in London. He returned to England in 1761, bought Ponsbourne manor for £13,500, was elected MP and spent most of his time in the City directing the company's business. He lost a fortune in the stock crash of 1769; in 1772 he owed about £18,000 and his estate was mortgaged. His son, Stephen inherited Ponsbourne in 1786 and laid out the grounds as a landscape garden.[110]

A rapid succession of purchaser-sellers bought and sold Colney House. In 1770, Philip Champion de Crespigny, a leading ecclesiastical lawyer, spent £5,000 on the purchase of the estate, £1,800 on the bare shell of a new house which he called Colney Chapel House, £600 on the kitchen garden and walls and £450 on the lake.[111] His first wife died while work was in progress and, on remarrying, his second wife wanted to move. In 1778, the unfinished building and 150 acres were sold for a bargain price of £6,500. The purchaser, Charles Bourchier, recently returned from Madras, where he preceded Rumbold as governor, was reputed to have lavished £53,000 on rebuilding the house and ornamenting the grounds but he did not settle. In 1795 he sold the property, which was subsequently acquired by the Margrave of Anspach and then by George King, son and heir of the Earl of Kingston. King succeeded to the earldom and lived there for five years before selling it to George Anderson, who held it for four years and sold it once more to Peter Hadow, another East India Company official.

Some small estates were bought or leased as temporary residences. The Duke of Bridgwater paid Samuel Whitbread £15,000 for Woolmers complete with furniture and stock. The duke intended to stay there for a short period while Ashridge was being rebuilt, but he died in 1803, before his house was ready for occupation.[112] Woolmers was inherited by his nephew, the Marquis of Stafford, who quickly sold it to another wealthy landowner, Sir John St Aubyn from Cornwall. The most mobile purchaser-sellers were property speculators who modernised places not for their own enjoyment but in order to obtain higher prices. In a market where many bidders were chasing few properties, it was unclear who were and who were not speculators.

Some owners of small estates clung tenaciously to their ancestral lands. A few families managed to add to their holdings, rebuild their houses and improve their grounds by cutting recurrent expenditure, borrowing from relatives, engaging in trade and marrying rich wives. The epic struggle of the Radcliffes to hold on to Hitchin Priory succeeded largely because of the determination shown by every generation to pass the estate to their children and grandchildren. Family finances were replenished by money earned from trading in the Levant, occasionally taken in the form of loans from members of the family resident in Aleppo. A large loan was used to improve the house and grounds in the early eighteenth century. The improver, Ralph Radcliffe, died childless in 1739 and instead of leaving the estate to his brother Edward, from whom he had borrowed over £6,000, he bequeathed it to an indigent younger brother, John. Edward demanded that John repay the money that was owed to him but John simply could not afford to do so. Edward allowed John and subsequently John's widow and their children to stay in the Priory but collected income from the estate until his own death in 1764. Three years later, John's younger son, also named John Radcliffe, inherited the estate together with a fortune of £150,000 from his uncle Arthur.

Some of this money paid for the purchase of land to enlarge the park, for Richmond's work on landscaping it and for John's election to parliament. When John died childless and impoverished in 1783, the Priory passed to his sister Penelope and, in 1802, to his niece, Anne Melicent Clarke, who unexpectedly became an heiress. Anne married Emilius Delme and he changed his name to Radcliffe as a condition of inheriting Hitchin Priory and an estate at High Down, Pirton.[113]

In 1800, the largest estates in Hertfordshire were approaching their maximum extent and owners were stretching their powers to the utmost. The nation and the county had become a one-party state, led and dominated by the landed interest. There were opposing factions within the whigs but there was no question about the authority of one faction or the other to raise taxes, call up the militia, enclose common land, divert public highways and return paupers to their places of settlement. The prestige of landowners was made manifest in the design of their houses and the layout of their parks and gardens. Government business was discussed informally at country house congresses, land tax and rents were collected in estate offices, justice was dispensed in magistrates' parlours and polite society was invited to country house balls. In the 1780s, the proud Countess of Salisbury regularly gave balls for 400 guests at Hatfield. Outdoors, in the park, hunts met, races were run, cricket matches played, militiamen camped and military exercises were conducted. In June 1800, King George III came to Hatfield Park to review the Hertfordshire militia, yeomanry and volunteer corps. The parade was watched by thousands of people and, after the ceremony, 1,500 troops sat down to a sumptuous dinner.[114] The occasion was hosted by the Marquess of Salisbury in his capacity as lord lieutenant of the county and colonel-in-chief of the militia. The field officers were all members of noble families and junior officers were drawn from the gentry. The gentry also provided horses for the cavalry. Many of the rank and file were volunteers; the rest were conscripted.

Landowners and the poor

At the height of their ascendancy, large landowners faced challenges both from the poor and also from the mercantile rich. Landed gentry were geographically more isolated than ever and mentally more detached from the daily lives of poor people, who were excluded from parks and deprived of means of subsisting on the natural resources of the locality. Between 1767 and 1811, roads, bridleways and footpaths were closed through twenty parks in Hertfordshire,[115] closures which forced labourers and their wives to walk longer distances to fields and market places. Between 1800 and 1810 Earl Cowper pulled down cottages and enclosed fields that had been communally ploughed and harvested at Panshanger, signalling that he could not bear the sight of villagers and did not care for the continuance of communal agriculture. In 1812, the earl took legal action against a local farmer, Mr Fowler, who claimed that he held a customary right to fish in the river Mimram. The court upheld Mr Fowler's claim and the earl had to pay compensation to gain fishery rights for his exclusive private enjoyment.[116]

Some landowners threatened to maim or kill all uninvited persons who set foot in their parks or woods on the pretext that they might be poachers. The seriousness of the landowner's threat and the plight of a poor man are illuminated in a deposition submitted to Hertford Quarter Sessions in 1791 by Joseph Ansell, a gardener from St Albans. Ansell had been walking along a common footpath through Parsley Wood near Rudwick Hall, with a little terrier at his heels, when he was suddenly arrested by John Dines, gamekeeper to Hale Esq. of Kings Walden. Dines was accompanied by John Cotton, who drew a sword and held it to Ansell's head while Dines searched the gardener's clothes, whereby he lost a shilling and a pocket handkerchief. He was then marched four miles to Kimpton Hoo, residence of Thomas Brand, a magistrate, where he was held in custody until 11 o'clock at night, being told that Mr Brand was playing cards and could not be interrupted. When Ansell was brought before the magistrate, the gamekeeper alleged that he had been found in a wood in which several snares had been set the night before, that he had a dog with him and Dines suspected him of being a poacher. In answer to Mr Brand's questions, Dines replied that Ansell had no snares upon him, that he was not beating for game, and that he was not out of the footpath. When asked whether the dog was hunting, Dines replied that he heard Ansell say 'chew' to the dog. Mr Brand said that was encouraging the dog and 'was quite sufficient'. Without hearing Ansell's own account, the magistrate convicted him of using a dog on a Sunday with intent to kill game and imposed a fine of £10. The deposition goes on to state that Mr Brand offered to excuse Ansell from paying the penalty if he would act as an informer by catching a hare and selling it to any person in St Albans who was not legally permitted to possess game. He said that many people from that town were destroying his game and he would give Ansell leave to go and catch a hare anywhere but warned him that steel traps and spring guns were set all over his own estate. Ansell was then dismissed and ordered to attend again two weeks later. When Ansell reappeared, he told Mr Brand that he had no intention of complying with his request and pleaded his inability to pay the fine. He also told the magistrate that he had sureties willing to testify on his behalf in an appeal against the conviction, 'whereupon Mr Brand, with many horrid oaths, swore that Ansell intended to make a fool of him and if he had known, he would have sent him to gaol before'.[117]

Ansell was summoned to appear at the first quarter session in 1791. His appeal against his conviction was granted and John Dines, his son Joseph, and John Cotton of Kings Walden were found guilty of assaulting him and each fined 13s 4d. The right of a gardener to exercise his dog on a public path without molestation and intimidation was vindicated. In a similar case, heard in April 1790, quarter session allowed an appeal by William Wright, yeoman of Hertford, against his conviction and fine of £10 for keeping and using certain dogs, namely one lurcher and two finders, and having a gun for destroying game.[118] In these cases, the court took a more lenient attitude towards alleged breaches of the game laws than individual magistrates. A selfish and vengeful pursuit of game preservation by a few landowners was alienating the loyalty and affections of many people.

The enlargement of private estates left the poor with fewer places where they could gather wood, bracken and furze for winter fuel. Common herds and flocks had largely disappeared and individuals now had to forage for pasture on small remnants of commons. In 1783, unstinted commons and wastes at Berkhamsted were reported to be overgrazed and 'distant farmers', with no property in the surrounding parishes, were keeping animals upon the common.[119] At other places, carters turned their ponies out on village greens and old people and youngsters tended cows and goats along roadside verges. Some marched their ducks and geese to and from village ponds, gleaned after harvest for grain to make bread and feed their chickens, and gathered plums, apples, hazel nuts and blackberries from hedgerows. The old and infirm sometimes resorted to begging. A few youths turned to crime, breaking hedges, damaging gates and stealing sheep. By far the largest number of indictments for theft were of one or two hens, ducks, rabbits, pigeons, a turkey, two sheafs of wheat, small quantities of potatoes, a piece of bacon and other items, mostly stolen from neighbours or small farmers. In 1783, quarter sessions were alarmed by a great rise in the number of larcenies and, in 1792, constables were instructed to use greater energy in enforcing the law.[120] John Carrington, a farmer, who served as chief constable for Bramfield, recognised that acute food scarcity in 1795–6 had caused Thomas Witty, a 32-year-old labourer with a wife and four children to feed, to steal a fat sheep out of a drove passing to London. Carrington made a determined effort to win the support of three members of parliament to recommend Witty's reprieve from a death sentence. The sentence was commuted to seven years' transportation to Botany Bay.[121]

The meagre pickings that could be obtained from the countryside by legal means were insufficient to sustain life; hence landowners were faced with increasing demands for poor relief. Some owners showed benevolence towards the poor by offering employment in their own parks, gardens and woodlands. A few of the newly hired were put to work excavating basins for ornamental lakes, repairing and setting up new palings and tending plantations where game was preserved. Other owners encouraged domestic industries such as straw-plaiting and lacemaking, which provided supplementary incomes for women and children.[122] The Earl of Clarendon helped his labourers by giving them nooks and corners of his fields in Sarratt for growing potatoes and, at Clothall Bury, labourers were allowed to plant potatoes on the fallows.[123] In addition to being paid wages, many labourers received bread, cheese and ale at harvest time. In rural parishes it was hard to find new employment for men seeking work and, when prices of bread and provisions rose faster than wages, it was extremely difficult for labourers to feed their children and other dependants. At Hitchin, in the hard winter of 1795, doles of flour and bread were given to the poor.[124] As a last resort, poor people seeking relief were removed to their places of settlement, where they had been born or spent their working lives.

The mercantile challenge

The challenge that wealthy merchants presented to ancient landed families was most clearly expressed in the marriage market. Daughters of brewers and nabobs came with larger dowries and jointures than daughters of high nobility. *The Gentleman's Magazine* announced brides' fortunes less frequently in the second half of the eighteenth century than in the first and the largest fortunes all belonged to mercantile families. In 1780, the brewer Samuel Whitbread's second daughter brought £30,000 to her marriage with Lord St John of Bletsoe. In 1793, East Indiaman Paul Benfield settled on his wife from County Durham a jointure of £3,000 a year in addition to £500 a year pin money and substantial endowments for their children. In 1796, a daughter and co-heiress of Richard Hassell of Barnet possessed a fortune of £10,000 when she married Rev. William Armstrong of Forty Hall, Enfield.[125]

Wealth inherited from a prominent Bristol tobacco merchant with interests in Virginia enabled Sir Lionel Lyde to pay for the controversial rebuilding of the parish church at Ayot St Lawrence in 1778–9. Sir Lionel's father-in-law, Cornelius Lyde, bought Ayot St Lawrence in 1723, at which time the old church, adjoining the manor house, was in a poor state of repair; it continued to deteriorate over the next fifty years. In 1772, the incumbent, churchwarden and principal inhabitants unsuccessfully petitioned the court of quarter sessions for £1,256 8s 10d to take down the ruins and repair and rebuild what could be saved.[126] Sir Lionel decided that he would build a new church at his own expense, to stand as an eyecatcher at the end of a vista about a quarter of a mile from his house. Nicholas Revett, an antiquarian and dilettante, designed a dramatic parkland ornament in the style of a classical Doric temple at Delos and added pavilions on either side. The deed of gift, assigning the new building to the rector and churchwarden of the parish, stipulated that worshippers were to enter and leave by way of a designated path through the park, concealed from the house, and also ruled that no villager was to be buried on that site.[127] The old church was treated as a picturesque ruin and parishioners continued to be buried in the old churchyard.

The consecration of the new St Lawrence church, in July 1779, was attended by neighbouring nobility and gentry and hundreds of people from all over the county. A procession to the church door was led by a band of twenty men and women, 'dressed in neat uniforms at the expense of Sir Lionel', and after the bishop had conducted the service the company was regaled with wine and cakes. In the afternoon, villagers 'diverted themselves in innocent rural games till the close of day, and at last parted highly delighted with the pleasure they had received'.[128] Similarly, in September 1783, Sir Lionel provided a lavish evening entertainment to celebrate Harvest Home. The park was lit by lamps of different colours and buildings were decorated with festoons of flowers and wheat ears. Among the guests were the French ambassador, the Earl and Countess of Salisbury, and leading nobility, gentry and clergy, as well as local harvesters. The gentry were saluted by music from the band of the militia as they alighted from their carriages. The fete opened with a musical act, performed by a group of country people singing 'Harvest Home' and other rural songs. The gentry then began to dance in a spacious tent that was floored and illuminated for their comfort. Tea and refreshments were served in one marquee and, in another, a local choir sang catches and glees in intervals between the dances. At midnight the company retired to the house for an elegant supper, while, in a large barn in the park, the harvesters sat down to a feast of lamb roasted whole. After supper, the gentry danced in the drawing room and broke up at four o'clock 'perfectly pleased with their entertainment'.[129] Old aristocrats gratefully accepted hospitality offered by a second-generation upstart, but the mixed company of old and new landowners did not dance or dine with the 'country people'. The new church at Ayot St Lawrence expressed the gulf between rich and poor: the Lydes would not be buried alongside ploughmen. No letters or diaries recorded the opinions of parishioners about the neglect and, later, the appropriation of the old church or about restrictions on access to the new church, just as no comments from harvesters have survived concerning the displacement of their traditional festivity by a social event for the gentry.

At the end of the eighteenth century, parks made significant contributions to the rural economy as producers of livestock and timber.
While farming prospered, landowners earned high profits from home
farms and were able to increase rents from tenants. On the other
hand, taste and fashion dictated that they spend large sums of money
to refront their houses in neo-classical Regency or picturesque gothick styles. Houses, parks and gardens were designed as theatre sets in
which landowners acted their parts as public figures. For a large
landowner it was important to have a house and park commensurate
with the size of his estate. For a small landowner, a park was a place
to display his wealth. Much money for constructing temples, lakes
and drives was drawn from outside Hertfordshire, from banking,
brewing, contracting for the army and navy and from trading in the
Levant, India and the Caribbean. Villagers did not voice their opinions about these symbols of power and wealth. William Wilshere of
Hitchin was probably alone in being obsessed with a fear that the
French Revolution would spread to England and that his house, aptly
named the Hermitage, would be burned down. He fortified his study
and built a secret chamber within which he fitted shelves to store food
and treasure and a passage to communicate with the outside world.[130]
Almost all landowners behaved with supreme confidence that their
way of life would continue to flourish for the foreseeable future.

Notes

1.   W. Hogarth, *The analysis of beauty* (London, 1753); E. Burke, *A
      philosophical enquiry into the origin of our ideas of the sublime and the
      beautiful* (London, 1757).

2.   D. Stroud, *Capability Brown* (London, 1950), pp.28–44; R. Turner, *Capability
      Brown and the eighteenth-century English landscape* (Chichester, 1999).

3.   Hertfordshire Gardens Trust and Williamson, *Parks and gardens of west
      Hertfordshire*, pp.30, 40–2.

4.   A. Young, *General view of the agriculture of Hertfordshire* (London, 1804),
      p.147.

5.   W.S. Lewis (ed.) *Horace Walpole's correspondence* (New Haven, 1941), pp.ix,
      285, letter to George Montague 4 July 1760, cited in Hertfordshire Gardens
      Trust and Williamson, *Parks and gardens of west Hertfordshire*, p.42.

6. T. Whateley, *Observations on modern gardening* (London, 1771), pp.5–6.

7. Hertfordshire Gardens Trust and Williamson, *Parks and gardens of west Hertfordshire*, pp.42–4.

8. N. Pevsner and B. Cherry, *The buildings of England: Hertfordshire* (Harmondsworth, 1992), p.253.

9. Hertfordshire Gardens Trust and Williamson, *Parks and gardens of west Hertfordshire*, pp.44–5.

10. Panshanger Papers (HALS D/EP 61/7).

11. H. Prince, 'The changing landscape of Panshanger', *East Hertfordshire Archaeological Society Transactions*, 14 (1959), pp.42–58.

12. Hertfordshire Gardens Trust and Bisgrove, *Hertfordshire gardens*, p.16; Younsbury Park Plan, c.1770 (HALS DE/A2845).

13. *VCH Hertfordshire*, vol. 3, p.358.

14. Turner, *Capability Brown*, pp.177–8.

15. *Ibid.*, p.178.

16. *Ibid.*, p.182.

17. S.R. (Sarah Rutherford), 'The Hoo, Kimpton', English Heritage unpublished report (1999) (HALS).

18. W. Le Hardy (ed.), *Calendar to the sessions books and other sessions records 1752–99*, Hertfordshire County Records, vol. 8 (Hertford, 1935).

19. D. Stroud, *Capability Brown*, 2nd edn. (London, 1975), pp.8–9, 245.

20. Pevsner and Cherry, *Hertfordshire*, p.271.

21. J.E. Cussans, *History of Hertfordshire*, W. Branch Johnson (ed.) (Hertford, 1972, first published 1870–81), *Hundred of Braughing I*, p.80.

22. D.A. Brown, 'Nathaniel Richmond (1724–1784) gentleman improver', (PhD thesis, Univ. East Anglia, 2000).

23. B. Howlett, *Hitchin Priory Park: the history of a landscape park and gardens* (Hitchin, 2004), pp.25–38.

24. Hertfordshire Gardens Trust and Williamson, *Parks and gardens of west Hertfordshire*, p.46, citing the receipt at Drummonds Bank, London DR/427/49.

25. Brown, 'Nathaniel Richmond'.

26. *Ibid.*

27. Jones, Hertfordshire in *The Gentleman's Magazine*, p.74.

28. Brown, 'Nathaniel Richmond'; N. King, *The Grimstons of Gorhambury* (Chichester, 1984), p.57.

29. Young, *General view*, pp.146, 147.

30. Lamer plan case (HALS 803236).

31. Brown, 'Nathaniel Richmond'; R. Beament, 'Lamer House and park, Wheathampstead' Report for the Hertfordshire Gardens Trust (2004), pp.16–25.

32. F. Cowell, 'Richard Woods (?1716–93): a preliminary account', Part I, Garden History, 14 (1986), pp.85–119, Part II, Garden History, 15 (1987), pp.19–54, Part III, Garden History, 15 (1987), pp.115–35. Most of the biographical details are in Part I, pp.85–7.

33. E. Gatland, 'Richard Woods in Hertfordshire' in Rowe, Hertfordshire garden history, pp.110–13; Cowell, 'Richard Woods' Part I, p.102; 'Plan of the Manor and Lands of Newsells', 1788 (HALS DE/Ry P3).

34. A. Young, A six month tour through the north of England (London, 1771), vol. I, pp.17, 82, 132–3, 260; vol. II, pp.73, 300–12, 430–5; vol. III, pp.1, 280, 286–96, 325–7.

35. W. Angus, Seats of the nobility and gentry in Great Britain and Wales (London, 1787).

36. D. Cecil, The young Melbourne (London, 1939), p.28.

37. Hertfordshire Gardens Trust and Williamson, Parks and gardens of west Hertfordshire, p.46.

38. H.M. Colvin, A biographical dictionary of British architects, 2nd edn. (London, 1978), p.817.

39. Hertfordshire Gardens Trust and Williamson, Parks and gardens of west Hertfordshire, p.46, citing D.C. Webb, Observations and remarks during four excursions made to various parts of Great Britain... in 1810 and 1811 (London, 1812), pp.162–7 and T. Baskerville, 'Sketches' (BL Add. Mss 9063.f.224).

40. Branch Johnson, Memorandoms, p.22. 'Bayfordbury Record Book', presented to the John Innes Horticultural Institution by Lady Clinton Baker in 1946. The bulk of the record was compiled in 1865 from notes derived from the following sources: 1759–71 from a memorandum book in the handwriting of William Baker; 1772–1803 from the written statements of John McKenzie, who superintended the several works detailed; 1803–21 from notes written by Rev. R. Baker, from scattered notes written by W. Baker jun. and from notes made at the time the plantations were made; 1822–30 no notes seem to have been preserved; 1830–4 from notes taken by Mr Lewis; 1834–65 from written statements taken at the time by John Slowe, who superintended the several alterations and works detailed for W.R. Baker Esq.

41. Hertfordshire Gardens Trust and Bisgrove, Hertfordshire Gardens, p.11.

42. VCH Hertfordshire, vol. 2, p.457.

43. Hertfordshire Gardens Trust and Williamson, Parks and gardens of west Hertfordshire, pp.48–9.

44. S. Switzer, Ichnographia rustica, 2nd edition (London, 1742), an appendix to vol. 3, pp.8–10; D. Jacques, Georgian gardens: the reign of nature (London, 1983), pp.23–5.

45. Whateley, *Observations*, pp.4–7.

46. W. Watts, *The seats of the nobility and gentry* (London, 1779), plate LIII.

47. P. Laxton, 'The geodetic and topographical evaluation of English county maps, 1740–1840', *Cartographic Journal*, 13 (1976), pp.37–54.

48. Hodson, *Printed maps*, p.57.

49. J.T. Coppock, 'Maps as sources for the study of land use in the past', *Imago Mundi*, 22 (1968), pp.37–49, esp. pp.42–4; H.C. Prince, 'The changing rural landscape', in G.E. Mingay (ed.), *The agrarian history of England and Wales*. Vol. VI 1750–1850 (Cambridge, 1989), pp.34, 36, 68.

50. P. Laxton, *John Rocque's map of Berkshire, 1761* (Lympne, 1973), Introduction.

51. Ashridge Estate Survey 1762 (HALS AH 2770), mentioned in Hertfordshire Gardens Trust and Williamson, *Parks and gardens of west Hertfordshire*, pp.18–9, 44–5, and also in B. Cowell, 'The Commons Preservation Society and the campaign for Berkhamsted Common 1866–70', *Rural History*, 13 (2002), pp.150, 152.

52. Young, *General view*, p.133.

53. Brocket Hall Account Books 1780–1821 (HALS DE/Lb 63829).

54. Young, *General view*, pp.186–93, 212–5.

55. Munsche, *Gentlemen and poachers*, pp.8–27.

56. C.T. Part, 'Sport, ancient and modern', in *VCH Hertfordshire*, vol. 1 (London, 1902), pp.359–60.

57. T. Williamson, *Polite landscapes: gardens and society in eighteenth-century England* (Stroud, 1995), p.134.

58. D.J.W. Sayer, 'The oak and the navy', *Quarterly Journal of Forestry*, 86 (1992), pp.40–4; E. Wade, *A proposal for improving and adorning the island of Great Britain: for the maintenance of our navy and shipping* (London, 1755); W. Hanbury, *An essay on planting and a scheme for making it conducive to the glory of God and the advantage of society* (Oxford, 1758).

59. W. Branch Johnson, *The Carrington diary 1797–1810* (London, 1956), p.85.

60. Jones, *Hertfordshire in The Gentleman's Magazine*, p.123.

61. Brocket Hall Account Books 1773–8, 1780–1821, 1837–45 (HALS DE/Lb 63828–33).

62. Beechwood, various 18th-century accounts (HALS DE/By 15685–97).

63. Great Gaddesden, Accounts of the Estate of Thomas Halsey, 1788 (HALS 14860–9).

64. HALS D/EH1 E1.

65. Knebworth, Lytton Papers 1768 (HALS DE/K).

66. H. Repton, *Observations on the theory and practice of landscape gardening* (London, 1803), pp.10–11.

67. S. Daniels, *Humphry Repton: landscape gardening and the geography of Georgian England* (New Haven and London, 1999), pp.1–25; also D. Stroud, *Humphry Repton* (London, 1962).

68. Notes on Repton's works in Hertfordshire are to be found in G. Carter, P. Goode and K. Laurie, *Humphry Repton landscape gardener 1752–1818* (Norwich, 1982), *Gazetteer* p.154; specific comments in Beament, 'Lamer House and park', pp.20–9.

69. *VCH Hertfordshire*, vol. 4, p.80.

70. W. Peacock, *The polite repository* (London, 1790–1809), 'Plates engraved from drawings of H. Repton of scenery improving under his direction'.

71. H. Repton, 'Tewin Water Red Book' 1799 (HALS D/Z42.Z1).

72. G.H. Moodey, 'Repton's work at Tewin Water', *East Hertfordshire Archaeological Society Newsletter*, 8 (1957).

73. The following account is based on Prince, 'Changing landscape of Panshanger', where details of estate records are cited.

74. Cowper MSS (HALS D/EP A18).

75. H. Repton, 'Panshanger Red Book', 1800 (HALS D/EP/P21A).

76. E. Johnson, Survey of Earl Cowper's estates in Hertfordshire, 1809 (HALS D/EP/P33).

77. Pevsner and Cherry, *Hertfordshire*, p.269.

78. Repton, *Observations*, p.78.

79. J. Britton, *The history and description of Cassiobury Park* (London, 1837).

80. J. Hassell, *A tour of the Grand Junction Canal* (London, 1819), p.21.

81. A. Fletcher, 'Notes on Repton's Red Book for New Barnes, 1802', unpublished report for Hertfordshire Gardens Trust.

82. B. Dix, 'Wall Hall, Aldenham, Archaeology', for Hertfordshire County Council Sites and Monuments Record (2000).

83. A. Farrington, *The records of the East India College, Haileybury and other institutions* (London, 1976), pp.61–7; R.G.C. Desmond, 'A Repton garden at Haileybury', *Garden History*, 6 (1978), pp.16–19.

84. H. Repton, *Fragments on the theory and practice of landscape gardening* (London, 1816), p.140.

85. H. Repton, *Sketches and hints on landscape gardening* (London, 1795); Repton, *Observations*; Repton, *Fragments*.

86. Repton, *Sketches and hints*, p.81.

87. R.P. Knight, *The landscape: a didactic poem in three books, addressed to Uvedale Price* (London, 1794), p.11.

88. T. Love Peacock, *Headlong Hall* (London, 1816).

89. Repton, *Observations*, p.94.

90. W. Marshall, *Planting and rural ornament* (London, 1796), vol. I, p.47.

91. C. Watkins and B. Cowell, *Letters of Uvedale Price*, Walpole Society, 68 (2006), p.310; Britton, *History of Cassiobury*, p.45.

92. U. Price, *Essays on the picturesque* (London, 1810), vol. II, p.246.

93. Repton, *Sketches and hints*, p.45.

94. Daniels, *Humphry Repton*, p.105.

95. J. Appleton, 'Some thoughts on the geography of the picturesque', *Journal of Garden History*, 6 (1986), pp.270–91.

96. E.W. Brayley and J. Britton, *The beauties of England and Wales* (London, 1808), vol. VII, p.122; later references at pp.145, 149, 203, 230, 266.

97. K. Harwood, 'Some Hertfordshire nabobs' in Rowe, *Hertfordshire garden history*, pp.62–3, 67–8.

98. BL Maps C:\Program Files\OS Drawings\OSD jpgs.

99. Y. Hodson, *Ordnance surveyors' drawings 1789–c.1840* (Reading, 1989), p.28.

100. *Ibid.*, p.27.

101. On the Ordnance Survey drawings (1799–1812) palings were represented at Albury Hall, Almshoe Bury, Ashridge Pk, Aspenden, Aston Pl, Ayot St Lawrence Pl, Balls Pk, Bayfordbury, Bedwell Pk, Beechwood, Briggens, Brocket, Broxbourne Bury, Cassiobury, Clothall Bury, Codicote Lo, Cokenhatch, Dyrham Pk, Gorhambury, Hatfield, Hexton Ho, High Cannons, Hitchin Priory, Julians, Kings Walden Bury, Kimpton Hoo, Kitwells, Knebworth, Knights Hall, Lamers, Lockleys, Millwards Pk, Moor Pk, Newsells, North Mymms, Offley Pl, Panshanger, Pishiobury, Ponsbourne, Popes, Porters, Putteridge Bury, Sacombe Pk, St Pauls Walden Bury, Stagenhoe, Tewin Water, Totteridge Pk, Tring Pk, Ware Pk, Watton Woodhall and Wyddial.

102. D. Paterson, *A new and accurate description of all the direct and principal cross roads in England and Wales* (London, 1808), pp.523–6; E. Pawson, *Transport and economy: the turnpike roads of eighteenth-century Britain* (London, 1977), pp.289–92; Munby, *Hertfordshire landscape*, pp.201–6.

103. W. Le Hardy and G.L. Reckett (eds.), *Calendar to the sessions books 1799 to 1833*, Hertfordshire County Records, vol. IX (Hertford, 1939), pp.537–66; Poll for the knights of the shire for the county of Hertford, 11-12 February 1805 (HALS, Gerish Collection).

104. *Census of population, 1801: enumeration* (Parl. Paper 1802). In descending order of size, the other places were: Hertford, 3,360; St Albans with St Stephen, 3,177; Cheshunt, 3,173; Hitchin, 3,161; Rickmansworth, 2,975; Ware, 2,950; Hemel Hempstead, 2,722; Hatfield, 2,442; Bishops Stortford, 2,305; and Tring, 2,156.

105. W.G. Rawlinson, *Turner's Liber Studiorum: a description and catalogue* (London, 1878), pp.iv–v.

106. Stone and Stone, *An open elite?*, citing Bodleian Library, Gough collection: Hertfordshire, interleaved Salmon, Hertfordshire, pp.60–1.

107. Harwood, 'Some Hertfordshire nabobs', pp.49–77. Parks acquired by men associated with the East India Company included Ayot St Lawrence, Balls Park, Broxbournebury, Cassiobury, Colney Park, Gobions, Haileybury, Haresfoot, Kings Walden Bury, Little Grove, Marshalswick, Moor Park, Muffets, Ponsbourne, Sacombe Park, Totteridge, Tyttenhanger, Wall Hall, Woodhall Park, Wormleybury, Youngsbury.

108. W.G.J. Kuiters, 'Rumbold, Sir Thomas (1736–91)', in *Oxford Dictionary of National Biography* (Oxford, 2004), vol. 48, pp.112–4.

109. P.J. Marshall, 'Benfield, Paul (1741–1810)', in *Oxford Dictionary of National Biography* (Oxford, 2004), vol. 5, pp.73–4.

110. L.S. Sutherland, *The East India Company in eighteenth-century politics* (Oxford, 1952), pp.49–80; P.J. Marshall, 'Sulivan, Laurence (c.1713–86)', in *Oxford Dictionary of National Biography* (Oxford, 2004), vol. 53, pp.294–5.

111. Stone and Stone, *An open elite?*, p.357.

112. *Ibid.*, pp.166–8.

113. Howlett, *Hitchin Priory Park*, pp.11–45.

114. Jones, Hertfordshire in *The Gentleman's Magazine*, pp.138–42.

115. B. Cowell, 'Patrician landscapes, plebeian cultures: parks and society in two English counties c.1750–1850', (PhD thesis, Nottingham Univ., 1998), pp.184–5. The parks where highways and footpaths were closed, with dates of closure, were: Gaddesden Place, 1767; Camfield Place, 1768; The Grove, 1768; Hitchin Priory, 1772; Porters, 1773; Hatfield, 1781; Bayfordbury, 1787; Albury Hall, 1788; Totteridge Park, 1789; Digswell House, 1791 and 1810; Theobalds Park, 1792; High Cannons, 1792 and 1807; Tewin Water, 1800; Hunsdon House, 1802; Ware Park, 1803; Edge Grove, 1803; Youngsbury, 1804; Hamels, 1808; Panshanger, 1810; and Kimpton Hoo, 1811.

116. Jones, Hertfordshire in *The Gentleman's Magazine*, p.114.

117. W.J. Hardy, *Notes and extracts from the sessions rolls, 1699 to 1850*, Hertford County Records, vol. 2 (Hertford, 1905), pp.169–71. In Ansell's deposition, the gamekeeper's name is spelled 'Dynes'; in the sessions record (n. 118, below) he is named 'Dines'.

118. Le Hardy, *Calendar to the sessions books 1752–99*, pp.398, 407.

119. Cowell, 'Berkhamsted Common', p.151.

120. Le Hardy, *Calendar to the sessions books 1752–99*, pp.311–12, 421.

121. Branch Johnson, *Carrington diary*, pp.158–9.

122. J.G. Dony, *A history of the straw hat industry* (Luton, 1942).

123. Young, *General view*, pp.221–5.

124. *VCH Hertfordshire*, vol. 4, p.218.

125. Jones, *Hertfordshire in The Gentleman's Magazine*, pp.158, 167, 170.

126. Le Hardy, *Calendar to the sessions books 1752–99*, pp.205–6.

127. 'Deed of gift from Sir Lyonel Lyde, Bart., and his sister, Mary Lyde, to the rector and churchwarden of the parish of Ayot St Lawrence' (HALS D/EX 809/1).

128. Jones, *Hertfordshire in The Gentleman's Magazine*, pp.41–2.

129. 'Harvest Home notes', Chauncy papers. (HALS D/E/Cy 1 F8).

130. R.L. Hine, *Hitchin worthies: four centuries of English life* (Hitchin, 1932, reprint 1974), p.328n.

Chapter VI

Parks in the Nineteenth Century

A T THE BEGINNING OF THE NINETEENTH CENTURY, country houses stood proudly in the midst of spacious parks, outward and visible symbols of the property, power and prestige enjoyed by landed families. The number and size of parks in Hertfordshire increased in the first two decades of the century but the appearance of peace and prosperity was an illusion for many owners, who faced serious economic and political problems. After 1815, owners of parks had to cope with falling returns from agriculture, rising unemployment, widespread distress among the labouring poor and violent clashes with poachers who raided their woods and plantations. At a national level, country landowners were unable to provide effective government for growing industrial towns. The long-term outlook for maintaining parks was not encouraging. Contrary to expectations, however, some parks continued to expand through the nineteenth century by adding to plantations; many were redesigned in a variety of styles; others were newly created later in the century. This chapter examines the complex interrelations between the development of parks and economic, social and political changes.

In 1816, agriculture sank into a depression as grain prices and livestock prices tumbled to less than half the levels attained during the years of wartime scarcity. Increased output from an enlarged area under cultivation aided by improved methods of farming resulted in disastrous falls in farmers' incomes. In Hertfordshire, farmers sought to reduce labour costs by employing fewer hands and cutting wages from about 10 shillings per week in 1815 to under 9 shillings in 1819.[1] Landowners sitting in parliament pushed through the Corn Law in 1815, which prohibited the import of foreign wheat until the price reached 80 shillings per quarter. To protect barley growers and dairy farmers, duties on imported malt, butter and cheese were raised. These measures had little effect on the market but angered many people, who saw landed aristocrats fending for themselves at the expense of the poor and hungry.

The depression occurred at a time when thousands of men were discharged from the navy, army and militia.[2] In addition to this sudden influx of young men seeking work, the population of Hertfordshire began to increase at an unprecedented rate. Almost all rural parishes recorded decennial increases in population in successive censuses from 1811 to 1841.[3] In order to provide relief for large numbers of unemployed, as well as their dependants, orphans, the old and the infirm, local poor rates increased by 38 per cent between 1803 and 1815 and increased by a further 16 per cent in the next three years. After 1818, poor rates were lowered as wheat prices fell but rose again in the years leading up to the new poor law of 1834. After that they declined sharply.[4] The burdens of poor rates and national taxes, mostly in the form of customs and excise duties on consumer goods, fell most heavily on farmers. Many appealed to their landlords, generally without success, for rent remissions; some slid into arrears; others defaulted on payments of tithes.

Rev. Thomas Newcome, rector of Shenley, owned a small park and a small agricultural estate. In 1822, he noted in his diary losses of tithe income through making allowances to farmers of 5, 10 or 15 per cent. In December 1822, the principal farmers in Shenley demanded further reductions of 45 per cent and even the gentry expected allowances of 10 or 15 per cent. In the same year, some parishioners attempted to deduct poor rates from Newcome's tithes. Adding to his trials, the tax collector demanded four guineas' excise duty on four horses. This the rector refused to pay, on the grounds that the horses were used for husbandry. For the future, he decided to employ a bailiff to collect tithes and deal with rates and taxes.[5] In the

1820s, the effects of the depression spread beyond agriculture, engulf-ing banks and other businesses. Thomas Newcome lost money when Messrs Chambers' bank in Marylebone went bankrupt in 1824. He began to borrow money in 1831 and eighteen years later he was still £1300 in debt.[6] In 1873, Newcome's two sons, Henry and Edward Newcome, owned respectively 50 and 39 acres in Shenley, all that remained of the paternal estate.

The labouring poor bore the brunt of the hardship. Expenditure on poor relief was lowest at those times and in those places where work was most difficult to find. Faced with rising numbers of unem-ployed, overseers of the poor applied to magistrates for orders to remove claimants who were not settled in their parishes. The number of removal orders issued in Hertfordshire peaked between 1815 and 1834, in which period over 1000 people were removed. After the passing of the new poor law which ordered the confinement of pau-pers in workhouses, compulsory removals tailed off rapidly.[7] Labourers living in arable districts in the north and east of Hertfordshire suffered the most severe distress, particularly in winter, when there was little work for them. In 1822, William Cobbett described the high land at Royston, on the border of Cambridgeshire, as having 'a hungry soil', which 'bears wheat sometimes'.[8] At this time, in Royston and Hinxworth, each farmer and landowner was required to find work for a number of unemployed labourers propor-tional to the size of the farm,[9] an arrangement that was costly for farmers and demoralising for regular wage-earners, who were com-pelled to work alongside paupers. In the south of the county, in areas of mixed arable and pastoral farming — for example, at Hatfield, Welwyn, Bayford and Little Berkhamsted — no poor relief was given to able-bodied unemployed men. Ignoring strong opposition from parish vestries, landowners appointed overseers and workhouse mas-ters from outside these parishes. At Hatfield, the new overseer brought in by the Marquess of Salisbury had been a pay sergeant in the Coldstream Guards; he kept accurate accounts and he and his wife managed the workhouse firmly and kept the place clean and tidy.[10] In this parish, those who were out of work had little choice but to leave and, from 1815 to 1834, seven families were removed compulsorily. The west of the county, from Redbourn through Hemel Hempstead to Chesham, was praised by Cobbett in 1822 as 'the very best corn land we have in England' and, in addition, some of the finest oaks, ashes and beeches grew in the hedges. The district was notable for its labourers being well-housed, their gardens neatly kept and productive, and children better clad, better fed and cleaner, than elsewhere.[11] Here, labourers' wages were higher than average for the county and overseers of the poor were diligent in keeping the rates down; no fewer than seventeen removal orders were issued in Redbourn, Hemel Hempstead and Bovingdon between 1815 and 1834.[12]

During a period in which magistrates were administering poor relief with deliberate harshness, labourers were charged with an increasing number of offences against parks, woods and game. Quarter sessions records list a continuous rise in prosecutions for poaching from 1816, reaching a peak in 1832. Almost all were local labourers accused of taking pheasants and hares in nearby woods. Exceptionally, in 1827, four men from London, including two provision dealers and an auctioneer, were found guilty of shooting without gun licences at Kings Langley. Local labourers were also charged with breaking fences, stealing wood and fishing.[13] Serious offences were tried at Hertfordshire Assizes, such as the rare case of an attempt to kill and destroy a fallow deer in Totteridge Park. On a moonlit night in the early hours of 26 July 1807, two men broke into the park and their dog chased but failed to bring down a deer. The cries of the deer and the barking of the intruders' dog roused Edward Arrowsmith's dogs in the stable yard and the poachers fled towards the park pales. As they were climbing over, two watchmen, who had been observing them, seized the older man, Thomas Champion, and his dog; the other man escaped.[14] At the trial of 53-year-old Champion in 1808, Mr Arrowsmith's right to keep deer was called in question, but the accused was convicted of poaching at night and sentenced to be transported for seven years. Champion died before he was shipped to Australia.[15]

In the period from 1815 to 1835, young men, singly or in small groups, were tried at the assizes for poaching with guns; in some cases keepers had been shot at or beaten. In 1820, four young men from Watford, armed with guns, were caught poaching at night in Furze Field Wood, Abbots Langley, and in Juniper Hill Wood, where they assaulted the Earl of Clarendon's keepers. Each of them was sentenced to seven years' transportation. Almost all poaching offences were committed in parks and woods belonging to large landowners; among these were the Earl of Clarendon at The Grove; Samuel Smith at Watton; Sir Abraham Hume at Wormley; Nicolson Calvert at Hunsdon; Elizabeth Bulwer Lytton at Knebworth; the Earl of Essex at Cassiobury; Sir Anthony Paston Cooper at Hemel Hempstead; Earl Cowper at Panshanger; the Countess of Bridgwater at Ashridge; the Marquess of Salisbury at Essendon; and Lord Melbourne at Brocket.[16]

In 1830, when landowners, parsons, overseers of the poor and farmers in many parts of southern England were terrorised by letters signed by 'Captain Swing', and when mobs were breaking threshing machines, demanding higher wages and demonstrating against unemployment, Hertfordshire remained relatively calm. In December 1830, there were wage riots at Royston, Hinxworth, Baldock and Ickleford. Unknown incendiarists threatened to burn down paper mills at Hemel Hempstead and Chorley Wood and, at Standon, five stacks of corn and hay were set on fire.[17] James Goddard, the Standon arsonist, was a man of previously unblemished character, and the death sentence was commuted to transportation for life.[18] The judges and the home secretary were in no mood to be lenient.

Owners of parks made few attempts to regain the trust of villagers. In the war against poachers, two small concessions were granted. To prevent injury to innocent walkers and stray animals, the use of spring guns was made illegal in 1827. Foxhunting squires had an interest in removing these weapons since foxes, hounds and hunters themselves were in danger of being injured. And to regulate a traffic that previously had been banned, licences to deal in game were introduced in 1831, as it was calculated that keeping licensed dealers under surveillance was easier than searching randomly for illicit receivers of game. In the treatment of poverty, the new poor law of 1834 was much more oppressive than the old and many labouring people regarded it as a dereliction of a duty owed to them by their masters. The new workhouse regime was mean and punitive; an affront to the old and infirm, and cruel to children.

In 1832, landowners conceded a share in national government to wealthy townsmen, who gained a right to vote and be represented in parliament by members for new urban constituencies. Merchants, manufacturers and other men of property were given responsibility for reforming turbulent, populous towns, while an increased number of county MPs representing rural constituencies remained firmly under the control of large landowners. In an increasingly hostile social milieu, a few old landed families and a multitude of new rich in Hertfordshire enlarged their parks, pleasure grounds and tree planta-tions, and clergymen, military officers and London merchants created many small new parks. A tradesman's view of who was who in Hertfordshire was presented in Pigot's *Directory*, in which the county was divided into districts headed by market towns; under each town, businesses and services were classified as 'gentry', 'churches', 'schools', different professions, trades, and so on. Within these classes, it listed names of individuals in alphabetical order.[19] Distinctions of title and rank that had been paramount twenty years earlier were no longer obligatory, and the mingling of titled and untitled families was reflected in the ownership of parks. The highest nobility continued to hold the largest parks but gentry and clergy were competing with mercantile families for possession of small and medium-sized places. All new places were created by the new rich. A map of the county surveyed in 1820 and 1821 shows a larger number of parks and a larger area of parkland than ever before.

A. Bryant's map, 1821

A. Bryant produced the most elegant of all Hertfordshire's county maps.[20] It was engraved on four sheets at a scale of 1 in 42,240 or 1.5 inches to a mile, and an examination of the map indicates that it was surveyed independently of the work of the Ordnance surveyors; Bryant possibly distrusted the accuracy of the depiction of settlement features on Ordnance maps.[21] His prospectus claimed: 'The superior-ity in point of Accuracy and Authenticity which this Map will derive from its being carried on, step by step, from Actual Survey, will render it an unerring Standard for every local purpose', and pointedly remarked that 'more than fifty years [had] elapsed since the Publication of any Map of the County'.[22] At the time at which that was written, the Ordnance Survey had made drawings but had not yet published sheets covering the north of the county.

Little is known about Bryant. Donald Hodson calls him 'Andrew', but Bryant himself used only the initial 'A'. His dates of birth and death and details of his personal life are unknown. In 1820, he styled himself 'surveyor' at 27 Great Ormond Street, London, but he seems not to have carried out surveys for private clients, and the name 'A. Bryant' does not appear as a surveyor of enclosure maps, estate plans or other manuscript plans in the Hertfordshire Archives.[23] He was engaged continuously from 1820 to 1830 in making thirteen county maps, which were published mostly at a scale of 1 in 42,240 or 1.5 inches to a mile.[24] In publishing county maps, Bryant faced direct competition from Christopher Greenwood, who also planned to produce maps for all counties in England. Greenwood and his brother John succeeded in mapping thirty-three English and four Welsh counties, but ran out of money before completing the task.[25] Bryant gave up after publishing his thirteenth map in 1835.

Bryant sought the patronage of the nobility, gentry and clergy of Hertfordshire and was apparently successful, as his prospectus listed the names of 223 subscribers. All noble landowners were included in the list and no fewer than thirty-one clergy responded to Bryant's invitation; incomes of established incumbents had increased from the late eighteenth century up to 1815, and twenty-six clergymen sat as justices of the peace in 1821.[26] In addition to the clergy, the subscription list recorded the ranks of seventeen naval and military officers. In total, the list provided names of owners and residents for eighty-seven parks. Names of owners and residents at other parks have been drawn from county histories, topographies, biographies, diaries, a directory and a list of magistrates. None of the sources is entirely satisfactory,[27] but cross-referencing has enabled identifications to be confirmed or rejected. In the post-war years, many new names appeared as owners or residents of parks.

Bryant's top priority was the representation of seats. He fulfilled his promise that 'the Residences of the Nobility and Gentry will be handsomely displayed and ornamented, and Parks, Plantations, Pleasure Grounds, Waters, Woods, &c. clearly described and tastefully executed'.[28] Tracts of parkland and pleasure grounds were stippled and, on the folded and mounted copy of the map examined in the British Library, they were tinted green. Omitting gardens and grounds under fifteen acres in extent, 217 places have been abstracted and listed. Bryant made no attempt to differentiate parks enclosed by pales from other pleasure grounds and gardens, and used palings to delineate parts of park boundaries at fifty places.[29] Some places that kept herds of deer were shown as partly enclosed by walls, hedges and belt plantations. At Hexton House, High Canons, Julians, Lamer and Pishiobury, palings had disappeared and trees were planted in groves where pheasants could be reared. In the absence of defining lines of palings or sunk fences, parks in 1821 were characterised by their distinctive landscape features, which were neatly depicted: ornamental arrangements of trees, grass and water.

Roads were carefully delineated, toll bars were identified and distances from London were inscribed in miles. Approach drives in parks were clearly indicated. Fox coverts, symbolised by small triangles, were novel features on Bryant's map, demonstrating the rise of organised foxhunting in the early nineteenth century. On the northern edge of Enfield Chase, eight coverts were scattered through woods between Hoddesdon and Northaw: one was located in the centre of Millwards Park; four were situated around Bricket Wood; four lay in spinneys south of Panshanger; three were in Sherrards Park Wood and other woods near Brocket; four were in Whippendell Wood and woods west of Cassiobury; four were located in spinneys near Albury Hall. Eleven more were scattered across woods and spinneys around Stevenage, on the edge of Benington Park and in Knebworth Great Wood, Wymondley Bury Wood, Almshoe Bury and Box Wood. One lay in the north-east corner of the county in Scales Park Wood. This new sport was served in other ways: stables at Beechwood and Broxbourne Bury were enlarged; at Knebworth, a new court containing the stable block

continued on p173

Table 6.1 Parks in Hertfordshire in 1821

Park	Grid Reference	Owner	Acres
Abbots Langley Manor	093019	Sir Edmund Filmer	25
Albury Hall	427254	John Calvert MP	310
Albury House, Cheshunt	355022	John Jessop	15
Aldenham Abbey	138995	Adml Sir Charles Morice Pole MP	110
Aldenham Lodge, Radlett	167004	John Finch Mason	90
Aldenham Park	168965	Sarah and Anne Noyes	90
Alswick Hall, Buntingford	378295	John Archer Houblon	40
Amwell Bury, Ware	364128	Col Charles Brown	30
Ardeley Bury	301271	Gen. Sir John Murray Bt	240
Ash Park, Bovingdon	020030	Nathaniel Snell	50
Ashlyns, Berkhamsted	991067	James Smith	140
Ashridge, Lt Gaddesden	994121	John Egerton, 7th Earl Bridgwater	1,750
Aspenden Hall	352284	Sir Stephen Lushington Bt	120
Aston Bury	276217	Edmund Darby	20
Aston Place	271225	Mr Hudson	50
Ayot St Lawrence Place	195170	Mrs Levi Ames	260
Ayot St Peters Rectory	218149	Rev. Charles Chester	40
Balams, Redbourn	103134	John Hawkins	20
Baldock Place House	243337	John Izard Pryor	60
Balls Park, Hertford	335120	Lord John Townshend	50
Barkway Vicarage	382355	Hon. John William Peachey	15
Bartletts, Berkhamsted	998074	Mrs Sarah Pechell	90
Bayfordbury	315104	William Baker	440
Bayford Place	314088	William Baker	30
Bedwell Park, Essendon	277076	Sir Culling Smith Bt	160
Beechwood Park, Flamstead	045144	Sir John Saunders Sebright Bt MP	410
Benington Lordship	297236	Rev. John Peter Chesshyre	70
Benington Place	312235	Charles Montgomery Campbell	130
Berkhamsted Place	991088	Hon. Harriet and Charlotte Grimston	80
Birds Place, Essendon	273079	John Currie	130
Blakesware, Ware	405163	William Plumer MP	20
Bonningtons, Stanstead Abbots	408131	Edmond Calvert	60
Bovingdon Lodge	025032	Thomas Smith	15
Bragbury End, Aston	270209	John Green	15
Bramfield Place	295155	Lord Henry Stuart	30
Bramfield Rectory	290158	Rev. Edward Bourchier	20
Brickendon Bury	330105	George Gould Morgan	220

continued over

Table 6.1 Parks in Hertfordshire in 1821 *continued*

Park	Grid Reference	Owner	Acres
Briggens, Hunsdon	412112	James Taylor	90
Broadfield Hall, Cottered	324310	Rev. Thomas Sisson	100
Broad Oak End, Stapleford	307138	Samuel Smith MP	40
Brocket, Hatfield	214130	William Lamb, 2nd Viscount Melbourne	650
Brookmans Park, North Mimms	253048	Samuel Robert Gaussen	210
Broxbourne Bury	353072	Jacob Bosanquet	270
Bush Hall, Hatfield	239100	Sir Robert Chester	90
Bushey Grove	130975	David Haliburton	70
Bushey Hall	136951	Thomas Clutterbuck	50
Bushey Manor	129955	Gen. Frederick Nathaniel Walker	25
Bygrave Place	264360	James Cecil, Marquess of Salisbury	25
Callipers Hall, Chipperfield	051008	Donald Mackay	20
Camfield Place, Essendon	268069	Rev. William Browne	120
Carpenders Park, Watford	125934	Samuel Moody	40
Cassiobury, Watford	095972	George Capel, 5th Earl of Essex	1,350
Champneys, Wigginton	947086	W. Hammond	50
Chesfield Lodge, Graveley	247275	Edward Parkins	130
Cheshunt Great House	345027	Rev. Charles Mayo	70
Cheshunt Nunnery	369040	Thomas Artemidorus Russell	50
Cheshunt Park	347045	Mrs Cromwell	90
Cheverells, Flamstead	056155	Sir John Saunders Sebright Bt MP	35
Childwick Bury, St Michael	140102	Capt. Joshua Lomax	140
Chipperfield House	036021	Billingsley Cunningham	20
Chipperfield Manor	048013	John Parsley	100
Chorleywood House	037970	Edmund Morris	20
Claramont, Cheshunt	330020	Sir Gore Ouseley Bt	110
Clay Hall, Walkern	305250	John Horsey Waddington	30
Clothall Bury	281321	James Cecil, Marquess of Salisbury	30
Codicote Lodge	214183	Francis Sapte	90
Cokenhatch, Barkway	396361	Gen. Sir William Clinton	100
Coles Park, Westmill	368260	Thomas Greg	120
Colney House, London Colney	173030	George Anderson	200
Corner Hall, Hemel Hempstead	059060	Henry Campbell White	30
Corney Bury, Buntingford	357309	William Butt	260
Dane End House, Lt Munden	334220	Nathaniel Snell Chauncy	80
Delrow, Bushey	142974	Gen. Sir Hew Dalrymple Bt	45
Digswell House, Welwyn	250151	Hon. Edward Spencer Cowper MP	160

continued

Table 6.1 Parks in Hertfordshire in 1821 *continued*

Park	Grid Reference	Owner	Acres
Digswell Rectory, Welwyn	230145	Ven. John Watson	50
Dyrham Park, Borehamwood	223 985	John Trotter	160
Eastbury, Rickmansworth	101926	James Howard	25
Edge Grove, Aldenham	144989	John Thellusson, Lord Rendlesham	100
Epping House, Lt Berkhamsted	293068	Sir William Horne	20
Felden, Bovingdon	043047	Hon. Henry Watson	25
Gaddesden Hoo, Gt Gaddesden	032124	Henry Greene	60
Gaddesden Parsonage, Gt Gaddesden	051126	Edward Protheroe	90
Gaddesden Place, Gt Gaddesden	038111	Rev. John F. Moore Halsey	330
Gadebridge, Hemel Hempstead	049081	Sir Astley Paston Cooper Bt	190
Gilston Park	441129	William Plumer MP	480
Gobions Park, North Mimms	252039	Thomas Nash Kemble	200
Goldings, Waterford	311143	Eric Macay, 7th Lord Reay	80
Goldingtons, Sarratt	038984	Lewis Munn	60
Gorhambury, St Michael	113080	James Grimston, Earl of Verulam	630
Gt Hadham Lordship	430200	Bishop of London	100
Gt Hormead Bury	399296	Lt Col Henry Stables	40
Gt Hyde Hall, Sawbridgworth	496154	Adml Sir Thomas Williams	160
Green Elm, Lt Munden	330224	Nathaniel Snell Chauncy	35
Grove Park, Sarratt	082988	Thomas Villiers, Earl of Clarendon	210
Hacksters End, Berkhamsted	018073	William Littleboy	15
Hadham Park, Lt Hadham	461223	James Cecil, Marquess of Salisbury	15
Haileybury, Hertford Heath	358108	East India Company College	80
Hamels, Braughing	376247	Catherine Mellish	340
Haresfoot, Northchurch	985062	Thomas Dorrien	130
Harpsfield, Hatfield	205091	George Gape	20
Hartsbourne Manor, Bushey	143935	Sir B. Thompson Bt	20
Hatfield House Park	236084	James Cecil, Marquess Salisbury	1,100
Hatfield Rectory	217083	Rev. Francis Joseph Faithfull	70
Hertingfordbury	310121	William Baker	80
Hexton House	108306	William Young	280
High Ash, Chorleywood	019948	Richard Taylor	50
High Canons Park, Ridge	209990	Enoch Durant	200
High Down, Pirton	144305	Emilius Delme-Radcliffe	25
High Elms, Leavesden	114019	John Ryler	60
Hilfield Lodge, Aldenham	153963	John Fam Timins	90
Hinxworth Place	238396	Robert Clutterbuck	25

continued over

Table 6.1 Parks in Hertfordshire in 1821 *continued*

Park	Grid Reference	Owner	Acres
Hitchin Priory	184286	Emilius Delme-Radcliffe	100
Hoo, Kimpton	187195	Thomas Brand, 20th Lord Dacre	330
Hunsdon House	420127	Nicolson Calvert MP	160
Ickleford House	180309	Thomas Cockayne	35
Ippolitts	197269	George Whittingstall	60
Julians, Rushden	307326	Adolphus Meetkerke	350
Kendalls Hall, Aldenham	173982	Capt. William Robert Phillimore	80
Kingshill, Northchurch	984069	Thomas Dorrien, jun.	40
Kings Walden Bury	161235	William Hale	260
Kitwells, Radlett	191994	Mrs Dorothea Tuite	80
Knebworth	231210	Mrs Elizabeth Bulwer Lytton	520
Knights Hall, Westmill	371256	Thomas Greg	40
Lamer House, Wheathamstead	181160	Sir Charles Benet Drake Garrard	220
Langleybury, Abbots Langley	077001	Rev. Sir John Filmer Bt	30
Laurel Lodge, Lt Bushey	146946	G. Isherwood	20
Lawrence End, Kimpton	142197	Maj. John Greenstreet	50
Lilley Lodge	112278	John Sowerby	60
Lilley Park	114263	John Sowerby	35
Lilley Rectory	118264	Rev. William Wade	15
Little Court, Buntingford	364293	Capt. Henry Harman Young	20
Lt Offley	129285	Richard Sheppard	25
Lt Munden, Bricket Wood	137008	Roger Parker	15
Lockers Park, Hemel Hempstead	049073	Ebenezer John Collett MP	50
Lockleys, Welwyn	237159	Sir George Shee Bt	190
Mackerye End, Wheathamstead	157157	Sir Charles Benet Drake Garrard	30
Maddocks House, Wareside	396146	George Proctor	200
Marchmont House, Hemel Hempstead	053086	Thomas Abbot Green	50
Marden Hill, Tewin	279140	Claude George Thornton	140
Markyate Cell	057174	Joseph Howell	210
Meesden Bury	440328	Rev. Armytage Gaussen	50
Merry Hill House, Bushey	138942	Sarah Noyes	20
Micklefield Hall, Rickmansworth	053974	Emmott Skidmore	110
Millwards Park, Hatfield	236065	James Cecil, Marquess of Salisbury	70
Moor Park, Rickmansworth	075933	Robert Williams MP	610
Moor Place, Much Hadham	423187	James Gordon	180
Mount Clements, Bushey	150938	Capt. Patterson	15
Munden House, Gt Munden	136003	Nathaniel Snell	50

continued

Table 6.1 Parks in Hertfordshire in 1821 *continued*

Park	Grid Reference	Owner	Acres
Nascot Fm, Watford	106968	Hon. Mrs Grey	40
Netherfield House, Stanstead Abbots	393115	William Henry Feilde	40
New Barns, St Peters	156054	Joseph Timperon	100
New Organ Hall, Radlett	167997	Earl of Portsmouth	110
Newsells, Barkway	386367	John Peachey, 2nd Lord Selsey	180
Node, Codicote	217202	Hon. Mary Leeson	60
North Mymms Park	217042	Henry Browne	500
Offley Holes	168263	Rev. Lynch Burroughs	50
Offley Place	145272	Rev. Lynch Burroughs	200
Offley Vicarage	137277	Rev. Thelwell Salusbury	30
Owles, Layston	377288	John Archer Houblon	20
Panshanger	290132	Peter Leopold, 5th Earl Cowper	560
Pishiobury, Sawbridgeworth	480134	Rowland Alston	260
Poles, Thundridge	352163	Robert Hanbury	100
Ponsbourne, Hatfield	304054	Jacob Hans Busk	230
Porters, Shenley	182008	Col Luke White	360
Potterells, North Mimms	236046	Justinian Casamajor	180
Preston Castle	175251	Thomas Harwood Darton	50
Putteridge Bury, Lilley	118245	John Sowerby	120
Radwell Hall	225375	Rev. Wollaston Pym	45
Rawdon House, Hoddesdon	373084	Mrs Ann Wood	30
Redheath, Watford	066971	John Finch	80
Rickmansworth Bury	061945	Matthew Wiggins	25
Rickmansworth Park	057955	John Walker	250
Rossway, Northchurch	960073	Robert Sutton	90
Rothamsted, Harpenden	125131	John Bennet Lawes	130
Russells Farm, Watford	091995	Rev. Hon. William Capel	100
Sacombe Park	339190	George Caswall	350
St Johns Lodge, Welwyn	229169	William Blake	130
St Pauls Walden Bury	187217	Thomas Bowes, 11th Earl Strathmore	180
Sandridge Lodge	166087	George Sullivan Marten	100
Sarratt Hall	044001	Ralph Day	15
Serge Hill House, Bedmond	107042	Samuel Reynolds Solly	30
Shenley Hill	194010	Thomas Bradbury Winter	60
Shenley Rectory	197013	Rev. Thomas Newcome	30
Shephall Bury, Stevenage	256229	Samuel Unwin Heathcote	40
Stagenhoe, St Pauls Walden	185227	Robert Thornton Heysham	140

continued over

Table 6.1 Parks in Hertfordshire in 1821 *continued*

Park	Grid Reference	Owner	Acres
Stags End, Gt Gaddesden	069120	Robert S. Bassel	30
Standon Lordship	392214	William Plumer MP	25
Stanstead Bury, Stanstead Abbots	400111	Rev. Thomas Feilde	50
Stocks House, Aldbury	966133	James Adam Gordon	70
Tarling Park, Gilston	449116	Mr Turvin	35
Temple Dinsley, Preston	181248	Thomas Harwood	65
Tewin Water	255145	Henry Cowper	200
Theobalds Park, Cheshunt	345011	Henry Meux	240
Theobalds Square, Cheshunt	355011	Elizabeth Frances Harman	80
Thorley Hall	476189	Edward Law, Lord Ellenborough	25
Tolmers, Cuffley	303048	Robert Taylor	110
Totteridge Park	233942	Mrs Louisa Arrowsmith	70
Totteridge Priory	247943	Frederick Holbrooke	25
Tring Park	926111	Giles Willis	320
Tyttenhanger House, Ridge	192047	Philip Yorke, Earl of Hardwicke	120
Walkern Rectory	292267	Rev. James Camper Wright	50
Ware Park	333144	John Hope Byde	260
Wellbury Hall, Offley	130285	Rev. Lynch Burroughs	60
Westbrook Hay, Bovingdon	025054	Rt Hon. Richard Ryder MP	180
White Barns, Furneux Pelham	432290	John Halden	30
Widford Bury, Hunsdon	412158	William Parker Hammond	15
Widford Rectory	413157	Rev. Francis Thomas Hamond	30
Willian Bury	226304	William Wilshere	25
Woodcock Hill, Northchurch	974080	Alexander Manson	25
Woodhall Park, Watton	318189	Samuel Smith MP	50
Woodhill, Hatfield	266058	William Franks	80
Woodside Place, Hatfield	250069	John Church	20
Woolmers Park, Hertingfordbury	286103	Sir Gore Ouseley Bt	290
Wormley Bury	355059	Sir Abraham Hume Bt	190
Wyddial Hall	373317	John Thomas Ellis MP	150
Wynches, Much Hadham	421176	W. Anthony	140
Youngsbury, Standon	378179	Daniel Giles	140

Sources: *Map of the county of Hertford from an actual survey by A. Bryant in the years 1820 & 1821* (BL Maps C.23.a.6). Most names of owners are taken from a List of subscribers, and their respective seats published with Bryant's map (HALS Wilshere Family Archives 63787). Additional names are identified in a subscription list for R. Clutterbuck, *The history and antiquities of the county of Hertford* (London, 1815); J.E. Cussans, *History of Hertfordshire* (Hertford, 1870–81); J.P. Neale, *Views of the seats of noblemen and gentlemen in England, Wales, Scotland and Ireland* (London, 1819) — vol. II illustrates Hertfordshire; *VCH Hertfordshire* (London, 1902–14); Pigot and Co., *Royal, national and commercial directory and topography of the county of Hertfordshire* (London, 1839); G.E.C., *Complete peerage*; R.G. Thorne, *House of Commons 1790–1820* (London, 1986); W. Le Hardy and G.L. Reckitt, *Calendar to the sessions books 1799 to 1833*, Hertfordshire County Records, vol. 9 (Hertford, 1939), pp.537–45 lists justices of the peace.

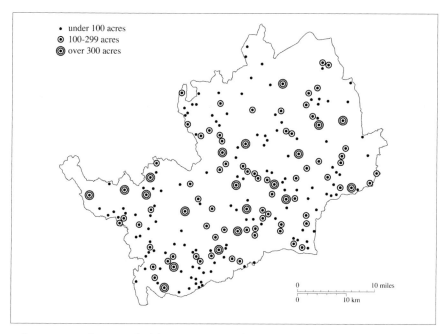

Figure 6.1: Parks in Hertfordshire in 1821. Two hundred and seventeen parks of different sizes have been located. Full details are listed in Table 6.1. Based on A. Bryant, Map of the county of Hertford from an actual survey, *1821. Drawn in the Geography Department, UCL*

continued from p166

was built in 1813 and, at Childwick Bury, Joshua Lomax built a new stable block before 1840.[30] Kennels for the Hatfield Hunt were furnished by the intrepid huntress, Lady Mary Emilia, Marchioness of Salisbury, who was master from 1793 until 1828. Foxhounds for Mr Calvert's Hunt were first accommodated at Albury Hall and, in 1802, the hunt was renamed the Puckeridge when Sampson Hanbury built new kennels at that place. In the 1830s, the Old Berkeley Hunt kept a pack of hounds at Parsonage Farm, Rickmansworth, while John Chesshyre kept harriers for hare coursing at Benington and Emilius Delme-Radcliffe kept both harriers and staghounds at Hitchin Priory.[31]

The total area occupied by 217 parks of more than fifteen acres in Hertfordshire in 1821 was 29,335 acres. That was about 12,000 acres more than the comparable total for 1799–1812, an overall increase of 70 per cent from the earlier date (Figure 6.1). Part of that remarkably large increase may be attributed to a change in the

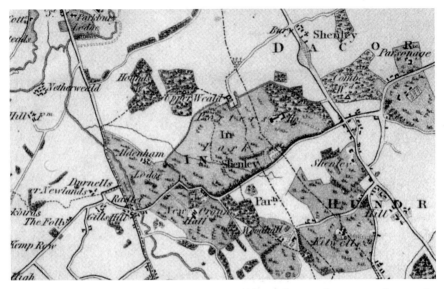

Figure 6.2: Parks around Shenley in 1821. Many villa residences were set in small areas of parkland. Detail from Bryant's Map of the county of Hertford. *Photograph by Matt Prince*

purpose of the maps: the Ordnance Survey maps were designed for military use, while Bryant's map was paid for by large landowners and other subscribers. It would be wrong to surmise that Bryant sought to flatter his patrons by showing their parks as larger than they actually were. Indeed, large ancient parks, belonging to those at the top of the subscription list, hardly expanded at all; it was the small parks and pleasure grounds, owned by non-subscribing new-comers, that showed the greatest increases in size. Freed from the constraint of an eighteenth-century concept of parkland as an enclosure, Bryant expressed a progressive nineteenth-century attitude, embracing a variety of styles, in discerning what constituted parkland. He recognised and mapped as small parks, gardens and pleasure grounds places where meadows had been transformed into lawns by planting trees that framed vistas or where distant prospects had been opened by grubbing up trees and hedgerows. He identified as gentlemen's residences houses that had been converted from manors or farmhouses by diverting public roads, putting up new facades or modernising interiors. It is significant that only two places still named 'farm', Russells Farm and Nascot Farm, near Cassiobury, were occupied by members of the old-established Capel family. Other former farms were pretentiously renamed 'Place' or 'Hall' or 'House'.

Out of these 217 parks, 128, more than half the total, were under 100 acres in size, and most of the 69 newly shown parks were small. A scatter of 7 new parks across south-west Hertfordshire, from Bovingdon, through Sarratt and Chipperfield to Chorleywood were all under 100 acres in size. A cluster of new parks between Berkhamsted and Northchurch, including Champneys, Kingshill, Rossway and Woodcock Hill, ranged in size from 25 to 140 acres. Similar clusters of new parks sprang up in the Lea valley between Cheshunt, Hoddesdon, Ware and Hertford. Other small parks appeared in the Colne valley around Shenley (Figure 6.2), Aldenham, Bushey, Watford and Rickmansworth. Oldfield described Boxmoor Hall, near Hemel Hempstead, as 'originally a Farm House increased to a little Villa by Mr Almon, once editor of the General Advertiser'.[32] Neale reported that Nicolson Calvert had 'judiciously restored' the whole of Hunsdon House 'in the castellated form of the original edifice', replacing eighteenth-century casements with mullioned windows.[33] At Ardeley Bury, a turret and battlements were added to the old manor house by its new owner, a retired general, and the much-altered Great House in Cheshunt was given a gothick face-lift by an incoming parson. Old rectories at Bramfield and Shenley were enlarged and surrounded by ornamental grounds; at Bishops Stortford, Church Manor House was one of the most extensive conversions of a parsonage.[34] Amwell Grove and a few other completely new villa residences were sited within newly laid-out gardens.[35] Some, such as Aldenham Abbey (formerly Wall Hall) and Preston Castle (formerly Hunsdon House, in Preston), were given new names with romantic associations. At this period, Hilfield Lodge, Aldenham, was known alternatively as Sly's Castle or Hilfield Castle. Bartletts (Berkhamsted Hall) and St John's Lodge (Danesbury) sounded upper-class and one new name, 'Tags End', was substituted in error for Stags End.

The landscape depicted on Bryant's map was still predominantly rural but woodlands were becoming more fragmented, heaths were fringed with houses and open fields were fast disappearing.

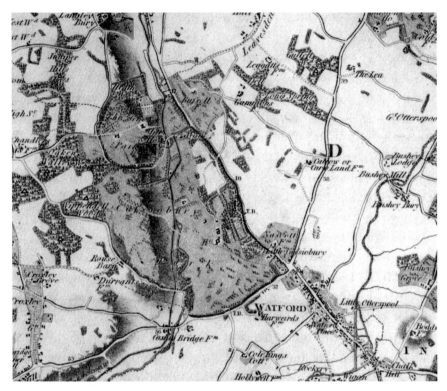

Figure 6.3: Cassiobury and adjoining parks in 1821. Cassiobury and the Grove occupied the whole of a quadrant north-west of Watford. Detail from Bryant's Map of the county of Hertford. *Photograph by Matt Prince*

Settlements were concentrated along lines of turnpike roads and waterways. Market towns were expanding and buildings were beginning to press against boundaries of parks such as Cassiobury, Hatfield and Hitchin Priory (Figure 6.3). Hertfordshire was ceasing to look like the exclusive domain of large landowners and beginning to look like countryside taken over by townsmen.

John Claudius Loudon

The death of Humphry Repton in 1818 marked the end of the age of extensive landscape gardening. Repton's successor as leader of taste was John Claudius Loudon (1783–1843), who called his style 'Gardenesque'. As early as 1812, Loudon drew plans for laying out gardens and pleasure grounds designed specifically for owners of small plots ranging in size from one to one hundred acres. His plans included flower gardens, kitchen gardens, conservatories, hothouses, formal terraces, parterres, straight canals, fountains, circular sunk fences and 'groves', which he defined as 'collections of trees on smooth surfaces without undergrowth'.[36] He considered geometrical layouts were especially suited to flat surfaces and he recommended constructing rockeries for alpine plants. The defining characteristic of the Gardenesque style was 'the display of the beauty of trees and other plants individually'.[37] Loudon appealed to plant collectors to create specialised rose gardens, herbaceous gardens, alpine gardens, American gardens, ferneries, shrubberies, arboreta and pineta. Ivy, creepers, araucarias, gingkos, magnolias, rhododendrons, azaleas, camellias, geraniums, petunias and many other colourful flowering plants were widely planted. A patriotic splash of red, white and blue emblazoned flower gardens and a luxuriance of evergreens darkened shrubberies and the walls of houses.

Loudon was a publicist and encyclopaedist, rather than a creative practitioner. His plans for flower gardens were modelled on Repton's later works at Cassiobury and Ashridge. He described visits to these places in the *Gardener's Magazine*. At Cassiobury, he remarked on the beauty of a flower garden in the Chinese style containing a conservatory in the form of a pagoda. He observed an extensive lawn with numerous flower beds planted with exotic trees and shrubs, including magnolias, rhododendrons and azaleas. This led towards a secluded valley lined with a rock garden. Passing through a grotto, the visitor entered a rose garden surrounded by a laurel hedge.[38] At Ashridge, Loudon admired the kitchen garden, under the care of T. Torbron from Kew, and a gothick conservatory near the house, but was disappointed that 'scarcely anything has been done to the grounds to render them a worthy accompaniment to such a splendid pile'.[39] In the fourth edition of his *Encyclopaedia of Gardening* (1826), Loudon wrote brief notes on twenty parks and gardens in Hertfordshire. He noted that Colney House had 'a well stocked kitchen garden' and praised Beechwood, Brocket and Hatfield for promoting scientific agriculture. He regarded trees as the greatest ornament and the most effective defence against bareness, remarking that parks such as Ashridge, Gorhambury, Beechwood, Colney

House, Tring and Watton Woodhall were well stocked with fine oaks and stately beeches. Hatfield contained 'some of the finest oak, ash, elm and other trees in the county', and Wormleybury was remarkable for 'new plants introduced from China and India'.[40]

A nephew of Rev. William Gilpin, writer on the Picturesque, William Sawrey Gilpin (1763–1843) turned from painting landscapes in watercolour to landscape gardening at the age of 58.[41] He enjoyed the patronage of Uvedale Price and his work was praised by Loudon. In Hertfordshire, he was involved in designing Cassiobury and, between 1825 and 1827, the Earl of Verulam called for his advice in developing the park and pleasure grounds at Gorhambury. Gilpin's principal contribution was:

> to recommend a sloping bank to be raised about four feet
> above the level of the lawn, at a short distance from the
> house, parallel with it; and upon this bank there is a broad
> terrace of nearly four hundred feet in length, the retaining
> wall of which forms a fence against the deer, while the
> varied masses of shrubs planted upon it unite it with the flat
> lawn beneath, and the whole forms a foreground to the
> scenery beyond. The terrace is connected by a flight of steps
> at each end, with the pleasure ground.[42]

The ground in front of the mansion at Gorhambury was covered by the 'dress lawn'. At a distance, below the terrace, lay Gilpin's Wood, screening the kitchen garden. Near the house, formality ruled; further away, nature reigned.

John Britton's backward-looking *History and Description of Cassiobury Park* glorified the great age and grandeur of woods in the upper park, to the west of the Gade. In particular, Britton admired the old beeches, some of which were 'of immense size and imposing aspect. The branches of a single beech spread over an area of 130 feet in diameter.'[43] Prince Puckler-Muskau, who toured through England in 1826, was captivated by the diverse novelties of Cassiobury but was dismayed by Hatfield, which he described as 'poor in works of art, and the park rich only in large avenues of oaks, and in rooks;

otherwise dreary, and without water, except a nasty green standing pool near the house'.[44] Loudon and Gilpin shared the progressive outlook of the German prince and the map-maker, Bryant, embracing a variety of styles and acknowledging the wishes of small proprietors.[45]

Railways and parks

The grandeur of early nineteenth-century parks in Hertfordshire belonged to an age of rural remoteness when they were jewels in an agrarian landscape. Visitors approached them at a slow pace by way of narrow, leafy lanes in horse and carriage. The novelist, Sir Walter Scott, travelling to stay for a few days with his kinsman, David Haliburton, at Bushey Grove in late May 1828, described his drive through Hertfordshire lanes, 'winding and turning among oaks and other large trees, just like pathways cut through a forest'.[46] In the course of his stay, Scott paid respectful visits to Moor Park, to The Grove and Cassiobury. The coming of the railway disrupted that leisurely scene. The earth was ripped open; unprecedented quantities of rock were moved; the volume of goods, the number of passengers and the speed at which they could be transported surpassed all previous records; the social and economic consequences were revolutionary. Railways transformed the environment in which parks were situated.

The first mainline railway to enter the county was planned to reduce the time taken to carry manufactured goods from the north by way of Birmingham to London. It would compete directly with the Grand Junction Canal. The proposal was fiercely resisted by the earls of Bridgwater, Clarendon and Essex, who were major shareholders in the canal and also owned land across which the railway would have to be built. Their opposition was partially abated by re-routing the line to pass half a mile east of Watford High Street, and then through a mile-long tunnel under Russell Farm, a park belonging to the Earl of Essex. At Berkhamsted, the line was drawn to lie out of sight of the Bridgwater estate. Other landowners sought compensation for threatened disturbance of their peace and quiet, for loss of visual amenity and for the cutting up of farms. The Old Berkeley Hunt protested that horse and hounds would be prevented from pursuing foxes over the tracks. One objector, Sir Astley Paston Cooper, owner of Gadebridge at Hemel Hempstead, complained: 'if this sort of thing be permitted to go on, you will, in a very few years, destroy the *noblesse*.'[47] As long as parliament remained unreformed, the landed interest was able to hold up the passage of the London and Birmingham Railway bill. It was finally passed in May 1833, at a high price. In addition to extortionate parliamentary and legal expenses, the company had to pay three times the original valuation for land.[48] When shares were issued in 1833, some noblemen and gentlemen swallowed their pride and subscribed 16 per cent of the capital. By 1837, the gentry had raised their holdings to 31 per cent of the total amount invested; merchants and tradesmen had bought 45 per cent, manufacturers 8 per cent, professions — including clergymen — 11 per cent, and women 5 per cent.[49]

Construction works for the railways were marvels of the modern world. They were new expressions of power and wealth, outshining parks, which appeared quaint and old-fashioned by comparison. John Bourne's drawings romanticised the awesome vastness of the cuttings, embankments and bridges, picturing teams of diminutive navvies at work in the middle distance. At Northchurch, a tunnel 345 yards in length and a two-and-a-half-mile long cutting were dug through the Chilterns. More than one million cubic yards of spoil were removed from the cutting, much of it being used to build a six-mile embankment north of Tring. The tunnel at Watford was over a mile long and its construction killed ten men when loose sand poured out of a fissure in the overlying chalk. The number of navvies employed by contractors was more than 12,000, frequently rising to nearly 20,000 to meet urgent schedules. Some men were recruited locally, which drained the pool of unemployed labourers. A few obtained permanent jobs as railway staff. The first section of the line to Boxmoor was opened in June 1837 and the whole length was completed in 1838.[50]

The London and Birmingham Railway had been opposed by an alliance of landowners and canal proprietors. The proposal to build a main line from London to York was obstructed by the joint forces of two railway companies, the London and North Western and the Midland Railway, but it enjoyed 'the hearty concurrence and support' of the major landowners.[51] The second Marquess of Salisbury signalled his approval by offering to build a Jacobean-style station at the entrance to Hatfield Park and the Lyttons donated land for a station to be built near Knebworth Park. The act authorising the Great Northern Railway was passed in 1846. Without delay, the contractors Peto and Betts began work from Peterborough to Werrington and Thomas Brassey embarked on the southern section to Kings Cross. Brassey spanned the Mimram valley at Digswell with a monumental viaduct, ninety feet high and 520 yards long, and removed half a million cubic yards of spoil from a cutting through the chalk at Hitchin. The first train ran into Kings Cross in 1852.

A third main line through Hertfordshire was proposed by the Midland Railway to extend its line from Bedford to a London terminus at St Pancras. The proposal was not contested by rival railway companies and was cautiously accepted by most landowners, and the act was passed in 1863. Costs of acquiring land in built-up areas of London and digging a long tunnel under Hampstead were exceptionally high, but there were few engineering difficulties in laying the track from Elstree to Harpenden. St Pancras was opened in 1868.

A fourth line, built by the Northern and Eastern Railway from Broxbourne, reached Bishops Stortford in 1842. Lord Braybrooke insisted that the track, on its way to Cambridge, be buried in two tunnels to preserve the views from his mansion at Audley End. Trains ran from Cambridge to Shoreditch in 1845 and to Liverpool Street after 1874.[52]

A few years after the excavators had finished their work, the bare slopes of cuttings were covered with vegetation and railways came to be accepted features in the landscape. Social and economic changes took longer to materialise. The gentry and clergy soon availed themselves of first-class travel facilities; some went to experience the poetic delights of the Lake District and explore the misty heights of wild Wales, while others began to stalk deer in the Scottish highlands and shoot grouse on moors in the Pennines and southern uplands in Scotland. Yet others made excursions to distant race meetings and county cricket matches and travelled by rail and steam packet to Paris and the French Riviera. Many attended parliament and business meetings in the City, stayed overnight at their town houses or clubs and returned by train the next day. Their mail and London newspapers were dispatched to reach Hertfordshire on the following morning. The railway turned some country squires into men about town or men of the world.

The availability of cheap third-class fares had a deeper impact on a large part of the rural population. The railway released the poor from ties of settlement that hitherto inhibited their movement and opened new horizons to seek marriage partners, move to new homes and find better-paid work. As early as 1838, *Osborne's Guide* remarked that the London and Birmingham Railway 'has already begun to produce material changes in society. Many, who but a few years since, scarcely penetrated beyond the county in which they happened to have been born are now induced to visit places far more remote.'[53] The population of seventy small parishes, including many in north-east Hertfordshire, decreased from the late 1840s and through the 1850s, and in forty-five parishes the decline continued until the end of the century, although the development of dormitory settlements around railway stations began to reverse the exodus at a few places in the 1890s. While remote villages shrank, towns increased in population, towns in west Hertfordshire expanding more rapidly than those in other parts of the county. The railways contributed to a loosening of the grip of landowners over rural society.

The architecture of country houses and the design of parks and pleasure grounds influenced the choice of architectural styles by railway companies. Buildings for the Great Northern Railway imitated the Jacobean style employed in the restoration of houses and gardens at Hatfield and Knebworth. At Hatfield in the 1840s, the restored Jacobean mansion was flanked by terraced gardens and a maze that were later mistaken for genuine seventeenth-century creations. In 1847, Sir Edward Bulwer-Lytton laid out gardens at Knebworth 'in the style favoured in the reign of James I, with stone balustrades, straight walks, statues, and elaborate parterres'. The garden was Lytton's own design but was laid out askew while he was away from home.[54] At the same period, a substantial amount of planting was carried out in the park in a seventeenth-century manner, including a new avenue of horse chestnuts leading north-east from the house.[55]

Another way of incorporating railways into parkland scenery was to open vistas towards them. Paper-making prospered at Apsley Mills and Nash Mills, alongside the London and Birmingham Railway and the Grand Junction Canal. John Dickinson and his partner, Charles Longman, proprietors of the paper mills, built houses on rising ground overlooking the mills. Dickinson's house at Abbots Hill was built in 1836. Situated in open parkland, it looked down on Nash Mills and, beyond the mills, to the canal and railway. On the other side of the valley, Charles Longman built his house, in the fashionable Jacobean style, at the top of a hill at Shendish in 1853. It looked down at the railway, main road and canal, with Apsley Mills behind.[56]

Edward Kemp, Robert Glendenning, James Pulham and William Paul
The grounds at Shendish, occupying 250 acres, were designed by Edward Kemp (1817–1891). Kemp was trained by Joseph Paxton at Chatsworth and, through Paxton's recommendation, he was invited to lay out public parks in Liverpool and other northern towns.[57] In 1858, he published a second edition of a guide for owners of small country houses on *How to Lay Out a Small Garden*. Shendish, by no means a small garden, was illustrated in that book. A short distance to the west of the house lay a disused chalk pit. Kemp converted the pit into a sunken dell, where 'rugged masses of natural vegetation', including wild clematis, were to be planted. A path to the dell led through elaborate formal gardens set within a 'home pasture' occupying about twenty acres and bounded by a curving sunk fence that concealed a public footpath which was conducted through an underpass under the main carriage drive:[58] in the climate of the 1850s it was prudent for a new landowner to avoid applying for a public right of way to be closed. In addition to the work on the gardens, a good deal of tree-planting was required to frame a view over the park towards the railway and mills.

In 1856, Henry Toulmin, a ship owner who had recently bought Childwick Bury, commissioned Kemp to redesign 117 acres of pleasure grounds. Kemp redirected the carriage drive in a curving sweep towards the new entrance before leading it into the new courtyard where the stables were situated. Large masses of rhododendrons were planted on either side of the drive and two Irish yews were placed on each side of the entrance. In front of the house, geometric flower beds were laid out to 'produce a little colour from the more important windows' and the west and south lawns were planted with 'some recently introduced specimen conifers', including cypresses, araucarias, junipers, Douglas firs and deodar cedars.[59] The upkeep of the estate was too expensive for Henry Toulmin's son, who sold it in 1883 to Sir John Blundell Maple, owner of the London furniture shop.

In 1872, nearly twenty years after he designed Shendish, Kemp was asked by Thomas Frederick Halsey to prepare a plan for the grounds of his ancestral home at Gaddesden Place. Kemp raised a terrace in front of the house, cut flower beds in the lawn below, levelled a square in order to create a croquet ground and laid down a straight gravel walk at a lower level. He planted an Atlas cedar, cedar of Lebanon, weeping ash and other specimen trees near the house.[60] While his design for the garden was formal, the rest of the park was not changed.

In 1844, Robert Hanbury, the brewer, rebuilt his house at Poles near Ware and commissioned Robert Glendenning (1805–1862) to redesign the grounds and supply new plants. Glendenning, like Loudon, was born in Lanarkshire. In the 1830s he collaborated with Loudon in setting up an arboretum at Bicton in Shropshire, where he was head gardener, and he began writing articles on specimen trees for Loudon's *Gardeners' Magazine*. After Loudon's death in 1843, Glendenning opened a nursery at Chiswick and contributed to the new *Gardeners' Chronicle*.[61] His plan for the grounds at Poles included a rose garden, rock garden and a French-style parterre with densely planted beds of flowers, which was sunken so that the house enjoyed uninterrupted views over parkland scenery. Hanbury's great passion was collecting orchids and Glendenning not only supplied him with specimens but designed hothouses for their propagation.[62] In 1865, James Pulham added new glasshouses with rockwork for a fernery.[63]

James Pulham (c.1820–1898) of Broxbourne specialised in making rockeries. He invented Pulhamite, an artificial stone, made by pouring Portland cement over heaps of clinker and rubble and shaping the surface to resemble beds of sandstone or limestone. One of his earliest commissions, about 1835, was for George Proctor who restored and romanticised the ruins of a Norman castle at Benington Lordship. Pulham built a mock-Norman gatehouse, a summer house and other embellishments using his artificial stone.[64] A year or so later, for John Warner of Woodlands, Hoddesdon, he erected cliffs and a cave to screen the new gas works. In 1845–6, Pulham formed a rock garden in a sheltered nook near the house at Bayfordbury.[65] At High Leigh, also in Hoddesdon, Pulham was called upon in 1871 to create a highly irregular rocky valley in the enlarged park of a Jacobean-style house built in the 1850s. He used large quantities of Pulhamite to simulate Alpine rock formations and construct a grotto and waterfalls.[66] Pulham was also employed at Rawdon House, Bayfordbury, Bedwell Park, Danesbury and Poles. At Carpenders Park, Brickendonbury, and Bushey House, at the end of the nineteenth century, extensive rockeries were built with Pulhamite. Even larger quantities were used to make rockeries at Aldenham House at the beginning of the twentieth century.[67] By that time, the material was being used all over the country. Kate Banister has noted seventeen gardens in Hertfordshire where the Pulham family worked.[68]

Another nurseryman, William Paul (1822–1905) of Cheshunt, supplied roses to many Hertfordshire gardens. In the 1850s, his nursery stocked more than half a million roses, as well as heathers, rhododendrons, azaleas and camellias. He had fields of asters, hyacinths and two acres of hollyhocks. In 1848, he wrote *The Rose Garden*, drawing upon his extensive knowledge of rose-growing in Hertfordshire. He remarked on 'a very pretty arrangement of roses introduced in the walks of the shrubbery' at John Warner's garden in Hoddesdon, where Pulham had built a rockwork cliff, and praised other collections of roses at Dane End, Munden, Ponsbourne Park and Mr Sabine's at North Mimms. He considered the Rosarium at Broxbournebury 'the best private collection of roses in England'. It covered half an acre and displayed 2,200 fine plants.[69] Paul particularly admired large blooms, bright colours and sweet scents; many varieties of roses that had been introduced since 1837 possessed these qualities. His *Handbook* for owners of villa gardens, published in 1855, was garnished with hints of Victorian common sense. He advised against growing vegetables, because 'in these days of rapid transit, they can usually be bought cheaper and better in the neighbourhood of every town'. He also recommended protecting the privacy of the principal garden so that the owner could enjoy walking in it in his 'dressing gown and slippers'. He regarded glass as an essential perquisite for a villa; 'no garden can be considered complete without it'.[70] Rose-growing appealed to owners of ancient parks as well as to villa residents: Ashridge and Cassiobury had fine rose gardens in the 1820s and, at Beechwood, Sir John Sebright planted a rose garden in Elizabethan style in 1857.[71]

Early Victorian gardeners followed the Gardenesque objectives set out by Loudon. General principles for laying out small gardens were listed by Kemp as simplicity, intricacy, convenience, snugness, seclusion, unity, congruity, connexion, symmetry and apparent extent.[72] From this wide-ranging agenda, emphasis was placed on displaying individual plants to their best advantage. Among the leaders of fashion were nurserymen, plant collectors and wealthy patrons, whose mission was to search for new plants across the world. They viewed botanical exploration as continuing the work of sixteenth- and seventeenth-century discoverers, which may account for a revival of Jacobean-style garden ornament in this period. Nurserymen specialised in collecting and propagating particular kinds of plants. Of those practising in Hertfordshire, Glendenning was an expert on conifers, Pulham specialised in rockeries and ferneries, Paul was an authority on roses and Thomas Rivers of Sawbridgeworth supplied a great variety of apples, pears and plums.

Victorians welcomed new inventions. Every owner was eager to acquire a small version of the palatial glasshouses designed by Joseph Paxton at Chatsworth and Decimus Burton and Richard Turner at Kew. Newly invented Portland cement was highly valued for making rockeries and paving; ingenious waterworks and powerful fountains were much sought after; Edwin Budding's lawn mower, patented in 1830, was manufactured on a large scale by Ransomes ten years later. Gardens and their accessories were conspicuously costly to make and maintain. Rare and exotic plants were expensive; glasshouses, heating and watering were expensive; and intensive employment of skilled labour was expensive. When enthusiasts died or funds were exhausted, gardens rapidly decayed.

William Andrews Nesfield

Novelty, variety and individualism, cloaked in decorative styles borrowed from different periods of the past, characterised designs for Victorian houses, gardens and parks. For a brief spell in the middle of the nineteenth century one practitioner, William Andrews Nesfield (1793–1881), attempted to stop the anarchy and impose strict geometrical order on garden layouts. He applied the same rules in planning grounds for gothick as for classical mansions, for flat as for sloping surfaces and for large as for small areas. He arranged parterres symmetrically on either side of an axial walk or avenue. Slopes were regularly sculpted into flights of terraces and balustraded in the manner of sixteenth-century Italian gardens.[73]

In 1841, Nesfield was invited by the Earl of Clarendon to lay out new gardens for The Grove that would complement alterations to the house, which had been designed by Edward Blore. Nesfield constructed a terrace with a rosarium on the west side of the house and placed an architectural garden with parterres on the south front.[74]

At Moor Park, in 1848, in conjunction with the architect William Burn, Nesfield replaced old formal gardens with a new, perfectly symmetrical Italian garden laid out on a broad terrace surrounded by balustrades, ornamented with urns, fountains and a fish pond, offering extensive views over the park. The parterres were planted with colourful flowers and masses of dwarf evergreens. During the 1860s, Lord Ebury introduced into the park many exotic trees, including Japanese cedar, Chinese tree of heaven, hemlock spruce, *abies nobilis*, evergreen oak and *catalpa syringaefolia*.[75]

The Italianate style won few adherents in Hertfordshire. The placing of precisely measured rectilinear garden structures next to vernacular forms of domestic architecture looked incongruous but some owners strongly preferred classical regularity. Coles at Westmill was rebuilt in an Elizabethan style in 1847 and, in 1853, the garden was laid out defiantly 'after the Italian fashion' with balustraded terraces.[76] At Putteridge Bury, in the 1850s, the head gardener, Robert Fish (1808–1873) created a floral avenue in the Italian manner. The avenue marched as a procession of matching pairs of pincushion beds, planted with matching mixtures of roses, fuchsias, calceolarias, cannas, pelargoniums, pinks, verbenas and lobelias.[77] In a heavily gothicised setting at Knebworth, a small Italian garden was formed at the end of the nineteenth century. The plot was set about with shady trees, adorned with regular flower beds, classical urns, statues and fountains; a particularly secluded glade was dedicated to the pastoral Roman poet, Horace.[78]

In the late 1860s, Nesfield was severely criticised for his austere treatment of the Royal Horticultural Society's garden in Kensington. Plantsmen disliked his predilection for broad gravel walks and ostentatious displays of balustrades, urns and statuary. The most extreme reaction against Nesfield's rigid rectilinearity was expressed by William Robinson (1838–1935), who called for a return to *The Wild Garden*. The guiding principle of Robinson's system was 'naturalizing or making wild innumerable beautiful natives of many regions of the earth in our woods, wild or semi-wild places, rougher parts of pleasure grounds, etc.'[79] In practice, Robinson advocated woodland embellishment, subdued rather than strident colours, the naturalising of exotics, displays of the distinctive foliage of hardy subtropical bamboos and pampas grass, the grouping of individual plants and space for plants to spread themselves in large masses. The sole commission he received in Hertfordshire was to plant a rose garden in a scheme planned by the architect, Sir Ernest George (1839–1922) as a setting for a Jacobean revival house at North Mymms Park, largely rebuilt in 1893.[80] He was not invited to create a wild garden but some of his recommendations were adopted. A few gardeners shared his appreciation of British wild flowers, 'from showy, self-asserting buttercups and poppies to modest grasses of exquisite grace' and, on his suggestion, woods were carpeted with snowdrops, primroses and bluebells.[81] Many owners preserved some formality in the immediate precincts of their houses and let natural forms of plants and the natural lie of the land shape the layout of their parks.

In the late Victorian era, parks and pleasure grounds were laid out in a wide variety of styles or none at all. Freedom and individuality were valued more highly than was conformity to accepted standards of good taste. Owners from different social backgrounds followed their own inclinations, taking advice from trained head gardeners, nurserymen and a few professional designers. Most owners flaunted their wealth; some signified their aristocratic status and many expressed their diverse personal interests in forestry, horticulture, plant collecting or field sports.

Parks for plant collectors and scientists

In the late nineteenth century, Hertfordshire was renowned for rose growing. William Paul's nurseries at Cheshunt and later at Waltham Cross supplied many gardens with roses; some of the rare specimens in the celebrated collection at Broxbournebury came from Paul's nurseries. Rivers' Nursery at Sawbridgeworth also supplied roses to the gentry. In 1894, a specialist orchid grower, Frederick Sander of St Albans, sent twenty plant collectors to tropical regions in Latin America and south Asia.[82] The collection of the Royal National Rose Society, founded in 1875, was later transferred to St Albans.

Some of the most valuable collections, however, were of trees. The formation of arboreta and pineta were long-term projects, undertaken by families who expected their children and grandchildren to continue the work of planting and replanting. Bayfordbury, the landscaped park containing the most famous arboretum and pinetum in Hertfordshire, was created by four generations of William Bakers.[83] The first (1705–1770), an alderman in the City of London, bought the property in 1757, built a new house at the top of the hill and began planting. The details of his and his descendants' tree-planting activities from 1759 to 1869 are recorded in a remarkably complete series of memoranda.[84] The earliest planting formed a dense belt of conifers around the grounds and, within the belt, many thousands of oaks and other timber trees were planted by William and his son, the second William (1743–1824), who succeeded to the estate in 1770. Between 1809 and 1812 the outside of the house was completely transformed and at the same time large quantities of Levant oaks, sweet chestnuts, beech and larch were acquired from Lee's celebrated nursery, founded on the site of an old vineyard in Hammersmith. The third William (1778–1813) predeceased his father and, when the second William died in 1824, the estate passed to his fourteen-year-old grandson, William Robert Baker (1810–1896), the fourth in succession, who lived in the family home for the next seventy-two years. At the age of twenty, William Robert began building greenhouses, cottages, lodges and a new village school, and in 1836 and 1837 the gardens were completely remodelled.

The famous pinetum at Bayfordbury was begun in 1837.[85] In that year, ground in the north-west corner of the park, sheltered by a belt of yew trees, was cleared, levelled and trenched to receive the first trees in the autumn. In consultation with John Claudius Loudon, a semicircular area of three acres was laid out with walks and planted with labelled specimens apparently placed on raised mounds to avoid damage by ground frost. During the next three years, from 1837 to 1840, at least ninety-two specimens are known to have been planted, because that number of labels supplied by Loudon have since been recovered. In 1848, the area was extended to include a disused pit on the north and a strip on the south where a rockwork cascade and a grotto were made. In 1855, two *sequoia Wellingtonia (gigantea)* were acquired. They were put in the ground in the baskets in which they had been received when they were only two inches high,[86] and grew to become the tallest and most vigorous trees in the collection. Loudon's principle that 'the object of ornamental gardening is to exhibit beauties either *singly* or *collectively*' guided William Robert Baker in manipulating and cultivating botanical freaks.[87] Among these were some trees that had been planted in the same holes and had grown together, producing amalgams of elm, oak and ash, and some thorn trees grafted on to elm and ash.

Apart from curiosities and rare specimen trees, the greatest changes at Bayfordbury during the nineteenth century were brought about by the regular planting and cutting of timber trees. Years such as 1856, when seventeen acres of timber and underwood were cleared and 200 spruce, 600 larch and 10,000 ash were planted, must have resulted in a striking change in the appearance of the park.[88] The gardens were altered in 1867 by the addition of ornamental vases, the building of an *erica* house and the planting of clumps of yuccas. In 1885, a rock garden was built, and ferns, bamboos, cannas, hardy cacti, gunneras and gourds were planted. After that, few notable changes took place. William Clinton Baker, the fifth generation, (1839–1903) was succeeded by the last of the line, Henry William Clinton Baker (1865–1935), both of whom struggled to meet the rising costs of maintaining the collections at Bayfordbury.

A more ostentatious collection of rare trees and shrubs was formed in the late nineteenth century by the Gibbs family at Aldenham House. A London banker, George Henry Gibbs inherited the estate in 1842 but did not reside there. After Elstree station opened in 1870, George Henry's son and heir, Henry Hucks Gibbs, moved in and travelled by train to and from his office in London. He extended and modernised the seventeenth-century mansion and began spending large sums of money on the grounds, assisted by his younger son, Vicary Gibbs, and head gardeners, Charles Penny and Edwin Beckett. Formal gardens adjoining the house were laid out on a lavish scale and, beyond the regular flower beds and rose garden, an extensive wilderness was prepared for planting forest trees. In 1873, Tykes Water was dammed to form a lake that supplied millions of gallons of water to irrigate the gardens and plantations. Vast quantities of ash, leaf mould and manure were ploughed in to relieve the tenacious London clay soil. Vicary Gibbs, a dedicated collector, assembled one of the world's finest collections of hardy trees and shrubs. Among the specialities, he planted more than 700 varieties of thorns. He continued to add to the collection until his death in 1932.[89]

The international banker Lionel Nathaniel Rothschild, who bought Tring Park in 1872, embarked on extensive alterations to the grounds, creating an Italian garden with fountain and terraced lawn, a topiary garden, an enclosed Dutch garden, a vinery, a palm house and greenhouses in which rare orchids were grown. The park was grazed by a collection of exotic animals, including zebras, kangaroos, emus and ostriches, in addition to a herd of fallow deer. Lord Rothschild's son, Walter, established a natural history museum at Tring where the evolution of animals and plants was studied.[90]

During the eighteenth century, interests in agricultural innovation had been pursued on experimental plots in Hatfield Park by the Cecils and in Beechwood Park by the Sebrights. In 1834, Sir John Bennet Lawes set up a laboratory at Rothamsted and began to conduct scientific investigations into the manuring of agricultural plants, at first in pots, then on the home farm. In 1843, field trials were started and eventually forty acres were devoted to trials of different rotations of crops and different applications of fertilisers. In 1842, Lawes patented his superphosphate, which soon began to earn good profits. The gardens were improved in 1863; two greenhouses were built and walls surrounding the old garden were pulled down. A continuous clover experiment that had been started in the old walled garden in 1854 was allowed to continue, now a bed in the new lawn. A lime walk, possibly planted in the seventeenth century, and an avenue, possibly of eighteenth-century origin, were incorporated in the informal layout of the grounds.[91]

Parks at Broxbournebury, Bayfordbury, Aldenham House, Rothamsted and Tring were internationally important sites of scientific and technological innovation. They served as training grounds for botanists, horticulturalists, foresters and agricultural scientists.

Deer parks in the late nineteenth century

Most parks in Hertfordshire were without deer throughout the nineteenth century. Browsing animals had been removed in order to protect growing trees, especially in young plantations. In some parks, flocks of sheep or herds of cattle replaced deer. During the second half of the nineteenth century, however, deer-keeping enjoyed a short-lived revival, despite the dangers that it could present: in August 1888, the owner of Putteridge Park, George Sowerby, was gored to death by one of his own deer. His death was particularly poignant because he was helping a young photographer by trying to place the stag in a good position for a picture.[92]

The largest herds were kept at the largest and oldest parks (Table 6.2), the revival apparently peaking before 1885. In 1892, Joseph Whitaker recorded a total of 1,540 fallow and 100 red deer grazing in parks that totalled 5,860 acres in area.[93] Of two parks where no

Table 6.2 Deer parks in Hertfordshire in 1892

Park	Acres	Fallow deer	Red deer	
Ashridge	1,100	300	100	1914: 986 acres
Cassiobury	1,028	150	—	1873: 700 fallow deer; 1883: 670 acres, 350 fallow; 1914: 735 acres
Gorhambury	300	5	—	
Grove	250	100	—	1914: 230 acres, 75 fallow
Hatfield	530	200	—	1867: 314 acres, 360 fallow
Kings Walden	300	—	—	1885: 250 acres
Knebworth	400	150	—	1883: 280 acres, 140 fallow; 1914: 155 acres, 200 fallow
Moor Park	500	225	—	1883: 250 fallow; 1914: 473 acres, 150 fallow
Putteridge	450	—	—	1883: well stocked
Rickmansworth	200	50	—	1914: 200 acres
Tring	350	60	—	1892: 25 kangaroos; 1914: 225 acres, 80 fallow
Woodhall	447	300	—	1914: 428 acres, 150 fallow
Total	5,845	1,540	100	

Sources: Data for 1892 are from J. Whitaker, *A descriptive list of deer parks and paddocks in England* (London, 1892); for 1867, from E.P. Shirley, *Some account of English deer parks* (London, 1867), p.144; for 1873 and 1883, from J.E. Harting, 'Hertfordshire deer parks', *Transactions of the Hertfordshire Natural History Society*, II (1883), pp.97–111; for 1914, from *VCH Hertfordshire*, vol. IV, pp.277–9.

deer were reported by Whitaker, J. E. Harting noted in 1883 that Putteridge Park was 'well stocked' and a sales catalogue for King's Walden in 1885 described the park as containing deer.[94] Harting also reported that at Cassiobury 300 deer had 'died out about 1850' in an epidemic.[95] Other parks that lost herds of deer before 1870 included Panshanger and Brocket; at Gorhambury, the last few deer disappeared shortly after 1892. In 1914, parks that still kept deer were smaller in area and held fewer animals than in 1892.[96] At the height of the revival no more than one park in twenty kept deer and the area they grazed was less than one-tenth of the total area of parkland.

The enclosure of deer parks required the regular maintenance and repair of fences. It is remarkable that in 1892, only two parks which contained deer, Ashridge and The Grove, were partly enclosed by iron railings, and only two others, Tring and Woodhall, had durable walls of brick and stone. The remainder had oak palings or other forms of wooden fences. In most places, deer ranged widely across large parks, although Whitaker's rounded acreages are somewhat larger than those recorded on the Ordnance Survey six-inch maps. At Hatfield, however, it was reported that deer were confined to an enclosure of 530 acres within a park that extended over more than 1000 acres.[97] They were removed from the park during the First World War. In 1914, only nine parks kept deer.[98]

Ordnance Survey first six-inch map 1863–81

In 1853, the Ordnance Survey began to map all cultivated and settled areas in England, Wales and Scotland at a scale of 1 in 2500 or about twenty-five inches to a mile, reaching Hertfordshire in 1863 and completing the county's mapping in 1881. Maps at a reduced scale of 1 in 10,560 or six inches to one mile were derived from the initial twenty-five-inch drawings. The six-inch maps have been examined in preference to the large-scale plans because they indicate 'ornamental grounds' by stipple, whereas the original plans have no distinctive symbol for parkland.

No specific instructions on how to identify ornamental grounds were given to surveyors or to draftsmen who prepared the six-inch maps. On the twenty-five inch plans, surveyors were required to fix the exact positions of individual trees in pastures and hedgerows, outline areas of close canopy woodlands, and supply 'all other ornament, permanent footpaths, rocks and steep slopes'.[99] In the drawing office, examiners of the twenty-five-inch plans had to provide all the information necessary for numbering parcels and measuring their areas. In the accompanying books of reference, an examiner was required to describe 'the nature of the different characters of ground, whether arable, pasture, wood, rough pasture, moor, moss, sandhills &c, and in cases of doubt, defining on the ground, to the best of his judgment by dotted lines the limits of parcels as he would recommend them to be computed'.[100] Ornamental grounds and parks were not classed among 'the different characters of ground', so that while the identification of large gardens immediately adjacent to country houses was not difficult, that of deer parks and other ornamental pastures on the twenty-five-inch plans was more problematic.[101] The practice of representing parkland by stippling originated from the Ordnance Survey six-inch maps of Ireland carried out between 1833 and 1846 and parkland on the six-inch maps in England was also stippled.[102] The delineation of gardens, both on the large-scale plans and on early six-inch maps, was highly decorative, but when the Ordnance Survey was forced to cut expenditure in 1884, elaborate ornamentation was stopped and the compilation of books of reference discontinued.[103]

An additional difficulty in defining areas to be stippled was the absence of a symbol for park palings. Fences and hedges of whatever height, including sunk fences, were represented by continuous lines; dotted lines were applied to indeterminate edges of unfenced roads and unfenced margins of woodland or clumps. In plotting individual trees and tracts of woodland and plantations, the surveyors followed strict instructions, and areas defined as woodland included plantations that might have been classed alternatively as parkland. By the late nineteenth century much land that had been planted within parks was occupied by fully grown woods. Some, such as Millwards, next to Hatfield Park, had disappeared entirely under woodland, while others,

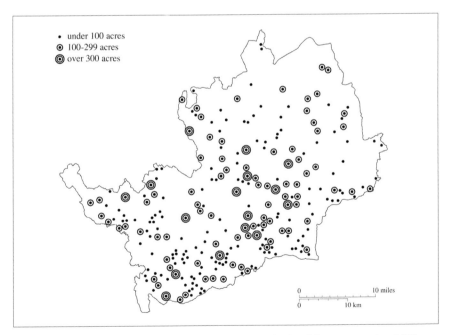

Figure 6.4: Parks in Hertfordshire in 1863–81. Two hundred and forty-nine parks of different sizes are recorded. Full details are listed in Table 6.3. Based on Ordnance Survey first edition six-inch map. Drawn in the Geography Department, UCL

such as Lilley Park, were shown as overgrown with birch heath; a large number of parks, including Whitney Wood near Stevenage, were deeply embedded in woodland. Large parts of Ashridge, Knebworth and Bedwell were thickly covered with trees. North Mymms Park, Broadfield and Danesbury were surrounded by woods; Panshanger, Marden Hill and Brocket were intricately intermixed with woods; Cassiobury was adjoined by extensive Whippendell Woods; Munden House adjoined Bricket Wood and Markham's Hill, mostly wooded, was attached to Wellbury House, Little Offley. Dozens of parks bore 'wood' name elements, varying from the basic form of Woodside and Woodhill parks in Hatfield to compound names, such as Kingswood and Borehamwood House. Tree names appeared in Hazelwood, Highfirs, Oak Lodge, The Elms, and The Cedars at Chorleywood and Cheshunt. In these places, stippled areas of ornamental grounds were filled in between blocks of woodland. Because of questions about which parcels of woodland were to be included in parks and which excluded, estimates of parkland acreages based on inspections of six-inch maps are not absolutely accurate.

Some ornamental grounds under fifteen acres in extent were stippled, but for purposes of comparison with earlier maps, the minimum size of parks listed in Table 6.3 has been set at fifteen acres. A total of 249 parks is listed, an increase of 32 since 1821 (Figure 6.4). Of that total, 152 were small parks, ranging from fifteen to a hundred acres, and 97 were over a hundred acres in size. The number of small parks increased from 128 shown on Bryant's map to 152 in 1863–81. The trend towards concentration of parks in south Hertfordshire, evident in 1799–1812 and 1821, continued to 1863–81. South of the rivers Lea and Colne, the number of parks, mostly small in size, increased from 61 in 1821 to 84 in 1863–81 (Figure 6.5). The number of new parks that appeared since 1821 in the south was 39. Of 58 parks newly recorded north of the Lea and Colne, a high proportion appeared in west Hertfordshire, on the sides of the Gade and Bulbourne valleys (Figure 6.6).

The total area of parkland in Hertfordshire shown on the first six-inch maps was 28,705 acres, about 630 acres less than that recorded

continued on p204

Table 6.3 Parks in Hertfordshire in 1863–81

Park	Grid Reference	Owner	Acres in park	Acres in Herts estate
Abbotshill, Abbots Langley	076044	John Dickinson	180	297
Abbots Langley Place	093019	Sir Samuel Canning Bt	20	7
Albury Hall	425252	Miss Fanny Dawson	220	671
Aldenham Abbey	138995	Col William Stuart	120	310
Aldenham House	168965	Henry Hucks Gibbs	120	1,257
Aldenham Lodge	167004	Thomas Part	30	
Ardeley Bury	301271	Charles James Bastard	90	859
Ashlyns, Berkhamsted	991067	Lt Col Robert Algernon Dorrien Smith	150	1,209
Ashridge, Lt Gaddesden	994121	Adelbert Egerton Cust, 3rd Earl Brownlow	1,120	8,551
Ashwell Bury	266400	Edward King Fordham	20	1,103
Aspenden Hall	352284	Sir Henry Lushington Bt	120	1,379
Aston House	271225	Donat John Hoste O'Brien	50	804
Ayotbury, Ayot St Peters	218153	Francis Thomas, 7th Earl Cowper	40	10,122
Ayot St Lawrence House	195170	George Henry Ames	170	872
Balls Park, Hertford	335120	John Stuart, 5th Marquis Townshend	230	1,565
Barvin Park, Northaw	290010	W.E. Balston	80	
Bayfordbury	315104	William Robert Baker	380	3,912
Bedwell Park, Essendon	277076	Mrs Frances Culling Hanbury	200	887
Beechwood	045144	Sir John Gage Saunders Sebright Bt	390	3,886
Benington Lodge	294233	William Wigram	30	224
Benington Lordship	297236	Leonard Proctor	50	1,294
Berkhamsted Hall	998074	Thomas Curtis	40	333
Berkhamsted Place	991088	Adelbert Egerton Cust, 3rd Earl Brownlow	70	8,551
Blackmore End, Kimpton	165175	Richard Birley Baxendale	60	348
Blakesware, Ware	405163	Mrs Frances Hadsley Gosselin	90	1,089
Bonningtons, Stanstead Abbots	408131	Lloyd B. Baxendale	130	348
Borehamwood House	189962	Henry Robinson	100	291
Bovingdon Lodge	025032	Mrs Salter	20	65
Boxmoor House, Hemel Hempstead	037057	Charlotte Catlin	20	62
Bragbury Hall, Aston	270212	Francis Pym	50	631
Bramfield Place	295155	Abel Smith MP	20	10,213
Brickendon Bury	330105	Russell Ellice	170	756

continued over

Table 6.3 Parks in Hertfordshire in 1863–81 *continued*

Park	Grid Reference	Owner	Acres in park	Acres in Herts estate
Brickendon Grange	319077	Mrs B. Cherry	40	55
Briggens, Hunsdon	414112	Charles James Phelips	90	1,868
Broadfield Hall, Cottered	324310	R.W. Wilkins	110	823
Brocket Hall	214130	Hon. Henry Frederick Cowper	510	0
Brookmans Park	253048	Robert William Gaussen	500	3,566
Broxbourne Bury	353072	Horace Smith Bosanquet	260	2,207
Burleigh, Cheshunt	315045	Joseph Levick	20	234
Burton Grange, Cheshunt	335037	Edmund T. Doxat	30	
Bury Green, Cheshunt	344016	George Augustus Crocker	25	
Bush Hall, Hatfield	239100	Lord Braye	30	650
Bushey Grange	130965	Rev. Humphrey Frederick Burchell Herne	60	207
Bushey Hall	127968	Edward Majoribanks	160	801
Bushey House	136951	George Lake	30	152
Bushey Manor	129955	Gen. Sir Edward Walter Forestier Walker	30	45
Caddington Hall, Markyate	068173	Anne Macnamara	30	1,443
Camfield Place, Essendon	268069	Edmund Potter	140	399
Carpenders Park, Watford	125934	Robert Russell Carew	90	254
Cassiobury	095972	Arthur Algernon Capel, 6th Earl of Essex	920	6,158
Cedars, Cheshunt	355011	Lady Prescott	40	475
Champneys, Wigginton	947086	Emily Anne Valpy	100	332
Chesfield Lodge, Graveley	247275	Col Robert Hindley Wilkinson	90	1,654
Cheshunt House	345027	William Herbert Mayo	30	888
Cheshunt Park	347045	Sir George Rendlesham Prescott	90	475
Cheverells Park, Flamstead	056155	Sir John Gage Saunders Sebright Bt	40	3,886
Childwick Bury	140102	Capt. Henry Joseph Toulmin	150	876
Chipperfield Manor	048013	Robert Blackwell	60	591
Chorleywood Cedars	039962	John Saunders Gilliatt	50	596
Chorleywood House	037970	Howard Gilliatt	90	596
Claramont, Cheshunt	330020	Samuel Warren	30	
Codicote Lodge	214183	Mrs Joseph Busk	60	
Coles Park, Westmill	368260	Robert Phillips Greg	150	1,573
Colney House	173030	Sir Andrew Lusk Bt MP	130	293
Copped Hall, Totteridge	246940	Mrs Harriet Kirby	120	139
Corner Hall, Hemel Hempstead	059060	George Haydon	20	2

continued

Table 6.3 Parks in Hertfordshire in 1863–81 *continued*

Park	Grid Reference	Owner	Acres in park	Acres in Herts estate
Corney Bury, Buntingford	357309	William Butt	100	978
Cottered Rectory	316291	Rev. John James Manley	15	326
Counters End, Hemel Hempstead	042073	Mrs William Henry Smith	20	1,098
Danesbury, Welwyn	234173	William John Blake	170	1,414
Delaport, Wheathamstead	175153	Charles Higby Lattimore	40	
Delrow, Bushey	142974	Adml Edward Gennys Fanshawe	30	49
Digswell House	250151	Thomas Powney Marten	120	164
Digswell Rectory	239149	Rev. George Edward Prescott	40	76
Durrants Farm, Watford	077965	Frank Bradshaw	25	811
Dyrham Park, South Mimms	223985	Frederick Trotter	210	400
Earlsbury Park, Barkway	396361	Col Henry Clinton	160	791
Easneye, Stanstead Abbots	380135	Thomas Fowell Buxton	60	1,809
Eastbury, Rickmansworth	101926	David Carnegie	190	320
Edge Grove, Aldenham	144989	Charles Sabine Augustus Thellusson	90	400
Elbrook House, Ashwell	267403	Edward King Fordham	20	1,103
Elms, Baldock	246335	Thomas Pryor	50	590
Essendon Place	273079	Robert, 6th Lord Dimsdale	120	1,357
Felden, Bovingdon	043047	Benjamin Brentnall	15	153
Frogmore Hall, Aston	289207	Rev. Thomas D Hudson	140	1,782
Frogmore Lodge, Colney Street	151036	Francis Wigg	20	236
Frythe, Welwyn	226150	Charles Willes Wilshere	80	2,417
Furneux Pelham Hall	427279	Mrs Elizabeth Calvert	120	827
Gaddesden Hoo, Gt Gaddesden	032124	Thomas Proctor	70	398
Gaddesden Place, Gt Gaddesden	038111	Thomas Frederick Halsey	250	2,100
Gadebridge, Hemel Hempstead	049081	Sir Astley Paston Cooper	60	980
Garston House, Watford	118004	Mrs Mary Ann Cobb	40	193
Gilston Park	441129	John Hodgson	230	2,079
Golden Parsonage, Gt Gaddesden	051126	Thomas Proctor	140	398
Goldings, Waterford	311143	Robert Smith	180	439
Goldingtons, Sarratt	038984	Thomas Clutterbuck	50	1,181
Gorhambury	113080	James Walter Grimston, 2nd Earl Verulam	500	8,625
Grange, Bishops Stortford	488224	James Odams	15	137

continued over

Table 6.3 Parks in Hertfordshire in 1863–81 *continued*

Park	Grid Reference	Owner	Acres in park	Acres in Herts estate
Gt Hormead Bury	399296	Ven. John Allen	30	476
Gt Hyde Hall, Sawbridgeworth	496154	Robert, 3rd Earl Roden	90	409
Grove, Sarratt	082988	Edward Hyde Villiers, 5th Earl of Clarendon	220	903
Grove Hill, Hemel Hempstead	063094	Shadrach Godwin	30	641
Haileybury, St Margarets	358108	East India College	50	53
Hamels, Braughing	376247	Catherine Martha Mellish	220	2,049
Hansteads House, Colney Street	142016	Richard Harrison	50	272
Haresfoot, Northchurch	985062	Lt Col Robert Algernon Dorrien Smith	140	1,209
Hartsbourne Manor, Bushey	143936	Joseph Sladen	80	215
Hatfield	236084	Robert, 3rd Marquess of Salisbury	1000	13,390
Hawkswick, St Albans	146101	Maj. Whittingstall	80	102
Haydon Hill House, Bushey	128948	Robert Percy Attenborough	60	
Hazelwood, Abbots Langley	089005	Gen. Henry, Lord Rokeby	40	349
Hertingfordbury	310119	William Robert Baker	110	3,911
Hexton House	108306	William Lautour Young	120	987
High Canons Park, Ridge	207990	Richard Durant	190	845
High Elms, Leavesden	114019	Robert Pryor	70	852
Highfield House, Berkhamsted	995074	Capt. Benjamin Hamilton	30	2
Highfield House, Hemel Hempstead	068084	Henry Newton Heale	40	43
Highfirs, Harpenden	149136	Charles Robert Fenwick	30	249
High Leigh, Hoddesdon	362087	Robert Gurney Barclay	40	231
High Wych, Sawbridgeworth	462139	William Barnard	20	2,036
Hilfield Lodge, Aldenham	153963	Rev. D.C. Timins	100	362
Hillside, Abbots Langley	087010	Henry C. Robarts	60	
Hillside, Ridge	188991	William Muller	50	122
Hitchin Priory	184286	Frederick Peter Delme Radcliffe	90	2,900
Hoo, Kimpton	187195	Thomas Brand, 22nd Lord Dacre	220	7,100
Hook, Northaw	279014	Nathaniel Brindley Acworth	50	115
Hunsdonbury	414131	James Sydney Walker	90	976
Hunsdon House	420127	James Wyllie	90	86
Julians, Rushden	307326	Adolphus Meetkerke	230	1,711
Kendalls Hall, Aldenham	173982	William Brough Phillimore	90	958
Kings Walden Bury	161235	Charles Cholmondley Hale	260	6,558
Kingswood, Garston	108001	John Henry James	30	108

continued

Table 6.3 Parks in Hertfordshire in 1863–81 *continued*

Park	Grid Reference	Owner	Acres in park	Acres in Herts estate
Kitwells, Ridge	191994	Richard Farmer Chattock	70	197
Knebworth Park	231210	Edward Robert, 2nd Lord Lytton	430	4,863
Kytes, Garston	117007	William Capel	30	6
Lamers, Wheathamstead	181160	Sir Charles Benet Drake Garrard	220	2,543
Langleybury, Abbots Langley	077001	William Jones Loyd	180	1,185
Langley House, Abbots Langley	094018	John Evans	20	117
Laurel Lodge, Lt Bushey	146946	Thomas Gapes	20	
Lawrence End, Kimpton	142197	George Oakley	110	1,448
Leahoe, Hertford	322120		40	
Leggatts, Northaw	266029	William Webb Moore	60	227
Letchworth Hall	217308	Julius Alington	150	884
Lt Berkhamsted House	294080	Lucinda, Lady Dimsdale	50	357
Lt Hadham Place	433225	Nicholas Segar Parry	60	592
Lt Offley House	129285	Richard Marsh	80	678
Littleheath House, Northaw	262023	James Bishop Hocombe	20	
Lockers Park, Hemel Hempstead	049073	Mrs Harvey Bathurst	20	1,144
Lockleys, Welwyn	237159	George Edward Dering	350	535
Loudwater House, Rickmansworth	051963	Joseph D'Aguila Samuda MP	150	
Lower Woodside, Hatfield	247063	John Church	100	238
Lye Farm, Bricketwood	132022	William Morten	40	
Marchmont House, Hemel Hempstead	053086	Lady Cooper	20	980
Marden Hill, Tewin	279140	Godfrey Henry Thornton	150	
Markyate Cell	057174	Rev. Francis William Adye	90	411
Marshalswick, St Albans	163085	George Robert Marten	100	645
Micklefield Hall	053974	Thomas Clutterbuck	60	1,181
Millwards Park, Hatfield	236065	Robert Cecil, 3rd Marquess of Salisbury	380	13,389
Mimmwood House, North Mimms	216028	P. Ashton	20	298
Moneyhill House, Rickmansworth	050941	Mrs Walker	30	
Moor Park, Rickmansworth	075933	Robert Grosvenor, Lord Ebury	460	2,620
Moor Place, Much Hadham	423187	Money Wigram	90	224
Munden House, Gt Munden	136003	Emily Hibbert	160	1,093
Nascot Farm, Watford	106968	Joceline F. Watkins	20	

continued over

Table 6.3 Parks in Hertfordshire in 1863–81 *continued*

Park	Grid Reference	Owner	Acres in park	Acres in Herts estate
Netherfield House, Stanstead Abbots	393115	Sir Charles Booth	30	58
New Barns, Sopwell	158052	Mrs Isabella Worley	90	301
Newberries, Radlett	172998	Thomas Bagnall	90	440
Newsells, Barkway	386367	Hon. Mrs Vernon Harcourt	160	1,769
Node, Codicote	217202	William Reid	50	70
Norcott Court, Aldbury	968107	Hon. Mrs Vernon Harcourt	25	1,769
Northaw House	275024	Col Francis Le Blanc	140	220
Northaw Place	270025	John Mounsey	40	78
Northchurch House	981098	Mrs Brooke	30	34
North Mymms Park	217042	Coningsby Charles Sibthorp	210	1,818
Nyn Lodge, Northaw	273025	John Pearson Kidston	20	451
Nyn Park, Northaw	279031	John Ashfordby Trenchard	120	776
Oak Lodge, Totteridge	228940	Francis H Huntington	25	
Oaklands, St Peters	182077	Charles Dymoke Green	90	323
Offley Holes	168263	Richard Marsh	40	678
Offley Place	145272	Mrs Salusbury Hughes	190	2,070
Offley Vicarage	137277	Rev. Thelwall Salusbury	30	137
Oxhey Grange	121942	William Thomas Eley	20	202
Oxhey Place	114933	Thomas Frederick Blackwell	120	1,094
Panshanger	290132	Francis Thomas, 7th Earl Cowper	860	10,122
Pendley, Tring	943118	Joseph Grout Williams	120	1,075
Pirton Hall	125329	Frederick Peter Delme Radcliffe	15	2,835
Pishiobury Park, Sawbridgeworth	480134	Andrew Caldecott	150	515
Plaw Hatch, Bishops Stortford	500218	James Odams	15	137
Pointers Grove, Totteridge	250940	Lt Col John Puget	20	593
Poles, Ware	352163	Robert Hanbury	160	1,694
Pondfield House, Lt Berkhamsted	297085	Emily Ann Eleanor Hanmer	40	
Ponsbourne Park, Hatfield	304054	Wynn Ellis	130	766
Porters, Shenley	182008	Thomas Borron Myers	350	1,135
Potterells, North Mimms	236046	Coningsby Charles Sibthorp	110	1,818
Presdales, Ware	358135	Charles Cass	60	170
Putteridge Bury, Lilley	118245	George Sowerby	410	2,805
Queensborough, Ippolitts	197269	Mrs Amos	60	220
Redheath, Croxley	066971	Henry Charles Finch	70	474

continued

Table 6.3 Parks in Hertfordshire in 1863–81 *continued*

Park	Grid Reference	Owner	Acres in park	Acres in Herts estate
Rickmansworth Park	057955	Joseph Arden	170	201
Rose Cottage, Berkhamsted	015079		20	
Rossway, Northchurch	960073	Charles Stanton Hadden	130	427
Rothamsted, Harpenden	125131	John Bennet Lawes	210	1,121
Rowney Abbey, Sacombe	347202	Lt Henry Sampson	30	
Russells Farm, Watford	091995	William Fowler Copeland	80	
Sacombe Park	339190	Samuel George Smith MP	190	358
St Edmunds College	372221	Roman Catholic Church	60	
St Pauls Walden Bury	187217	Claude, 13th Earl of Strathmore & Kinghorne	60	1,795
Sennoweville, Bushey	145942	John Hall Morse Boycott	60	11
Serge Hill House, Bedmond	107042	William Hammond Solly	50	1,170
Shendish, Kings Langley	059043	Arthur Hampton Longman	130	737
Shenley Grange	189004	William Brough Phillimore	20	958
Shenley Hill	194010	Forster Alleyne McGeachy	50	365
Shenley Lodge	202023	Henry Edward Chetwynd Stapylton	50	
Shephallbury	256229	Unwin Unwin Heathcote	70	2,882
Stagenhoe, St Pauls Walden	185227	James, 14th Earl of Caithness	120	614
Stags End, Gt Gaddesden	069120	Edward Heneage	20	79
Stanborough, Garston	110997	Henry Cobb	30	193
Stanstead Bury, Stanstead Abbots	400111	Capt. Lewis Upton	15	553
Stevenage Parsonage	238262	Rev. William Jowitt	30	
Stocks House, Aldbury	965133	Richard Bright MP	40	168
Temple Dinsley, Preston	181248	William Henry Darton	50	550
Terlings Park, Gilston	448117	James Duke Hill	20	33
Tewin Water	255145	Francis Thomas, 7th Earl Cowper	110	10,122
Theobalds Park, Cheshunt	345011	Sir Henry Meux	160	2,702
Tolmers, Cuffley	303048	John Remington Mills	70	3,672
Totteridge Park	233942	Rev. Nicholas Fiott Lee	100	2
Tring Park	926111	Baron Lionel Nathan de Rothschild	240	3,643
Tyttenhanger, Ridge	192047	Countess of Caledon	60	1,947
Upp Hall, Braughing	409241	Mrs Maria Tower	35	991
Walkern Hall	300249	Mrs Louisa Mary Browne	70	1,785
Ware Park	333144	William Parker	180	1,208
Warren Wood, Hatfield	269064	Charles Butler	30	64

continued over

Table 6.3 Parks in Hertfordshire in 1863–81 *continued*

Park	Grid Reference	Owner	Acres in park	Acres in Herts estate
Wellbury House, Lt Offley	135291	Francis Gosling	110	309
Westbrook Hay, Bovingdon	025054	Hon. Granville Dudley Ryder	230	1,793
Weston Park	262293	Marlborough Robert Pryor	80	965
White Barns, Furneux Pelham	432290	Joseph Gurney Barclay	30	1,112
Whitney Wood, Stevenage	231262	Andrew Whyte Barclay	20	36
Wiggenhall, Oxhey	112953	Jonathan King	20	335
Woodcock Hill, Northchurch	973080	Frank John Moore	15	227
Woodgreen Park, Cheshunt	326020	James Bentley	50	275
Wood Hall, Ridge	182993	Frederick Samuel Child	50	
Woodhall Park, Watton	316182	Abel Smith MP	460	11,213
Woodhill, Hatfield	266058	William Franks	100	190
Woodlands, Northaw	272036	John Warner	15	33
Woolmers Park, Hertfordbury	286103	William Herbert Wodehouse	160	240
Wormley Bury	355059	Mrs Mary Grant	50	515
Wyddial Hall	373317	Edward Heaton Ellis	120	1,133
Wynches, Much Hadham	422176	William Hollis Anthony	60	515
Youngsbury, Standon	370179	Arthur Giles Giles-Puller	130	2,889

Sources: Ordnance Survey first edition six-inch map. Field survey conducted at a scale of 1 in 2500 between 1863 and 1881 (BL Maps). Names of most owners listed in *Return of Owners of Land 1873, England and Wales* (Parliamentary Papers LXXII (1874)). Additional names taken from J.E. Cussans, *History of Hertfordshire* (Hertford, 1870–81); E.R. Kelly (ed.) *Post Office directory of the six home counties: Essex, Herts, Middlesex, Kent, Surrey and Sussex* (London, 1874), pp.xii–xiii and *VCH Hertfordshire* (London, 1902–14).

continued from p196

in 1821. That small difference must be interpreted in the light of the differing aims of Bryant's survey and the Ordnance Survey. The Ordnance surveyors were under instructions to map woodlands and were allowed to exercise their discretion in mapping parklands. Change in the landscape is, therefore, probably exaggerated on the map, with the oldest and largest parks appearing to have shrunk. At the other end of the scale, the formation of new small parks added to the county's total area of ornamental grounds.

In the 1870s, the largest parks in Hertfordshire were owned by families that had held them for a long time. Hatfield (1,000 acres), together with Millwards (380 acres), was the largest of all and had been continuously in the hands of the Cecils since 1607. Ashridge

Figure 6.5: Parks around Broxbourne in 1876. Large houses were surrounded by small parks and extensive woodlands. Broxbournebury had an exceptional collection of roses supplied by William Paul. Detail from Ordnance Survey first edition six-inch map, Hertfordshire Sheet XXXVI. © British Library Board — all rights reserved

(1,120 acres), the second largest park, was owned by the Brownlows, who possessed large ancestral estates in Shropshire and Lincolnshire. The three neighbouring parks of Panshanger (860 acres), Tewin Water (110 acres) and Digswell (120 acres) together constituted the third largest tract of parkland, owned by Earl Cowper. Another member of the family, Henry Cowper, lived at Brocket (510 acres), the fifth largest park in the county. Cassiobury (920 acres) was the fourth largest park, owned by the Earl of Essex, whose estate included Russells Farm (80 acres). The Earl of Verulam's Gorhambury and Robert Gaussen's Brookmans Park were both 500 acres in extent and

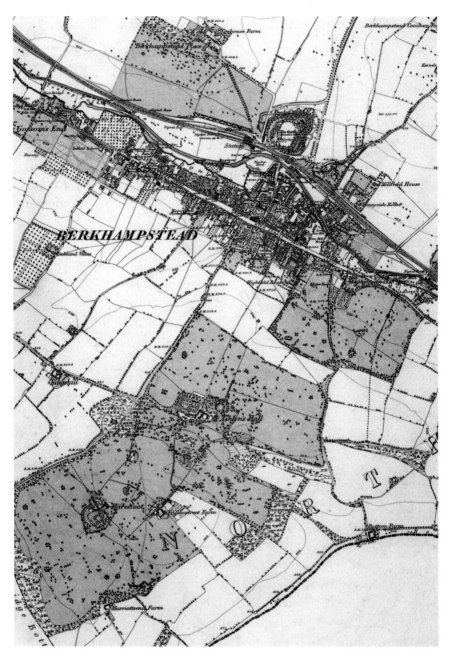

Figure 6.6: Parks around Berkhamsted in 1875. Large new houses were sited within moderate-sized parks. Detail from Ordnance Survey first six-inch map, Hertfordshire Sheet XXXIII. © British Library Board — all rights reserved

Lord Ebury's Moor Park and Abel Smith's Woodhall were 460 acres. The tenth largest park was Lord Lytton's Knebworth, 430 acres. The next three largest parks exemplify the effect of woodland encroaching on parks in the period between 1821 and 1863–81. Beechwood (390 acres), a well-wooded old park belonging to a leading county family, appears to have lost 20 acres since 1821. Bayfordbury (380 acres), where generations of Bakers had regularly planted large numbers of trees, appears to have lost 60 acres since 1821. Lockleys (350 acres), newly enlarged by George Edward Dering, son of a family from Kent, appears to have gained 160 acres since 1821. The two long-established parks became more wooded, while the park of a newcomer expanded its boundaries over open land.

Once old halls and farmhouses had been taken over by newcomers and converted into villa residences set in ornamental grounds, they were not subsequently bought by local farmers. They passed from one newcomer to another and, in the last quarter of the nineteenth century, some were acquired by building developers. An early encroachment took place at Oxhey Park in 1866–72, when William Henry Smith cut up 200 acres of his estate into building lots.[104] The dissolution of the landed interest came about by the break-up of a few great estates and, finally, by the disposal of many small properties.

Parks, landowners and politics

In the face of mounting opposition, owners of large parks and hereditary estates continued to hold the highest offices in government throughout the nineteenth century. They dominated the House of Lords and held an overwhelming majority of seats in the House of Commons. In 1820, two owners of large parks and estates, Sir John Saunders Sebright and Hon. William Lamb, represented the county of Hertfordshire, two townsmen, William Tierney Roberts and Christopher Smith, represented the city of St Albans and two other landowners, Viscount Cranborne and Nicolson Calvert, represented the borough of Hertford in the House of Commons. The Parliamentary Reform Act of 1832 redistributed seats in the House of Commons and enfranchised large towns, but gave landowners total control over Hertfordshire. In the new parliament, elected in 1833,

the three members returned for the county, Sir John Saunders
Sebright, Nicolson Calvert and James, Viscount Grimston, all owned
large parks and estates, as did two members for St Albans, Sir Francis
Vincent and Henry George Ward of Eastwick. The two members for
Hertford were sons of peers, Hon. J.C. Talbot and Hon. Philip Henry
Stanhope. In 1852, St Albans lost its one remaining seat following a
bribery scandal. In 1868, with an enlarged franchise, the county again
elected three leading landowners, Hon. Henry Frederick Cowper,
Henry Brand and Abel Smith; another landowner, Robert Dimsdale,
was returned for the borough of Hertford. In 1880, with yet more
electors, Abel Smith, Hon. Henry Frederick Cowper and Thomas
Frederick Halsey were again returned for the county and Arthur
Balfour, a Scottish landowner and nephew of the third Marquess of
Salisbury, was elected for the borough of Hertford. In 1895, owners
of parks and large estates still won three out of four seats.

For most of the nineteenth century, Hertfordshire aristocrats were
also prominent among cabinet ministers. Lord Melbourne was prime
minister in 1834 and from 1835 to 1841.[105] Lord Melbourne's sister
Emily, widow of the fifth Earl Cowper, married the third Viscount
Palmerston, who was war minister 1809–28, foreign secretary
1830–34 and 1835–41, home secretary 1851–54 and prime minister
for two terms from 1855 to 1858 and again from 1859 until his death
in 1865.[106] The Earl of Clarendon was president of the board of trade
in 1846–7, and foreign secretary from 1855 to 1858 and again from
1868 to 1870. The second Marquess of Salisbury was lord privy seal
in 1852 and lord president of the council in 1858–9. His son, the
third marquess, was secretary of state for India in 1866 and 1874–78,
foreign secretary 1878–80, prime minister and foreign secretary in
1885, 1886–92 and, for a third term, in 1895–1902.[107]

In local affairs, new administrative boards took over duties previously performed by owners of parks in their capacity as justices of the
peace. Following the Poor Law Amendment Act of 1834, poor relief
was administered by boards of guardians for unions of civil parishes;
the boards collected poor rates and built and managed new workhouses
and infirmaries. Changes in the administration of local highways were
enacted in 1835 and a county police force was established in 1841.[108]

The judicial powers of local magistrates were gradually curtailed, while punishments for serious offences were moderated; the death penalty was abolished for a long list of minor offences in the 1830s and transportation to Australia from Hertfordshire ceased in 1866.[109] From the 1830s onwards, the rule of magistrates seated in their parks and country houses was superseded by elected boards and permanent officials, including policemen, overseers and surveyors. After 1888, local government was conducted by an elected county council that met in Hertford.

Owners of parks were, however, called upon to head lists of subscribers to parochial charities. John Edwin Cussans praised the exceptional benevolence of a few old gentry, such as the Honourable Mrs Vernon Harcourt of Newsells in Barkway:

> At her sole expense this lady rebuilt the tower of the church and restored the naves and aisles: she has established a benefit society, and erected baths for the use of the poor: she contributes liberally towards a reading room which was built on the site presented by her late husband; and in many ways testifies her regard for the poor of the district.[110]

The Earl of Essex, Earl Brownlow, Colonel Arthur Blake and a wealthy banker, Robert Smith, improved the housing of workers by paying for commodious cottages to be built on their estates. Other landowners sought to encourage self-help among the poor by cutting their dependence on charitable donations. In many parishes, benefactions from clergy and the new rich were more generous than those from established landed families. By the end of the nineteenth century, many owners of parks had largely withdrawn from local affairs, spending more time away from Hertfordshire, attending meetings of boards of directors in London, performing duties in the British empire and travelling to Europe for pleasure.

Social isolation of landowners

Continuing sources of resentment against owners of parks were the enclosure of commons, the harsh treatment of the poor in the new workhouses and the unrelenting persecution of poachers. A landmark case in the history of enclosures was the battle for Berkhamsted Common.[111] Decades of disputes between users of the common and the owner of Ashridge culminated in 1866 when, in order to safeguard the privacy of his park against daily incursions by strangers, Earl Brownlow enclosed 430 acres of common without proper authority. The response of the commoners, backed by another local landowner, Augustus Smith of Ashlyns, was forceful and immediate. On the night of 6 March 1866, a team of 122 navvies hired by the newly formed Commons Preservation Society assembled at Euston station where they drank a great deal of beer before boarding a special train at midnight. They travelled to Tring, and marched three miles to Berkhamsted, sobering up on the way. Then they speedily removed two miles of iron railings and left them in neat piles to be discovered by Lord Brownlow's agent early the following morning. The ensuing battle in the court of chancery took over three years to reach a decision in favour of the commoners. The announcement in January 1870, confirming the right of public access, made no provision for the custody, management and regulation of the common for outdoor recreation and the condition of the land continued to deteriorate through overgrazing, destruction of heather, uncontrolled burning and digging of stone for road repairs.

Private enclosure ended in the 1870s but no effective means of preserving public open spaces was put in place. As late as 1870, when 350 acres of common in Aspenden parish were enclosed, a small patch of two acres near the railway was set aside as a public recreation ground without arrangements for its future upkeep being made.[112] By 1888, however, the political climate had changed and a democratic process was invoked to solve the management problem. In that year, Sir John Bennet Lawes, lord of the manor of Rothamsted, called a meeting of commoners and proposed that a Harpenden Common Preservation Committee should take responsibility for protecting and policing the common that adjoined his park. In the twentieth century, all the town's commons, greens and wastes were acquired by the urban district council.[113]

The grievance of poor people against landowners for abandoning a system of outdoor relief was alleviated by new opportunities for moving away from poverty-stricken districts to better-paid work in towns and overseas. Wages of agricultural labourers increased by about 30 per cent between 1830 and 1870, during a period of growing prosperity, but after early successes in recruiting members in north Hertfordshire between 1872 and 1875, Joseph Arch's National Agricultural Labourers' Union failed to obtain significant wage rises thereafter.[114] The union was swept away during the agricultural depression in the late nineteenth century but the pay and working conditions of farmworkers did not suffer as a result, because a labour surplus changed to a labour shortage. The number of agricultural labourers in Hertfordshire decreased continuously from 21,945 in 1851 to 10,228 in 1901. At the same time, numbers of poor receiving outdoor relief fell from 9,014 in 1851 to 6,218 in 1899.[115] Migration reduced the magnitude of rural poverty and, with the passage of time, a sense that the poor had been let down and forsaken by rich landowners gradually faded.

Hostility towards owners of parks for enforcing the game laws grew deeper and stronger in the course of the nineteenth century. The casual pursuit of wild pheasants, partridges and hares by one or two gentlemen and their dogs, going into the fields and firing at birds as they flew away, changed during the nineteenth century into formal shoots at which sportsmen wore correct dress and carried powerful guns. Strict preservation of game was practised not only on great estates of the nobility but in parks and woods acquired by city merchants: owners of shooting estates consolidated their holdings into compact ring-fenced territories, employed permanent staffs of gamekeepers and watchers and reared birds in hatcheries. In the 1820s, Lord Verulam formally notified his tenants and announced to the general public that all game birds were reserved exclusively for the owner and that he had sufficient keepers to enforce the rule.[116] In the 1820s, the organisation of grand battues, where beaters drove flocks of plump, hand-reared pheasants towards a line of guns, enabled huge bags to be taken. The slaughter was increased in the 1860s following the introduction of fast breech-loading double-barrelled shotguns, and landowners opened game books to keep a tally of the number of birds killed. In January 1823, the record for the largest single day's bag was held by Ashridge, with 525 pheasants shot by twelve guns.[117] The game book for Gorhambury registered exceptionally good seasons in 1822 and 1827, falling away in the following years. 1830–1 was a very bad season: birds were scarce, cover bad and poaching more prevalent than before. Lord Verulam lamented: 'It would be far better to have no care for game than incur the expence of so much mortification.' 1832 was even worse and he minuted: 'expences on the rise, rents declining, preserving given up'. Far from giving up, preservation revived in 1848 and bags continued to increase up to the season of 1886.[118] At the end of the century, shoots at Hatfield, Kimpton Hoo, Kings Walden, Beechwood, Brocket and Panshanger were notable for the celebrity of those taking part and the size of the bags.[119] At Panshanger, over 7,000 pheasants, 1,000 partridges and 250 hares were shot in 1914.[120]

F.M.L. Thompson has described the uneven geographical distribution of game preservation in England, based on numbers of gamekeepers recorded in late nineteenth-century censuses of occupations;[121] Hertfordshire had a higher than average density per acre of gamekeepers.[122] For the early nineteenth century, certificates issued to gamekeepers were recorded in quarter sessions books, which show that, in 1805, about 291 gamekeepers held certificates and, in 1821, there were about 248.[123] The 1851 census recorded 227 gamekeepers in the county, somewhat fewer than the number of certificate holders in the early nineteenth century.[124] Later censuses recorded increasing numbers of gamekeepers: 313 in 1871, 346 in 1891 and 402 in 1901.[125] In the 1880s and 1890s, as the agricultural depression deepened, rents from farms declined and landowners turned to shooting as a source of income. Invitations to British and foreign aristocrats and other rich men to join shooting parties commanded high prices. Entertainment was generous and guests expected the sport to be outstanding. At Gorhambury in the 1890s, the third Earl of Verulam could not afford to maintain such excellent amenities. He gave up the hand rearing of pheasants and let the shooting first to J.B. Taylor for £1,500 and then to Lord Bingham for £2,000 per year.[126]

Farmers felt strongly aggrieved by increasing demands made on them by game preservation. Not only were they excluded from invitations to the grand battues, but they suffered costly damages from birds that fed on their grain crops and hares and rabbits that consumed their turnips and carrots and ruined their meadows. After prolonged agitation, the Ground Game Act in 1880 permitted farmers accompanied by not more than one other person to shoot hares and rabbits in their fields but it gave them no protection against depredations by pheasants and partridges.

In addition to this grievance, farmers and other ratepayers were not satisfied that officers in the county constabulary were acting impartially in dealing with suspected poachers. The police had a duty to apprehend those who assaulted gamekeepers and their assistants, and they received support from most people in their efforts to stop gangs of townsmen from raiding pheasantries and intimidating estate servants. Questions about civil liberties arose, however, when police or gamekeepers arrested, searched and interrogated local residents on suspicion of poaching in parks and woods. Problems multiplied as police numbers increased. The census returns indicate that there were 123 policemen in Hertfordshire in 1851, 191 in 1871, 223 in 1891 and 423 in 1901.

Owners of parks themselves were divided in their attitudes towards game preservation. There was friction between owners of shooting estates and foxhunters. To safeguard chicks, gamekeepers surreptitiously destroyed foxes as well as rats, stoats, weasels and other predators. At the beginning of the nineteenth century, the game-preserving Earl of Essex charged his half-brother, Hon. Rev. William Capel, master of the Old Berkeley Hounds, with trespassing and wilfully damaging his park at Cassiobury. Following a successful prosecution at Hertford assizes in 1809, the earl warned the Old Berkeley not to enter any part of his extensive estate in future.[127] The action set a precedent for other landowners who might decide to refuse permission for hunts to invade their properties.

Foxhunting, however, did not isolate landowners from the rest of society as remotely as shooting had done. Farmers and other tenants were required to give the hunt access to their fields and woods. Many farmers actively cooperated and some came to hunt meets and took part in the chase alongside lords, ladies, parsons, lawyers, doctors and tradesmen. The master and members were obliged to pay farmers for damages to their gates, hedges and trampled crops and were expected to compensate for losses of lambs and poultry worried by foxes. In return, farmers had to refrain from killing foxes and were expected to take down barbed wire fences during the hunting season. Hunts strove to maintain friendly relations with local farmers, and while disputes flared up from time to time they did not disturb the camaraderie in the field.

In the late nineteenth century, hunts in Hertfordshire were hemmed in by railways, towns and spreading suburbs. Owners of villa residences in Bushey, Radlett, Totteridge, as well as owners of valuable nurseries, market gardens and dairies in Hoddesdon and Cheshunt warned hunts not to cross their land. The costs of maintaining kennels and stables rose and some landowners diverted funds to game preservation. The fortunes of the Hertfordshire Hounds declined after being taken over by joint masters in 1875. The Puckeridge was forced to cut costs and accept subscriptions from brewers and bankers. The presence of many city businessmen, who owned little or no property in the county, deterred local gentry and farmers from joining and, after 1875, membership dwindled. The Old Berkeley had been a subscription pack since 1801, but in 1881 the country was split, the Old Berkeley West taking Buckinghamshire and the Old Berkeley East south-west Hertfordshire. The greatly diminished territory of the Old Berkeley East between Bricket Wood, Aldenham and Stanmore continued to provide good hunting down to 1914.[128] At the end of the nineteenth century, foxhunting was no longer universally viewed benignly as a traditional country sport in which different ranks of society united to rid their fields of noxious vermin. A few observers came to regard hunts adversely, as occasions when large numbers of townsmen dressed up to take pleasure in killing a sacrificial fox.

In the 1870s, most owners resided at their principal seats but, for various reasons, some residences were deserted. Those who owned more than one house let members of their families live in others. After the death of Lord Melbourne in 1848, Brocket Hall passed by way of his sister Emily, who had been married first to Earl Cowper and later to Lord Palmerston. The Palmerstons occupied Brocket until 1869 and, after Emily's death, the hall reverted to the Cowpers, who let it to a relative, Henry Frederick Cowper. Some owners let their properties to genteel tenants who were not family members. Russells Farm, next to Cassiobury, belonged to the Earl of Essex, who let it in 1862 to Alderman William Taylor Copeland, one of the original directors of the London and Birmingham Railway.[129] A few owners left their country houses and became absentee rentiers. In 1874, the *Post Office Directory* listed the names of 170 residents of principal seats in Hertfordshire.[130] Of these resident occupiers, 20 were not named as owners by Cussans or the *Victoria County History* and were not included in the *Return of Owners of Land*, 1873. Most, but not all, owners named in Cussans' *History of Hertfordshire* and in the *Victoria County History of Hertford* were holders of titles of lords of manors, many of whom possessed mansions and substantial areas of land; a few had nothing more than vestiges of hereditary feudal rights. On the other hand, many new purchasers of land and creators of parks had no ancient titles. The appearance of occupiers and care-takers alongside resident owners indicated that some people had climbed over tenurial and social barriers that had been firmly maintained earlier in the century; in the 1870s, not all parks belonged to a distinctive and exclusive group of landowners and gentlemen.

Return of owners of land, 1873

Large expanses of parkland apparently not producing much that was useful, and grand mansions standing unoccupied for long periods, looked conspicuously out of place to the eyes of inquisitive Victorian ramblers. During the 1860s, radicals expressed disquiet at the undue power and influence wielded by the families that owned these places. Based on the number of 'land proprietors' listed in the 1861 census, it was inferred that a mere 30,677 men and women owned the whole of England and Wales. Of these, John Bright asserted that 'fewer than one hundred and fifty men owned half the land', which, in his opinion, was neither more nor less than 'a practical monopoly on land'.[131] In 1865, Sanford and Townsend mapped the possessions of 202 aris-tocrats, showing that Hertfordshire was particularly attractive to the nobility because of its proximity to London.[132] In Hertfordshire, 240 'land proprietors' were enumerated in the 1851 census, 245 in 1861 and 204 in 1871, the last of these numbers being slightly smaller than the number of parks recorded on contemporary Ordnance Survey maps. To counter 'reckless exaggerations' about 'what was called the monopoly of land', in 1872 Lord Derby asked the House of Lords to

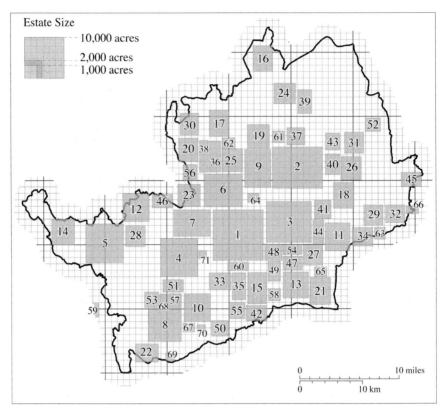

Figure 6.7: Areas of land in Hertfordshire belonging to owners of more than 2,000 acres in the United Kingdom in 1873. Areas on the map represent areas on the ground true to scale, 1km² being equivalent to 247 acres. The boundaries of estates are depicted diagramatically.

institute a definitive survey of landownership. The government agreed to instruct local government boards to abstract from more than five million valuation lists for poor-rate assessments the names and assessed values of owners of all rateable properties, excluding properties in the Metropolis. As soon as the *Return of owners of land, 1873, England and Wales* was published, Lord Derby and his supporters claimed a triumphant vindication of their argument that there were hundreds of thousands of landowners. In fact, nearly one million individuals owned some land in England and Wales.[133] Land reformers, on the other hand, were quick to point out how much property was concentrated in the hands of very few owners. The powerful position enjoyed by a small number of grandees raised serious questions about how they justified the receipt of enormous unearned incomes, how far

Owners of Hertfordshire estates in 1873, in descending order of size, were:

1. Marquess of Salisbury	25. Charles Willes Wilshere	49. Lord Dimsdale
2. Abel Smith	26. Duke of Wellington	50. Henry Hucks Gibbs
3. Earl Cowper	27. Horace Smith Bosanquet	51. William Hammond Solly
4. Earl of Verulam	28. Thomas Frederick Halsey	52. Joseph Gurney Barclay
5. Earl Brownlow	29. John Hodgson	53. Earl of Clarendon
6. Lord Dacre	30. Mrs Salusbury Hughes	54. Mrs Frances Hanbury
7. Charles Cholmondley Hale	31. Catherine Martha Mellish	55. Richard Durant
8. Earl of Essex	32. William Barnard	56. John Gerard Leigh
9. Lord Lytton	33. Countess of Caledon	57. Frank Bradshaw
10. Lord Rendlesham	34. Charles James Phelips	58. John Trenchard
11. William Robert Baker	35. Coningsby Charles Sibthorp	59. Lord Chesham
12. Sir John Saunders Sebright	36. Earl of Strathmore	60. Lord Braye
13. John Remington Mills	37. Mrs Louisa Mary Browne	61. Francis Pym
14. Baron Nathan Rothschild	38. Lionel Ames	62. Earl of Caithness
15. Robert William Gaussen	39. Adolphus Meetkereke	63. Lewis Upton
16. Earl Spencer	40. Henry Edward Surtees	64. George Edward Dering
17. Frederick Delme Radcliffe	41. Robert Hanbury	65. Sir George Prescott
18. Arthur Giles Puller	42. Earl of Strafford	66. Earl Roden
19. Unwin Heathcote	43. Robert Greg	67. Charles Sabine Thellusson
20. George Sowerby	44. Marquess of Townshend	68. Lord Rokeby
21. Sir Henry Meux	45. John Arthur Houblon	69. David Carnegie
22. Lord Ebury	46. Anne Macnamara	70. Col. William Stuart
23. Sir Benet Drake Garrard	47. Arthur Maurice Blake	71. Sir Edmund Beckett.
24. Earl of Strathnairn	48. James Gape	

Based on Return of owners of land 1873. *Full details are listed in Table 6.4.*
Drawn in the Geography Department, UCL

strict family settlements impeded a free market in land and how far tenants were disadvantaged in dealing with overbearing landlords.

Hertfordshire was an exceptional county in having many aristocratic seats belonging to twenty-seven peers and peeresses, but very few great estates.[134] Of twenty-three owners of estates of more than 10,000 acres in extent, only three held 10,000 acres or more within the county. The other twenty owners possessed additional areas of land in other counties. The total area in Hertfordshire owned by the twenty-three grandees was 94,316 acres, or 24.5 per cent of the surface of the county, excluding 5,302 acres of waste land. That was almost exactly the same as the average of 24.5 per cent calculated by John Bateman for all counties in England and Wales, and much lower than John Bright's rash guess.[135] A first examination of the *Return* by the officials who compiled it, found no fewer than 250,000 errors in its transcription. The largest number of errors occurred in the recording of names and addresses in the original valuation lists. The rental values, in contrast, were filled up with more care, as they were the basis on which rates were assessed. Most of the errors were corrected before the *Return* was published,[136] and Bateman cleared up further errors and omissions by correspondence with owners. In Hertfordshire, he added over 1,700 acres to the possessions of the Earl of Strathmore, made small adjustments to acreages of other estates and corrected some names and addresses, including seven variants of the name of Lord Braye.[137] He also made a few mistakes. He failed to bring together scattered holdings belonging to railway companies and Oxford and Cambridge colleges, and used a confusing method of classifying landowners whereby he attempted to combine social groupings, 'peers and peeresses', 'squires', and 'yeomen', with size categories measured in acres and value categories based on notional gross annual rents.

A new ordering of estates, strictly by acreage, is presented in Table 6.4. Estates are arranged in order of total holdings of individuals in all counties of the United Kingdom. The list names seventy-nine owners of more than 2,000 acres, and follows the name of each owner by the address of the owner's seat in Hertfordshire or elsewhere; it also records other counties in which the owner had properties, acreages of the Hertfordshire estate and the owner's entire estate in the UK and, finally, the annual value of rents received respectively from Hertfordshire and from the estate as a whole. The new tabulation shows that the seventy-nine owners of more than 2,000 acres held a total of 186,204 acres or 48.4 per cent of the surface of the county, excluding wastes.

Areas of land in Hertfordshire held by owners of more than 2,000 acres in the United Kingdom in 1873 are represented on Figure 6.7. The map omits seven owners who were not residents in the county.[138] Henry Cowper is also omitted because he occupied Brocket Park as a tenant of Earl Cowper. Large estates covered a broad tract of land extending from Tring in the west to Sawbridgeworth in the east, the nine largest estates, at Hatfield, Woodhall at Watton, Panshanger, Gorhambury, Ashridge, Hoo at Kimpton, Kings Walden, Cassiobury and Knebworth, being clustered in the centre of the county in the valleys of the Lea, Beane, Mimram, Ver and Gade. In north-east Hertfordshire, from Hitchin to Bishops Stortford, a higher proportion of land belonged to estates under 2,000 acres in size. Enclosure of open

continued on p222

Table 6.4 Owners of more than 2,000 acres of land in the United Kingdom holding estates in Hertfordshire in 1873

Landowner	Seat	Estate (other than Herts)	Acres		Gross annual value £	
			Herts	Total UK	Herts	Total UK
Earl Brownlow	Ashridge	Salop, Lincs., Bucks., Beds.	8,551	58,335	12,760	86,426
Earl Cowper	Panshanger	Beds., Notts., Essex, Derbys.	10,122	37,869	13,540	60,392
Countess of Caledon	Tyttenhanger, Ridge	Tyrone, Armagh	1,948	34,060	2,567	22,321
Earl Spencer	Althorp, Northants	Northants, Warks., Norfolk, Bucks.	3,017	27,185	5,600	46,764
Earl of Strathmore	St Pauls Walden Bury	Forfar, Perth, Sussex	1,800	24,686	3,569	28,502
Lord Rendlesham	Rendlesham, Suffolk	Suffolk	3,969	24,028	5,500	25,024
David Carnegie	Eastbury House	Perth, Middx.	314	22,994	404	4,859
Marquess of Salisbury	Hatfield	Dorset, Lancs., Essex	13,390	20,223	18,372	33,413
Marquess of Townshend	Balls Park, Hertford	Norfolk, Warks.	1,565	19,910	1,645	22,560
Duke of Wellington	Standon Lordship	Hants, Somerset, Berks.	2,247	19,116	3,922	22,162
John Archer Houblon	Hallingbury, Essex	Essex, Lincs.	1,450	15,515	1,647	19,487
Baron Nathan de Rothschild	Tring Park	Bucks., Northants, Middx.	3,643	15,378	5,413	28,901
Sir Henry Meux	Theobalds, Cheshunt	Wilts., Middx.	2,702	15,110	6,017	23,507
Earl of Caithness	Stagenhoe, St Pauls Walden	Caithness	614	15,073	973	5,451
Earl of Strafford	Wrotham Park, Barnet	Middx., Kent, Londonderry	1,634	14,994	2,751	16,349
Earl of Essex	Cassiobury	Essex, Meath Roscommon	6,158	14,870	7,805	18,936
Earl Roden	Hyde Hall, Sawbridgeworth	Down, Louth, Essex	409	14,596	698	13,077
John Remington Mills	Tolmers, Cuffley	Norfolk, Leics., Kent	3,672	13,800	4,993	17,991
Lord Dacre	Hoo, Kimpton	Essex, Cambs., Suffolk	7,100	13,317	9,527	16,632
George Edward Dering	Lockleys, Welwyn	Galway, Durham	536	12,761	1,045	6,306
Lord Chesham	Latimers, Bucks.	Hunts., Bucks., Lancs., Lincs.	775	11,487	1,014	15,625
Abel Smith	Woodhall Park, Watton		11,213	11,213	14,617	14,617

continued over

Table 6.4 Owners of more than 2,000 acres of land in the United Kingdom holding estates in Hertfordshire in 1873 *continued*

Landowner	Seat	Estate (other than Herts)	Acres		Gross annual value £	
			Herts	Total UK	Herts	Total UK
Earl of Verulam	Gorhambury	Essex	8,625	10,117	11,919	14,101
Earl of Mexborough	Methley Park, W. Yorks.	W. Yorks., Notts.	1,769	9,534	1,854	34,565
Henry Edward Surtees	Lordship Farm, Lt Munden	Durham, Northumb.	1,706	9,456	2,283	7,102
Charles Sabine Thellusson	Edge Grove, Aldenham	N. & W. Yorks., Wilts.	400	8,981	684	14,064
Sir Edward Dyke	Aylesbury	Kent, Sussex	223	8,865	648	11,474
Frank Bradshaw	Durrants Farm, Watford	Devon, Somerset	811	8,122	1,394	10,342
Charles Cholmondley Hale	Kings Walden Park	Beds.	6,558	7,999	10,130	11,790
Coningsby Charles Sibthorp	North Mymms Park	Lincs.	1,818	7,700	2,331	10,300
Sir John S. Sebright	Beechwood	Beds.	3,886	7,210	6,155	13,567
John Gerard Leigh	Luton Hoo, Beds.	Beds.	824	6,507	1,141	12,945
Charles Eyre	Welford Park, Newbury	Berks.	409	6,146	592	7,713
George Sowerby	Putteridge Park	Beds.	2,805	6,001	4,098	7,767
Hon. Henry F. Cowper	Brocket Park	W. Yorks.	0	5,720	0	6,333
Anne Macnamara	Caddington Hall	Beds.	1,443	5,400	1,769	8,000
Richard Edward Arden	Sunbury Park, Middx.	Pemb., Carm., Middx., Bucks.	113	5,378	251	4,336
Christopher Tower	Huntsmore Park, Bucks.	Essex, Bucks., Beds.	266	5,287	347	9,833
Sir Henry Stanhope	Holm Lacy, Hereford	Hereford	152	5,191	256	6,480
Col William Stuart	Aldenham Abbey	Beds., Leics., Somerset	310	4,951	930	7,485
Lord Rokeby	Hazelwood, Abbots Langley	N. Yorks., Northumb.	348	4,863	911	9,180
Lord Lytton	Knebworth		4,863	4,863	5,366	5,366
Lord Braye	Bush Hall, Hatfield	Leics., Northants	650	4,658	759	8,317
Arthur Maurice Blake	Danesbury, Welwyn	Leics., Northants	1,414	4,343	2,282	7,331
John Henry Blagrave	Calcot Park, Reading	Berks., Somerset	396	4,249	632	8,709
Lionel Ames	Ayot St Lawrence House	Norfolk, Beds.	1,732	4,152	2,056	5,358

continued

Table 6.4 Owners of more than 2,000 acres of land in the United Kingdom holding estates in Hertfordshire in 1873 *continued*

Landowner	Seat	Estate (other than Herts)	Acres		Gross annual value £	
			Herts	Total UK	Herts	Total UK
Sir George R. Prescott	Cheshunt Park	Sussex, Kent	475	4,078	2,013	5,465
Mrs Frances C. Hanbury	Bedwell Park, Essendon	Northants	887	3,970	1,192	7,096
Arthur Giles Puller	Youngsbury, Standon	Essex	2,889	3,965	4,480	6,055
Thomas Frederick Halsey	Gaddesden Place	Dorset, Kent	2,100	3,911	3,381	5,839
William Robert Baker	Bayfordbury		3,912	3,912	6,631	6,631
Frederick Delme Radcliffe	Hitchin Priory	Beds.	2,900	3,826	4,600	5,890
Joseph Gurney Barclay	White Barns, Furneux Pelham	Suffolk, Essex	1,112	3,816	2,070	4,766
Francis Pym	Bragbury Hall, Aston	Beds., Hunts.	631	3,630	1,020	7,587
Robert William Gaussen	Brookmans Park		3,566	3,566	4,246	4,246
Charles Willes Wilshere	Frythe, Welwyn	Beds.	2,417	3,449	4,793	6,347
Henry Hucks Gibbs	Aldenham Park	Oxon	1,257	3,405	2,406	6,177
Sir Edmund Beckett	Batch Wood Hall, St Albans	Lincs., E & W Yorks.	274	3,396	274	7,517
James John Gape	Harpsfield Hall, Hatfield	Cambs.	1,360	3,246	1,435	3,199
Unwin Heathcote	Shephallbury	Derbys., Notts.	2,882	3,043	3,723	4,335
Charles James Phelips	Briggens, Hunsdon	Essex	1,868	2,925	3,299	4,840
Earl of Strathnairn	Wallington Manor	Cambs., Essex, Bucks.	2,491	2,918	3,171	3,603
Mrs Louisa Mary Browne	Walkern Hall	Beds., Cambs.	1,785	2,784	2,964	4,499
Lord Ebury	Moor Park	Middx.	2,620	2,723	5,634	5,803
Sir Benet Drake Garrard	Lamers, Wheathamstead		2,543	2,543	3,185	3,185
Richard Durant	High Canons Park	Devon	845	2,404	1,403	4,553
Robert, Lord Dimsdale	Essendon Place	Essex, Devon	1,357	2,382	1,653	3,641
Lewis Upton	Stanstead Bury	Louth	553	2,382	1,117	2,903
Robert Hanbury	Poles, Ware	Essex, Wilts.	1,694	2,351	1,523	4,280

continued over

Table 6.4 Owners of more than 2,000 acres of land in the United Kingdom holding estates in Hertfordshire in 1873 *continued*

Landowner	Seat	Estate (other than Herts)	Acres		Gross annual value £	
			Herts	Total UK	Herts	Total UK
Robert Phillips Greg	Coles Park, Westmill	Ches., Lancs.	1,573	2,324	1,928	5,996
John A. Trenchard	Nyn Park, Northaw	Wilts., Glos, Oxon	776	2,319	615	3,048
Adolphus Meetkerke	Julians, Rushden	Norfolk, Cambs., Lincs.	1,711	2,305	1,942	3,077
Earl of Clarendon	Grove, Sarratt	Warks.	903	2,298	1,833	3,741
William Hammond Solly	Serge Hill, Bedmond	Kent, Warks.	1,170	2,279	2,059	3,448
Horace Smith Bosanquet	Broxbourne Bury		2,207	2,207	4,451	4,451
William Barnard	High Wych, Sawbridgeworth	Essex	2,036	2,133	3,126	3,644
John Hodgson	Gilston Park	Essex	2,079	2,091	3,244	3,248
Mrs Salusbury Hughes	Offley Place		2,070	2,070	2,884	2,884
Catherine Martha Mellish	Hamels, Braughing		2,049	2,049	3,025	3,025

continued from p218
arable fields in this district was not completed until 1834 and some farmland remained in the hands of owner-occupying farmers.[139] Few large estates were situated on the uplands between Berkhamsted and Chorleywood, along the western border of Hertfordshire, another region where more land belonged to independent small farmers.

At the apex of the landowning elite in Hertfordshire in 1873 stood the Marquess of Salisbury, who held 13,390 acres in the county and 6,833 acres elsewhere, including a valuable 20 acres in Westminster, making a total of 20,223 acres. Estates in the United Kingdom held by Earl Brownlow (58,335 acres, of which 8,551 acres lay in Hertfordshire) and Earl Cowper (37,869 acres, of which 10,122 were in Hertfordshire), were much larger overall. The Countess of Caledon had extensive possessions in Ireland, the Earl of Strathmore owned vast areas in Scotland and Lord Rendlesham possessed a large tract in the Sandlings of east Suffolk. Earl Spencer, the Marquess of Townshend and the Duke of Wellington owned small second homes in Hertfordshire and the Earl of Strafford, Earl Roden, Lord Chesham and John Gerard Leigh managed their Hertfordshire properties from seats in adjoining counties. Hon. Henry Frederick Cowper lived at Brocket Hall and represented Hertford in parliament, but his entire estate was situated in West Yorkshire. In addition to seventeen peers and peeresses, six commoners owned estates of more than 10,000 acres. They were David Carnegie, John Archer Houblon, Sir Henry Meux, John Remington Mills, George Edward Dering and Abel Smith, and were mainly descended from Scottish, Flemish and Huguenot families who had made fortunes as bankers, brewers and grocers in London; one was a member of a landed family from Kent married to a Hertfordshire lady.

Below the great landowners were sixteen owners of estates ranging from 5,000 to 9,999 acres in size, holding 6.0 per cent of the land in Hertfordshire; twenty-one owners of estates between 3,000 and 4,999 acres, occupying another 9.5 per cent of the county; and nineteen owners of estates over 2,000 and under 2,999 acres, taking a further 8.4 per cent. In total, 56 owners of medium-sized estates possessed 91,888 acres, covering 23.9 per cent of the surface of the county, excluding wastes. Among owners of more than 2,000 but less than 10,000 acres, Lord Lytton, William Baker, Robert Gaussen, Sir Charles Benet Drake Garrard and others possessed estates lying wholly within Hertfordshire. Some close relatives owned estates in the same locality. Charles Thellusson was related to Lord Rendlesham who owned neighbouring land in Aldenham and Charles Eyre was a member of the Houblon family who had changed his name. In 1873, consolidation of landownership in the hands of great and medium-sized owners had reached its zenith. The greatest estates had increased in size after 1815 by acquiring farms and small estates put up for sale as a result of the post-war depression. Expansion had slowed down after 1840. Between the drawing of the Tithe surveys around 1840 and 1873, a few great estates had grown by small additions whilst properties under 2,000 acres had continued to diminish in size and number.

The significance of ordering landowners by size of estate in 1873 is that it corresponds in two ways with the size of parks recorded on the Ordnance maps of 1863–81. Sizes of parks tended to be related to

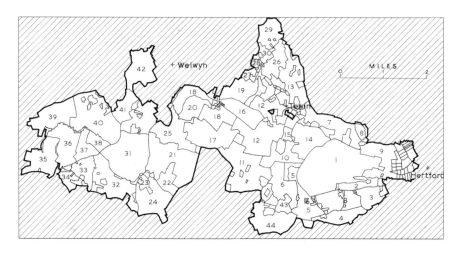

Figure 6.8: Panshanger and Brocket estates, 1862–71. The estate extended from Hertford to the western edge of Welwyn. Panshanger Park is located at number 1; Marden Hill, 14; Tewin Water, 16; Digswell House, 20; Brocket Park, 31. Based on plans of estates of Earl Cowper (HALS DE/P/P64). Drawn in the Geography Department, UCL

the total extent of lands all over the United Kingdom from which their owners drew rents, but they were also related more directly to the size and rentals of possessions in Hertfordshire. The largest park in the county, Hatfield, belonged to the Marquess of Salisbury, the eighth greatest landowner, whose Hertfordshire estate was larger than any other. The second largest park, Ashridge, belonged to Earl Brownlow, the leading landowner, whose Hertfordshire estate ranked fifth. Earl Brownlow also possessed a principal seat and an extensive park at Belton in Lincolnshire. Earl Cowper, the second greatest landowner, owned Panshanger, the fourth largest park, and three smaller parks in the Mimram valley. The unification of the Brocket estate and Panshanger along the line of the Great North Road after the death of Lord Palmerston's widow is represented in Figure 6.8. The third largest park, Cassiobury, belonged to the Earl of Essex, who ranked sixteenth among great landowners, but eighth in order of owners of Hertfordshire estates.

Owners of smaller parks possessed estates of many different sizes. Some belonged to gentry families, whose small parks were surrounded by extensive farming estates. Some belonged to churchmen and junior members of aristocratic and gentry families, most of whom had estates under 2,000 acres. Others belonged to families who had retired to Hertfordshire after serving in India, the colonies or in the army and navy. Some planned to stay and planted trees; others were prepared to re-sell and move. Still others were formed by Londoners who built comfortable villas and laid out elaborate gardens and pleasure grounds. William Phillimore, who owned Kendalls Hall and a small park in Aldenham, was an exceptionally rich Londoner. He was the only landowner apart from the Marquess of Salisbury to possess a valuable estate in London, fifty-four acres of most sought-after building land in Kensington. Some newcomers bought estates in order to preserve game and enjoy country sports. Many were only interested in buying sufficient land to ensure their privacy. The relationship between the size of parks and the size of estates may be summed up in two broad generalisations. Old-established parks occupied less than one-tenth of the area of an estate. New parks generally occupied more than one-tenth, some more than half an estate.

Parks, landowners and economic decline

Soon after 1873, observers realised that the economic base on which the wealth of landowners rested was no longer secure and it was questionable whether they could continue to afford the luxury of maintaining their parks. In 1873, the quantity of wheat imported from the New World exceeded the amount produced in Britain for the first time and, after 1874, cereal prices began to decline. The fall in prices preceded four bad seasons. A wet spring in 1878 delayed sowing and three notoriously wet summers in 1879, 1880 and 1882 ruined crops before they could be harvested. Agricultural distress was caused as much by a succession of harvest failures as by low grain prices. Farmers who survived the wet years were hit again by a succession of bad seasons caused by record droughts from 1892 to 1895. In Hertfordshire, where grain-growing was a major source of farm incomes, landlords had little choice but to accept lower rents, and between 1874–8 and 1894–8 rents fell by 40 per cent on most estates in the county. The second Earl of Verulam's income fell from £17,000 in the 1870s to £14,000 in 1889.[140] At the end of the nineteenth century, the diehard conservative Marquess of Salisbury was drawing more than half his income from urban property and the Earl of Verulam supplemented his dwindling rental income with director's fees and dividends.[141] Areas of heavy soils suffered most, with some poorly drained arable land being allowed to tumble down to rough pasture. Some farms close to railway stations took up dairying and a few began to grow vegetables. At Much Hadham, rents in 1901 ranged from 30s an acre on the best land in a good position to between 10s and 7s 6d on land more than three miles from a railway station.[142]

A consequence of rent reductions was that the capital value of land depreciated by more than 15 per cent between 1878 and 1890.[143] Landowners who were heavily mortgaged were put under increasing pressure to reduce their debts, and those whose estates were entailed by strict family settlements were not free to sell land; it was landowners themselves who mustered sufficient votes in parliament to secure the passage of the Settled Land Act, 1882, removing most restrictions on sales of freehold land. The act permitted a tenant for life to sell any settled land except the principal mansion and park, for which the trustees of the settlement had to give their consent. Once land was released from entails, hard-pressed owners of large estates were able to dispose of outlying properties and smaller owners were free to sell all their land.

Of ten parks within five miles of St Albans in 1890, F.M.L. Thompson found that only three remained in the same hands in 1912:

> and they were the houses of the old nobility and gentry, Lord Verulam, Lord Cavan and the Cherry Garrards. The others housed temporarily such newcomers as Lord Grimthorpe, lawyer, banker and church restorer, Sir John Blundell Maple, upholsterer and furniture store keeper and John Barnato Joel, South African diamond dealer.[144]

Rider Haggard gloomily remarked that some owners in Hertfordshire were 'crippled by losses of income' and that 'possession of land is becoming, or has already become, a luxury for rich men, to whom it is a costly toy, or a means of indulging a taste for sport'.[145]

As a result of insecurity, the land market was much brisker at the end of the nineteenth century than it had been at the beginning. Among willing buyers were rich Londoners and a new group of building developers. After a railway station was opened at Radlett in 1868, a search for eligible building sites began and two landowners, Robert Phillimore of Kendalls Hall and Thomas Part of Aldenham Lodge, decided to develop plots here and there on their properties between 1894 and 1914. Most of the new houses were set in large gardens.[146] Around St Albans, Watford and Rickmansworth, residential development advanced, meeting determined resistance from owners of large parks at Gorhambury, Cassiobury and Moor Park. At Hatfield the Marquess of Salisbury succeeded in preventing builders from gaining access to the old town and railway station.

Another blow to the fortunes of great estates was a shift in the world market for timber trees. Since the sixteenth century, the navy had depended on parks for a large part of its supply of oak timber from free-growing trees which produced crooked pieces, as well as elm timber, which lasted well when permanently submerged. Naval demand reached a height in 1815. The era of wooden warships ended abruptly in 1862, when an American ironside destroyed a Confederate man o'war at the Battle of Hampton Roads. After that, the world's navies began to re-equip themselves with ironclad dreadnoughts. A rapidly expanding merchant fleet continued to consume large quantities of oaks and elms from parks to build wooden sailing ships until the 1880s but, by that time, bridges were constructed with steel and factories, warehouses and offices were framed with steel girders. In house-building and furniture-making, softwoods imported from Scandinavia and North America competed with home-grown beech and ash. Imported softwoods also provided the pulp from which paper was manufactured. The market for firewood declined as railways brought coal to towns and villages for heating houses, raising steam and making gas.

Contrary to the world-wide market trend, there was still a demand for the special qualities of hardwood timber grown in Hertfordshire, and poles used for fencing and making garden furniture were supplied to local manufacturers. At the end of the nineteenth century, sales of timber and wood from Hertfordshire estates paid the wages of foresters, their staffs and costs of replanting, thinning and felling, while leaving small surpluses to add to estates' incomes. The agricultural returns for 1891 recorded a total of 23,151 acres of woodland in Hertfordshire, including 307 acres planted since 1881. In 1895, a woodland census indicated an increase of about 1,400 acres, bringing the total area of woods and plantations up to 24,543 acres. The increase continued from 1895 to 1905, when 26,586 acres were reported. The total included 8,167 acres of coppice, 1,104 acres of new plantations and 17,297 acres of other woods.[147] Some of the new planting was of pines and larch but most soils were not well adapted to growing conifers. Unlike agriculture, forestry was still contributing a little to the upkeep of parks at the beginning of the twentieth century.

During the nineteenth century, private parks in Hertfordshire reached their maximum extent, covering 7.5 per cent of the surface area in 1821 and 7.3 per cent in 1863–81. Some large parks shrank a little during this period but many continued to increase in size through the impetus of planting programmes initiated by earlier generations. Small parks increased in number primarily because many newly rich families wanted to enter the county elite.

The largest parks were among the oldest. Echoing the original purpose of a park, ten still contained deer at the end of the century. Stately avenues at Cassiobury and restored Renaissance gardens at Hatfield reminded visitors of their antiquity, while the mature beeches at Beechwood and Ashridge were magnificent. At Brocket and Panshanger, broad stretches of water and enveloping woods, composed as landscape gardens about a century earlier, reached maturity. All these features lent large parks an old-time charm.

Newly formed Victorian parks and smaller ornamental grounds exhibited a great variety of styles. Innovation was their chief characteristic, displayed not only in a bewildering medley of designs but also in choices of plants and in the use of machinery and accessories. Collectors introduced into parks new plants from all parts of the world and new kinds of structures were erected to propagate alpine, tropical and aquatic plants. Glasshouses, wheelbarrows, lawn mowers, water sprinklers and a range of specialist implements were invented. Gardening became a skilled occupation and the number of gardeners employed in Hertfordshire increased from 1,215 in 1851 to 3,100 in 1901.

During the nineteenth century, a final stage was reached in the appropriation of parkland as private property. The enclosure movement left few vestiges of common land open to villagers. Within parks, customary rights to graze livestock, gather winter fuel, and pick hazelnuts, blackberries and mushrooms were abolished. Permits to fish had to be paid for and taking of game was strictly prohibited. Claims by owners to possess wild birds and wild animals that happened to nest and burrow within the boundaries of their property continued to be contested by local residents. The demarcation of private property boundaries and the restriction or exclusion of access to the grounds of country mansions were persistent themes in nineteenth-century park-making. Public rights of way were systematically closed or diverted and entry to parks was controlled through gates and lodges.

From 1846 onwards, free trade policy enabled townspeople to buy cheap food from overseas and left Hertfordshire farmers and landowners struggling to find alternative sources of income. The principle of free trade extended to releasing landowners from strict family settlements and opening the land market to competitive trading. In the last two decades of the nineteenth century, owners of parks were able to sell land and reinvest the proceeds in government stock, building development, railways, foreign mining and manufacturing enterprises, all of which earned higher returns than farm rents.

Owners of parks in 1900 had different political aspirations, different economic objectives and different attitudes to society from their predecessors in 1815. In 1900, the ownership of broad acres still conferred great advantages in seeking political power but gave no assurance of electoral success. Economically, large landowners were severely handicapped in competition with businessmen: parks were valued as costly pleasure grounds rather than as profitable assets. Socially, owners were more detached from villagers and their servants than they had been in 1815. Their parks also stood apart from the rest of the landscape. The three characteristics of parkland that remained unchanged throughout the century were spaciousness, verdure and privacy, but these qualities were thrown into sharp contrast with other forms of land use as the built-up area marched towards them.

Notes

1. G.E. Mingay (ed.), *The agrarian history of England and Wales*. Vol. VI 1750–1850 (Cambridge, 1989), p.1095.

2. A total of 338,000 left the armed services between 1813 and 1819: B.R. Mitchell and P. Deane, *Abstract of British historical statistics* (Cambridge, 1962), p.396. It is not known how many ex-servicemen returned to Hertfordshire but in July 1814 the Hertford Militia, numbering 7,000 was disembodied. Accounts and estimates of the disembodied militia. *Parliamentary Papers 1814–15*, vol. IX; J.H. Busby, 'Local military forces in Hertfordshire, 1793–1814', *Journal of the Society of Army Historical Research*, 31 (1953), pp.15–24.

3. Return of the population of Great Britain in 1811; *Census of Great Britain 1851*, vol. I, Population Tables (London, 1854); D.J.M. Hooson, 'Some aspects of the growth and distribution of population in Hertfordshire since 1801', (PhD thesis, Univ. London, 1955).

4. Poor rate assessment and expenditure on the poor in each county of England and Wales 1748 to 1839, *Parliamentary Papers (1839)* XLIV.1; Mingay, *Agrarian history*, 1750–1850, p.975.

5. F. Kilvington and S. Flood (eds.), 'Diary of Thomas Newcome, rector of Shenley, 1822–1849', in J. Knight and S. Flood (eds.), *Two nineteenth-century Hertfordshire diaries* (Hertford, 2002), pp.134–9.

6. Knight and Flood, *Two nineteenth-century diaries*, pp.122, 152, 157, 215, 245.

7. J. Hill, *Hertfordshire poor law removal orders* (Hertford, 2003), pp.135–6.

8. W. Cobbett, *Rural rides in Surrey, Kent and other counties in the years 1821 to 1832* (London, 1912), vol. I, p.79.

9. S.G. Checkland and E.O.A. Checkland (eds.), *The Poor Law Report of 1834* (Harmondsworth, 1974), pp.129–30.

10. *Ibid.*, pp.345–7, 453.

11. Cobbett, *Rural rides*, vol. I, pp.86–8.

12. Hill, *Hertfordshire removal orders*, pp.106–10.

13. Le Hardy and Reckitt, *Calendar to the sessions books 1799 to 1833*, vol. 9, pp.188–586.

14. 'Memorandum on the stealing of deer from Totteridge Park' (HALS 68417).

15. K. Griffin, *Transported beyond the seas: an alphabetical listing of criminals prosecuted in Hertfordshire who received transportation sentences to Australia 1784–1866* (Hertford, 1997), p.18.

16. *Ibid.*, pp.11–62.

17. E.J. Hobsbawm and G. Rude, *Captain Swing* (Harmondsworth, 1969), pp.115, 119, 134–5, 209.

18. Griffin, *Transported beyond the seas*, p.29.

19. The first edition of *Pigot's Hertfordshire directory* (London, 1823) contained no classified list of gentry. Gentry were listed separately in Pigot and Co's *Royal, national and commercial directory and topography of the county of Hertfordshire* (London, 1839).

20. *Map of the county of Hertford, from actual survey by A. Bryant in the years 1820 and 1821* (BL Maps C.23.a.6).

21. Hodson, *Printed maps of Hertfordshire*, p.116.

22. A. Bryant, *Preparing for publication: a new map of the county of Hertford* (London, 1821), p.1 (HALS 63787).

23. P. Walne, *A catalogue of manuscript maps in the Hertfordshire Record Office* (1969) (HALS 912.4258).

24. The British Library holds Bryant's maps of the counties of Hertford (published in 1822), Surrey (1823), Oxfordshire (1824), Gloucestershire (1824), Buckingham (1825), Bedford (1826), Suffolk (1826), Norfolk (1826), Northampton (1827), Lincolnshire (1828), East Riding, Yorkshire (1829), Chester (1831) and Hereford (1835).

25. J.B. Harley, *Christopher Greenwood county map-maker and his Worcestershire map of 1822* (Worcester, 1962), pp.1–24.

26. Le Hardy and Reckitt, *Calendar to the sessions books 1799 to 1833*, pp.537–45.

27. Clutterbuck's History is too early, Cussans is too late, Neale's Views provides only two names, the Victoria County History provides few dates, Pigot's Directory is late and not wholly reliable and the county list of magistrates contains no addresses. Biographies and diaries are generally accurate and record precise dates.

28. Bryant, *Preparing for publication*, p.1.

29. Palings were represented on the map at Albury Hall, Ashlyns, Ashridge, Aspenden Hall, Ayot St Lawrence, Bartletts, Bayfordbury, Bedwell Pk, Beechwood, Brickendon Bury, Briggens, Brocket, Broxbourne Bury, Camfield Pl, Cassiobury, Cheshunt Ho, Codicote Lo, Coles Pk, Corney Bury, Gilston Pk, Gorhambury, Grove Pk, Hamels, Haresfoot, Hatfield, Hunsdon Ho, Kimpton Hoo, Kings Walden Bury, Knebworth, Lockleys, Moor Pk, Moor Pl, Newsells, North Mymms Pk, Offley Pl, Panshanger, Porters, Rickmansworth Pk, Sacombe Pk, St Johns Lo, St Pauls Walden Bury, Sandridge Lo, Tewin Water, Theobalds Pk, Totteridge Pk, Tring Pk, Ware Pk, Woodhall Pk, Woolmers Pk and Wynches.

30. Smith, *Hertfordshire houses*, pp.113, 158.

31. Part, 'Sport ancient and modern', pp.349–59.

32. H.G. Oldfield, Dimsdale collection of Hertfordshire drawings (HALS D/EOf 1–9), vol. III, p.349; L.L. Leitner, 'John Almon, 1737–1805, bookseller and political journalist', in *Oxford Dictionary of National Biography*, vol. 1, p.885.

33. J.P. Neale, *Views of the seats of noblemen and gentlemen in England, Wales, Scotland and Ireland* (London, 1819), vol. II.

34. Smith, *Hertfordshire houses*, p.33.

35. *Ibid.*, pp.29, 60.

36. J.C. Loudon, *Hints on the formation of gardens and pleasure grounds; with designs in various styles of rural embellishment* (London, 1812), p.31.

37. J.C. Loudon (ed.), *The landscape gardening and landscape architecture of the late Humphry Repton, Esq.* (London, 1840), pp.viii–ix.

38. J.C. Loudon, *Gardeners' Magazine*, 12 (1836), pp.279–87.

39. *Ibid.*, pp.289–92.

40. J.C. Loudon, *Encyclopaedia of gardening; comprising the theory and practice of horticulture, floriculture, arboriculture and landscape gardening*, 4th edn. (London, 1826), p.1071.

41. S. Piebenga, 'William Sawrey Gilpin (1762–1843): picturesque improver', *Garden History*, 22 (1994), pp.175–96.

42. W.S. Gilpin, *Practical hints upon landscape gardening* (London, 1832), p.47.

43. Britton, *The history and description of Cassiobury Park*, p.26.

44. *A German Prince (Herman Puckler-Muskau) Tour in Germany, Holland and England in the years 1826, 1827 and 1828: a series of letters* (London, 1832), vol. IV, pp.257–8.

45. J.C. Loudon, *The suburban gardener and villa companion* (London, 1836).

46. J.G. Tait and W.M. Parker (eds.), *The journal of Sir Walter Scott* (Edinburgh, 1950), p.551.

47. R. Leleux, *The east midlands. Vol IX. Regional history of the railways of Great Britain* (Newton Abbot, 1976), p.13.

48. J. Francis, *A history of the English railway: its social relations and revelations* (London, 1851), vol. I, p.189.

49. M.C. Reed, *Investment in railways in Britain 1820–44: a study in the development of the capital market* (London, 1975), p.137.

50. J.C. Bourne, *Drawings of the London and Birmingham Railway with an historical and descriptive account by John Britton* (London, 1839), pp.10–20.

51. C.H. Grinling, *The history of the Great Northern Railway, 1845–1902* (London, 1903), p.15.

52. D.I. Gordon, *The eastern counties. Vol. V. Regional history of the railways of Great Britain* (Newton Abbot, 1968), p.111.

53. *Osborne's London and Birmingham Railway guide* (Birmingham, 1838), p.i.

54. B. Elliott, *Victorian gardens* (London, 1986), p.68.

55. A. Rowe, *A history of Knebworth's parks* (Ware, 2005), pp.18–21.

56. Hertfordshire Gardens Trust and Williamson, *Parks and gardens of west Hertfordshire*, p.71.

57. Elliott, *Victorian gardens*, pp.53, 99–105, 171.

58. E. Kemp, *How to lay out a small garden*, 2nd edn. (London, 1858), pp.241–5.

59. *Ibid.*, pp.356–9.

60. Hertfordshire Gardens Trust and Williamson, *Parks and gardens of west Hertfordshire*, pp.83.

61. R. Desmond, *Dictionary of British and Irish botanists and horticulturalists* (London, 1977), p.255; Elliott, *Victorian gardens*, pp.36, 111, 114.

62. Hertfordshire Gardens Trust and Bisgrove, *Hertfordshire gardens*, p.24.

63. Elliott, *Victorian gardens*, p.185.

64. K. Banister, 'The Pulham family of Hertfordshire and their work' in A. Rowe (ed.), *Hertfordshire garden history: a miscellany* (Hatfield, 2007), p.137.

65. S. Festing, 'Pulham has done his work well', *Garden History*, 12 (1984), pp.140–1.

66. Hertfordshire Gardens Trust and Bisgrove, *Hertfordshire gardens*, pp.22, 25.

67. Hertfordshire Gardens Trust and Williamson, *Parks and gardens in west Hertfordshire*, pp.97, 98.

68. Elliott, *Victorian gardens*, pp.97, 99; Banister, 'Pulham family', pp.134–54.

69. W. Paul, *The rose garden* (London, 1848), pp.21, 22, 36–9, 47, 48.

70. W. Paul, *The handbook of villa gardening* (London, 1855), pp.11, 13, 16.

71. Plan for a rose garden at Beechwood, 1857 (Sebright Papers, Maps HALS 18690).

72. Kemp, *Small garden*, pp.47–138.

73. Elliott, *Victorian gardens*, pp.71–4, 138–47; C. Ridgway, 'William Andrews Nesfield: between Uvedale Price and Isambard Kingdom Brunel', *Journal of Garden History*, 13 (1993), pp.69–89.

74. Hertfordshire Gardens Trust and Williamson, *Parks and gardens in west Hertfordshire*, p.78.

75. *Ibid.*, pp.79–80.

76. Hertfordshire Gardens Trust and Bisgrove, *Hertfordshire gardens*, p.24.

77. Elliott, *Victorian gardens*, pp.128–31.

78. 'Knebworth, Herts', *Country Life*, 19 (7 April 1906), p.490.

79. W. Robinson, *The wild garden, or our groves and shrubberies made beautiful by the naturalization of hardy exotic plants: with a chapter on the garden of British wild flowers* (London, 1870), p.7.

80. Pevsner, revised Cherry, *Hertfordshire*, p.263.

81. Robinson, *Wild garden*, p.236.

82. A. Amherst, *A history of gardening in England* (London, 1896), p.298; H. Smith, 'A Victorian passion: the role of Sander's orchid nursery in St Albans', in Rowe, *Hertfordshire garden history*, pp.155–73.

83. J.J. Baker, 'Bayfordbury', *Transactions of the East Hertfordshire Archaeological Society*, 3 (1907), p.265.

84. 'Bayfordbury Record Book', presented to the John Innes Horticultural Institution by Lady Clinton Baker in 1946.

85. W.H. Baker and A.B. Jackson, *Illustrations of conifers* (London, 1909–1913).

86. 'Bayfordbury Record Book', pp.43, 54, 60.

87. J.C. Loudon, *A treatise on improving and managing country residences* (London, 1806), p.330.

88. 'Bayfordbury Record Book', p.61.

89. *Gardeners' Chronicle* (5 June 1875), pp.720–2; A. Lawrence, *The Aldenham House gardens: a brief history of the school grounds* (Elstree, 1988).

90. Hertfordshire Gardens Trust and Williamson, *Parks and gardens in west Hertfordshire*, pp.97–100.

91. Hertfordshire Gardens Trust and Williamson, *Parks and gardens in Hertfordshire*, p.97.

92. A. Hillyard, 'Lilley Bottom', *Hertfordshire Countryside* (January, 2005), p.39.

93. J. Whitaker, *A descriptive list of deer parks and paddocks in England* (London, 1892), pp.19–26, 75–8, 118–22.

94. J.E. Harting, 'Hertfordshire deer parks', *Transactions of the Hertfordshire Natural History Society*, II (1883), pp.97–111, ref. on p.104; Sales particulars, Kings Walden, 1885 (HALS D/ERy B292).

95. Harting, 'Hertfordshire deer parks', p.102.

96. *VCH Hertfordshire*, vol. 4, p.279.

97. Whitaker, *Deer parks and paddocks in England*, p.75.

98. *VCH Hertfordshire*, vol. 4, 277–9; *VCH Hertfordshire*, vol. 1 (London, 1902), p.358. The nine deer parks were Ashridge, Cassiobury, Grove, Hatfield, Knebworth, Moor Park, Rickmansworth, Tring and Woodhall.

99. Ordnance Survey, *Account of the methods and processes of the Ordnance Survey of the United Kingdom; drawn up by officers of Royal Engineers employed under Lieut.-Gen. Sir Henry James, R E, F R S, Director-General* (London, 1875), p.46.

100. *Ibid.*, p.46.

101. R. Oliver, *Ordnance Survey maps: a concise guide for historians* (London, 2005), p.95.

102. J.H. Andrews, *A paper landscape: the Ordnance Survey in nineteenth-century Ireland* (London, 1975), pp.102, 129.

103. J.B. Harley, *Ordnance Survey land-use mapping: parish books of reference and the county series 1:2500 maps, 1855–1918*, Hist. Geog. Research Series 2 (Norwich, 1979), pp.40–1.

104. Cussans, *History of Hertfordshire*, 'Hundred of Cashio', vol 3, part 2, p.175.

105. D. Cecil, *Lord M., or the later life of Lord Melbourne* (London, 1954), pp.112–301.

106. D. Steele, 'Temple, Henry John, third Viscount Palmerston (1784–1865) prime minister', in *Oxford Dictionary of National Biography*, vol. 54, pp.55–67.

107. D. Cecil, *The Cecils of Hatfield: a portrait of an English ruling family* (London, 1973), pp.217–67.

108. W. Le Hardy (ed.), *Calendar to the sessions books 1833–43*, Hertfordshire County Records, vol. 10 (Hertford, 1957), p.305.

109. Griffin, *Transported beyond the seas*, p.74.

110. Cussans, *History of Hertfordshire*, 'Hundred of Edwinstree', vol. 1, p.21.

111. Cowell, 'Berkhamsted Common', pp.145–61.

112. Cussans, *History of Hertfordshire*, 'Edwinstree', vol. 1, p.107.

113. Munby, *Hertfordshire landscape*, p.188.

114. N. Agar, 'The Hertfordshire farmer in the age of the industrial revolution', in D. Jones-Baker, *Hertfordshire in history* (Hertfordshire Local History Council, 1991), pp.258–60.

115. *VCH Hertfordshire*, vol. 4, p.219; *Poor Law Reports. Parliamentary Papers* (1852) XXIII, p.39; (1899) LXXXIII (1), p.619.

116. F.M.L. Thompson, *English landed society in the nineteenth century* (London, 1963), p.137.

117. *Ibid.*, p.137 citing Gorhambury MSS, 1st Lord Verulam's Diary, 17 January 1823.

118. *Ibid.*, pp.139–40 citing Gorhambury MSS, Game Books 1821–1923.

119. Part, 'Sport, ancient and modern', pp.360–1.

120. Prince, 'Panshanger', p.52; Panshanger MSS, Game Record 1899–1923 (HALS).

121. F.M.L. Thompson, 'Landowners and the rural community', in G.E. Mingay (ed.), *The Victorian countryside* (London, 1981), vol. II, pp.457–74.

122. *Ibid.*, vol. II, pp.459–62.

123. Le Hardy and Reckitt, *Calendar to the sessions books 1799 to 1833*, vol. 9, pp.623–40; Le Hardy, *Calendar to the sessions books 1833–43*, vol. 10, pp.497–532.

124. *Census of Great Britain 1851, vol. II, Ages, civil condition and occupations of the people* (London, 1854), pp.162–6.

125. *Census of England and Wales 1871, vol. III, Ages, occupations, birthplaces* (London, 1873), pp.127–32; *Census of England and Wales 1891, vol. III, Ages, condition as to marriage, occupations* (London, 1893), pp.99–101; *Census of England and Wales 1901, County of Hertford, Table 32 Occupations* (London, 1903), pp.46–7.

126. Thompson, *English landed society*, p.305.

127. *VCH Hertfordshire*, vol. 4, p.355; E.W. Bovill, *English country life, 1780–1830* (London, 1962), pp.223–30.

128. *VCH Hertfordshire*, vol. 4, pp.350–7.

129. H. Williams, *History of Watford and trade directory* (London, 1884), p.38.

130. E.R. Kelly (ed.), *Post Office directory of the six home counties: Essex, Herts, Middlesex, Kent, Surrey and Sussex* (London, 1874), pp.xii–xviii.

131. D. Spring, 'Introduction', in J. Bateman, *The great landowners of Great Britain and Ireland*, reprint of 4th edn. (1883) (Leicester, 1971), p.8; G.B. Smith, *Life and speeches of John Bright* (New York, 1881), p.137.

132. J.L. Sanford and M. Townsend, *The great governing families of England* (Edinburgh, 1865).

133. *Return of owners of land, 1873, England and Wales, exclusive of the Metropolis. Parliamentary Papers.* (1874) LXXII.

134. The twenty-seven peers and peeresses who owned properties in Hertfordshire were Lord Braye, Earl Brownlow, Earl of Caithness, Countess Caledon, Lord Chesham, Earl of Clarendon, Earl Cowper, Lord Dacre, Lord Dimsdale, Lord Ebury, Lord Ellenborough, Earl of Essex, Viscountess Glamis, Lord Lytton, Earl of Mexborough, Lord Rendlesham, Earl Roden, Lord Rokeby, Baron Rothschild, Marquess of Salisbury, Earl Spencer, Earl Strafford, Earl Strathnairn, Earl of Strathmore, Marquess of Townshend, Earl of Verulam and Duke of Wellington.

135. J. Bateman, *The great landowners of Great Britain and Ireland*, reprint of 4th edn. (1883) (Leicester, 1971), pp.xiii–xvii, 515.

136. *Return of owners*, p.6.

137. Bateman, *Great landowners*, p.55.

138. Non-resident landowners in 1873 were the Earl of Mexborough, Sir Edward Dyke, Charles Eyre, Richard Arden, Christopher Tower, Sir Henry Stanhope and John Blagrave.

139. M. Turner, *English parliamentary enclosure: its historical geography and economic history* (Folkestone, 1980), p.198.

140. Thompson, *English Landed society*, pp.304, 310.

141. F.M.L. Thompson, 'Business and landed elites in the nineteenth century', in F.M.L. Thompson (ed.), *Landowners, capitalists and entrepreneurs: essays for Sir John Habakkuk* (Oxford, 1994), p.166.

142. H. Rider Haggard, *Rural England, being an account of agricultural and social researches carried out in the years 1901 and 1902* (London, 1906), vol. I, p.535.

143. Thompson, *English Landed society*, p.318.

144. F.M.L. Thompson, 'English landed society in the twentieth century. II, New poor and new rich', *Transactions of the Royal Historical Society*, 6th series, 1 (1991), p.16, comparing the 1890 and 1912 editions of Kelly's directory of Hertfordshire. The ten houses checked were Aldwickbury, Batchwood, Childwickbury, Gorhambury, Lamer House, Mackerye End, Marshalswick, Oaklands, Sandridgebury and Wheathampstead House.

145. Rider Haggard, *Rural England*, vol. I, pp.421, 441, vol. II, p.543.

146. J.T. Coppock, 'Dormitory settlements around London', in J.T. Coppock and H.C. Prince (eds.), *Greater London* (London, 1964), pp.279–89.

147. *VCH Hertfordshire*, vol. 4, pp.279–80.

Chapter VII

Heritage of Parks
in the Twentieth Century

AFTER 1880, INCREASING NUMBERS OF PARKS in Hertfordshire were sold to purchasers who converted their land and buildings to new uses. Many country houses ceased to be lived in as family homes. Some were demolished or had wings and outbuildings pulled down. Other mansions were adapted to institutional functions as schools and hospitals. When resident families departed, parks disappeared. Ornamental lakes were expensive to maintain and produced no income; belt plantations were not conducive to efficient forest management; clumps threw shadows across patches of grass and obstructed mowing of meadows. For use as public parks and recreation grounds or as golf courses, private parks could be adapted without much alteration, but for most other uses, parkland features had to be cleared away.

Until 1930, few efforts were made to save parks as sites of historic interest. Owners felt no obligation to open their gates to the general public and neither local nor central government had the powers or resources to preserve parks and country houses. During the inter-war years, the idea that the countryside could be used as a place of recreation gained widespread support from ramblers' and cyclists' organisations; many people agreed that urban expansion should be controlled and access to open spaces secured for outdoor recreation. Lord Phillimore reasoned that because few people actually worked in rural areas and their contribution to national wealth was small, the countryside ought to be thrown open as 'a vast park or pleasure ground for the townsman, where he should be able to recuperate from his efforts and be solaced by its natural beauties'.[1] Prevailing tastes among urban visitors favoured natural, in preference to peopled, landscapes, and in cultivated countryside tourists preferred to see old cottages, snug inns and neatly tended fields rather than grand mansions and majestic avenues. Those who were devoted to preserving country houses and their grounds were unable to stem the pressures for new developments, including house- and road-building.

In the period after the Second World War, the government took the initiative in drawing a green belt around London, designating the Chilterns an area of outstanding natural beauty, protecting sites of special scientific interest and authorising the treasury to acquire houses and grounds of national importance in lieu of death duties. The Forestry Commission agreed to share the costs of managing woodlands dedicated by their owners to timber production. Parish councils were directed to map footpaths and other rights of way and the Ancient Monuments Commission began to schedule important architectural works built after 1714.

The fate of parks in the twentieth century depended on the determination of owners to hold on to their landed estates. In the first half of the century, when agriculture was depressed and landowners were heavily taxed, parks disappeared rapidly. Between 1945 and 1970, agriculture and land values recovered and fewer parks were destroyed. After 1970, the outlook for parks darkened, but many were saved by adapting to new uses as golf courses, colleges, hotels and spacious grounds for genteel apartments.

Destruction of parks

The dismemberment of parks and estates accelerated when landowners, caricatured by radicals as 'idle rich', were targeted by the Chancellor of the Exchequer David Lloyd George and successive liberal governments from 1906 to 1914. The 'People's Budget' of 1909 introduced new taxes and supertax, and also contained a clause requiring the Inland Revenue to carry out a survey and valuation of land in the United Kingdom. The House of Lords rejected the bill, precipitating a constitutional crisis. A general election in 1910 returned another liberal government with a slender majority, which carried out its pledge to remove the power of the House of Lords to veto money bills. It again empowered the Inland Revenue to value land and impose an increment value duty on increased site values after April 1909.[2] Many conservatives complained that these punitive measures were 'unjust attacks' upon landlords, making owners of land bear a disproportionate share of the nation's tax burden. Some owners decided to sell out before land prices collapsed.[3]

The dissolution of Cassiobury began in the 1880s, when the number of gardeners and other estate staff was reduced. By 1900, the seventh Earl of Essex was spending less and less time at Cassiobury and offered the house, together with shooting and fishing rights, for letting. In 1908, a 184-acre tract of the home park was sold for the building of large detached houses, and the developers offered to sell 75 acres of this tract to Watford Council for use as a public park. A poll among ratepayers rejected the proposal but the council obtained permission from the Local Government Board to raise loans for the purchase of a total of 190 acres in 1909 and 1913.[4] In 1922, works of art and furnishings were disposed of; in 1923, the house and the rest of the grounds were sold to a syndicate, the Cassiobury Estate Company, which in turn sold more land to Watford Borough Council to extend the municipal park and recreation ground. The mansion and most of the ornamental cottages were demolished in 1927. Much of the upper park to the west of the Gade was leased to the West Herts Golf Club. Whippendell Woods were acquired by the council in 1930 and 1935.[5]

At Knebworth, the Lyttons also tried to reduce their household expenditure in the 1880s but two successive members of the family bore the high costs of serving as viceroys of India. In 1897, the second earl's sister Emily married the architect Sir Edwin Lutyens, who planned alterations at Knebworth House and sketched designs for new gardens. The earl could not afford to carry out all these plans but a design for a five-ringed herb garden drawn by Gertrude Jekyll in 1907 was implemented seventy years later.[6] As debts mounted, the earl moved out and let Knebworth to aristocratic families, including a divorced Russian grand duke. By 1930, suitable tenants could no longer be found and Lord Lytton joined with other owners of parks in asking the government to relieve them of their crushing tax burdens.

The mansion at Brookmans Park was burnt down in 1891 and not rebuilt. After a long period of neglect, the park was converted to a golf course in 1930. The wild wooded garden created in 1914–15 by a wealthy printer, Edward Wormald, at Sheepwell House, Potters Bar, was abandoned and sold in 1924 to Queenswood School from Clapham, who were looking for spacious premises outside London.[7] In 1927, Rickmansworth Park was sold to the Royal Masonic School for Girls and the house was demolished. At about the same time, other parks were converted into schools and playing fields. A part of Kendals in Aldenham was taken by Radlett Preparatory School in 1926; Edge Grove in Aldenham, greatly enlarged in Edwardian times, was converted into another private school; Lockleys, in Welwyn, extensively restored in 1911 by Sir Reginald Blomfield for Mrs Neale, was acquired by Sherrardswood School; Hamels, on the death of Ethelburt Furness in 1933, was bought by a private girls' school called Crofton Grange; and Woodhall Park, Watton, disposed of its deer and was abandoned in 1934 to become Heathmount School.[8] The Grove, which the sixth Earl of Clarendon had sold in 1926, became a girls' school; in the Second World War it was occupied by the London Midland and Scottish Railway, before being taken over by British Railways as a services training centre.

During the First World War Boxmoor House, Bragbury, Codicote Lodge, Goldings, Hatfield House, Knebworth and Kingswalden Bury were lent as hospitals for wounded soldiers,[9] and Bushey Hall, Cassiobury Park, Gorhambury and Hatfield Park were used as grounds for training and exercising troops. Many houses, parks and gardens were damaged or neglected in this period, but materials and labour could not be spared for repairs and maintenance. During the course of the war, some park owners and their heirs were killed. Five of the third Marquess of Salisbury's ten grandsons were killed in action,[10] and Lady Desborough of Panshanger lost her two sons, Julian and Billy Grenfell. Many smaller properties also suffered losses

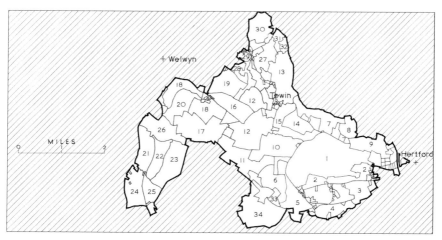

Figure 7.1: Panshanger estate in 1919. A compact block of land extended from Digswell to Hertford with a western limb that stretched from Welwyn to Stanborough. The park is number 1 on the map. Based on Panshanger sales particulars (HALS DE/P P99–100). Drawn in the Geography Department, UCL

of heirs in the First World War. The sale of Danesbury in 1919 was caused by the death of two sons in the war.[11] Part of the land was taken for a golf course and part was converted into a hospital.

After the war the payment of estate duties and taxes, as well as restrictions on raising rents, forced many owners of parks to sell up. A rush of country house sales turned into an avalanche. Land sales reached a record high in 1919 and the volume of sales continued to rise higher and higher for the next five years.[12] Early in 1919, Lord Salisbury even sold his London home in Arlington Street. Lady Desborough had to sell most of the Cowper family's art collection and 4,000 acres of the Panshanger estate in 1919.[13] Figure 7.1 shows the boundaries of the estate before the sale, stretching continuously from Welwyn through Tewin and from Hertingfordbury to Hertford. The Welwyn Garden City Company bought 1,458 acres lying astride the main line from London to Edinburgh and built one of London's first satellite new towns there.[14] At the eastern end of the Panshanger estate, land at Sele was acquired for building private houses on the outskirts of Hertford and the county council bought several fields to convert into smallholdings.

In 1921, Lord Brownlow died without an heir and the Ashridge estate was put on the market. It did not immediately find a buyer. A trust formed by Urban Broughton to commemorate Bonar Law acquired the house, gardens and much of the park in 1927 to found a college for the study of conservative political ideas. Additional funds for the college were provided by the sale of some land on the western side of the park for building a few houses on large-sized plots and the eastern side of the park was leased to Ashridge Golf Club. In 1926, a public appeal organised by local residents and supported by leaders of the three main political parties raised £40,000 to enable the National Trust to buy 1,800 acres of woodland, common and down-land from the Ashridge estate to form a tract of open space leading up to Ivinghoe Beacon.[15]

Few contemporary observers expressed concern or regret at the dis-appearance of parks and country houses between 1880 and 1930. Many owners were pleased to be rid of loss-making estates; farmers looked for-ward to becoming independent freeholders or mortgagees instead of subservient tenants; and many townsmen thought that the appearance of the landscape was improved by the removal of alien Georgian man-sions and stiffly formal ornamental grounds. Ramblers and naturalists sought to reopen footpaths that would enable them to wander freely through shady woods and sunlit pastures. Hikers and cyclists preferred the wide open spaces of moors, downs and heaths to gloomy parklands.

Arts and Crafts gardens in the south and west
Professional and managerial people seeking to escape from Victorian London, many of whom thought that fresh country air and vigorous outdoor exercise were the keys to healthy living, seized opportunities to purchase land and build modern homes in old-fashioned cottagey styles with mock Tudor facades and Arts and Crafts decorative motifs. Ray Pahl describes the acquisition of building plots among former woods and parks in Tewin; in the 1920s and 1930s, the parkland residents formed a distinct new group in rural society, remaining aloof from the older, village, community.[16] Influences of the garden designers Gertrude Jekyll (1843–1932) and Thomas Mawson (1861–1933) and the archi-tects Charles Voysey (1857–1941), Hugh Baillie Scott (1865–1945) and Sir Edwin Lutyens (1869–1944) lay heavily over early twentieth-century homes and gardens in Berkhamsted, Potten End, Elstree,

Bushey and Chorleywood. The extension of the Metropolitan Railway in 1892 from Moor Park through Rickmansworth and Chorleywood and onward to Amersham was followed by the break-up of parks and the building of detached residences set in well-wooded gardens an acre or more in extent. Spacious gardens in 'Metroland', hidden from view behind high yew or holly hedges, were thickly planted with varieties of cedars, magnolias and masses of rhododendrons. Near the houses there was ample space for tennis courts, croquet lawns, summer houses, lily ponds, paved walks, pergolas and garages. When they were not at work or at home gardening, middle-class commuters found a new use for parks as golf courses.

Golf and parks

Golf became an important sport in Hertfordshire in 1890, when five golf clubs at Bushey Hall, Boxmoor, West Herts, Berkhamsted Common and Chorleywood Common were recognised by the Royal and Ancient Golf Club of St Andrews. All five courses were situated in west Hertfordshire and two of them, Bushey Hall and West Herts — the latter in the upper park at Cassiobury — lay in parks. The course at Bushey Hall, designed by Scottish professional golfer and open champion James Braid, was situated in a district where many Scottish people had settled. No golf was played on Sundays at Bushey Hall. Weekend golfers were attracted, therefore, to the nearby West Herts course at Cassiobury. The most celebrated golfer, Harry Vardon, five times world open champion, together with James Braid and John Henry Taylor, played at Bushey Hall in 1897. Braid designed eight golf courses in Hertfordshire and Vardon five. Vardon ended his career as the professional at South Herts Golf Club in Totteridge Park in 1903 and stayed there until he died in 1937.[17] By 1910, eighteen golf clubs had been established in Hertfordshire, fourteen of which were situated in the west and south of the county; ten lay in former parks.

No golf club was founded between 1910 and 1922. After the First World War, four, including Moor Park, opened in 1922–3 and five more, including Brookmans Park and Ashridge, were opened from 1930 to 1937. In 1932–3, twenty-two places were named 'Golf Course' on Ordnance Survey fifth edition one-inch maps, fourteen of which were sited in parks.[18] Samuel Ryder (1858–1936), a seedsman and herbalist who was once mayor of St Albans, was a captain of Verulam Golf Club, situated in sixteenth-century Sopwell Park. In 1927, he presented a gold cup to be awarded to the winner of a professional golf competition between world players. It was named the Ryder Cup after him.[19]

After a very long interval, spanning the Second World War and a period of post-war austerity, a spate of new golf clubs opened in the 1970s, and yet more in the 1980s, culminating in the founding of fourteen new clubs in the 1990s. By 2006, Hertfordshire had sixty-one golf clubs, the membership of which totalled more than 30,000.[20] No fewer than thirty-two golf courses, covering about 3,000 acres of land, occupied former parks.[21] A large majority of parkland courses were situated in west and south Hertfordshire, where population had increased most rapidly. Only recently has the north-east begun to catch up with the rest of the county.

Popular attitudes to parkland: Ordnance Survey fifth edition one-inch maps, 1932–3

In the early years of the twentieth century, the pleasures of parks came to be experienced by a new generation of visitors and users. Golfers trudging for miles in parks might occasionally pause and look up to admire venerable oaks, beeches, limes and chestnuts that sheltered fairways or curse a large tree or broad expanse of water that stood in the way of a long drive. On summer days, cyclists and motorists came to picnic in or near parks that were located at the sides of roads. New attitudes to parks in the landscape were reflected in the aptly named Popular one-inch Ordnance maps.

The Ordnance Survey carried out a full revision of the large-scale plans of Hertfordshire in 1913–14 in preparation for the publication in colour of the Popular Edition one-inch maps at a scale of 1 in 63,360.[22] In 1932–3, a newly revised fifth edition was published. The new maps were designed for road users and were recommended by the newly established Youth Hostels Association, as well as by ramblers', cyclists' and motorists' organisations. The maps differentiated eleven categories of roads from Ministry of Transport A roads (red)

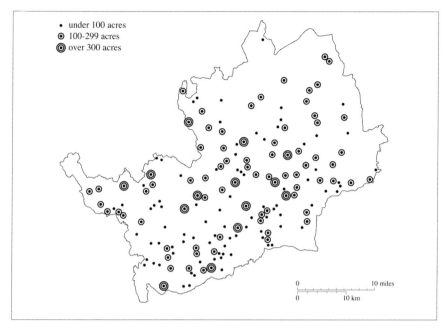

Figure 7.2: Parks in Hertfordshire in 1932–3. Based on Ordnance Survey, fifth popular edition one-inch maps. Full details are listed in Table 7.1. Drawn in the Geography Department, UCL

and B roads (yellow) to unclassified roads less than 14 feet wide (uncoloured) and unmetalled tracks and bridleways, marked by pecked lines. Relief was indicated by contours drawn at fifty-foot intervals. Parks and ornamental grounds were tinted by pale green ruled lines; woods were coloured deep green. Within parks, deciduous trees were indicated by black bushy topped symbols and conifers by spiky topped symbols; lines of avenues were sketched. Richard Oliver remarks that 'no O.S. definition of "ornamental ground" has been found: presumably surveyors were expected to recognise it when they saw it'.[23] Uses of country houses and parks were labelled as 'hotel', 'school', 'college', 'sanatorium' and 'golf course'. Tring Park, Kings Walden Park and Woodhall Park, Watton, were named as 'deer park'.

The map identified 165 places as parks and ornamental grounds, of which 81 were over 100 acres in size and 84 between 20 and 100 acres. The distribution of parks in 1932–3 is represented on Figure

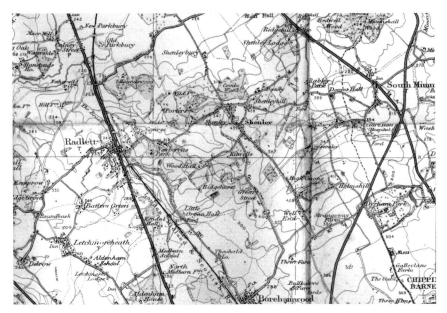

Figure 7.3: Parks around Radlett in 1932–3. House building had begun west of Watling Street, near Radlett station. Detail from Ordnance Survey fifth edition one-inch map, Sheet 106. Digital image by the Geography Department, UCL

7.2. The total number of parks had fallen by 84 since 1863–81, when a total of 249 had been recorded. Of the 84 parks lost, 68 were under 100 acres in size, the other sixteen were larger; owing to suburbanisation, losses to the south of the rivers Lea and Colne were proportionately greater than those to the north of the vale of St Albans. Because large parks persisted and did not shrink much in size, the total acreage of parkland in Hertfordshire was 23,270 acres in 1932–3, amounting to a reduction of 5,395 acres since 1863–81. That represents a decrease from 7.3 per cent of the surface area of the county, excluding waste land, to 6 per cent of the surface in 1932–3.

In detail, many small parks, especially in the south and west of the county, had been broken up into building plots. In Cheshunt, Hoddesdon, St Albans, Potters Bar, Radlett, Aldenham, Bushey, Oxhey, Watford and Rickmansworth many new detached houses had been built in parks and grounds of former mansions (Figure 7.3). New housing estates depicted on the one-inch map may be traced back to

continued on p253

Table 7.1 Parks in Hertfordshire in 1932–3

Park	Grid Reference	Owner	Acres
Abbotshill, Abbots Langley	075045	Lady Marjorie Louise Dalrymple	80
Albury Hall	427254	Francis Maurice Grosvenor Glyn	130
Aldenham House	168966	Lord Aldenham (unoccupied)	360
Aldwickbury, Harpenden	152139	Edward Ernest Maylor Hett	120
Ardeley Bury	301272	John Howard Carter	90
Ashendene, Epping Green	302069	Herman Walter de Zoete	50
Ashlyns Hall, Berkhamsted	991067	Reginald Hugh Nichols	100
Ashridge, Lt Gaddesden	993122	Bonar Law College	1,030
Ashwell Bury	266400	Mrs W.A. Fordham	30
Aspenden Hall	351285	Sir Arthur Douglas Lushington Bt	120
Astwick Manor, Hatfield	203100	John Lloyd	30
Ayotbury, Ayot St Peter	218154	Sir Alfred Reynolds	30
Ayot House, Ayot St Lawrence	195170	Hon. Ronald Nall Cain	130
Balls Park, Hertford	335120	Sir Lionel Lawson Faudel Phillips Bt	220
Barvin Park, Northaw	289010	St Raphaels Colony for Epileptics	60
Batchwood, St Michaels	137088	unoccupied	70
Bayfordbury	315105	Adml Sir Lewis Clinton Baker	350
Bedwell Park, Essendon	277076	Sir Francis Edward Fremantle	210
Beechwood	046145	Sir Giles Edward Sebright Bt	380
Benington Lordship	297238	Arthur Francis Bott	50
Benington Park	310236	Harry Whitworth Hall	120
Berkhamsted Place	990087	Capt. Lucius Abel Granville Ram	40
Blakesware, Ware	405163	Lord Gerard	250
Bonningtons, Stanstead Abbot	407132	Archibald Herbert James	130
Borehamwood House	189962	Sir George Lewis Barstow	60
Bovingdon House	011030	F. Dudley Ryder	50
Bragbury, Aston	270212	Mrs Jessie Nancy Warner	40
Brickendonbury	330105	unoccupied	180
Briggens, Hunsdon	414112	Lord Hunsdon	60
Broad Colney Convent	174028	Anglican Community of All Saints	70
Brocket Park	212130	Charles Nall Cain, Lord Brocket	500
Broxbourne Bury	354073	Maj. George Richard Smith Bosanquet	280
Bushey Hall	124965	Bushey Hall Golf Club	100
Bushey House	133951	Lord John Henry Bethell	30
Caddington Hall, Markyate	069173	Mrs C. Green	50
Camfield Place, Essendon	266069	Lord Almeric Hugh Queenborough	140
Carpenders Park	125934	Highfield Girls' School	30

continued over

Table 7.1 Parks in Hertfordshire in 1932–3 *continued*

Park	Grid Reference	Owner	Acres
Cassiobury Park	087965	West Herts Golf Club	280
Champneys, Wigginton	947087	Health Home	110
Cheshunt Park	347045	Misses Debenham	50
Chesfield Park, Graveley	245278	Mrs Charles Poyntz Stewart	110
Childwick Bury	139102	Jack Barnato Joel	310
Chipperfield Manor	049013	Norman Kelly	40
Chorleywood House	037970	Lady Ela Russell	80
Codicote Lodge	213182	Everard Martin Smith	60
Cokenach, Barkway	396361	Douglas Crossman	160
Coles Park, Westmill	369259	John George Murray	130
Corney Bury, Buntingford	357309	Edgar Semmons Noy	110
Culverwood House, Lt Berkhamsted	296086	Miss V.L. Bates	60
Danesbury, Welwyn	234173	Michael Bruce Urquhart Dewar	150
Darley Ash, Bovingdon	020030	Alice Sophia Gladstone	30
Delaport, Wheathampstead	175154	Mid Herts Golf Club	70
Digswell Place	230143	Hester Byng, Countess of Cavan	90
Easneye, Stanstead Abbots	380135	John Henry Buxton	140
Edge Grove, Aldenham	144989	John Pierpont Morgan	70
Essendon Place	274079	Lord Frederick William Lewis Essendon	70
Fanhams Hall, Ware	371156	Brig.Gen. Henry Page Croft (unoccupied)	70
Frogmore Hall, Aston	290207	Vernon Austen Malcolmson	130
Frythe, Welwyn	226150	Miss Wilshere	60
Furneux Pelham Hall	427279	Lord Rolf Cunliffe	60
Gaddesden Hoo	032124	Mrs Mary Douglas Wood	70
Gaddesden Place	038111	Mrs T.S. Pryor	220
Gadebridge, Hemel Hempstead	049080	Humphrey David Pelham Lindsay	90
Garston Manor	111016	Col William H. Briggs	60
Gilston Park	441130	Francis Edward Salvin Bowlby	150
Golden Parsonage, Gt Gaddesden	050126	Arthur Cory Wright	150
Goldings, Bengeo	311142	Dr Barnardo's Home	180
Goldingtons, Sarratt	037983	Peter Clutterbuck	40
Gorhambury	113079	James W. Grimston, 4th Earl of Verulam	480
Grove, Sarratt	081988	Grove School, Miss Harman, principal	220
Gt Hyde Hall, Sawbridgeworth	496155	Sir Walter Lawrence	90
Hamels, Braughing	375245	Ethelburt Furness	200
Haresfoot, Northchurch	985062	Thomas Geoffrey Blackwell	150
Hatfield Park (inc. Millwards)	235084	James, 4th Marquess of Salisbury	1360

continued

Table 7.1 Parks in Hertfordshire in 1932–3 *continued*

Park	Grid Reference	Owner	Acres
Hawkswick, St Albans	147100	George William Long	110
Haydon Hill, Bushey	129949	Robert Percy Attenborough	50
Hazelwood, Abbots Langley	089006	Francis Fisher	40
Hertingfordbury	310119	Rev. Roland Audley Smith	30
Hexton Manor	108305	Sir James Hill Bt	140
High Canons, Ridge	207990	William Walker	70
Highfield, Hemel Hempstead	069083	Arthur Harrison	40
High Leigh, Hoddesdon	362087	Robert Barclay	90
Hilfield Lodge, Aldenham	152962	Claude Graham-White	110
Hoo, Kimpton	189196	Thomas Brand, 3rd Viscount Hampden	230
Hook, Northaw	281012	Lt.Col Alexander Douglas Cameron	60
Houndswood, Radlett	163014	William Sandford Windover	30
Hunsdonbury	414131	Ernest Ward Thomas	40
Hunsdon House	418127	Mrs Montgomerie	70
Julians, Rushden	307327	Edward J. Marchal	220
Kendal Hall, Aldenham	172982	John Venning	70
Kingswalden Park	160234	Maj. John Fenwick Harrison	200
Kitwells, Shenley	191994	Thomas Henry Riches	70
Knebworth	230209	Victor Alexander, 2nd Earl of Lytton	400
Lamer Park, Wheathamstead	182161	Apsley Benet Cherry Garrard	190
Langleybury, Abbots Langley	077002	Edward Henry Loyd	180
Lawrence End, Kimpton	142197	Lt Col Richard Oakley	190
Lt Berkhamsted House	294080	Joseph P. Rochford	30
Lt Hadham Place	433225	Lt Cmdr Richard Henry Langton	50
Lt Offley	130286	Hugh Clutterbuck	80
Lockleys Park, Welwyn	237160	Sherrardswood School	290
Lower Woodside, Hatfield	246062	Harold Walduck	90
Lye House, St Stephens	131022	Nellie Victoria Withrington	50
Marchmont House, Hemel Hempstead	052086	Mrs Talbot	40
Marden Hill, Tewin	280140	Maj. Cecil E. Banbury	110
Markyate Cell	058176	Ernest Albert Sursham	80
Micklefield Hall	053975	T.R. Clutterbuck	90
Moor Park, Rickmansworth	074932	Moor Park Golf Club	350
Moor Place, Much Hadham	421189	Ronald Collet Norman	130
Munden House, Gt Munden	137003	Arthur Holland Hibbert, Viscount Knutsford	140
Netherfield House, Stanstead Abbots	392114	Henry Lawrence Prior	50

continued over

Table 7.1 Parks in Hertfordshire in 1932–3 *continued*

Park	Grid Reference	Owner	Acres
Newberries Park, Radlett	171998	Sir Arthur du Cros	130
Newsells Park, Barkway	388370	Sir Humphrey De Trafford Bt	130
Node, Codicote	216202	Carl Holmes	50
Northaw Place	270025	Sir Philip Henry Devitt Bt	30
North Mymms Park	218042	Mrs Burns	370
Nyn Park, Northaw	278031	Mrs Arthur	120
Oaklands, St Peters	182077	Hertfordshire Agricultural Institute	60
Offley Place	146268	Arthur William Acland	130
Oxhey Place	115931	Thomas Anthony Blackwell	50
Panshanger	290132	Lord Desborough	860
Pendley Manor, Tring	942117	Dorian Williams	140
Pishiobury Park, Sawbridgeworth	481134	unoccupied	160
Poles, Ware	351163	Roman Catholic Convent School	150
Potterells, North Mimms	236047	Horace James Seymour	90
Potwells, North Mimms	216028	Mrs Burns	40
Presdales, Ware	357135	Lt Col Osmond Robert McMullen	70
Priory Park, Hitchin	184287	Ralph Hubert Delme Radcliffe	90
Putteridge Bury, Lilley	118245	Sir Felix Cassel Bt	410
Queenswood, Potters Bar	265037	Queenswood Residential Girls School	90
Redheath, Croxley	066971	Lord Ebury	50
Ridgehurst, Shenley	188991	unoccupied	90
Rossway, Northchurch	960072	Lady Hadden	120
Rothamsted, Harpenden	125132	Maj. Ralph Bennett Sidebottom	280
Rowney Priory, Sacombe	347203	David Augustus Bevan	50
Russells, Watford	091992	Alexander Hedderwick	60
Sacombe	339190	E. Allen Hay	200
Sergehill, Bedmond	107041	Maj. Thomas Augustus Motion	40
Shenley Hill	194009	Lt Col Wilfred Hubert Wild	40
Shenley Lodge	202023	John Charrington	50
Shephallbury	255225	Hon. Thomas Morgan Grenville Gavin	70
Sopwell	155054	Verulam Golf Club	70
Springfield, Northaw	273024	Charles Gordon Maynard	120
Stagenhoe, St Pauls Walden	185228	Lady Whitehead	120
St Edmunds College, Standon	372220	Roman Catholic College	90
St Pauls Walden Bury	187217	Hon. Sir David Bowes Lyon	100
Temple Dinsley, Preston	181248	Almina, Countess of Carnarvon	70
Tewin Water	255145	Sir Otto Beit	100

continued

Table 7.1 Parks in Hertfordshire in 1932–3 *continued*

Park	Grid Reference	Owner	Acres
Tolmers, Cuffley	302048	Tolmers Park Hospital	70
Tring Park	925111	Lady Rothschild	250
Tyttenhanger Park, Ridge	191047	Countess of Caledon	60
Walkern Hall	300250	Miss Cotton Browne	70
Wall Hall, Aldenham	137995	John Pierpont Morgan	110
Ware Park	333145	Hertfordshire County Sanatorium	180
Warrenwood, Hatfield	269065	Capt. Hubert Lavie Butler	40
Wellbury Park, Lt Offley	136291	Bernard Kenworthy Browne	90
Westbrook Hay, Bovingdon	026055	Allan Campbell Macdiarmid	190
Weston Park	262294	Maj. Oliver G. Villiers	170
Woodcockhill, Northchurch	973080	Alfred James White	60
Wood Hall, Radlett	182995	Sir George Duncombe	50
Woodhall Park, Watton	316182	Maj. Edward Pelham Smith	440
Woodhill House, Hatfield	265059	Reginald Henry Macaulay Abel Smith	100
Woolmers Park, Hertingfordbury	285103	Charles Edward Wodehouse	160
Wormleybury	356057	Maj. Albert Pam	210
Wyddial Hall	374318	Sir Charles Brabazon Heaton Ellis	130
Youngsbury, Standon	371179	Christopher Bernard Giles-Puller	120

Sources: Ordnance Survey fifth Popular edition one-inch maps, 1932–3. Names of most residents listed in Kelly's *Directory of Hertfordshire* (1933); *Who's Who in Hertfordshire* (1936); *Registers of Electors* (1932) for Hemel Hempstead, Hitchin and St Albans divisions.

continued from p248

sales of land recorded in sales catalogues from 1880 onwards. A typical example was the sale in 1921 of the Marshalswick estate, lying north of St Albans, that included 72 acres of gardens and grounds and 100 acres of surrounding land. The property was divided into seven lots and, following the sale, plans were drawn by Watford estate agents Stimpson, Lock and Vince for a 'superior residential estate for houses, bungalows and weekend cottages', preserving 'the lovely matured timbers and woodlands, such as time only can create'.[24] The presence of neighbouring parks and plantations were amenities that added to the value of new houses. Parks also provided space for playing fields where mansions were replaced by school buildings. In Bushey, the manor house was pulled down about 1920 and the Junior Royal Masonic School was built in the small park. Bushey Grange was demolished about 1935 and its grounds were later occupied by Queen's School and the Metropolitan Police Sports Club.[25]

Remaining large parks continued to be encroached on by woods and plantations so that open park pastures, lightly tinted areas on the map, continued to decrease. This process had begun in the eighteenth century and was depicted on successive maps. Stands of hardwood timber were not seriously depleted during the First World War and, after the war, demand for beech in furniture-making, sales of oak to make barrel staves and cartwheels, and of oak bark for tanning declined as alternative materials were substituted. In 1919, the Forestry Commission was established to increase the nation's reserves of timber and announced that a priority was the expansion of the area to be planted with softwoods. It managed a tract of woodland belonging to the Crown which bordered the Gorhambury estate between St Albans and Hemel Hempstead, and planted beech, larch, firs and other trees there. A census of woodlands carried out by the Forestry Commission in 1924 recorded that Hertfordshire contained about 26,000 acres, consisting mostly of hardwoods — one of the few remaining plantations of pure beech in the county stood in Beechwood Park. In 1938, another survey conducted by the National Home Grown Timber Council recorded 26,548 acres occupied by woodland in that year, almost the same acreage as reported in 1905.[26] During the interwar period, private owners restocked parks with quick-growing conifers that yielded saleable produce in less than half the time taken by broadleaved trees. Parks in the county were already embellished with conifers and new planting did not radically alter their appearance.

Remarkably, against the prevailing trend towards parkland decline, nine parks appear to have been created since 1863–81.[27] These were substantially larger than the one- or two-acre gardens laid out by Jekyll and Mawson for middle-class clients. Houndswood at Radlett, a medium-sized country house designed by Norman Shaw in 1871–2, was enlarged around 1900 and a new park was created. Cokenach, which had been a large house in the nineteenth century, was further enlarged by Douglas Crossman in 1925.[28] The newcomers spent money they had made in business, banking, shop-keeping and in the professions.[29]

In 1908, when Herbert George Fenwick bought Temple Dinsley, he invited Sir Edwin Lutyens to enlarge the house to the extent of entirely changing its external appearance.[30] In the following three years, in collaboration with Gertrude Jekyll, Lutyens redesigned the pleasure grounds, creating a pergola garden, a paved rose garden and an orchard set in thirty acres of parkland. The property was sold in 1919 and after two further sales, it was acquired by the Princess Helena College in 1935. Lutyens and Jekyll collaborated again in 1911–12 to design another formal garden, covering about fifteen acres, within a much larger park at Putteridge Bury. It included a rose garden and a circular lawn enclosed by yew hedges.[31]

Fanhams Hall, Ware, a Queen Anne house of moderate size, was converted by W. Wood Bethell in 1900–1 into a much larger neo-Tudor mansion. The owner, Captain Richard Benyon Croft, imported two Japanese gardeners every summer for ten years to carry out a design under the direction of Professor Suzuki from Japan. The grounds contained an authentic Japanese tea house brought from an exhibition in Paris. Another Japanese layout was started in 1905 by Herbert Goode, a wealthy china and glass merchant, for his garden at Cottered. In 1923, the architect Seyemon Kusumoto was commissioned to complete Goode's work. David Ottewill describes Cottered as 'probably the most impressive example of a Japanese garden in England'. It had cascades, pools and a 'path of life' leading across a bridge, through an archway and up to a shrine set in a grove of pine trees.[32] A third Japanese garden was created at the Node near Codicote.[33]

In the 1930s, old-established noble families still held the largest parks and estates. Earls Brownlow, Essex, Clarendon and Lord Ebury had gone; Panshanger, Brocket, Gorhambury and Knebworth estates were greatly diminished. On the other hand, Hatfield remained pre-eminent in size and continuity of ownership. Knebworth and Gorhambury were still fairly large and lived in by descendants of the Lyttons and Grimstons. Old families of gentry possessed a majority of parks; bankers, financiers, politicians and a few manufacturers held a small minority. In the inter-war years, retired military officers out-numbered India merchants, brewers and clergymen.

Public interest in parks and open spaces in the inter-war period
Without a prospering agricultural base, landed estates and the parks
and pleasure grounds financed by farm rents could not be preserved.
When agricultural prices plunged and taxes remained high after the
First World War, most family estates with parks were doomed to
extinction. Townspeople complained about the loss of countryside
amenities but lacked powers to prevent the spreading disorder of
uncontrolled house- and road-building.

During the First World War, the Ministry of Agriculture guaran-
teed minimum prices for food producers and encouraged farmers to
grow more cereals. Price support continued until 1921, when world
wheat prices collapsed and the government could no longer afford to
protect farmers. As prices for agricultural produce continued to fall,
farmers' incomes were reduced and rents went unpaid. The depression reached its lowest point in the winter of 1932–3. The
government responded by providing deficiency payments for wheat in
1932; in the following two years, sugar beet, fat cattle, potatoes,
bacon pigs and milk were subsidised and marketing boards were set
up to boost sales. Farmers remained impoverished, few able to raise
money to buy tractors, pay for electrification, install piped water, or
buy milking machines and fertilisers, all of which were essential to
meet competition from foreigners. A few farmers who were owner-
occupiers sold a field or a road frontage for building houses or
bungalows. Tenants who abandoned farming left their landlords with
tracts of vacant, derelict land. By employing trained farm managers
some landowners hoped to raise productivity, but their financial
resources were severely constrained by high taxes and ruinous death
duties. The net result was that Hertfordshire lost more than one-tenth
of its agricultural land between 1914 and 1935, the greatest losses
occurring in the south.[34]

Townspeople seeking relaxation in cared-for countryside were
horrified by what they saw. When Londoners entered south
Hertfordshire, they were confronted by uncut hedges, choked ditches,
neglected pastures overgrown with bracken, brambles and elder
saplings. Abandoned arable land was infested with rabbits and disused gravel pits were piled high with stinking refuse. Motorists and

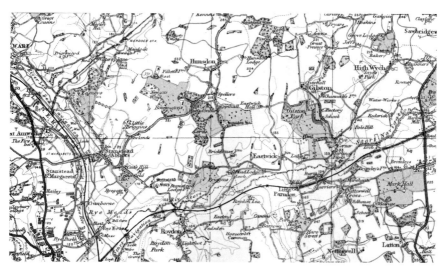

Figure 7.4: Parks in the Stort valley in 1932–3. A tract of unspoilt countryside in which areas of woods and plantations were closely associated with parks. Detail from Ordnance Survey fifth edition one-inch map, Sheet 96. Digital image by the Geography Department, UCL

picnickers scattered trails of litter over commons. Across this unsightly landscape, strips of land were taken for building semi-detached houses, bungalows, factories and warehouses, widening the North Orbital Road, constructing by-passes around Watford, Barnet and Ware, putting up obtrusive advertising hoardings, raising pylons to carry electric power lines and quarrying for gravel.[35] Protests against the disfigurement of the countryside were directed at agricultural dereliction, break-up of estates, jerry building and ribbon development, but Clough Williams-Ellis and other protesters were too strident to win many supporters.[36] Their cheerless, negative denunciations of blots on the landscape touched raw nerves of people who were striving to improve their living conditions and bring roads, electricity, piped water, main drainage and comfortable housing to neglected rural areas.

More positive approaches designed to protect the most beautiful old landscapes, keep the farmed countryside tidy and prevent suburban sprawl were promoted by the Council for the Preservation of Rural England, founded in 1926. Annual reports to members of the CPRE recorded additions of land in Frithsden and Hudnall to the

National Trust property at Ashridge and announced piecemeal acquisitions by public authorities of Lockleys at Welwyn, Gadebridge at Hemel Hempstead and other areas of parkland. Many localities, such as the Stort valley around Hunsdon, remained unspoilt (Figure 7.4). Parks there had changed little for over a century.

A small number of politicians sought powers to control building development in rural areas and to preserve open spaces for public enjoyment and recreation. A regional plan for Hertfordshire, submitted to the county council in 1927, proposed creating a belt of open spaces consisting of parkland, woodland and farmland along the southern boundary of the county to stop the spread of suburbs from Middlesex.[37] County councillors and officials representing Hertfordshire were appointed to the Greater London Regional Planning Committee set up by the Minister of Health, Neville Chamberlain, in November 1927. Recommendations made by Raymond Unwin in the committee's report required compensation be paid to landowners for loss of development values following the imposition of green belt restrictions.[38] In a time of deepening economic depression, government and local authorities could not afford to pay the full costs of compensation and owners of parks were unwilling to enter into agreements with each other to redistribute gains and losses of development values in areas subject to planning controls.[39] As a matter of principle, most freeholders objected to planning as an infringement of property rights.

In 1936, when it was clear that the Greater London Regional Planning Committee would not be able to find a basis for agreement on its green belt proposals, the London County Council withdrew from the committee and launched its own plan, offering to make grants of up to two million pounds over three years to county councils in the home counties to purchase a reserve supply of public open spaces and recreational areas that would form a green belt or girdle of open lands around the metropolis. In 1938, the Green Belt (London and Home Counties) Act ensured the permanent preservation of lands acquired under the scheme.[40] In Hertfordshire, land protected by the act included Chorleywood Common, Moor Park golf course, Whipendell Woods, Wall Hall, High Canons, Dyrham

Park, woods in Northaw and Great Wood, Cuffley, amounting in total to about 2,200 acres.[41] The primary aim was to secure open land for recreation, but landscaped parks were also acquired.

A few landowners followed a different approach to the preservation of rural amenities, inspired by the writings of Christopher Hussey, Ralph Dutton and other aesthetes. Hussey asserted that the picturesque style was a peculiarly English way of harmonising art and nature which achieved its highest perfection in late eighteenth-century landscape gardens.[42] He applauded the efforts of generations of owners who had acted as guardians of these precious elysiums in a series of articles in *Country Life* from 1920 onwards. Among places singled out for special attention was St Paul's Walden Bury, occupied and faithfully restored in 1932 by Sir David Bowes-Lyon, president of the Royal Horticultural Society.[43] Ralph Dutton's book *The English garden* (1937) credited Capability Brown with extending the gardener's art 'to the almost unlimited spaces of the park, encouraging owners to undertake vast schemes of planting' that now urgently needed renewal.[44] The Institute of Landscape Architects, founded in 1929, set out to apply the principles of eighteenth-century landscape gardeners to modern design. There was little scope for a revival of landscape design in Hertfordshire, where parks continued to disappear at an alarming rate.

If parks were to be saved, owners would have to be relieved of taxes or paid allowances to maintain them. A first step in that direction was taken in 1931, when lands given to the National Trust were exempted from death duties.[45] In 1934, the Earl of Lothian, who had unexpectedly inherited Blickling Hall, Norfolk, accompanied by a demand for death duties that left him insolvent, persuaded the National Trust to take a further initiative, requesting the government to exempt their endowment income from taxes, permit former owners to lease back houses and parks and also grant tax concessions to individual private owners. Responding to these requests, Neville Chamberlain offered tax concessions on condition that all houses and parks participating in his scheme would be opened to the public. The National Trust reluctantly agreed to form a country house committee, which was chaired by Lord Esher with James Lees-Milne as its enthusiastic and energetic secretary. The Marquess of Salisbury and Lord Brocket, neither of whom approved Chamberlain's proposal, were co-opted to advise the committee in negotiating with the government. The committee's two main tasks were to compile a list of places of national importance that ought to be saved and to invite owners to join the scheme. No owner was willing to submit to the enforced 'servitude' of opening his house and grounds, calculating that costs of preparing to cater for visitors were likely to exceed receipts and would certainly disrupt a family's domestic privacy.[46] Almost all owners would have preferred to vacate their large, draughty, inconvenient houses, move to farmhouses on their estates and bequeath to their heirs what remained of their possessions after payment of death duties. In Hertfordshire no owner was ready to surrender his park to the National Trust. A part of the Ashridge estate had been acquired by public subscription in 1926 and Shaw's Corner at Ayot St Lawrence did not pass to the Trust until 1944, after the death of the playwright, George Bernard Shaw.

In the face of public and private hardship and pervasive insecurity and despondency, inter-war attempts to save parks as beauty spots or sites of historic importance achieved little beyond raising the problem for future discussion. Owners' first duty towards their own heirs took precedence over their inclinations to serve as trustees for the general public. They needed to make their land yield a profit, not revenue for the exchequer. Taxpayers were even more stubborn in refusing to assist impoverished aristocrats and very few were swayed by the charms of landscaped parks. Legal barriers surrounding private property were swept away arbitrarily by wartime regulations, when houses, parks and agricultural estates were commandeered for national defence.

Parks at war, 1939–45

During the Second World War, owners and their heirs suffered fewer casualties than in the First World War but more parks and country houses were damaged or fell into disrepair. The war brought an end to the slump in agriculture, and strenuous efforts to boost food production benefited farmers and landowners. Land that had gone out of cultivation and parks that had been under permanent grass for many years were ploughed up. Machinery was pooled and labour directed to work on the land. Later in the war, plans were drawn up for post-war reconstruction and the protection of a green belt around London.

A register of buildings and parks to be requisitioned on the out-break of war was secretly compiled by the committee for imperial defence in December 1938. As in the First World War, Hatfield House was voluntarily offered to the nation as a military hospital. Interior walls and decorations were covered with hardboard panels and win-dows were protected by ramparts of sandbags in the courtyards. Ashridge was also opened as a military hospital, while Brocket was converted into a maternity hospital for women evacuated from east London. Later in the war, Canadian troops were billeted there and some soldiers carved their names and addresses into the balustrade of James Paine's bridge. Some houses received schools and colleges evac-uated from London; others were requisitioned for government offices and armed forces from home and overseas: Bushey Hall was occupied by the headquarters of the United States Eighth Air Force Fighter Command from 1942 to 1945 and Dyrham Park became the head-quarters of the Polish army. Knebworth was requisitioned by the Froebel Institute as a teacher training college from October 1939 to August 1946. The waterworks and the drainage system had to be enlarged to cope with 100 women students. After the war, the Earl of Lytton, who had lost his two sons, the younger killed in North Africa in 1942, received a token rent and an additional £1,950 for dilapida-tions. When he died in 1947, his estate passed to his daughter, Lady Hermione Cobbold, wife of the governor of the Bank of England.[47] Rothamsted was occupied by the British army, who 'left the whole fabric in a very dilapidated condition and the back premises almost derelict',[48] while Moor Park was successively headquarters of the ter-ritorial army, women's Auxiliary Territorial Service and the second airborne corps, both house and park being extensively damaged by their military occupants. That was not the worst that could happen: Newsells Bury was burnt to the ground in 1943.[49] The BBC's Latin America and Near East services occupied Aldenham Park and the park was allowed to deteriorate to the extent that, after the war, the owners brought an action against the BBC for gross negligence.[50] Payments of rent to displaced owners and compensation for damage and losses to their property were niggardly and long delayed.

A revival of agriculture began some months before war broke out. From September 1939, farming operations were placed under state control and run by county war agricultural executive committees vested with powers to order farmers to plough up pastures and bring land up to a satisfactory standard of cultivation. Exceptionally bad farmers could be dispossessed by the authority of an executive committee. In Hertfordshire, farmers willingly co-operated in the plough-up campaign and owners of large parks, including Gorhambury, Beechwood, Panshanger, Ashridge and the smaller Hitchin Priory, reclaimed large areas that had not raised crops for over a hundred years (Figure 7.5). At Gorhambury, fruit and also pigs raised in the park were sent to Enfield Rolling Mills to supplement the rations of Lord Forrester's employees; in 1956, fruit trees and bushes were grubbed up and the park was again laid down to pasture. The war agricultural executive committee allocated rations of fertilisers and animal feedstuffs, controlled pests and diseases, organised pools of tractors and other machinery, supervised the employment of farmworkers and found accommodation for the Women's Land Army and, later, prisoners of war.[51] From the beginning, acreages sown with wheat, barley, oats, temporary grasses, potatoes, sugar beet and brussels sprouts expanded rapidly, the total area of arable land in the county increasing from 140,000 acres in 1938 to 220,000 acres in 1945.[52] The plough-up campaign brought lasting improvements to agriculture, more than doubling the number of tractors, as well as accelerating the spread of harvesters, milking machines, artificial fertilisers and rural electrification. Oaklands County Farm Institute contributed to modernisation by recruiting and training skilled personnel to work in agriculture.[53]

An interdepartmental committee under the chairmanship of Lord Justice Scott reported on land utilisation in rural areas in August 1942.[54] Its strongest recommendation was that good agricultural land should be avoided for housing development. It called for footpaths to be clearly signposted, nature reserves protected and green belts conserved as tracts of ordinary country where farmers and foresters

Figure 7.5: Fruit trees planted at Gorhambury during the Second World War. An aerial photograph taken in 1950 shows about five acres of fruit trees and extensive areas of gooseberries and blackcurrants. Reproduced by kind permission of the seventh Earl of Verulam

would be able to conduct their normal business. A green belt would also include golf courses and other open spaces, some of which were owned by local authorities under the provisions of the 1938 Green Belt Act. Dudley Stamp, who served as vice-chairman on the Scott committee, wrote a chapter on land classification and agriculture in Sir Patrick Abercrombie's *Greater London Plan 1944*. He deplored the 'undignified sprawl of towns and suburbs into the surrounding country' and called for an urban fence, beyond which 'it is most important that the farmer should be encouraged to perform his unpaid function as the nation's landscape gardener and steward of the countryside'.[55] His optimistic view of farmers' attitudes towards the appearance of the countryside captured a new spirit of confidence. The men and women who were growing food earned the goodwill of the whole nation and won support from the government in their endeavours to re-equip their farms and improve soil quality through cultivating, draining and applying fertilisers.

Abercrombie modelled his green belt on the examples of garden cities. Letchworth and Welwyn Garden City had been the first to acquire land to form rings of open spaces and pleasant countryside encircling built-up areas. The plan for a green belt around London envisaged a ring about five miles wide beyond the edge of the suburbs. In Hertfordshire, it was to extend from Rickmansworth, in the west, along the county boundary to Hoddesdon.[56] Abercrombie attributed the special attraction of old parks to their historic associations and idyllic scenery. He admired their fine architecture set in gardens and parks, their sheets of water and 'superb trees, sometimes in a state of extreme picturesque decline'. He probably exaggerated the degree of popular enthusiasm in claiming 'it is the conscious work of man harmonised and softened by nature that commands such ardent popular admiration'.[57] Less ardently, most commentators agreed that parks ought to be safeguarded as valuable features in the countryside.

At the end of the war, farmers in Hertfordshire were in a much stronger position to compete in world markets than they had been in the 1930s. However, owners of parks were in a much weaker position, facing heavy costs for repairs and modernisation, shortages of materials and labour and little prospect of being able to hire domestic staff. During and after the war, the government treated landowners more harshly than farmers. Rents from agricultural land were strictly controlled from 1939 to 1958 and lagged far behind land prices, farm incomes and maintenance costs.[58] Rents received by landlords were taxed as unearned income whereas farmers, computing their tax liabilities, were able to deduct expenses for new machinery and improvements from income. The outlook for owner-occupied agricultural land appeared to be much brighter than for privately owned country houses.[59]

Parks and planning

The post-war Labour government retained controls over private land and widened planning legislation to cover rural areas as well as towns. Historic country houses were recorded and listed and a new Ministry of Town and Country Planning was made responsible for deciding whether they could be altered or demolished. In the budget of 1946, Hugh Dalton dealt a further blow to private landowners by raising the

top rate of death duty from 65 per cent to 75 per cent. He also established a national land fund endowed from the sale of war surplus
stores. The proceeds were to be spent on creating national parks and
aiding the Ramblers' Association, the Youth Hostels Association and
the National Trust. The National Trust, under its new chairman the
Earl of Crawford, sought assistance from the government to extend
the Trust's ownership of houses and parks. Dalton agreed that the
Trust should receive grants to buy open land and should be given custody of houses acquired in lieu of death duties. Dalton's successor at
the exchequer, Sir Stafford Cripps, was prepared to continue the policy of using the national land fund to pass land and houses to the Trust
but was alarmed by the prospect of spending money on an unknown
number of unworthy properties. He appointed a senior civil servant,
Sir Ernest Gowers, to head an inquiry into the selection and means of
preserving houses and parks of outstanding historic value.

In 1950, the Gowers report concluded that neither public ownership
nor alternative uses would ensure the preservation of the unique and
irreplaceable qualities of country houses and their landscaped settings.
Long-term care could only be provided by families living in them. The
report recommended sweeping tax reductions and supplementary grants
to be disbursed by independent historic buildings councils.[60] In response,
the government set up historic buildings councils for England, Wales and
Scotland and encouraged owners to hand over their land and houses to
the National Trust with an option of staying in residence. It also offered
maintenance grants to a few private owners on condition that the properties would be opened to the public, but the chancellor absolutely
refused to make tax concessions to private owners. When a Conservative
government was returned to power in 1951, a 'limited salvage operation
of a few of the very best houses' was the most the treasury was prepared
to pay for.[61] In Hertfordshire, recipients of grants from the national land
fund included Ashridge, Gorhambury and Moor Park.[62] Some owners
were unwilling to open their gates to tourists in order to qualify for
grants, and many were aggrieved at losing the potential development
value of lands that were scheduled not to be built on.

The implementation of Abercrombie's plan for a green belt around
London was devolved to county councils under the terms of the 1947

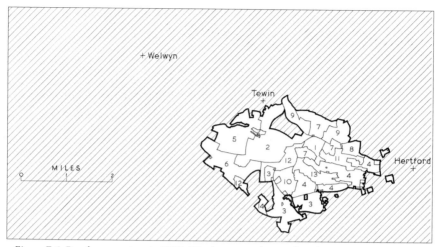

Figure 7.6: Panshanger estate in 1953. The house, gardens and park were divided into lots. Humbert and Flint, 'Particulars of the sale of the Panshanger estate', 15 July 1953. Drawn in the Geography Department, UCL

Town and Country Planning Act. The Hertfordshire county development plan, prepared in 1951, designated an area almost identical to that proposed by Abercrombie but excluded two enclaves where the London County Council built housing estates at south Oxhey, taking land from Oxhey Place, and at Borehamwood, swallowing the whole of Borehamwood House and its grounds. The two post-war new towns in Hertfordshire, Stevenage and Hemel Hempstead, did not build over former parks. At Hemel Hempstead, Geoffrey Jellicoe designed a long water garden, a haven of tranquillity leading towards picturesque Gadebridge, which had been a public park since the 1930s. The county plan deployed the green belt as a defence against the spread of suburbia, but made few provisions for either expanding recreational space or preserving farmland, woodland and parkland.[63] Agriculture was by far the most extensive user of green belt land, much of which was managed for dairying. It was not a neat and tidy pastoral landscape. Many smallholdings were used as riding schools, nursery gardens and poultry farms, and part-time hobby farmers occupied a higher proportion of land in the green belt than further from the metropolis.[64] Woodland and parkland constituted major land uses both in the green belt and elsewhere in Hertfordshire, with areas of special scenic value being protected from building development. Parks

at Ashridge, Great Gaddesden, Sarratt and Chorleywood were protected in the Chilterns area of outstanding natural beauty; Newsells
Park lay in the north Hertfordshire scenic area; and parks lying
between Welwyn and Hertingfordbury were protected by the Mimram
valley scenic area. A large area between Hatfield and Hoddesdon,
south to Northaw, was in the green belt but additionally protected as
an area of special beauty and its oak and hornbeam woods were scheduled as sites of special scientific interest and nature reserves.
Knebworth woods were also a nature reserve. In addition, Balls Park,
Tyttenhanger, Moor Park, Hitchin Priory, Rothamsted, Gorhambury
and Aldenham House were among places scheduled as buildings of
outstanding architectural and historic interest.[65]

The imposition of planning controls did not prevent the destruction of parks and country houses rising to unprecedented levels from
1950 to 1970. Albury Hall, Broadfield Hall, Bushey Hall, Coles Park,
Kimpton Hoo, Newberries and Panshanger were destroyed in the
1950s. Aspenden Hall was gutted and Cheshunt Great House was
pulled down in the 1960s.[66] Panshanger was devastated in 1953
(Figure 7.6). Furniture, family portraits, the contents of the library
and the estate records were removed before the sale by auction of the
entire estate, including William Atkinson's gothick mansion, gardens,
park, lakes, woods, outlying farms and houses in Tewin and
Hertingfordbury.[67] By the end of the year the mansion had been
demolished. In the following years, a dual carriageway, the A414
from Hatfield to Hertford, cut obliquely across the Mimram valley
and gravel was dug from the uplands in the south of the park. The
name Panshanger was taken by an aerodrome, a golf complex and a
residential neighbourhood in Welwyn Garden City, all situated to the
west of the nineteenth-century park. Repton's landscape scheme was
irreparably damaged and the county's plans for conserving the
Mimram valley scenic area suffered a serious setback.

Some parks were saved from destruction by being adapted for
institutional uses. In 1943, after the American millionaire John
Pierpont Morgan died, Hertfordshire County Council bought Wall
Hall and converted it into an emergency teacher training college. The
college later became a part of the University of Hertfordshire. In

2003, it was closed and houses and luxury apartments were built in the grounds.[68] The county council and subsequently the university also acquired Balls Park, which was used for training teachers. The house has now been refurbished for offices and part of the park is to be built over. Bayfordbury was restored by the John Innes Horticultural Institution until it was transferred to Hatfield Polytechnic, then to the University of Hertfordshire; the park has recently been divided into plots for speculative building. In 1951, Rothamsted house and gardens were adapted as residential accommodation for staff and visitors at the agricultural experimental station; the park was used for field trials. In 1959, Ashridge passed to Ashridge Management College Trust. In the same year, Haberdashers' Aske's School acquired Aldenham Park.[69] Beechwood, Langleybury and Temple Dinsley were also transformed into school grounds.

Other parks provided prestigious locations and spacious settings for commercial enterprises. Tyttenhanger, which had remained in the hands of the Caledon family, was bought in 1973 by John Boddington as offices for a firm of architects. In 1978, the Childwick Bury estate was sold, the house and grounds being acquired by film director, Stanley Kubrick, and the remainder of the estate broken up and sold in forty-nine lots.[70] The park and adjoining land were used as a stud farm. Hitchin Priory Park was cut across by a major road, the house and a remnant of the park being converted into a training centre for National Mutual Life.[71] Fanhams Hall became a staff college for building society managers and was later converted into a hotel.[72] Some of these places were listed as 'houses in adaptive use' by John Cornforth in *Country houses in Britain: can they survive?*[73] Cornforth's report analysed in detail the financial problems facing owners of houses and parks in the post-war period, and concluded that they could not survive without massive subsidies and substantial reductions in taxation.

Parks and tourism

A serious obstacle to preserving houses, parks and gardens in Hertfordshire was the unwillingness of owners to open their gates to tourists. An amenity highly prized by owners was privacy; an amenity sought by ramblers, naturalists and admirers of landscape beauty was access. Conflicts between owners' desires for privacy and public demands for access were inevitable.

In 1934, Knebworth was open every weekday throughout the year, Hatfield was open on Wednesday and Thursday afternoons between Easter and the August bank holiday and Ashridge was open on Saturday afternoons only between April and October.[74] In 1972, Gorhambury, Moor Park, Walkern Hall and St Pauls Walden Bury, in addition to Knebworth, Hatfield and Ashridge, admitted visitors and the tourist industry was commercially organised. When the fifth Marquess of Salisbury inherited Hatfield House in 1947, he set about creating a self-contained family residence in one wing and rearranging the state rooms for opening to tourists. No fewer than 30,000 were received in 1949 and numbers continued to rise. Later, the great hall of the old royal palace of Hatfield was restored for holding banquets, wedding receptions and parties. Craft workshops were opened in the palace yard and the east garden, patiently improved by Lady Salisbury, was opened for garden enthusiasts on Thursday afternoons during the summer.[75]

In 1969, after trying unsuccessfully to interest public or corporate bodies in buying Knebworth, David Lytton Cobbold decided that it might be possible to make the place earn its keep as a stately home. He persuaded Hertfordshire County Council to build a new spur road from the A1(M) into the park and support an application for Knebworth to become the first privately owned country park, aided by grants from the Countryside Commission. He laid out an adventure playground for children, built a narrow-gauge steam railway, created a tropical bird garden and reintroduced two herds of deer in the park. Later, he hosted pop concerts, jousting tournaments and car rallies in the park and formed a dinosaur trail among the rhododendrons and redwoods. He spent £150,000 on a restaurant and tourist centre and employed fourteen additional staff to take care of the house. Visitor numbers increased to 178,000 in 1972.[76] At both Hatfield and Knebworth, large sums of money were spent on guides, domestic staff and facilities for visitors. Knebworth, in particular, had to carry out costly building repairs to remedy serious outbreaks of dry rot. In 1974, Cornforth was doubtful whether more than a handful of country houses would be able to break even on investments in tourist attractions.[77]

Parks made a further contribution to the tourist industry by being turned into hotels and country clubs. Bushey Hall was among the first to open as a hotel in 1890; others followed, mostly after 1945. Sopwell House Hotel occupied the grounds of New Barns, landscaped by Humphry Repton. Pendley Manor, at Tring, rebuilt about 1874, was converted into an adult education centre before becoming a hotel.[78] In 1976, Bedwell Park at Essendon was turned into Hatfield London Country Club, a golf course with a country house hotel. Thirty years later, a developer announced the building of eight new townhouses and four apartments at Essendon Park, 'set in the spectacular rural idyll that is Hatfield London Country Club'.[79] In 1985, Hanbury Manor Country Club and golf course took over Poles, formerly the residence of the Hanbury family, brewers and bankers. At The Grove, near Watford, a luxury hotel and championship golf course were established in 2003 in a 300-acre park landscaped in the nineteenth century. At Ponsbourne Park, Potters Bar, a hotel occupied a seventeenth-century house with 200 acres of parkland. The Manor of Groves, set in 150 acres of parkland at High Wych, near Sawbridgeworth, was advertised as being close to Stansted airport.[80] Brocket Hall, one of the most beautiful landscape gardens in Hertfordshire, was elegantly restored as a setting for a conference centre and two championship golf courses. Champneys, at Tring, adorned with fine specimens of Wellingtonias planted in the late nineteenth century, was adapted as an exclusive health farm. At Tring Park, Walter Rothschild's zoological collection was taken over and opened to the public by the Natural History Museum.

The construction of motorways and trunk roads assisted the expansion of tourist traffic. Hertfordshire was crossed by the M1, A1(M) and the M25, which served some parks and cut through others. In 1974, Tring Park was slashed in two by the A41 by-pass, demolishing the back walls of an eighteenth-century temple and leaving its Ionic portico standing alone.[81] New roads were the most visible non-conforming uses in the green belt whose development was authorised by central and local planning authorities.

Parks and landed estates in recession

From 1940 until 1970, agriculture was protected by government measures that supported prices and allowed tax relief for investments in modernisation. Owners increased production and earned regular profits from their efforts. The greatest benefits were gained by large farmers. Under this benign regime, many landowners took in hand land that had previously been let to tenants and consolidated small farms into larger units, employing professionally qualified farm managers and spending large sums of money on powerful machines, fertilisers, pesticides and feedstuffs. For thirty years, the price of agricultural land rose steadily, keeping returns on the notional value of fixed capital low.

During the 1970s, the British economy suffered severe inflation and agriculture was particularly hard hit. The market for highly priced farm produce shrank and rising subsidies paid under the European Common Agricultural Policy failed to make good the deficit.[82] In trimming budgets, the first priority for landowners was to save their estates. Although many made great sacrifices to hold on to their parks and country houses, few were foolish enough to bankrupt their estates to do so. They knew that 'if the land goes, the house and family would soon follow'.[83] When it came to a final choice, the park and house had to go. The economic crisis reopened the rift between rural landowners seeking to preserve their estates and a largely urban public calling upon owners to protect the beauties of the countryside and conserve wildlife. Owners insisted that they could not afford to act as stewards of rural landscape without payment; they had to bear costs of repairs and maintenance for historic parks and houses that rose much faster than the general rate of inflation.[84] As politicians pressed for stronger environmental safeguards, landowners demanded adequate compensation for losses incurred in changing land use management.[85]

In Hertfordshire, an additional incentive to retain possession of their land was the persistent pressure for building development. In 1975 and 1977 building land in the metropolitan green belt was valued about fifty times higher than agricultural land and prices of all farmland in the home counties were much higher than in the rest of

Britain.[86] Even a remote possibility of obtaining planning permission to build acted as a deterrent to investing in environmental conservation. Standards of maintenance were visibly poorer on the edge of built-up areas than elsewhere.[87]

The economic crisis confronting landowners coincided with a surge in public anxiety about losing parks as landscape heritage. A Labour government elected in 1974 was forced to reduce public expenditure and raise taxes. The Chancellor of the Exchequer, Denis Healey, proposed to introduce a capital transfer tax and a wealth tax on capital assets, including houses worth more than £100,000. A parliamentary select committee heard a stream of witnesses opposed to the scheme and in 1975 received a petition signed by a million visitors to country houses. The government was persuaded to exempt country houses and parks from capital transfer tax and the proposed wealth tax was dropped. In 1978, farm rents received by private landlords were subject to income tax schedule A, which included, above certain levels, the addition of an investment income surcharge rising to a top rate of 98 per cent. No allowance could be made for maintenance expenditure, nor could Value Added Tax be recovered on materials or labour used in repair work. On the other hand, both owner-occupiers and tenant farmers could claim allowances for expenditure on buildings and machinery. For private farmers, the top rate of income tax was 75 per cent and for public farming companies the top rate of corporation tax was 52 per cent. Owner-occupiers also enjoyed substantial advantages over owners of tenanted estates in the imposition of the new capital transfer tax, and in 1979 the Northfield committee concluded that many private owners of let land would 'face difficulties in attempting to hand on tenanted estates intact to their successors'. The committee recommended that capital transfer tax and capital gains tax should be indexed against inflation, that landlords should be allowed a management charge against tax and should be allowed to recover VAT paid on repairs and maintenance work.[88]

Early in 1979, a new National Heritage Memorial Fund was established as an independent trust with an endowment of £12,400,000, to be supplemented by annual grants. Later that year, a new Conservative government, led by Margaret Thatcher, committed itself to cutting public spending, including that on heritage. Michael Heseltine reassured landowners that they would benefit from reduced taxation and would be able to keep their homes, parks and works of art with little or no assistance from the state. More money might be earned from car owners visiting places of historic interest; between 1980 and 1990, membership of the National Trust rose from one to two million and visits to country houses increased to an even greater extent. A market research survey conducted in 1993 reported that a third of the entire adult population of Britain had visited a stately home in the previous year.[89] Although parks in Hertfordshire were near to London, they were less frequently visited than those in other parts of the home counties.

At Knebworth, David Lytton Cobbold forecast in 1974: 'the struggle will continue on a year-to-year basis with the auctioneer's hammer always poised – Going, Going …?'[90] In 1986, David's wife Christine reported on twenty years of strenuous efforts to hold on to the house and park. In the summer of 1981 they:

> had to face up to the fact that we had lost a lot of money opening to the public – it had become a nonsense … We discussed it with the children who begged us to struggle on. They loved the house – Henry in particular who hoped to inherit it one day – and we must not sell it whatever happened.[91]

After protracted negotiations with North Hertfordshire District Council to grant planning permission for two separate sites to be developed as residential building land in order to endow a charitable trust that would pay for the upkeep of the house and park, the plan was finally approved in September 1984. The sale of the land for building realised over a million pounds and Knebworth House Education and Preservation Trust was established to secure the house and grounds for the foreseeable future. When the first Lord Cobbold died in 1987, David succeeded to the title and in 2000, his son Henry married and took over the house and the running of the park and estate. The recent history of Knebworth demonstrates how difficult it has been for an enterprising businessman, encouraged by his wife and children, to achieve the aim of making a place pay its way as a tourist attraction.

In 1980, Heather Clemenson carried out a postal questionnaire survey addressed to a sample of 500 owners of more than 3,000 acres of land in England and compared the sizes of their estates with those recorded in the *Return of Owners of Land, 1873*. The results of the survey indicated a 'continual and steady decline in the number and extent of privately owned historic estates'; the extent of the decline had been 'greater for estates of private owners in the 3,000 to 10,000 acre size range' than for 'great landowners, especially the long-established landed aristocracy'. The survey concluded that 'the sale and break-up of estates had even greater impact on country houses than on the ownership of estate land'. The loss of country houses and parks by owners of less than 10,000 acres had been greater than for the largest landowners.[92]

Landowners and parks in 2001

From the last quarter of the nineteenth century until the end of the twentieth century, the territorial base that paid for the upkeep of parks and country houses was whittled away. Of seventy-nine owners in Hertfordshire who held estates of more than 2,000 acres in 1873, only three survived in 2001 and their holdings were reduced to a fraction of their former size.[93] Kevin Cahill ranks the sixth Marquess of Salisbury as the county's leading private landowner in 2001, possessing 3,500 acres in Hertfordshire, 3,500 acres in Dorset and a most valuable 20 acres in Westminster. In 1873, the third marquess had owned a total of over 20,000 acres. The trunk of the Cecils' estate, like an aged oak, remained firmly rooted in Hatfield Park. Outlying branches had been lopped off and some land near the old town of Hatfield had been sold at a high price for housing and industrial development. Cahill credits the seventh Earl of Verulam as owning about 2,000 acres in 2001, compared with the 8,625 acres in Hertfordshire and over 10,000 acres in Essex owned by the second earl in 1873. Almost all outlying properties belonging to the

Grimstons had been sold to cover losses incurred by the fourth earl through the failure of companies drilling for oil in South America and growing tobacco in Rhodesia, in which he had invested heavily.[94] In 1931, the Crown had purchased 3,400 acres adjoining Gorhambury. At Knebworth, a leaking mansion and a neglected park were partly restored out of Lord Lytton Cobbold's earnings as a banker and company director in the City, but in 2001 the estate was reduced to 2,000 acres, compared with the 4,863 acres owned by Lord Lytton in 1873. Large tracts of land had been sold to maintain the exalted lifestyles of two heirs, father and son, who were both viceroys of India.

In 1933, twenty-two gentry families lived in moderate-sized parks but all had departed before the end of the century.[95] When Viscount Hampden sold Kimpton Hoo and its extensive agricultural estate in 1938, he wrote to his tenants expressing his regret:

> It was with great reluctance that I came to the decision to sell, but as I am unable to live at the Hoo and my son feels that he will also be unable to do so, we came, very regretfully, to the conclusion that we ought not to refuse the offer from such a purchaser as Oxford University, with the assurance that the character of the estate will be retained. I am sorry for breaking the connection which I trust you will agree has been a happy one, and I wish you all possible success under the changed conditions.[96]

After the sale, Oxford University continued to let farms to sitting tenants. The house was occupied by the London and North Eastern Railway Company throughout the Second World War and later by Imperial Chemical Industries. Failing to find a new tenant after ICI ended its lease, the university ordered the mansion to be demolished. The site was then used as a slaughterhouse by a local game merchant and afterwards by a fish packer.[97] From 1958, the park reverted to a wilderness. Recently, the bridge designed by William Chambers has been restored and executive homes have been built near the site of the Hoo.

Most owners of estates under 2,000 acres divested themselves of parks and took their farmland in hand, employing managers or farming companies where they were unable to farm themselves. A few transferred their holdings to trusts or companies in overseas tax havens.[98] During the late twentieth century, most small parks changed hands frequently. Owners and occupiers followed one another in rapid succession. Once a stately home had ceased to be a private residence, it passed from one use to a different use with each change of ownership. Schools became corporate offices or hotels; hospitals and colleges were converted into apartments. Some houses, left unoccupied for a year or more, were eventually pulled down. The demand for vacant seats at the end of the century remained weak.

At the beginning of the twenty-first century, public bodies, notably the Crown Estate, Hertfordshire County Council and the National Trust, owned larger areas of land than the largest private owners. The biggest institutional landowner in Hertfordshire in 2001 was the Crown Estate, which owned 6,922 acres. The county council owned 4,927 acres of farmland and woodland, including some purchased under the 1938 Green Belt Act. The National Trust owned 4,155 acres, mainly to the north of Ashridge, and the diocese of St Albans held 3,785 acres in many scattered parcels.[99] Despite these figures, public bodies acquired only a small amount of parkland and very few country houses. The county council transferred ownership of Wall Hall, Balls Park and Bayfordbury to the University of Hertfordshire and all three eventually fell into the hands of developers. With the exception of the National Trust, public institutions were not diligent guardians of landscape heritage.

Very much contrary to the dominant trend, Sir Thomas Henry Milborne-Swinnerton Pilkington, grandson of John Fenwick Harrison, director of the Harrison family business, and inheritor of the family seat at Kings Walden Park, commissioned Raymond Erith and Quinlan Terry to design a pure Georgian country house. The old house was pulled down in 1969 and the new building was completed in 1971. Nikolaus Pevsner described its appearance in the late twentieth century as 'the unexpected phenomenon' and Robert Hewison commented that it might have been 'conceived as the last country house'.[100] The new Kings Walden Bury fitted perfectly into the setting of an ancient park (Figure 7.7). In front of the house, a large expanse of

Figure 7.7: Kings Walden Bury, rebuilt in 1971. The Palladian mansion, designed by Raymond Erith and Quinlan Terry, stands on rising ground, backed by mature trees. In front of the house stretches an open lawn and scattered trees. Photograph by Matt Prince. Reproduced by kind permission of Sir Thomas Pilkington

lawn stretched as far as a ha-ha. In the spacious park, magnificent oaks, ancient sweet chestnuts and an avenue of limes were preserved. Monterey pines, Wellingtonias and other specimen trees diversified the wooded slopes, recalling a vision of an eighteenth-century landscape.[101]

Parks and landscape heritage

Parks in Hertfordshire lie within fifty miles of central London; most are within an hour's drive from the north-west suburbs. Visitors have been drawn to the county not by the prospect of endless vistas and vast spaces encompassed by great landscape gardens fashioned in the late eighteenth century, but by intimate glimpses of smaller parks. Brocket and Gorhambury are jewels in a wooded landscape. Hatfield has some of the most venerable oaks and exquisite gardens, reflecting the art of the seventeenth century and the skill of a twentieth-century connoisseur. Kings Walden Park is adorned with mighty oaks and St Pauls Walden Bury possesses a small, sensitively restored eighteenth-century landscape garden. Ashridge has fine beeches, wild deer roaming through its glades and Repton's gothick gardens. Knebworth is a showplace with formal gardens, a spacious park and many attractions for young people. Golfers may wander through artfully contrived changing scenes at Moor Park and The Grove.

For seekers after relict features, Hertfordshire has much to offer. Benington Lordship presents a romantic garden around fragments of a Norman keep and a sham Norman gatehouse built about 1835. The ruins of a genuine Norman castle at Berkhamsted stand outside the boundary of a park that belonged to the Crown in the early fourteenth century. Ryehouse Gatehouse Museum occupies Sir Andrew Ogard's fifteenth-century manor house. Remains of Theobalds Palace lie in the grounds of Cedars Park at Waltham Cross and vestiges of the seventeenth-century deer park have been discovered at other sites in Cheshunt. The most fantastic folly in Hertfordshire is a tall archway set between two square castellated towers at Brookmans Park. This solitary memento of a celebrated park was built in the early eighteenth century as the southern gate to Sir Jeremy Sambrooke's Gobions Park.[102] Another surprising relic is a church designed by Nicholas Revett in 1778 as a likeness of a Grecian temple. It served as an eye-catcher for Ayot St Lawrence House. In Tring Park, another Grecian temple has been truncated by the A41 by-pass and at Moor Park, a temple to the four winds erected in honour of Admiral Lord Anson was destroyed in 1930. Year by year, follies, grottoes, temples, bridges and other parkland structures have crumbled and have been swept away.

Without constant attention, parks change as trees grow old and decay. Lakes become choked with reeds and silt up. Parkland pastures and driveways become overgrown. Deer, foxes and pheasants return to their old haunts in the absence of hunters and gamekeepers. Parks will be saved if they are lived in by people who cherish them and have sufficient resources to spend on their repair and modernisation. For five hundred years, the fortunes of parks have depended on the success or failure of large private estates, but private landowners now have little hope of regaining large areas of Hertfordshire in order to restore their landscape amenities. Modernisation and adaptation will continue to change the appearance of parks and landscape heritage will have to be cared for by new guardians.

Notes

1. Lord Phillimore, 'Agriculture and the preservation of the countryside', *Journal of the Town Planning Institute*, 18 (1932), pp.171–4.

2. B. Short, *Land and society in Edwardian Britain* (Cambridge, 1997), pp.9–37.

3. D. Cannadine, *The decline and fall of the British aristocracy* (New Haven and London, 1990), pp.48–87.

4. H.A. Clemenson, *English country houses and landed estates* (London, 1982), pp.197–8.

5. H. Poole, *A fair and large house at Cassiobury Park 1546–1927* (Watford, 1985), pp.49–50; L. Ellis, *Future proposals for Cassiobury Park* (Watford, 1972), section 2, para 2.2.

6. J. Brown, *Gardens of a golden afternoon: the story of a partnership: Edwin Lutyens and Gertrude Jekyll* (London, 1982), pp.65, 198.

7. A. Shellim, 'Garden creation in war-time: the legacy of the great war at Queenswood School' in Rowe, *Hertfordshire garden history*, pp.192–207.

8. Pevsner revised by Cherry, *Hertfordshire*, pp.67, 281; H.A. Tipping, 'Lockleys, Hertfordshire', *Country Life*, 48 (1920), pp.48–55; Wratten, Radlett and Aldenham, p.32; R. Bisgrove, *The gardens of Britain: Berkshire, Oxfordshire, Buckinghamshire, Bedfordshire and Hertfordshire* (London, 1978), p.194.

9. J.G.E. Cox, *'Be Proud': Hertfordshire and the Great War* (St Albans, 2002), p.136.

10. Cecil, *The Cecils of Hatfield*, p.294.

11. Danesbury sale particulars, 1919 (HALS D/EryB 486).

12. Cannadine, *Decline and fall of the British aristocracy*, p.111.

13. *Ibid.*, pp.115, 122.

14. F.J. Osborn, *Green belt cities* (London, 1946), p.57; 'Particulars of the sale of lands belonging to the Panshanger estate', 1919 (HALS DE/P P99–100).

15. J. Sheail, *Rural conservation in inter-war Britain* (Oxford, 1981), p.6; D. Coult, *A prospect of Ashridge* (Chichester, 1980), pp.2, 209–14.

16. R.E. Pahl, *Urbs in rure: the metropolitan fringe in Hertfordshire* (London, 1965), pp.45–6.

17. J. Hoppit, 'Vardon, Henry William (1870–1937)', in *Oxford Dictionary of National Biography*, vol. 56, p.138; R. Fisher, 'James Braid (1870–1950)', in *Oxford Dictionary of National Biography*, vol. 7, p.281; I. Stuart, *Golf in Hertfordshire* (Hitchin, 1970), pp.15–142.

18. Twenty-two places were named 'Golf Course' on Ordnance Survey one-inch maps in 1932–3. Those sited in parks are indicated as 'Pk' in the following list: Ashridge Pk, Batchworth Pk, Berkhamsted Common, Brookmans Pk,

Bushey Hall Pk, Chorleywood Common, Hadley Wood (Beech Hill Pk), Harpenden Common, Hartsbourne Manor Pk, Letchworth Pk, Mid Herts (Delaport Pk), Moor Pk, Old Fold Manor, Oxhey Pk, Porters Pk, Potters Bar, Royston, Sandy Lodge, South Herts (Totteridge Pk), Verulam (Sopwell Pk), Welwyn Garden City, and West Herts (Cassiobury Pk).

19.   J. Corbett, *A history of St Albans* (Chichester, 1997), pp.117–8.

20.   R. Laidlaw (ed.), *The R & A golfer's handbook 2006* (London, 2006), pp.679–83.

21.   In 2006 the thirty-two golf courses in former parks were: Aldwickbury Pk, Ashridge, Batchwood Hall, Batchworth (Moor Pk), Briggens, Brocket Hall, Brookmans Pk, Bushey (Ho), Bushey Hall, Chadwell Springs (Presdales), Danesbury Pk, Dyrham Pk, East Herts (Hamels), The Grove, Hadley Wood (Beech Hill Pk), Hanbury Manor (Poles), Hartsbourne Manor, Hatfield London (Bedwell Pk), Hertfordshire (Broxbournebury), Lamerwood (Lamer Pk), Letchworth (Hall), Little Hay (Westbrook Hay), Mid Herts (Delaport), Moor Pk, Oxhey Pk, Porters Pk, Rickmansworth (Moor Pk), Shendish Manor, South Herts (Totteridge Pk), Stevenage (Aston Ho), Verulam (Sopwell), and West Herts (Cassiobury).

22.   Y. Hodson, *Popular maps: the Ordnance Survey Popular Edition one-inch map of England and Wales 1919–26* (London, 1999), pp.61, 171, 323, 328–9, 335–7.

23.   Oliver, *Ordnance Survey maps: a concise guide for historians*, p.95.

24.   *Herts Advertiser,* 5 September 1925.

25.   B. Wood, *Bushey* (Stroud, 1997), pp.10, 36; sales particulars: Humbert and Flint, Bushey Grange estate for sale by auction, July 1925 (Bushey Museum).

26.   L.G. Cameron, *Hertfordshire: report of the Land Utilisation Survey of Britain, Part 80* (London, 1941), pp.317–20.

27.   The nine new parks were Aldwickbury, Bovingdon House, Cokenach, Culverwood Ho, Darley Ash, Fanhams Hall, Houndswood, Ridgehurst and Queenswood.

28.   Pevsner and Cherry, *Hertfordshire*, pp.88, 275; Smith, *Hertfordshire houses*, p.24.

29.   Thompson, 'English landed society in the twentieth century', p.16.

30.   A.S.G. Butler, *The architecture of Sir Edwin Lutyens* (London, 1950), vol. I, pp.39–41; Brown, *Gardens of a golden afternoon*, pp.121, 126, 159.

31.   *English Heritage Register of Parks and Gardens* (2002) GD 1914; *Hertfordshire Sites and Monuments Record* (2003), 7337.

32.   D. Ottewill, *The Edwardian garden* (New Haven, 1989), p.56.

33.   T. Williamson, 'The character of Hertfordshire's parks and gardens' in Rowe, *Hertfordshire garden history*, p.22, also pp.145, 152.

34. R.McG. Carslaw, *An economic survey of Hertfordshire agriculture*, Univ. Cambridge, Farm Economic Branch Report 18 (Cambridge, 1931); E. Whetham, *The agrarian history of England and Wales*. VIII, 1914–39 (Cambridge, 1978), pp.184–5, 310–11; J.T. Coppock, 'Land-use changes in the Chilterns, 1931–51', *Transactions of the Institute of British Geographers*, 20 (1954), pp.113–40; J.T. Coppock, 'Crop and livestock changes in the Chilterns, 1931–51', *Transactions of the Institute of British Geographers*, 28 (1960), pp.179–98.

35. W.B. Thomas, 'The home counties', in C. Williams-Ellis (ed.), *Britain and the beast* (London, 1937), pp.200–11.

36. C. Williams-Ellis, *England and the octopus* (Penrhyndeudraeth, 1928); Williams-Ellis, *Britain and the beast*; Sheail, *Rural conservation*, pp.240–1.

37. W.R. Davidge, *The Hertfordshire regional planning report, 1927* (Hertford, 1928).

38. *First report of the Greater London Regional Planning Committee* (Westminster, 1929).

39. D. Thomas, *London's green belt* (London, 1970), pp.55–6.

40. *Ibid.*, pp.80–2.

41. E.G. Sharp, 'The acquisition of London Green Belt estates: a study of inter-authority relations' (PhD thesis, Univ. London, 1986).

42. C. Hussey, *The picturesque: studies in a point of view* (London, 1927).

43. Hussey, *English gardens and landscapes*, pp.84–8.

44. R. Dutton, *The English garden* (London, 1937), p.4.

45. Hansard, 5th series 254 (24 June 1931), pp.533–4.

46. P. Mandler, *The fall and rise of the stately home* (New Haven, 1997), pp.295–308.

47. C. Seebohm, *The country house: a wartime history, 1939–45* (London, 1989), pp.97–101.

48. D.H. Boalch, *The manor of Rothamsted and its occupants* (Harpenden, 1978), p.36.

49. J.M. Robinson, *The country house at war* (London, 1989), pp.73–4, 79, 80, 162, 166–7.

50. Hertfordshire Gardens Trust and Williamson, *Parks and gardens of west Hertfordshire*, p.100.

51. B. Short, C. Watkins, W. Foot and P. Kinsman, *The National Farm Survey, 1941–1943: state surveillance and the countryside in England and Wales in the Second World War* (Wallingford, 2000), pp.25–39.

52. H.W. Gardner, *A survey of the agriculture of Hertfordshire*. County Agricultural Survey 5 (London, 1967), p.4.

53. *Ibid.*, pp.168–70.

54. Ministry of Works and Planning, *Report of the committee on land utilisation in rural areas,* Cmd 6378 (London, 1942) (Scott Report).

55. P. Abercrombie, *Greater London plan 1944* (London, 1945), p.95.

56. *Ibid.*, pp.24–5.

57. *Ibid.*, p.104.

58. R. Gasson, *The influence of urbanization on farm ownership and practice* (Wye, 1966), p.9; B. Short, 'Agency and environment in the transition to a productivist farming regime in England and Wales', in H. Clout (ed.), *Contemporary rural geographies: land, property and resources in Britain* (London, 2007), p.39.

59. H. Newby, C. Bell, D. Rose and P. Saunders, *Property, paternalism and power: class and control in rural England* (London, 1978), pp.37–8.

60. HM Treasury, *Report of the committee on houses of outstanding historic or architectural interest* (23 June 1950) (Gowers Report).

61. Mandler, *Fall and rise of the stately home*, pp.330–47.

62. J. Cornforth, *Country houses in Britain: can they survive?* (Crawley, 1974), pp.32–3.

63. Thomas, *London's green belt*, pp.88–92; E.H. Doubleday, *Hertfordshire: survey report and analysis of county development plan* (Hertford, 1951), pp.3, 124.

64. Gasson, *Influence of urbanization*, pp.16–33; R. Munton, S. Whatmore and T. Marsden, 'Reconsidering urban-fringe agriculture: a longitudinal analysis of capital restructuring on farms in the Metropolitan Green Belt', *Transactions of the Institute of British Geographers*, 13 (1988), pp.324–36.

65. Doubleday, *Hertfordshire: county development plan*, pp.118–21, 173.

66. R. Strong, M. Binney and J. Harris, *The destruction of the country house 1875–1975* (London, 1974), p.189.

67. Humbert & Flint, *Particulars of the sale of the Panshanger estate*, 15 July 1953.

68. D. Tilley and J. Beagle (eds.), *Wall Hall: from farmhouse to university* (Aldenham, 2003), p.30.

69. Lawrence, *Aldenham House gardens*, pp.40–5.

70. Strutt & Parker, Childwick Bury estate sale particulars (July 1978) (HALS DZ/91 E1).

71. Howlett, *Hitchin Priory Park*, p.9.

72. Bisgrove, *Gardens of Britain*, p.74.

73. Cornforth, *Country houses in Britain*, pp.53–6.

74. R. Dutton and A. Holden, *English country houses open to the public* (London, 1934), pp.52–8.

75. Mandler, *Fall and rise of the stately home*, pp.369, 417.

76. Strong et al., *Destruction of the country house*, pp.164–6.

77. Cornforth, *Country houses in Britain*, pp.98–9.

78. Pevsner and Cherry, *Hertfordshire*, p.370.

79. Advertisement in 'New homes and interiors', *Jewish Chronicle Supplement* (4 May 2007) 12.

80. Automobile Association, *AA 2007 hotel guide*, pp.346, 351, 353, 355.

81. Pevsner and Cherry, *Hertfordshire*, p.370.

82. T. Marsden, J. Murdoch, p.Lowe, R. Munton and A. Flynn, *Constructing the countryside* (London, 1993), p.61.

83. Cornforth, *Country houses in Britain*, p.20.

84. *Ibid.*, p.80.

85. Marsden et al., *Constructing the countryside*, pp.92–6.

86. R. Goodchild and R. Munton, *Development and the landowner* (London, 1985), p.149.

87. *Ibid.*, p.154.

88. Ministry of Agriculture, Fisheries and Food, *Report of the committee of inquiry into the acquisition and occupancy of agricultural land* (London, 1979) Cmnd 7599 (Northfield Report), pp.72–73, 84–86, 245.

89. Mandler, *Fall and rise of the stately home*, p.411; *Northfield Report*, pp.84–86, 245.

90. Strong et al., *Destruction of the country house*, p.166.

91. C.L. Cobbold, *Board meetings in the bath: the Knebworth House story* (London, 1986), p.170.

92. Clemenson, *English country houses and landed estates*, pp.127, 152.

93. K. Cahill, *Who owns Britain* (Edinburgh, 2001), p.241.

94. King, *Grimstons of Gorhambury*, pp.154–5.

95. The twenty-two parks and their residents in 1933 were: Abbotshill (Lady Marjorie Dalrymple); Aspenden (Sir Arthur Lushington); Bayfordbury (Adml Sir Lewis Baker); Beechwood (Sir Giles Edward Sebright); Briggens (Lord Hunsdon); Broxbourne Bury (Major Richard Smith Bosanquet); Easneye (John Henry Buxton); Frythe, Welwyn (Miss Wilshere); Kimpton Hoo (Viscount Hampden); Lamer Park (Apsley Cherry Garrard); Langleybury (Edward Henry Loyd); Lawrence End (George Oakley); Micklefield Hall (T.R. Clutterbuck); Munden House (Viscount Knutsford); Priory Park, Hitchin (Ralph Delme Radcliffe); Tyttenhanger (Countess of Caledon); Walkern Hall (Miss Cotton Browne); Warrenwood (Captain Hubert Butler); Woodhall Park, Watton (Major Edward Pelham Smith); Woolmers, Hertingfordbury (Charles Edward Wodehouse); Wyddial Hall (Sir Charles Heaton Ellis); and Youngsbury (Christopher Giles-Puller).

96. Reported in the *Hertfordshire Mercury* (27 May 1938).

97. English Heritage, *Report on The Hoo, Kimpton, North Hertfordshire* (1998) GD 1909.

98. *Northfield Report*, pp.84–6.

99. Cahill, *Who owns Britain*, p.241.

100. 'Kings Walden Bury, Hertfordshire', *Country Life*, 154 (1973), pp.858–61; Pevsner and Cherry, *Hertfordshire*, p.46; R. Hewison, *The heritage industry: Britain in a climate of decline* (London, 1987), p.74.

101. Hertfordshire Gardens Trust, Kings Walden Bury, Site Survey 2001–03 (HALS Acc 3898).

102. B. Jones, *Follies and grottoes,* 2nd edn. (London, 1974), p.345.

Bibliography

Primary Sources

The British Library map collection keeps county maps by Christopher Saxton, 1577; John Norden, 1598; John Seller, 1675; John Oliver, 1695; John Warburton, 1725; Andrew Dury and John Andrews, 1766; Ordnance Survey two-inch drawings, 1799–1812; A. Bryant, 1821; Ordnance Survey first edition six-inch maps, 1863–81; Ordnance Survey fifth popular edition one-inch maps, 1932–3, which provide the basis for identifying and locating parks at different dates. The map collection also contains indispensable guides for interpreting and evaluating the work of individual map-makers.

The Institute of Historical Research has an outstanding library of English Local History which serves the editors of the Victoria County Histories.

The Witt collection at the Courtauld Institute of Art keeps photographic reproductions of historical paintings of parks and landscapes by many artists.

Hertfordshire Archives and Local Studies (HALS) holds tithe surveys, directories, poll books and electoral registers which assist in identifying names and addresses of owners and occupiers of parks. Historical records, including deeds, accounts, maps and drawings from private estates have been deposited at HALS. Notable among these are manuscripts relating to Brocket, Great Gaddesden, Lamer, Newsells, Panshanger and other parks. Drawings of houses by H. G. Oldfield and John and John Chessell Buckler are also kept in HALS.

A most important collection of studies of individual parks written by members of the research group of Hertfordshire Gardens Trust, directed by Anne Rowe, are deposited at HALS, in Acc. 3898. The collection includes files on Abbots Hill, Ashridge, Ayot House, Beechwood, Cassiobury, Childwickbury, Danesbury, Golden Parsonage, The Grove, Hitchin Priory, Kimpton Hoo, Kings Walden Bury (by Anne Rowe), Knebworth (by Anne Rowe), Lamer (by R. Beament), Langleybury, Marshalswick, Moor Park, Offley Place, Rossway, Rothamsted, Shendish Manor, St Pauls Walden Bury, Temple Dinsley, Tring Park, Tyttenhanger, Wall Hall and Woodcock Hill.

Collections of papers relating to Bayfordbury, Beechwood, Gorhambury, Hatfield and Knebworth are kept in private archives.

Watford Museum, Bushey Museum and Watford Central Library are valuable repositories of information on local history.

Hertfordshire County Council Environment Department has compiled a Sites and Monument Record which contains details of parks and gardens of historic importance. English Heritage keeps a register of scheduled buildings, parks and gardens.

Secondary Sources

Abercrombie, P., *Greater London plan 1944* (London, 1945)

Addison, J., *The Tatler*, 161 (18–20 April 1710)

Addison, J., *The Spectator*, 414 (25 June 1712)

Agar, N., 'The Hertfordshire farmer in the age of the industrial revolution', in D. Jones-Baker, *Hertfordshire in history* (Hertfordshire Local History Council, 1991)

A German Prince (Herman Puckler-Muskau) *Tour in Germany, Holland and England in the years 1826, 1827 and 1828: a series of letters* (London, 1832)

Amherst, A., *A history of gardening in England* (London, 1896)

Andrews, J.H., *A paper landscape: the Ordnance Survey in nineteenth-century Ireland* (London, 1975)

Angus, W., *Seats of the nobility and gentry in Great Britain and Wales* (London, 1787)

Antrobus, J.J., *Bishops Hatfield: some memories of its past* (Hatfield, 1912)

Appleton, J., 'Some thoughts on the geography of the picturesque', *Journal of Garden History*, 6 (1986)

Armitage, H.A., *A history of Moor Park* (London, 1964)

Bacon, F., 'Of gardens' (1625)

Baker, J.J., 'Bayfordbury', *Transactions of the East Hertfordshire Archaeological Society*, 3 (1907)

Baker, W.H. and Jackson, A.B., *Illustrations of conifers* (London, 1909–1913)

Banister, K., 'The Pulham family of Hertfordshire and their work' in Rowe, A. (ed.), *Hertfordshire garden history: a miscellany* (Hatfield, 2007)

Barber, P., 'Maps and monarchs in Europe 1550–1800', in Oresko, R., Gibbs, G.C. and Scott, H.M. (eds.), *Royal and republican sovereignty in early modern Europe* (Cambridge, 1997)

Barton, P.R., 'Woodland management in the late seventeenth century', *Hertfordshire Archaeology*, 7 (1986)

Bateman, J., *The great landowners of Great Britain and Ireland*, reprint of 4th edn. (1883) (Leicester, 1971)

Batho, G., 'Landlords in England: the crown', in Thirsk, J. (ed.), *The agrarian history of England and Wales*. Vol. IV 1500–1650 (Cambridge, 1967)

Bean, J.M.W., 'Landlords: the market for land', in Miller, E. (ed.), *The agrarian history of England and Wales*. Vol. III 1348–1500 (Cambridge, 1991)

Beer, E.S. de (ed.), *The diary of John Evelyn*, 6 vols (Oxford, 2000)

Bendall, S., *Dictionary of land surveyors and local map-makers of Great Britain and Ireland*. Vol. 2. Dictionary (London, 1997)

Bickham, G., *The beauties of Stow* (London, 1750)

Bisgrove, R., *The gardens of Britain: Berkshire, Oxfordshire, Buckinghamshire, Bedfordshire and Hertfordshire* (London, 1978)

Blith, W., *The English improver improved; or the survey of husbandry surveyed* (London 1652)

Boalch, D.H., *The manor of Rothamsted and its occupants* (Harpenden, 1978)

Bourne, J.C., *Drawings of the London and Birmingham Railway with an historical and descriptive account by John Britton* (London, 1839)

Bovill, E.W., *English country life, 1780–1830* (London, 1962)

Bowden, P., 'Agricultural prices, farm profits and rents'; also 'Statistical appendix' Tables I, VIII, IX, XI, XII, XIII, in Thirsk, J. (ed.), *The agrarian history of England and Wales*. Vol. IV 1500–1650 (Cambridge, 1967)

Branch Johnson, W., *The Carrington diary 1797–1810* (London, 1956)

Branch Johnson, W., *The industrial archaeology of Hertfordshire* (Newton Abbot, 1970)

Branch Johnson, W. (ed.), *Memorandoms for… the diary between 1798 and 1810 of John Carrington, farmer, chief constable, tax assessor, surveyor of highways and overseer of the poor of Bramfield in Hertfordshire* (Chichester, 1973)

Brayley, E.W. and Britton, J., *The beauties of England and Wales*, vol. 7 (London, 1806)

Britton, J., *The history and description of Cassiobury Park* (London, 1837)

Brooks, C.W., 'Sir Harbottle Grimston, second baronet (1603–1685)', in *Oxford Dictionary of National Biography*, vol. 24 (Oxford, 2004)

Brown, D.A., 'Nathaniel Richmond (1724–1784) gentleman improver', (PhD thesis, Univ. East Anglia, 2000)

Brown, J., *Gardens of a golden afternoon: the story of a partnership: Edwin Lutyens and Gertrude Jekyll* (London, 1982)

Bryant, A., *Preparing for publication: a new map of the county of Hertford* (London, 1821)

Burke, E., *A philosophical enquiry into the origin of our ideas of the sublime and the beautiful* (London, 1757)

Busby, J.H., 'Local military forces in Hertfordshire, 1793–1814', *Journal of the Society of Army Historical Research*, 31 (1953)

Bushaway, R.W., 'Rite, legitimation and community', in Stapleton, B. (ed.), *Conflict and community in southern England* (Stroud, 1992)

Butler, A.S.G., *The architecture of Sir Edwin Lutyens* (London, 1950)

Cahill, K., *Who owns Britain* (Edinburgh, 2001)

Cameron, L.G., *Hertfordshire: report of the Land Utilisation Survey of Britain*, Part 80 (London, 1941)

Cannadine, D., *The decline and fall of the British aristocracy* (New Haven and London, 1990)

Carslaw, R.McG., *An economic survey of Hertfordshire agriculture*, Univ. Cambridge, Farm Economic Branch Report 18 (Cambridge, 1931)

Carter, G., Goode, P. and Laurie, K., *Humphry Repton landscape gardener 1752–1818* (Norwich, 1982)

Cecil, D., *The young Melbourne* (London, 1939)

Cecil, D., *Lord M., or the later life of Lord Melbourne* (London, 1954)

Cecil, D., *The Cecils of Hatfield: a portrait of an English ruling family* (London, 1973)

Chauncy, H., *The Historical antiquities of Hertfordshire*, 2 vols (Bishops Stortford, 1826)

Checkland, S.G. and Checkland, E.O.A. (eds.), *The Poor Law Report of 1834* (Harmondsworth, 1974)

Clark, A. (ed.), *'Brief lives', chiefly of contemporaries set down by John Aubrey, between the years 1669 & 1696*, 2 vols (Oxford, 1898)

Clay, C., 'Two families and their estates: the Grimstons and the Cowpers from c.1660 to c.1815', (Ph.D. thesis, Cambridge, 1966)

Clay, C., 'The evolution of landed society after the Restoration', in Thirsk, J. (ed.), *The agrarian history of England and Wales. Vol. V 1640–1750. Agrarian change* (Cambridge, 1985)

Clemenson, H.A., *English country houses and landed estates* (London, 1982)

Clutterbuck, R., *The history and antiquities of the county of Hertford*, 3 vols (London, 1815–27)

Cobbett, W., *Rural rides in Surrey, Kent and other counties in the years 1821 to 1832*, 2 vols (London, 1912)

Cobbold, C.L., *Board meetings in the bath: the Knebworth House story* (London, 1986)

Colvin, H.M., *A biographical dictionary of English architects 1660–1840* (London, 1954), 2nd edn. (London, 1978)

Cook, M., *The manner of raising, ordering and improving forrest trees; also, how to plant, make, and keep woods, walks, avenues, lawns, hedges, etc.* (London, 1676)

Cooper, A.A. (3rd Earl of Shaftesbury), *The moralists: a philosophic rhapsody* (London, 1709)

Coppock, J.T., 'Land-use changes in the Chilterns, 1931–51', *Transactions of the Institute of British Geographers*, 20 (1954)

Coppock, J.T., 'Crop and livestock changes in the Chilterns, 1931–51', *Transactions of the Institute of British Geographers*, 28 (1960)

Coppock, J.T., 'Dormitory settlements around London', in J.T. Coppock and H.C. Prince (eds.), *Greater London* (London, 1964)

Coppock, J.T., 'Maps as sources for the study of land use in the past', *Imago Mundi*, 22 (1968)

Corbett, J., *A history of St Albans* (Chichester, 1997)

Cornforth, J., *Country houses in Britain: can they survive?* (Crawley, 1974)

Couch, S.M., 'The practice of avenue planting in the seventeenth and eighteenth centuries', *Garden History*, 20 (1992)

Coult, D., *A prospect of Ashridge* (Chichester, 1980)

Cowell, B.,'Patrician landscapes, plebeian cultures: parks and society in two English counties c.1750–1850', (PhD thesis, Nottingham Univ., 1998)

Cowell, B., 'The Commons Preservation Society and the campaign for Berkhamsted Common 1866–70', *Rural History*, 13 (2002)

Cowell, F., 'Richard Woods (?1716–93): a preliminary account', 3 parts, *Garden History* 14, 15 (1986–7)

Cox, J.C., 'Forestry', in *VCH Hertfordshire*, vol. 4 (1914)

Cox, J.G.E., *'Be Proud': Hertfordshire and the Great War* (St Albans, 2002)

Crump, W.B., 'The genesis of Warburton's "Map of Yorkshire" 1720', *Thoresby Society Miscellanea*, 28 (1928)

Cussans, J.E., *History of Hertfordshire* (1870–81), W. Branch Johnson (ed.) 3 vols. (Hertford, 1972)

Dalton, C., 'The gardens at Quickswood, the hunting lodge of the earls of Salisbury' in Rowe, A. (ed.), *Hertfordshire garden history: a miscellany* (Hatfield, 2007)

Daniell, H.C.N., 'Popes Manor, Essendon', *East Herts Archaeological Society Transactions*, 7 (1923)

Daniels, S., *Humphry Repton: landscape gardening and the geography of Georgian England* (New Haven and London, 1999)

Davidge, W.R., *The Hertfordshire regional planning report, 1927* (Hertford, 1928)

Defoe, D., *The complete English tradesman* (London, 1726)

Defoe, D., *A tour through England and Wales*, 2 vols (London, 1927, first published 1724–26)

Delano-Smith, C. and Kain, R.J.P., *English maps; a history* (London, 1999)

Desmond, R., *Dictionary of British and Irish botanists and horticulturalists* (London, 1977)

Desmond, R.G.C., 'A Repton garden at Haileybury', *Garden History*, 6 (1978)

Doggett, N., 'Sir Henry Chauncy (1632–1719)', in *Oxford Dictionary of National Biography*, vol. 11 (Oxford, 2004)

Doggett, N. and Hunn, J., 'Excavations at Golden Parsonage, Gaddesden Row', *Hertfordshire's Past*, 13 (1982)

Dony, J.G., *A history of the straw hat industry* (Luton, 1942)

Doree, S.G., 'Nathaniel Salmon: Hertfordshire's neglected historian', in Jones-Baker, D. (ed.), *Hertfordshire in history: papers presented to Lionel Munby* (Hertfordshire Local History Council, 1991)

Doubleday, E.H., *Hertfordshire: survey report and analysis of county development plan* (Hertford, 1951)

Dutton, R. and Holden, A., *English country houses open to the public* (London, 1934)

Dutton, R., *The English garden* (London, 1937)

Dyos, H.J. and Aldcroft, D.H., *British transport: an economic survey from the seventeenth century to the twentieth* (Harmondsworth, 1974)

Edelen, G. (ed.), *William Harrison, the description of England, 1577–1587* (Ithaca, NY, 1968)

Elliott, B., *Victorian gardens* (London, 1986)

Ellis, L., *Future proposals for Cassiobury Park* (Watford, 1972)

Ellis, W., *Chiltern and Vale farming explained, according to the latest improvements necessary for all landlords and tenants of either ploughed-grass or wood-grounds* (London, 1733)

Evans, I.M. and Lawrence, H., *Christopher Saxton. Elizabethan map-maker* (Wakefield, 1979)

Evelyn, J., *Silva, or a discourse of forest trees and the propagation of timber,* Hunter, A. (ed.) (York, 1801)

Farrington, A., *The records of the East India College, Haileybury and other institutions* (London, 1976)

Fea, A. and Marshall, B. (eds.), *Memoirs of Lady Fanshawe* (London, 1905)

Fisher, R., 'James Braid (1870–1950)', in *Oxford Dictionary of National Biography*, vol. 7 (Oxford, 2004)

Fletcher, A., 'Tring Park, part I (1680–1800)', *Hertfordshire Gardens Trust Annual Report 1998–1999*

Francis, J., *A history of the English railway: its social relations and revelations,* 2 vols (London, 1851)

Fuller, T., *The history of the worthies of England*, Nutall, P.A. (ed.), 3 vols (New York, 1965)

Gairdner, J., *Letters and papers of Henry VIII*, vol. 6 (London, 1882)

Gardner, H.W., *A survey of the agriculture of Hertfordshire*. County Agricultural Survey 5 (London, 1967)

Gasson, R., *The influence of urbanization on farm ownership and practice* (Wye, 1966)

Gatland, E., 'Richard Woods in Hertfordshire' in Rowe, A. (ed.), *Hertfordshire garden history: a miscellany* (Hatfield, 2007)

G.E.C., *The complete peerage of England, Scotland and Ireland,* 13 vols (London, 1912)

Gibbs, H.C., *The parish registers of Hunsdon, county Hertford* (London, 1915)

Gilpin, W.S., *Practical hints upon landscape gardening* (London, 1832)

Glennie, P., 'Continuity and change in Hertfordshire agriculture 1550–1700: I. Patterns of agricultural production', *Agricultural History Review*, 36 (1988)

Goodchild, R. and Munton, R., *Development and the landowner* (London, 1985)

Gordon, D.I., *The eastern counties. Vol. V. Regional history of the railways of Great Britain* (Newton Abbot, 1968)

Gover, J.E.B., Mawer, A. and Stenton, F.M., *The place-names of Hertfordshire*, English Place-Name Society XV (Cambridge, 1938)

Greaves, R.L., 'Arthur Capel, first Earl of Essex (1632–1683)', in *Oxford Dictionary of National Biography*, vol. 9 (Oxford, 2004)

Green, D., *Gardener to Queen Anne. Henry Wise (1653–1738) and the formal garden* (Oxford, 1956)

Griffin, K., *Transported beyond the seas: an alphabetical listing of criminals prosecuted in Hertfordshire who received transportation sentences to Australia 1784–1866* (Hertford, 1997)

Grinling, C.H., *The history of the Great Northern Railway, 1845–1902* (London, 1903)

Habakkuk, J., *Marriage, debt and the estates system: English landownership 1650–1950* (Oxford, 1994)

Hadfield, M., *A history of British gardening* (London, 1985)

Hammersley, G., 'The crown woods and their exploitation in the sixteenth and seventeenth centuries', *Bulletin of the Institute of Historical Research*, 30 (1957)

Hanbury, W., *An essay on planting and a scheme for making it conducive to the glory of God and the advantage of society* (Oxford, 1758)

Handley, S., 'John Anstis (1669–1744)', in *Oxford Dictionary of National Biography*, vol. 2 (Oxford, 2004)

Hardy, W.J., *Notes and extracts from the sessions rolls, 1699 to 1850, Hertford County Records,* vol. 2 (Hertford, 1905)

Harley, J.B., *Christopher Greenwood county map-maker and his Worcestershire map of 1822* (Worcester, 1962)

Harley, J.B., *Ordnance Survey land-use mapping: parish books of reference and the county series 1:2500 maps, 1855–1918*, Hist. Geog. Research Series 2 (Norwich, 1979)

Harley, J.B., 'Christopher Saxton and the first atlas of England and Wales 1579–1979', *The Map Collector*, 8 (1979)

Harris, E. (ed.), *Thomas Wright: arbours and grottos* (London, 1979)

Harting, J.E., 'Hertfordshire deer parks', *Transactions of the Hertfordshire Natural History Society*, II (1883)

Hartlib, S., *Design for plenty; by a universal planting of trees* (London, 1652)

Harwood, K., 'Some Hertfordshire nabobs' in Rowe, A. (ed.), *Hertfordshire garden history: a miscellany* (Hatfield, 2007)

Hassell, J., *A tour of the Grand Junction Canal* (London, 1819)

Henderson, P., 'Sir Francis Bacon's water gardens at Gorhambury', *Garden History*, 20 (1992)

Henning, B.D., *The history of parliament: the House of Commons 1660–1690* (London, 1983)

Hertfordshire Gardens Trust and Bisgrove, R., *Hertfordshire gardens on Ermine Street* (Abbots Langley, 1996)

Hertfordshire Gardens Trust and Williamson, T., The *Parks and gardens of west Hertfordshire* (Letchworth, 2000)

Hewison, R., *The heritage industry: Britain in a climate of decline* (London, 1987)

Hill, J., *Hertfordshire poor law removal orders* (Hertford, 2003)

Hill, T., *The profitable art of gardening* (1568)

Hillyard, A., 'Lilley Bottom', *Hertfordshire Countryside* (January, 2005)

Hine, R.L., *Hitchin worthies: four centuries of English life* (Hitchin, 1932, reprint 1974)

Historical Manuscripts Commission, *The manuscripts of his Grace the Duke of Portland at Welbeck Abbey* (London, 1897), vol. 4

HM Treasury, *Report of the committee on houses of outstanding historic or architectural interest* (23 June 1950) (Gowers Report)

Hobsbawm, E.J. and Rude, G., *Captain Swing* (Harmondsworth, 1969)

Hodson, D., *Printed maps of Hertfordshire, 1577–1900* (Folkestone, 1974)

Hodson, D., 'John Warburton 1716–25 and 1749', in Hodson, D. (ed.), *County atlases of the British Isles published after 1703*, 3 vols (Tewin, 1984)

Hodson, D., *Four county maps of Hertfordshire* (Stevenage, 1985)

Hodson, Y., *Ordnance surveyors' drawings 1789–c.1840* (Reading, 1989)

Hodson, Y., *Popular maps: the Ordnance Survey Popular Edition one-inch map of England and Wales 1919–26* (London, 1999)

Hogarth, W., *The analysis of beauty* (London, 1753)

Holmes, C.A., *The Eastern Association in the English Civil War* (London, 1974)

Hooson, D.J.M., 'Some aspects of the growth and distribution of population in Hertfordshire since 1801', (PhD thesis, Univ. London, 1955)

Hoppit, J., *A land of liberty? England 1689-1727* (Oxford, 2000)

Hoppit, J., 'Vardon, Henry William (1870–1937)', in *Oxford Dictionary of National Biography*, vol. 56 (Oxford, 2004)

Hoskins, W.G., 'The rebuilding of rural England, 1570–1640', *Past and Present*, 4 (1953)

Howlett, B., *Hitchin Priory Park: the history of a landscape park and gardens* (Hitchin, 2004)

Hussey, C., *The picturesque: studies in a point of view* (London, 1927)

Hussey, C., *English gardens and landscapes 1700–1750* (London, 1967)

Jacques, D., *Georgian gardens: the reign of nature* (London, 1983)

Jones, A. (ed.), *Hertfordshire 1731–1800, as recorded in the Gentleman's Magazine* (Hertford, 1993)

Jones, B., *Follies and grottoes* (London, 1953), 2nd edn. (London, 1974)

Kelly, E.R. (ed.), *Post Office directory of the six home counties: Essex, Herts, Middlesex, Kent, Surrey and Sussex* (London, 1874)

Kemp, E., *How to lay out a small garden*, 2nd edn. (London, 1858)

Kilvington, F. and Flood, S. (eds.), 'Diary of Thomas Newcome, rector of Shenley, 1822–1849', in Knight, J. and Flood, S. (eds.), *Two nineteenth-century Hertfordshire diaries* (Hertford, 2002)

King, N., *The Grimstons of Gorhambury* (Chichester, 1984)

'Kings Walden Bury, Hertfordshire', *Country Life*, 154 (1973)

Kip, J. and Knyff, L., *Britannia illustrata, or views of several of the royal palaces as also of the principal seats of the nobility and gentry of Great Britain elegantly engraven* (London, 1707)

Kitchen, F., 'John Norden, c.1547–1625: estate surveyor, topographer, county mapmaker and devotional writer', *Imago Mundi*, 49 (1997)

'Knebworth, Herts', *Country Life*, 19 (7 April 1906)

Knight, R.P., *The landscape: a didactic poem in three books, addressed to Uvedale Price* (London, 1794)

Kuiters, W.G.J., 'Rumbold, Sir Thomas (1736–91)', in *Oxford Dictionary of National Biography*, vol. 48 (Oxford, 2004)

Laidlaw, R. (ed.), *The R & A golfer's handbook 2006* (London, 2006)

Lawrence, A., *The Aldenham House gardens: a brief history of the school grounds* (Elstree, 1988)

Laxton, P., *John Rocque's map of Berkshire, 1761* (Lympne, 1973)

Laxton, P., 'The geodetic and topographical evaluation of English county maps, 1740–1840', *Cartographic Journal*, 13 (1976)

Le Hardy, W. (ed.), *Calendar to the sessions books and other sessions records 1752–99, Hertfordshire County Records*, vol. 8 (Hertford, 1935)

Le Hardy, W. (ed.), *Calendar to the sessions books 1833–43, Hertfordshire County Records*, vol. 10 (Hertford, 1957)

Le Hardy, W. and Reckett, G.L. (eds.), *Calendar to the sessions books 1799 to 1833, Hertfordshire County Records*, vol. 9 (Hertford, 1939)

Leitner, L., 'John Almon, 1737–1805, bookseller and political journalist', in *Oxford Dictionary of National Biography*, vol. 1 (Oxford, 2004)

Leleux, R., *The east midlands. Vol IX. Regional history of the railways of Great Britain* (Newton Abbot, 1976)

Lewis, W.S. (ed.), *Horace Walpole's correspondence* (New Haven, 1941)

London Topographical Society, *Survey of building sites in the City of London after the Great Fire of 1666*, by Peter Mills and John Oliver, 5 vols (London, 1962–67)

Longman, G., *A corner of England's garden: an agrarian history of south-west Hertfordshire 1600–1850* (Bushey, 1977)

Loudon, J.C., *A treatise on improving and managing country residences* (London, 1806)

Loudon, J.C., *Hints on the formation of gardens and pleasure grounds; with designs in various styles of rural embellishment* (London, 1812)

Loudon, J.C., *Encyclopaedia of gardening; comprising the theory and practice of horticulture, floriculture, arboriculture and landscape gardening*, 4th edn. (London, 1826)

Loudon, J.C., *The suburban gardener and villa companion* (London, 1836)

Loudon, J.C., *Gardeners' Magazine*, 12 (1836)

Loudon, J.C. (ed.), *The landscape gardening and landscape architecture of the late Humphry Repton, Esq.* (London, 1840)

Mandler, P., *The fall and rise of the stately home* (New Haven, 1997)

Marsden, T., Murdoch, J., Lowe, P., Munton, R. and Flynn, A., *Constructing the countryside* (London, 1993)

Marshall, P.J., 'Benfield, Paul (1741–1810)', in *Oxford Dictionary of National Biography*, vol. 5 (Oxford, 2004)

Marshall, P.J., 'Sulivan, Laurence (c.1713-1786)', in *Oxford Dictionary of National Biography*, vol. 53 (Oxford, 2004).

Marshall, W., *Planting and rural ornament* (London, 1796)

Mead, W.R., *Pehr Kalm: a Finnish visitor to the Chilterns in 1748* (Aston Clinton, 2003)

Minet, W., *The manor of Hadham Hall* (Little Hadham, 1914)

Mingay (ed.), G.E., *The agrarian history of England and Wales. Vol. VI 1750–1850* (Cambridge, 1989)

Ministry of Agriculture, Fisheries and Food, *Report of the committee of inquiry into the acquisition and occupancy of agricultural land,* Cmnd 7599 (London, 1979) (Northfield Report)

Ministry of Works and Planning, *Report of the committee on land utilisation in rural areas,* Cmd 6378 (London, 1942) (Scott Report)

Mitchell, B.R. and Deane, P., *Abstract of British historical statistics* (Cambridge, 1962)

Moodey, G.H., 'Repton's work at Tewin Water', *East Hertfordshire Archaeological Society Newsletter,* 8 (1957)

Morden, R., *The new description and state of England* (London, 1704)

Mowl, T., 'John Drapentier's views of the gentry gardens of Hertfordshire', *Garden History,* 29 (2001)

Munby, L.M. (ed.) *The history of King's Langley* (King's Langley, 1963)

Munby, L.M., *Hertfordshire population statistics, 1563–1801* (Hitchin, 1964)

Munby, L.M., *The Hertfordshire landscape* (London, 1977)

Munsche, P.B., *Gentlemen and poachers: the English game laws 1671–1831* (Cambridge, 1981)

Munton, R., Whatmore, S. and Marsden, T., 'Reconsidering urban-fringe agriculture: a longitudinal analysis of capital restructuring on farms in the Metropolitan Green Belt', *Transactions of the Institute of British Geographers,* 13 (1988)

Neale, J.P., *Views of the seats of noblemen and gentlemen in England, Wales, Scotland and Ireland,* vol. II (London, 1819)

Newby, H., Bell, C., Rose, D. and Saunders, P., *Property, paternalism and power: class and control in rural England* (London, 1978)

Norden, J., *Speculi Britanniae pars. The description of Hartfordshire* (1598)

Norden, J., *The Surveior's dialogue* (London, 1607)

Oliver, R., *Ordnance Survey maps: a concise guide for historians* (London, 2005)

Ordnance Survey, *Account of the methods and processes of the Ordnance Survey of the United Kingdom; drawn up by officers of Royal Engineers employed under Lieut.-Gen. Sir Henry James, R E, F R S, Director-General* (London, 1875)

Osborn, F.J., *Green belt cities* (London, 1946)

Osborne's London and Birmingham Railway guide (Birmingham, 1838)

Ottewill, D., *The Edwardian garden* (New Haven, 1989)

Overton, M., *Agricultural revolution in England. The transformation of the agrarian economy 1500–1850* (Cambridge, 1996)

Pahl, R.E., *Urbs in rure: the metropolitan fringe in Hertfordshire* (London, 1965)

Part, C.T., 'Sport, ancient and modern', in *VCH Hertfordshire,* vol. 1 (London, 1902)

Paterson, D., *A new and accurate description of all the direct and principal cross roads in England and Wales* (London, 1808)

Paul, W., *The rose garden* (London, 1848)

Paul, W., *The handbook of villa gardening* (London, 1855)

Pawson, E., *Transport and economy: the turnpike roads of eighteenth-century Britain* (London, 1977)

Peacock, T.L., *Headlong Hall* (London, 1816)

Peacock, W., *The polite repository* (London, 1790–1809)

Pevsner, N. and Cherry, B., *The buildings of England: Hertfordshire* (Harmondsworth, 1992)

Phillimore, Lord, 'Agriculture and the preservation of the countryside', *Journal of the Town Planning Institute*, 18 (1932)

Piebenga, S., 'William Sawrey Gilpin (1762–1843): picturesque improver', *Garden History*, 22 (1994)

Pigot and Co., *Royal, national and commercial directory and topography of the county of Hertfordshire* (London, 1839)

Poole, H., 'Social life at Cassiobury', in Poole, S. (ed.), *A fair and large house at Cassiobury Park 1546–1927* (Watford, 1985)

Pope, A., 'Of the use of riches.' *Epistle IV, to Richard Boyle, Earl of Burlington* (1731)

Powell, W.R., 'Salmon, Nathanael (1675-1742)', in *Oxford Dictionary of National Biography*, vol. 48 (Oxford, 2004)

Price, U., *Essays on the picturesque* (London, 1794)

Prince, H., 'The changing landscape of Panshanger', *East Hertfordshire Archaeological Society Transactions*, 14 (1959)

Prince, H.C., 'The changing rural landscape', in G.E. Mingay (ed.), *The agrarian history of England and Wales. Vol. VI, 1750–1850* (Cambridge, 1989)

Radzinowicz, L., *A history of English criminal law and its administration from 1750*, 2 vols (London, 1948)

Rawlinson, W.G., *Turner's Liber Studiorum: a description and catalogue* (London, 1878)

Read, C., 'Lord Burghley's household accounts', *Economic History Review*, 2nd ser. 9 (1956)

Read, C., *Lord Burghley and Queen Elizabeth* (London, 1960)

Reed, M.C., *Investment in railways in Britain 1820–44: a study in the development of the capital market* (London, 1975)

Repton, H., *Sketches and hints on landscape gardening* (London, 1795)

Repton, H., *Observations on the theory and practice of landscape gardening* (London, 1803)

Repton, H., *Fragments on the theory and practice of landscape gardening* (London, 1816)

Richardson, T., *The Arcadian friends: inventing the English landscape garden* (London, 2007)

Rider Haggard, H., *Rural England, being an account of agricultural and social researches carried out in the years 1901 and 1902*, 2 vols (London, 1906)

Ridgway, C., 'William Andrews Nesfield: between Uvedale Price and Isambard Kingdom Brunel', *Journal of Garden History*, 13 (1993)

Robinson, J.M., *The country house at war* (London, 1989)

Robinson, W., *The history and antiquities of Enfield*, 2 vols (London, 1823)

Robinson, W., *The wild garden, or our groves and shrubberies made beautiful by the naturalization of hardy exotic plants: with a chapter on the garden of British wild flowers* (London, 1870)

Rogers, J.C., 'The manor and houses at Gorhambury', *St Albans and Hertfordshire Architectural and Archaeological Society Transactions*, New Ser. 4 (1933–5)

Rothschild, M., *The Rothschild gardens* (Stroud, 1996)

Rowe, A., 'Country house chameleon: the story of Hamels Mansion', *Hertfordshire's Past*, 43:4 (1998)

Rowe, A., *Garden making and the Freman family; a memoir of Hamels, 1713–1733* (Hertford, 2001)

Rowe, A., *A history of Knebworth's parks* (Ware, 2005)

Rowse, A.L., 'The Elizabethan discovery of England', in Rowse, A.L., *The England of Elizabeth: the structure of society* (London, 1950)

Salmon, N., *The History of Hertfordshire* (London, 1728)

Sanford, J.L. and Townsend, M., *The great governing families of England* (Edinburgh, 1865)

Saussure, C. de (ed. and trans. by Madame van Muyden), *A foreign view of England in the reigns of George I and George II: letters to his family* (London, 1902)

Sayer, D., 'The oak and the navy', *Quarterly Journal of Forestry*, 86 (1992)

Sedgwick, R., *The history of parliament: the House of Commons 1715–1754*, 2 vols (London, 1970)

Seebohm, C., *The country house: a wartime history, 1939–45* (London, 1989)

Sharp, E.G., 'The acquisition of London Green Belt estates: a study of inter-authority relations', (PhD thesis, Univ. London, 1986)

Sheail, J., *Rural conservation in inter-war Britain* (Oxford, 1981)

Shellim, A., 'Garden creation in war-time: the legacy of the great war at Queenswood School' in Rowe, A. (ed.), *Hertfordshire garden history: a miscellany* (Hatfield, 2007)

Shirley, E.P., *Some account of English deer parks* (London, 1867)

Short, B., *Land and society in Edwardian Britain* (Cambridge, 1997)

Short, B., 'Agency and environment in the transition to a productivist farming regime in England and Wales', in H. Clout (ed.), *Contemporary rural geographies: land, property and resources in Britain* (London, 2007)

Short, B., Watkins, C., Foot, W. and Kinsman, P., *The National Farm Survey, 1941–1943: state surveillance and the countryside in England and Wales in the second world war* (Wallingford, 2000)

Simpson, A., *The wealth of the gentry 1540–1660: East Anglian studies* (Cambridge, 1961)

Skelton, A., 'The development of the Briggens estate, Hunsdon, since 1720', *Hertfordshire Archaeology*, 12 (1994–6)

Smith, G.B., *Life and speeches of John Bright* (New York, 1881)

Smith, H., 'A Victorian passion: the role of Sander's orchid nursery in St Albans' in Rowe, A. (ed.), *Hertfordshire garden history: a miscellany* (Hatfield, 2007)

Smith, J.T., *English houses: the Hertfordshire evidence* (London, 1992)

Smith, J.T., *Hertfordshire houses: selective inventory* (London, 1993)

Spain, J., 'Joseph Sabine (1661–1739)', in *Oxford Dictionary of National Biography*, vol. 48 (Oxford, 2004)

Spring, D., 'Introduction', in J. Bateman, *The great landowners of Great Britain and Ireland*, reprint of 4th edn. (1883) (Leicester, 1971)

Standish, A., *New directions of experience, authorized by the king's most excellent majesty, as may appear, for the planting of timber and firewood* (London, 1614)

Steele, D., 'Temple, Henry John, third Viscount Palmerston (1784–1865) prime minister', in *Oxford Dictionary of National Biography*, vol. 54 (Oxford, 2004)

Stone, L. and Stone, J.C.F., 'Country houses and their owners in Hertfordshire, 1540–1879', in Aydelotte, W.O., Bogue, A.G. and Fogel, R.W. (eds.), *The dimensions of quantitative research in history* (London, 1972)

Stone, L. and Stone, J.C.F., *An open elite?* England 1540–1880 (Oxford, 1984)

Strong, R., *The Renaissance garden in England* (London, 1979)

Strong, R. Binney, M. and Harris, J., *The destruction of the country house 1875–1975* (London, 1974)

Stroud, D., *Capability Brown* (London, 1950), 2nd edn. (London, 1975)

Stroud, D., *Humphry Repton* (London, 1962)

Summerson, J., 'The building of Theobalds', *Archaeologia*, 97 (1959)

Sutherland, L.S., *The East India Company in eighteenth-century politics* (Oxford, 1952)

Switzer, S., *Ichnographia rustica* (London, 1718)

Tait, J.G. and Parker, W.M. (eds.), *The journal of Sir Walter Scott* (Edinburgh, 1950)

Temple, W., *Upon the gardens of Epicurus, or of gardening in the year 1685* (London, 1692)

Thirsk, J., 'The farming regions of England: four Home Counties', in Thirsk, J. (ed.), *The agrarian history of England and Wales*. Vol. IV, 1500–1650 (Cambridge, 1967)

Thirsk, J., 'Enclosing and engrossing', in Thirsk, J. (ed.), *The agrarian history of England and Wales*. Vol. IV, 1500–1650 (Cambridge, 1967)

Thomas, D., *London's green belt* (London, 1970)

Thomas, W.B., 'The home counties', in Williams-Ellis, C. (ed.), *Britain and the beast* (London, 1937)

Thompson, E.P., *Whigs and hunters: the origin of the Black Act* (London, 1975)

Thompson, F.M.L., *English landed society in the nineteenth century* (London, 1963)

Thompson, F.M.L., 'Landowners and the rural community', in G.E. Mingay (ed.), *The Victorian countryside* (London, 1981), vol. II

Thompson, F.M.L., 'English landed society in the twentieth century. II, New poor and new rich', *Transactions of the Royal Historical Society*, 6th series, 1 (1991)

Thompson, F.M.L., 'Business and landed elites in the nineteenth century', in F.M.L. Thompson (ed.), *Landowners, capitalists and entrepreneurs: essays for Sir John Habakkuk* (Oxford, 1994)

Thomson, A., 'Progress, retreat and pursuit: James I in Hertfordshire', in Jones-Baker, D. (ed.), *Hertfordshire in history: papers presented to Lionel Munby* (Hertfordshire Local History Council, 1991)

Thorne, R.G., *House of Commons 1790–1820* (London, 1986)

Tilley, D. and Beagle, J. (eds.), *Wall Hall: from farmhouse to university* (Aldenham, 2003)

Tipping, H.A., 'Lockleys, Hertfordshire', *Country Life*, 48 (1920)

Todd, H.J., *The history of the College of Bonhommes at Ashridge* (London, 1823)

Turner, M., *English parliamentary enclosure: its historical geography and economic history* (Folkestone, 1980)

Turner, R., *Capability Brown and the eighteenth-century English landscape* (Chichester, 1999)

Tyacke, S., *London map-sellers 1660–1720* (Tring, 1978)

Vickers, B. (ed.), *Francis Bacon: essays or counsels, civil and moral* (London, 2002)

Victoria County History, Hertfordshire, 4 vols (London, 1902–14)

Wade, E., *A proposal for improving and adorning the island of Great Britain: for the maintenance of our navy and shipping* (London, 1755)

Wagner, A., *Heralds of England: a history of the office and College of Arms* (London, 1967)

Walne, P., *A catalogue of manuscript maps in the Hertfordshire Record Office* (Hertford, 1969)

Walpole, H., *The history of modern taste in gardening* (London, 2007)

Warburton, J., *Proposals for publishing by subscription a new, large, beautiful and most correct map of London, Middlesex, Essex and Hertfordshire (and the rest of the counties in England and Wales) by actual survey and dimensuration, with the coats of arms and seats of the nobility and gentry, as in those of Yorkshire and Northumberland already published by John Warburton, Esq., Somerset Herald of Arms and F.R.S.* (London, 1721)

Warburton, J., *London and Middlesex illustrated by a true and explicit Account of the Names, Residence. Genealogy and Coat Armour of the Nobility, Principal Merchants and other Eminent Families trading within the Precincts of this most opulent City and County, All Blazon'd in their proper Colours* (London, 1749)

Warrand, D. (ed.), *Hertfordshire families* (London, 1907)

Watkins, C. and Cowell, B., *Letters of Uvedale Price*, Walpole Society, 68 (2006)

Watts, W., *The seats of the nobility and gentry* (London, 1779)

Webb, D.C., *Observations and remarks during four excursions made to various parts of Great Britain… in 1810 and 1811* (London, 1812)

Whateley, T., *Observations on modern gardening* (London, 1771)

Whetham, E., *The agrarian history of England and Wales. Vol VIII, 1914–39* (Cambridge, 1978)

Whitaker, J., *A descriptive list of deer parks and paddocks in England* (London, 1892)

Whybrow, G.H., *The history of Berkhamsted Common* (London, 1934)

Wilkerson, J.C., *John Norden's survey of Barley, Hertfordshire, 1593-1603* (Cambridge, 1974)

Willen, D., *John Russell, first earl of Bedford: one of the king's men* (London, 1981)

Williams, H., *History of Watford and trade directory* (London, 1884)

Williams-Ellis, C., *England and the octopus* (Penrhyndeudraeth, 1928)

Williams-Ellis, C. (ed.), *Britain and the beast* (London, 1937)

Williamson, T., *Polite landscapes: gardens and society in eighteenth-century England* (Stroud, 1995)

Williamson, T., 'The character of Hertfordshire's parks and gardens' in Rowe, A. (ed.), *Hertfordshire garden history: a miscellany* (Hatfield, 2007)

Willis, P., *Charles Bridgeman and the English landscape garden* (Jesmond, 2001)

Wood, B., *Bushey* (Stroud, 1997)

Woodcock, T., 'John Warburton (1682–1759)', in *Oxford Dictionary of National Biography*, vol. 57 (Oxford, 2004)

Worms, L., 'John Seller, (1632–1697)', in *Oxford Dictionary of National Biography*, vol. 49 (Oxford, 2004)

Wotton, H., *The elements of architecture* (London, 1624)

Wratten, D., *The book of Radlett and Aldenham* (Buckingham, 1990)

Youings, J., *The dissolution of the monasteries* (London, 1971)

Youings, J., *Sixteenth-century England* (Harmondsworth, 1984)

Young, A., *A six month tour through the north of England*, 4 vols (London, 1771)

Young, A., *General view of the agriculture of Hertfordshire* (London, 1804)

Index

FORTHCOMING

Medieval Parks of Hertfordshire by Anne Rowe

A holistic approach to landscape history has been adopted in this ground-breaking study of parks created in Hertfordshire between the eleventh and the fifteenth centuries. Over sixty medieval parks have so far been identified from documentary records; a large number for a relatively small county. The documentary history for each park has been compiled, including, where available, detailed records of their management in medieval times gleaned from a surprisingly rich resource of manorial accounts. This information is presented in the form of a gazetteer together with the cartographic and field evidence which has been used to locate the park in today's landscape.

This book is based on original research which opens a window into medieval Hertfordshire and explores a significant aspect of the county's landscape history.

ISBN: 978-1-905313-48-8
Publication date: 2009
Paperback

Visit our website for details of new and forthcoming titles:
www.herts.ac.uk/UHPress

BESTSELLER

Hertfordshire Garden History: A miscellany edited by Anne Rowe explores the rich heritage of the county's parks and gardens. The contributors have discovered the county's lost gardens, unearthed fascinating facts about its stately parks and shed light on the horticultural entrepreneurs who shaped garden landscapes in Hertfordshire and beyond.

If you are eager to be enthralled by the county's wonderful garden history, covering Tring Park, Brocket Park, Newsells Bury, John Scott's grotto, Quickswood, Benington Lordship and much more, then order your copy today.

ISBN: 978-1-905313-38-9
July 2007
Paperback £16.99 / US$33.95

(+p&p UK £2.75, Europe £5.00, rest of world £8.00)

To order direct
Email: UHPress@herts.ac.uk
Tel: +44 (0)1707 284654
Fax: +44 (0)1707 284666
Website: www.herts.ac.uk/UHPress